For Love of Life
and Country

For Love of Life and Country

Dean Hunter

VANTAGE PRESS
New York

Published by Vantage Press, Inc.
516 West 34th Street, New York, New York 10001

Manufactured in the United States of America
ISBN: 0-533-14468-X

Library of Congress Catalog Card No.: 2002095214

0 9 8 7 6 5 4

To so many good friends who encouraged me to write my stories that it would be impossible to mention them all. But I must give special thanks to the five people that proofread the manuscript: Ms. Joyce Blank, Mr. Harry Robertson, Dr. Mike Altman, Dr. Bruce Alexander, and Dr. Tom Baker. I could have never completed this work without the assistance of my wife and companion, Cynthia, who is a consummate teacher and discriminating editor. Her vision, guidance, and encouragement gave *For Love of Life and Country* the breath and soul that makes America what it is.

Contents

For Love of Life
and Country

1

Jerry Shank

Rolling my fighter upside down at 1800 feet and pulling the nose into the vertical position, I called, "Camel Three is in hot!" The tracer rounds from the Vietcong's antiaircraft guns were floating lazily up toward my aircraft. The date was March 24, 1964, and the place was near a large mangrove swamp just north of the Thuan River in the Delta Area of South Vietnam. I was flying as Camel Three in a three-ship formation of heavily loaded modified D-model T-28 fighter-bombers.

Right below us there was a large land battle going on between the South Vietnamese army forces and a large contingent of Vietcong (VC) forces. Our flight of three T-28s had been scrambled only ten minutes ago from a small U.S. Army remote jungle airstrip called Soc Trang. Our mission was to provide ground support for the South Vietnamese forces. The situation at the time was becoming critical for the South Vietnamese forces, as they were being overrun in many places by the VC mercenaries.

Climbing out of Soc Trang we leveled off at 1800-foot altitude and picked up a heading to the target area. Camel Lead Capt. Andy Anderson contacted the Forward Air Controller (FAC), who proceeded to advise us of the tactical situation on the ground. The FAC told us that he would mark the first target with a white phosphorus rocket. While the FAC was performing his target identification run we arrived overhead, and flying in trail we set up a large left-hand circular orbit over his aircraft's position. No sooner had the FAC cleared us in when Camel Lead called in hot for his first pass. We were carrying two 500-pound general-purpose iron bombs plus two other 250-fifty pound shrapnel bombs with daisy cutter fuses on them. During air-to-ground combat maneuvers it is always critical to keep a set of guns on the target area. The reason for this is to provide maximum protection for the fighter when he is most vulnerable to enemy ground fire during his pull-off from the bomb run.

As Camel Lead winged over, he told the flight to set up their ordnance switches to release the two 500-pound bombs on the first run. I watched Camel Lead's bombs strike the target area as Camel Two, flown by Cap. Jerry Shank, was rolling in. Five seconds later I winged over and began my bomb run. I did not see Camel Two, but there was a tremendous explosion where he was to have dropped his bombs. In my peripheral vision I saw VC troops running from the area where Camel Two's bombs had struck. At first thought it appeared that Camel Two's bombs had struck a VC ordnance storage shed, as the resulting explosion of fire and smoke was so large. In the same instant I saw what looked like an aircraft landing gear floating up through the smoke and fire. In addition, as I continued my bomb run I thought that I saw a piece of an aircraft wing flipping end over end in the air. This of course was all happening in microseconds. The FAC was talking all the time and requested me to adjust my weapons' drop forty feet northwest of Camel Two's bombs. There was a lot of chatter on the radio during this time period, and for me as a pilot it was critical to remain focused on the bomb run. Releasing my ordnance, I started my pull-up when it hit me instantly—where was Camel Two? I continued my climb frantically searching the skies above me for Camel Two.

In terms of emotions it is difficult to describe a moment like this. Camel Two, Capt. Jerry Shank, was my bunkmate, and we had flown probably forty or more combat missions together. The sudden grief of losing someone so close struck me like a lightning bolt. In situations like this a person quickly loses sight of the total war effort and cares only for the condition of his immediate buddies. While Camel Lead was trying to contact the Command Post with the information that Camel Two was down, I rolled in without the FAC's approval and attacked the VC positions with a ruthless abandonment. The VC were now running away from the bombed area across a mangrove swamp and jumping into small boats located in the nearby river trying to escape. Bombing from an extremely low altitude, I sank four of the boats with my two remaining 250-pound shrapnel bombs. I then began strafing other boats as fast as I could get my aircraft turned around. Both Camel Lead and I quickly expended all of our machine-gun ammunition on the escaping VC.

Camel Lead called his last strafing pass, and we both took up a heading for Soc Trang. Upon landing, we both, after securing our aircraft, ran for the nearby Army's Dust-Off helicopter that was sitting beside the runway with its engine running. Climbing onboard the helicopter, Camel Lead Capt. Andy Anderson quickly explained what had happened and requested the helicopter pilot's assistance. Without hesitation the pilot signaled for the crew chief to get onboard as he increased the power to the engine. We lifted off and with Camel Lead's directions took up a flight course directly to the scene of the accident. Arriving over the crash site minutes later we asked the pilot of the helicopter to put us down as near to the crash site as possible. Bullets were flying everywhere, with some of them striking the helicopter as the pilot descended as low as he could to the ground. Captain Anderson, the crew chief, and I all jumped off the helicopter as the pilot approached the ground. The helicopter pilot said that he would orbit overhead and would call for Army gunship assistance.

The three of us quickly made our way to the crash scene, paying no attention to what was going on around us. There was no doubt in my mind as I reviewed the facts that I had indeed seen Camel Two hit the ground in a vertical flight position. When we arrived at the large hole in the ground there was nothing to see except a large crater filled with smoking dirt and debris. Circling the crater I saw what looked like a piece of a pilot's flight glove. I picked it up and placed it in my pocket and quickly forgot about it, as the VC guns were getting too hot for us to remain where we were.

We left the crater and ran west toward the mangrove swamp. Flopping down on the berm next to the swamp, I told Camel Lead that I was certain that I had seen a piece of Camel Two's wing and felt that it might be somewhere in the mangrove swamp that we were looking at. We had recently been involved in a congressional committee hearing where we tried to explain to the U.S. congressmen present that the wings were coming off our aircraft, oftentimes while they were in level flight. The representatives of course did not believe us. The entire flight operations of the First Air Commando Squadron in 1963–64 was a clandestine cover-up from the top of our government down. We were flying old, tired, and obsolete aircraft while many times carrying 500-pound and sometimes 750-pound bombs on aircraft that were designed for two 100-pound bombs on each wing. Oftentimes we had to return to the home base and land the aircraft with all of the heavy ordnance still attached under the wings. This added weight put an incredible amount of additional stress on the wings of the T-28s. Getting no relief from the congressional committee, the T-28 section decided after Jerry's loss that we would restrict our pull-offs from bomb runs to one and a half Gs instead of the usual four or more Gs. This change in combat tactics would expose our aircraft to approximately five times the amount of enemy ground fire that we would normally take on a bomb run pull-off. However, after looking at the three-to-four-inch deep wrinkles in our wings that occurred on pull-offs we decided that this lesser-G pull-off would be the better of two evils.

Looking over the swamp, I told Captain Anderson that if we could locate the wing it would certainly validate our plea with higher headquarters. Since there were three of us, we decided that Andy would proceed to the river's edge and follow that south while I would trek down the middle of the swamp. The crew chief was to walk the berm south watching the other two as much as possible. The swamp was approximately one-quarter mile long, varying in width from one to two hundred yards in places. As I got out into the middle of the swamp, the area immediately in front of me was filled with jungle brush and large mangrove trees. This swamp that we were now in was also the same swamp that the VC had run through while we were strafing them, and there was plenty of blood and bodies to prove it. We decided to start the search from our current position while heading south. Reflecting back, we all looked like western cowboys, as we were armed to the teeth with submachine guns and pistols.

Months earlier several T-28 pilots had been shot down and captured by the VC simply because they couldn't keep the VC away armed only with pistols. As commando pilots, we were only issued pistols when we checked into our personnel equipment section. The T-28 section subsequently struck a deal with the Green Beret Forces stationed at Nha Trang, trading liquor for a number of submachine guns. I had selected what was called a tanker's M3A1 grease gun. It was a short .45-caliber submachine gun and held a thirty-round clip. To that clip I had taped two other thrity-round clips upside down, giving me a total of ninety rounds. I had fired the weapon a lot and felt quite comfortable with it. In addition, the gun fit perfectly inside the right side of the T-28's cockpit.

I had only gone about forty yards into the interior of the dark swamp before receiving the scare of my life. I guess it was my Marine Corps training, but for some unexplained reason I wasn't as scared as I should have been. As I stepped around a large spiny green bush a VC jumped up right in front of me. He had a long rifle with a rifle grenade in the end of the barrel pointed directly at my chest. My instant reaction was, *My God, this is it.* As the VC was straining to pull the trigger on his weapon, our eyes locked for perhaps a second or so. During this same moment in time I had my submachine gun pointed directly at the VC. I was, like he was, pulling the trigger on my weapon so hard that I actually bent the trigger, yet the gun would not fire. Suddenly, without warning, the VC stood straight up, yelled something, threw his rifle down, and took off running through the swamp. Hot as it was, I broke out in a cold sweat while fear cascaded throughout my entire body. Getting over my stunned condition, as this weapon had never failed me before, I glanced down to try to figure out why the gun would not fire. The reason was simple—I had not put a round into the chamber, plus the dustcover for the automatic ejection system was closed. I knew from previous experience that sometimes in critical combat situations like this the adrenaline in your body goes wild and your brain is slow to react—mine most certainly was!

I quickly flipped the dustcover open and jacked a round into the chamber as I watched the VC running ahead of me. For some unexplained reason I just could not shoot him in the back. Maybe because to my knowledge like my boyhood hero, John Wayne, I had never shot anyone in the back and maybe because—I'll never know—I held my gun straight up in the air and emptied the thirty rounds into the trees ahead of me. I may never know who that VC was, but I'm sure that he, like me, will never forget our jungle encounter. The other two guys upon hearing my grease gun go off started yelling was I OK? I quickly realized that there could be more VC in the swamp, and suddenly this looking around for a piece of wing didn't seem to be such a good idea. I turned right and ran as fast as I could toward the berm. Captain Anderson arrived shortly after I did, and we decided that we best get the heck out of there. As we ran south down the berm, the crew chief popped a yellow flare to attract the helicopter pilot's attention, and it worked. By the time we reached the end of the berm the helicopter was on the ground waiting for us. Reflecting back over this troublesome incident years later, I like to think that somewhere outside Hanoi there is a grandfather or maybe a college professor telling this same story about this crazy American he met in combat to his grandchildren or students.

Later back at our base I remembered the glove in my pocket. When I took it out I discovered that there was a finger with a wedding band still on it inside the glove. Washing the ring off, I discovered Camel Two's initials on the inside of the wedding band. I called our headquarters at Bien Hoa and reported my find to our section commander. He told me to gather up all of Captain Shank's possessions and to bring them up to Bien Hoa the next morning. After I reported in the next morning, Major Lengfield told me to stop off at Ton Son Knut Air Base on my way back to Soc Trang and to drop off Captain Shank's finger at the U.S. military mortuary. I had never been in a mortuary before, and the experience was very unpleasant. The mortician took me to Captain Shank's casket and told me to toss the finger inside. While I was standing there two airmen closed and sealed the casket. Several days later Major Lengfield informed us that he had received a telegram from Captain Shank's wife and the only thing that she wanted was his wedding ring. What a psychic phenomenon this was for all of us!

That same evening after I arrived back at Soc Trang and the so-called dust had settled, I sat and just stared at Jerry's bunk. My thoughts made me realize just how precious life was and that I could have just as easily been the one who went in. The loss of Jerry Shank really affected me, and I couldn't exactly explain it to others. I spent a lot of time that night just thinking about my life to date. So many things had happened over the years, and how come I was still here? Lying there on that lonely bunk that night, I tried to review the things that had influenced my life over the years. Had I ever stopped and given thought about how important the phrase is "For Love of Life and Country"? It has been the creed that has inspired my entire life to date. As you read through the pages of this book, keep that creed in your mind. Reflect on your life as I have on mine, and you, too, will come to realize how important those words are: "For Love of Life and Country." Return with me now to the year 1931.

2

1931

The year 1931 was incredibly exciting! Herbert Hoover was president and declared "The Star Spangled Banner" the national anthem. The stock market had crashed, and the Great Depression was beginning. Bread cost a nickel. A can of salmon cost a dime. Beer was an illegal substance, newspapers were three cents a copy, and gas was a dime a gallon and came in three colors. Across the country new Fords averaged $400 each. In addition, the Empire State Building was dedicated. The first nonstop flight across the Pacific was completed, and Notre Dame's famous football coach Knute Rockney was killed in an aircraft crash. The following people were born: James Dean, Mikhail Gorbachev, Willy Mays, Barbara Walters, and W. Dean Hunter.

Growing up, I discovered that I was in a generation that still idealized women, the American flag, apple pie, and John Wayne. My name is W. Dean Hunter and this is my story. At least it's my story up to this particular juncture in one man's life. Recently I retired from my second career of twenty-four years in education, which included teaching and coaching sports programs at the collegiate, secondary, and middle school levels, plus spending time as a high school principal. Since I'm a senior citizen now, there can't be too many chapters left, which is perhaps why I want to tell my story.

I don't mind telling you that up to this point in time it's been one heck of a ride. Like a lot of fellows who are on the short side of the grand trek, I've been known to tell a story or two about the things I've seen and the places I've been. More often than not the reaction from other people is, "How the devil did you manage to do all that?" I can tell you that a good number of those I served with, both in the Marine Corps and in the Air Force, fell along the way. From my personal experience I think that much of an individual's capacity to survive in this world is his capacity to love life. It is often said that death is a teacher. If that's the case, however, I must have been asleep in class, for I should now be the wisest man in the world.

I spent my early years as a World War II wannabe. The great conflict was over before I was old enough to fight. Back then, all of us kids played war games and pretended we were warriors. I always had a thing for the Marine Corps because their classy uniforms and tough discipline mesmerized me. My idol was John Wayne, and I must have seen *The Sands of Iwo Jima* a dozen times.

To this day, I can still sing all three verses of the "Marine Corps Hymn." The nation was tired of war when I reached my teens, but ours was a very patriotic country back then. We still all wanted to do our part—me probably more than anyone else. I couldn't wait to get into a uniform. One of my proudest moments was when I became a corporal in the Marine Corps and could wear a set of dress blues with a red stripe down the pants. The words of General MacArthur "Duty, Honor, Country" called out loudly to me. Most Marines who served during WW II knew that General MacArthur disliked the Marine Corps, but as time moved forward I found myself completely immersed in his "Duty, Honor, Country" philosophy. My feelings were that General MacArthur should have been a Marine. What an inspiration and hero he was to all young American men. To think that both he and his father were recipients of the Medal of Honor. This was a time in America when as soon as you were old enough to go to war, you went.

Two wars, and more than my share of combat, on land and in the air, have cooled my craving to fight and to prove myself. But it has done nothing to dampen the love I have for this great nation. I'm red, white, and blue—always have been, always will be. I'd like to think that my time in uniform also helped me to become a better American—to love life more for what it is and to be a better citizen. I also hope that it has helped me in the areas that really count, i.e., to be a better husband and father. You see, I may have served in harm's way, but I was also spared. I often wondered why some died and others lived. If you get nothing else from this book, I hope it's a sense of how lucky we are to be Americans and how much we owe to our flag and to this great nation.

In order to provide the reader with some background information on me, it will be necessary to spend a little time discussing my family. I was fortunate and came from a very loving family. Even though Dad and I had a difficult time telling each other that we loved each other, we did, in fact, truly love each other. Dad came from a generation of men where it wasn't considered manly to say, "I love you," to another male—it was always just assumed.

Sometimes it is difficult to describe how much I loved my mother. Mother was born Georgia Elaine Frazier in Greenforest, Arkansas, in 1906. There were four other sisters and one brother in her family. Grandfather Frazier was a typical Arkansas farmer with simple needs. I think his early military life, having fought in the Spanish American War, influenced my life to a great degree. I always admired the pictures of him in his official Army uniform. Grandma Frazier was unique in that she cooked on a wood stove all of her life. They did not get electricity in their home until 1955, and they never experienced the pleasure of running water in their house. Mother grew up in this small farming community in Arkansas until she reached age eighteen. She decided to come out west to California, where she not only found employment but also met Dad, and they got married.

Mom was always a very religious person who enjoyed life to the fullest extent. She was a member of the Spiritualist Church and eventually became a minister in that religion. During the 1940s she was a devout disciple of the Spiritualist Amy Semple McPherson, who conducted revivals in tents in Los Angeles for congregations in excess of 70,000 persons. Mother never forced her religion on the family; however, she did insist that both my sister, Zelda, and I attend Sunday school on a regular basis. We both received seven-year pins for perfect attendance from the Methodist church in Coronado. When we lived up in San Gabriel Canyon during the Great Depression years, I do remember Mom conducting seances in our home at night. However, Zelda and I were never allowed to attend these strange meetings

During the war years, Mom worked for the Civil Service Division of the U.S. Navy. She became an aircraft mechanic at North Island Naval Air Station and eventually had her own crew. She was a person of many talents, and I loved her dearly. Even though she knew nothing about the game of football, she faithfully attended every game that I played while I was in high school. Like Dad being in the Masonic Lodge, Mom was heavily involved in the Eastern Star Lodge.

How many times have you thought of your father's past and wondered how he got where he was? I have always cherished my father's birth certificate. It says that he was born somewhere in Sonora County, Texas, in a covered wagon in 1893. How exciting life must have been then. Dad never got beyond the third grade in terms of formal education, but what an incredible and exciting life he lived. I have always told myself that if I could just live one-half as an exciting life as his, then I, too, will have lived a full life.

Dad came from a large family and was the second oldest of nine children, and his mother died with the birth of his youngest brother. Dad grew up in Tombstone, Arizona, when Tombstone was at the mecca of wild life on the western frontier. He wore six-guns on his hips from his sixteenth birthday on. From what I have been able to piece together, by his eighteenth birthday he was given the option of going to Leavenworth for his involvement with some missing horses or joining the U.S. Army. He chose the Army. He reported to the famous "Rainbow Division" from California and found himself in the same infantry company as Sgt. Alvin York. Sergeant York later became one of the most famous winners of the Medal of Honor from WW I.

Because of Dad's mechanical abilities, he soon left his rifle company and was reassigned to one of the newly formed machine-gun companies. Things were happening fast in the war, and the air was rapidly becoming a part of the battlefield. Dad volunteered for and was subsequently reassigned to the U.S. Army Air Corps as an aerial machine gunner. He didn't remember the number, but he flew a number of combat missions in a Curtis Hayrack B-11 type aircraft. The B-11 was unusual in that it was constructed with what looked like metal pipes with no fuselage covering and had a pusher-type engine. He told me that the missions were exciting because they would fly very low over the German trenches strafing the enemy as they flew along. Whenever he ran out of ammunition for his machine gun, he would drop small bombs that were stacked around his legs in the forward cockpit. He also said that it was common to dump garbage and honey buckets on the Germans. He did say that his pilot sitting behind often complained about what was flying back on his windscreen. Dad didn't mention the danger, but he did say that they went through a lot of aircraft in a short time.

According to Army records, Dad was killed in action in 1918 while serving in France. The U.S. government sent a $10,000 NSLI life insurance check to his father in Arizona. He decided not to cash the check because he did not believe that his son was dead. It seems that there were two Charles R. Hunters in the same theater of operations in France. To keep their record separated, Dad changed his middle name from Riley to Ralph. Later when Dad was discharged and came back to Tombstone upon seeing him both of his two sisters at home fainted. His father returned the $10,000 check to the government. Nonetheless, beyond Dad's sixtieth birthday he was still having problems trying to convince the government that he was alive.

After his discharge, Dad, like many other young servicemen, was afflicted with the wanderlust. He didn't know what to do with his life. He met race driver Barney Oldsfield, who was racing automobiles in nearby Phoenix, and raced a number of races as Barney's brakeman. Dad moved on to Los Angeles and became an automobile mechanic when he met my mother. He was thirty-eight when I was born in 1931. Later we moved to Coronado, and Dad worked for the Civil Service as a heavy-duty mechanic. Frequently during the war years while I was both in elementary and junior high Dad would bring his big Navy truck by school and take me with him out to fix a Caterpillar tractor that had broken down somewhere in San Diego County.

Mom never approved of Dad doing this because most of the machines that broke down were located on the Navy's bombing and gunnery range at nearby Ream Field. I loved it because Dad always let me drive the tractors and I got to push a lot of sand around. This procedure stopped as I approached high school due to my involvement in sports programs.

I don't think anyone appreciated Dad's heroism as much as I did. During World War II Dad volunteered to fly out to Guadalcanal for the Navy. The Marines had just landed on Guadalcanal in what was to become one of their more famous assaults during WW II. One of the Marine Corps's main objectives was to capture Henderson Airfield. It seems that the Japanese had moved a large steamroller out onto the runway and then fixed it so that it couldn't be started or moved. Dad's job was to get this machine running and off the runway. He was under direct Japanese fire the whole time that he was working on the steamroller. When he got the machine running and started to move off the runway the Japanese zeroed in on him with artillery fire in an effort to stop him. As he cleared the runway an artillery shell exploded a building close to him and a piece of the structure struck him in the back. The Navy presented Dad with a Civilian Citation for heroism on Guadalcanal. Although Dad never complained, he lived with back pain for the remainder of his life as a result of this incident.

Strange, the things you remember about your dad! He was a kind man yet very stern, and if I did something wrong he was quick to get after me with a switch. Mom was a member of the Eastern Star Lodge while Dad was a Thirty-second Degree member of the Masonic Lodge. Dad supported Mom in everything she did and you could feel the lasting love they held for each other.

In 1946, when I was between the eight and ninth grades and had just turned fourteen, Dad helped me buy my first car. How proud I was of that automobile. It was a 1937 Dodge club coupe. In short order I had chopped the body down—lowered the rear end—and painted it a metallic green. I added fender skirts to the rear wheels and twin spotlights on each side of the windshield. I topped this off with foxtails on the twin antennas and installed dual Smitty mufflers that were so loud that you could hear me coming three blocks away. I was in "Hog Heaven," as the saying went! Dad also helped me soup the engine up for higher performance. We installed a dual manifold with twin carburetors, a three-quarter racing cam, a hotter ignition system, plus two racing fuel pumps. This car really roared down the highway and seemed indestructible. It lasted through all of my abuse in high school and beyond.

High school was really exciting for me. As a result of my experience as a Boy Scout, I learned to set goals early on. My first goal was to attend the Naval Academy and become a fighter pilot. In sports I lettered in varsity football and C-level basketball. In football our defensive coach was always on my case because I was so slow in running. If I hadn't been so good at sacking quarterbacks he probably would have kicked me off the football team. I was so bad at running that I absolutely could not run the required one mile for his PE class. As I will explain later, I could have qualified for any Pacific Coast Conference (PAC) Ten track team in terms of running after my experience as a young Marine in Korea. While still in school as a trumpet player, I envisioned myself as being another Harry James. I loved music and delighted in playing first chair in the trumpet section of the school band. As I came from a small school (student body wise), playing football and being in the band involved some unusual problems. I never got to listen to motivational talks by our coaches. However, I wasn't alone in this venture, as five other teammates had to also remain on the field and play with the marching band in our football uniforms. Imagine that in high school today? After school I organized a seven-piece pep band and we played at games for the newly formed semipro San Diego Bombers football team. During my senior year I was elected vice president of the student body and was involved in almost every club in school. I packed a lot into my high school years in terms of building character, defining values, and developing good morals.

Coronado originally was an island, which made it a unique town, especially during the war years. North Island, the largest naval air station on the West Coast, was located just to the north of Coronado. During the war, the Navy expanded their facilities by filling in the waterway between the two islands, making them into one large island. Coronado was very definitely considered a Navy town. There were seventy-six people in my graduating class, of whom thirty-two were boys. After high school, sixteen of those thirty-two boys went on to successful careers in the Navy. The war years were very emotional times, and patriotism flourished in Coronado. There were a total of seven students in my class whose fathers were not naval officers. Four of the seven eventually wound up in the Air Force as pilots, while the remainder went into the U.S. Army. The interesting thing is that all seven of us belonged to the same Boy Scout troop. By 1948 I was the only one in Troop 75 to achieve the rank of Eagle Scout. It is my firm belief that the Boy Scout Program provided me with leadership habits, the ability to set goals, and a work ethic that has had a significant impact upon my entire life.

One of my good friends on the football team, Dale Lemly, graduated two years ahead of me and went on to the Naval Academy. After Dale left, I used to cut his father's lawn each week and on occasion wash his car. General Lemly asked me one day what I was going to do after graduation. I told him that I wanted to go to the Naval Academy and to become a Marine aviator, but that I couldn't get into the academy because my father was not an officer in the

Navy. General Lemly told me that I could join a Marine Corps Reserve unit in San Diego and after one year of weekend warrior duty I could apply for Bainbridge Prep School in Maryland. He said that nearly 98 percent of students graduated from Bainbridge were accepted into the Naval Academy. In January of 1950, with my parents' consent, I joined the U.S. Marine Corps Reserve's 11th Tank Battalion.

After graduation I went with one of my classmates to the University of California, where I fully intended to play football for Coach Pappy Waldorf. After two weeks of indoctrination my classmate and I both headed north to Arcata, California. My Uncle Hack was a salesman for Firestone Tires and he was able to get both of us jobs in a logging camp. I spoke with the Marine Reserve unit in San Diego before we left, and they told me that it was OK to miss several training camps so long as I was working away from home. They said that I could make up the time when I returned at the end of the summer.

Pete, my buddy, and I went to work for the Maple Creek Lumber Company. It was the type of lumber company that subcontracted their products with large lumber mills located in Arcata, California. Pete and I held just about every job there was, from pulling the green chain to off-bearing the main head rig. I was fortunate to get out of the mill and work in the woods, where I set choker cables around logs for large Caterpillar tractors to pull into the loading area. Eventually, I became what they called a first loader and loaded logs onto waiting trucks. Pete and I built a house in our spare time, which was quite an accomplishment since neither of us knew anything about carpentry. In late July I received a "Priority" telegram from the 11th Tank Battalion telling me that I had twenty-four hours to report for active duty. It seems that a war was in the making and that there was an immediate need for tanks and heavy armored vehicles. The U.S. Marine Corps's 11th Tank Battalion was the first unit in the United States to be called to active duty by President Truman.

3

Korea

I was excited and felt that my time had finally arrived. Pete and I both quit our jobs and raced down U.S. 101 as fast as that old Dodge would go. The 11th Tank Battalion had already left for Camp Pendleton when we arrived. Collecting what little gear I possessed, I had my parents drive me up the coast to Oceanside and drop me off at the main gate of Camp Pendleton. The guard at the main gate told me to report to Tent Camp Two. I insisted that Mom and Dad leave me at the main gate, because I was too proud to accept a ride any farther. What a stupid mistake that turned out to be, for Tent Camp Two was located seventy-five miles back in the boondocks and I had a terrible time getting there. When I finally arrived, things were happening fast. After I was assigned to a tent, a sergeant came around and told us that we would be falling out at 0600 the following morning for shots.

I'll never forget the sight that I beheld the following morning. There must have been close to 2,000 Marines lined up in this small valley, all funneling down to ten or twelve Medical Corpsmen. A sergeant told us that we would be getting thirteen shots and to be sure that we kept moving or we might get the same shot twice. He was absolutely right, as the medics never looked up; they just slammed the needles into our arms. If you hesitated at all you got nailed twice, and many guys in line had several needles sticking in their arms as they moved down the lines. At the end of the line a technical sergeant, commonly called a gunny in the Marine Corps, was organizing calisthenics so the serum could move rapidly through our bodies.

We left later that afternoon in "cattle cars" onboard a long train headed for San Diego. While we were on our way to San Diego, the Navy was pulling an old WW II Victory-type troop transport ship out of mothballs. The seamen were still removing the white plastic

15

from the ship as we arrived. We divided into work details and spent the next six days loading the ship with combat supplies.

Even though many of us didn't have complete uniforms we learned that it didn't make a difference at the time. At departure time there was quite a celebration at dockside. It reminded me of the boys coming home from WW II. There were bands playing, with people throwing streamers into the air and Red Cross workers passing out doughnuts and coffee. Just as I was about to go up the gangplank, my mother rushed up and handed me what appeared to be a box of "Sees" candy. I was embarrassed, as I had been told that Marines did not eat "pogie bait" (candy). I remember trying to hide the box with the idea of throwing it off the other side of the ship after I got onboard, when Mom couldn't see me.

I was unable to do this, as there was an officer at the head of the gangplank assigning us to various sleeping compartments inside the ship. We didn't have time to do anything except follow his confusing orders. There were long lines leading down into the bowels of the ship to the quarters where we would be staying. A sailor gave each of us upon arrival a piece of canvas measuring two feet by four feet, plus a section of manila rope. He told us to string this canvas on the tubular racks attached to the bulkheads, which would then be our bunks for the duration of the trip. The problem was that none of us knew how to accomplish this task properly. The result was when the guy immediately above you got into his bunk he would sink down and it was impossible for you to get into your bunk. The first night out to sea one of the guys on the top bunk got seasick and the barf dribbled down through the ropes of everyone below him. You can imagine the smell, plus the mess. As quick as one guy got sick, several more would follow. I stashed my gear on my bunk carefully, hiding the box of candy, and got out of there.

The interior of the good ship *Daniel S. Pope* was a far cry from anything that you would want to take a cruise on. At departure we were supposed to have 3,000 Marines onboard, and we wound up with 4,300, making crowded conditions all the more difficult and deplorable. For some strange reason someone decided that all Marines should get up at 0430 each morning even though there was nothing to do, nor anywhere to go. We got in line at 0500 for breakfast and it usually took two to three hours of winding through the long corridors just to reach the mess hall. Word quickly reached us that the captain of the ship was upset because the Marines were writing graffiti on the walls and in passageways where we waited. Actually, some of the graffiti was quite entertaining and certainly relieved the boredom of the long waits. Arriving at the mess hall was another experience. The ship was constantly rolling and so many Marines had thrown up that the slop was rolling back and forth on the floor of the mess hall. To compound this problem the food, if one could call it food, would make you sick just to look at it. The scrambled eggs as well as the potatoes were green in color and smelled like sulfur. The coffee, if you could drink it, was the consistency of paint.

It took us seventeen days, most of them rough, to cross the Pacific to reach Japan. Since I couldn't stand the smell in the crowded sleeping quarters, I went topside each night and tied myself to a stanchion so I wouldn't fall overboard. The officers didn't bother those of us who did this, as they understood how bad it was belowdecks even in their quarters. The daily routine was one of complete boredom. You either got into a card game that lasted all day, read someone else's book, or spent your time in the chow lines.

There were all kinds of card games going on, with poker being the most popular. I recall one incident that stuck out in my mind since I wasn't a poker player. I had become a very close buddy with a kid by the name of Red K. Red had three stripes on his arms to my zero, but that didn't affect our friendship. In all military units there are always some shady characters who are worthless, and this unit was no exception. Red mentioned one evening that he had a buddy by the name of George who was a professional gambler that he introduced to me. George met the description of the persons described earlier except Red felt that he was honest. In any event, George had been in the same game for over three days and nights. George came to me one night and asked me to loan him forty dollars. He said that he would return my forty dollars and one-half of whatever he won. Forty dollars was a lot of money to a guy who only made seventy-two dollars per month, but I finally agreed to George's request. The next morning I found my sleeping bag stuffed with money. When I counted it up there was a total of $1,840. I never hesitated to finance George after that.

About the third day out from San Diego, I was hungry and remembered the box of candy that I had hidden on my bunk. I decided to sneak down there and eat some of the candy without anyone seeing me. The shock of opening that Sees box of candy was traumatic, for inside was a brand-new Colt .45-caliber automatic pistol! I quickly realized from listening to old Marines how important it was to own a pistol, so I concealed it for the remainder of the trip. I was almost overcome with emotion as I thought about what my mother had done, since she was a minister and all. As a Spiritualist minister she had to know something that I didn't, because this particular pistol was to save my life on two separate occasions later on.

We were told after several days at sea that we would be going to a place called Korea. Oddly enough, no one seemed to know exactly where it was located. That didn't really matter, as the atmosphere onboard ship was far too exciting just thinking about combat and fighting for your country. The boredom finally subsided on the seventeenth day as we sighted the island of Japan. The following day our ship docked in Yokohama and the confusion was much like it was back at Camp Pendleton. We fell out into platoons and were marched off to nearby barracks. It was somewhat comical, as upon arrival many of us did not have complete uniforms. There just wasn't time during the chaos at Camp Pendleton, so I found myself wearing a pair of Levi's with a University of California sweatshirt. I did have a Marine Corps hat and a pair of boots. One of the sergeants told us not to worry, that we would be properly outfitted before we left Japan.

The next morning we were again formed into platoons and marched off to an Army post exchange. Here we were issued brand-new sets of U.S. Army class A-type uniforms. They told us that where we were going it was cold and we would be happy to have these Army uniforms. There were forty-one guys much like myself who had not been in the unit long enough to get complete uniforms. None of us had been in long enough to attend summer camp with the battalion. I was a little concerned, as my new Marine Corps job description listed me as an assistant tank driver and machine gunner. The only tanks and machine guns that I had ever seen were in the hands of my hero, John Wayne. The sergeant who was responsible for us told us not to worry. He said that we would not be accompanying the battalion into combat but would be reassigned to a special weapon support company that was being formed. We were then marched to a warehouse where supply people outfitted us for combat. Because of my size I was issued a twenty-one-pound Browning Automatic Rifle (BAR), and I was both proud and impressed at first. Later I had reason to question the receipt of the BAR. I quickly learned from some of the old Marines that the life expectancy of a BAR man in combat was seven seconds. This was due to the fact that there were very few automatic firing weapons at the time and the minute you fired your BAR every enemy soldier around was trying to kill you. At the time right then I was too young to be scared.

The following day we were loaded onboard a landing craft infantry-type boat (LCI) that departed immediately for Korea. En route I received a quick course in how to fieldstrip and take care of the BAR. Firing the BAR from the LCI was a lot of fun, and the atmosphere was one of sheer excitement. Three days later on the afternoon of September 15, 1950, we boarded smaller landing craft and went ashore as a part of the second wave in the Inchon Landing. Our target area was Red Beach which was located on the northern half of the harbor.

The Korean "Conflict" was indeed a curious war. For those of us who missed WW II, we were eager to get involved in fighting for our country. It was to be my first war, and I really matured rapidly. The Korean War is often tagged as "the Forgotten War." I can assure you that some fifty years later, after suffering some 54,245 fatalities, it was anything but a forgotten war to those of us who saw action there. As a young Marine involved in this war I developed a strong feeling of patriotism and love for this nation. These feelings were forged during two tours of combat in Korea, and I have never wavered in my responsiveness toward this great nation.

General MacArthur's operational plan for the Inchon Landing was brilliant. It worked even though many officers said that it would not because of the hazards involved. Like our armies in Europe, especially at Normandy, the landing was planned for a high-tide approach. It didn't work out at Normandy and it didn't work out here, either. The harbor of Inchon was unusual in that it had one of the world's highest tides, i.e., thirty-four feet. When the tide starts to go out the vertical volume of thirty-four feet of water really gets to moving fast. The speed of the landing craft at approximately three to five miles per hour was extremely slow and couldn't keep up with the outward flow of the water. As a result most of the landing craft wallowed or were grounded in the shallow water and mud. We had to walk in many cases almost a quarter of a mile to get to the safety of the harbor wall. It was nearly impossible for the vehicles to move at all, and most vehicles were abandoned. I'm sure that many of them are still buried in the mud of the harbor today. Even though we lost a lot of equipment, the actual plan of the assault landing at Inchon enabled our forces to cut the NKPA (North Korean Peoples Army) supply lines in half. The final success of MacArthur's plan was deemed brilliant by our own Joint Services Command (JCS).

The actual landing was not as bad as I had expected. The Army Rangers had landed twenty-four hours ahead of the Marine forces and had knocked out all of the enemy heavy machine guns located on the small islands in the harbor. Rumor control indicated that the Rangers had taken over 400 prisoners. No one could confirm it, but I sure was glad that the Rangers were there. Once we were ashore, the next obstacle that we faced was a sixteen-foot-high wall that ran all along the waterfront. We had some wooden ladders, but not enough to get all the Marines over the top of the wall.

Our engineers and the Navy Seabees finally were able to set charges and to blow several holes large enough for us to get through. The holes really became a problem for us, and I'm sure that we lost more people to our own guns than to the enemies. The sailors in their beached landing craft were racking the walls and holes with .50 caliber bullets in an effort to assist us. We had no communications with these sailors and we just had to wait until the excitement wore down or they ran out of ammunition for us to get through the holes. The day was one of complete excitement, and the only thing missing was the music that normally accompanies war movies.

There was little enemy opposition as we moved through the town of Inchon. Once Inchon had been secured our next objectives were the two airfields located north and east of our position. Our force split with half going after Kimpo Airfield, which was located approximately ten miles northeast of our position. The remainder of the battalion, which included myself, marched on toward Suwon

Airfield, which was approximately twenty-five miles to the southeast of us.

About ten to twelve miles east of Inchon we experienced our first real combat in the form of a mortar barrage. At first I wasn't sure what was happening, simply because I didn't know what a mortar was. It didn't take but a few seconds to realize that one could get killed fast by simply standing around waiting for orders. The adrenaline suddenly peaked out as the mortar shells began to get closer and closer to me. I saw the entrance to an old bunker about thirty feet away and took off for it. I never hesitated and flung my body through the entrance. Guys around me later said that I came out faster than I went in. I have always had this great fear of spiders, and as I dived through the opening I went through three or four spiderwebs. There was instant panic and I exited the bunker like a madman, throwing myself flat on the ground outside. I found it incredible how quiet it is after an attack like that. I came through this first attack without a scratch. However, I wasn't as lucky during the next one.

We were crossing the end of a large valley about three hours later when the next attack hit us. As the mortars began to fall I glimpsed two Marines lying perpendicular to a large log about twenty feet away. I didn't hesitate as I dashed the twenty feet and hurled my body between them. I remember pulling my helmet down as far as it would go and holding on for life as the ground blew up around us. When the mortars stopped falling there was an uncommon quiet that I can only describe as an absolute silence.

The Marine lying next to me punched me and said, "Christ, doesn't your foot hurt?" My foot didn't hurt at all until he brought it to my attention. I glanced down and my first reaction was that my foot had been blown completely off. The ground around my foot and my pant leg were all covered with blood and my boot wasn't where it was supposed to be. Panic set in big-time, and the Marine next to me started yelling for a medic. What happened next was almost unbelievable! The medic when he arrived was what Marines call an old-salt type Marine who was probably all of twenty-three years old. I made no effort to look as the pain was terrible, but I could hear the medic snipping and swearing, and quite frankly, I was too scared to look. It seems that a spent round had hit the instep of my boot and promptly taken the lower half of the boot

21

and shoe sole with it. The medic cleaned off the blood, put a Band-Aid on my foot, and told me to get my butt over to the nearest dead Marine and take his right boot.

Somehow this experience was more traumatic than any experience I had encountered before. Perhaps it was the sight of my own blood that got to me. I quickly laced up the boot that I had taken off the dead Marine and attempted to catch up with my platoon. I began to realize that a guy could get himself killed real easy around here. Having never been in a violent fight of any kind or seen real dead people, I found myself enveloped in both sweat and fear.

Later that same evening we dug in farther down this same valley. Sleep was out of the question, as artillery shells were bursting in the distance and occasional automatic weapons' fire close by would scare the living hell out of you. I lay there on the ground that night with my BAR locked and loaded and ready for instant action. The night sounds have a way of really getting to you, especially if you are already scared out of your wits. We learned the next morning that Kimpo Airfield was secured quickly by members of our battalion who had gone north out of Inchon. The securing of Suwon Airfield was to be a different story. The fighting wasn't what you would call heavy, but it was heavy enough for guys like me who were new to the theater.

Once Suwon was secured we set up camp around the perimeter of the base while the engineers worked around-the-clock on the runway. We had both two-man tents plus a number of eight-man tents. I felt more comfortable in one of the eight-man tents, as there were more guys around me. One of our more difficult jobs was to train the remnants of the Republic of South Korean (ROK) forces that were with us. What made it difficult was that most of us had no combat training to begin with. Trying to teach someone else who couldn't understand your language became a problem. The ROKs were happy to be with us regardless of what we asked of them. We issued the ROKs M-1 rifles and tried to show them how to both use and clean the weapons. Since there were still enemy forces in the immediate area and we couldn't understand their language, we decided to use the ROKs as outer perimeter guards at night. This seemed to work well, but somehow elements of the NKPA managed to kill a number of the ROK guards. They would then exchange uniforms with them and God only knows how long some of them lived with us. It was quite common to hear a lot of small-arms fire, especially at night, when sentries were more excited. They usually shot first and asked questions later. My habits had not changed in the least, and I found it nearly impossible to sleep at night. This particular habit was to later save my life.

Maybe I had seen too many western movies and somehow had got the idea there. Possibly it was fear, but I found myself lying on my back at night with my .45 pistol cocked with a round in the chamber and all the safeties off. One night several weeks after our arrival, as usual I lay down with my .45 on my chest and some sixth sense awakened me. At first I was afraid to even breathe, wondering what had alarmed me. Suddenly a person appeared over my sleeping bag and I could tell from the garliclike smell that it wasn't another Marine. I saw the flash of a large knife coming down toward me. Without hesitating, I rolled left and fired a shot right through my sleeping bag. It was an NKPA soldier and my bullet caught him right between his teeth.

The sudden explosion of my .45 brought complete pandemonium in that tent. By the time we got some lights on and got organized, eight Marines in our area had died by having their throats slit or by being bayoneted. The first reaction was, *Oh, my God, I've hurt someone,* then the ever-present fear struck me again. I had just killed another human. His body was still on my sleeping bag. Parts of his brain, bits of teeth, and other gore were all over the immediate area and me. I was too scared to move and had to be talked up. After that no one slept the remainder of the night. The other Marines in the tent thanked me for saving their lives, but I was still too scared and sick to my stomach to respond. Later the next morning as we got things sorted out I found myself playing the role of the tough Marine, but inside I was putty. From that night on I really do not remember sleeping anytime while in Korea. How many times I lay awake thanking my mother for the insight of giving me that pistol. How did she know?

Several days later I had an opportunity to discuss my feelings with my platoon sergeant. He laughed and told me that it was natural to be scared. I told him that my concern was not fear but that I was not properly trained by the Marine Corps for combat. I told him that I didn't mind fighting for my country, but I felt that my country should prepare me first. I requested permission to discuss my problem with the company commander. I was informed by the executive officer that the company commander didn't have time for such petty things. The lieutenant told me I was acting cowardly and dismissed me. I finally did get a chance to speak with the company commander, but he, too, told me I was out of place. I then requested permission from him to speak to the battalion commander. The company commander got mad and told me outright that I was acting like a coward and to return to my post.

That evening an Army major stumbled into our area. There was a bullet scar on his steel helmet and he had blood on his uniform. He really looked like he had gone through some sort of hell. It seems that one of his companies had been hit hard by a large force of the NKPA and had panicked. He was asking our company commander for assistance so he could return and pick up his wounded and dead soldiers. Our commander turned around to face us, and before he could say anything every man was on his feet and volunteering to go. I had never experienced anything in my life as emotional as this moment. How proud I was to be a Marine at that particular moment. We had been informed that no matter what happened in combat, Marines never deserted their wounded or left their dead on the battlefield. We formed up and left with the Army major leading the way. It was not a happy mission, as we spent the entire night tending to the wounded and placing others in body bags. We were fortunate that the NKPA forces had moved on.

In the few weeks that we were there in and around Suwon, I couldn't believe the courage and fighting spirit of the ROK soldiers who were assigned to us. I was astounded by their ability to handle and deal with pain. I also got the impression that all Korean soldiers were somehow involved with the field of dentistry. After each firefight with the NKPA, the ROK soldiers would go out into no man's land with empty helmets, a hammer, a screwdriver, plus a pair of pliers. Later they would return with the helmets full of human jaws and teeth. They would then sit down, as only a person who has been raised sitting on his haunches instead of a chair can, and begin to sort through the matter in the helmets. While this was going on they built fires and placed several pots of boiling water in the now-burned-down ashes. Into these pots they placed bits of the jawbones and all of the teeth, and then boiled them for hours.

24

As the fires got hotter, the metal that was in the jawbones and teeth would begin to melt. The soldiers would then remove the jawbones and broken teeth, leaving just the metal residue in the container. Next they would separate the silver from the gold and pour it into separate pots and let it start to cool down. This was where it really got interesting and I learned something about the Korean culture. At that time the soldiers would then take turns squatting down and examining each other's mouths. One of them would then take the dirty screwdriver and a hammer and begin to chip a large part of his buddy's teeth out. As quickly as the cooled liquid would allow, one soldier would then dip his fingers into either the gold or silver, quickly rubbing a small glob until it had the pliability of putty. He would next work it into his buddy's mouth. This process went on all night without a whimper from either man. I couldn't get over how they were able to withstand the pain. However, by morning each soldier had a mouth full of new gold and silver teeth. I later learned that among this group it was considered a sign of wealth to have lots of gold or silver in your mouth.

Slowly I was gaining more confidence, but I still remained a very scared young man. One morning I was outside the tent feeling depressed and sorry for myself when a Red Cross worker passed by and asked me what was wrong. I explained that I was having trouble sleeping at night and that I could not get rid of the fear associated with combat. I also told him that I was totally unprepared for combat. Being a Marine was a proud thing, but I had never been trained to fight like a Marine and, quite frankly, I was scared to death. I told the gentlemen that I really wanted to return to the States and to go through Marine Corps boot camp so that I would know how to take care of myself and to be able to fight like a Marine. I finished by saying that I wasn't afraid to fight or die for my country, but it would be nice if only I knew how to professionally.

He told me that he could not help me unless I knew someone with significant rank who would listen to my plea. I then told him that I knew a brigadier general in the Marine Corps. After listening to my story, this Red Cross worker decided that he would help me and subsequently wrote a night letter to General Lemly explaining my situation. Our platoon sergeant somehow got a copy of this night letter and the next day really chewed me out. He told everyone around that he considered me a coward, especially since I had gone outside of military channels for help. Needless to say, I got on every shit detail for the next ten days. About ten days later a set of orders arrived transferring me back to the States and to Marine Corps boot camp. I avoided the platoon sergeant as much as possible prior to my departure, as he didn't like me and made no bones about how he felt. The company commander was a little friendlier and hoped that he would see me again in the distant future. I thanked him as I boarded a C-54 aircraft that next afternoon that was returning to the States.

4

Boot Camp

The C-54 aircraft that brought me home from Korea landed at Marine Corps Station El Toro, located in Santa Ana, California. The following day I joined a number of other Marine Corps reservists who had come in from Arkansas. We boarded buses to San Diego and to the Marine Corps Recruit Depot (MCRD). Marine Corps boot camp was to become eleven weeks of hell that changed my life forever. Not only did I become a true Marine, but I also learned something of becoming a man.

Upon my arrival at MCRD a corporal met the buses calling out our names and assigning us to a platoon. Another young corporal called us to attention and marched us off with our duffel bags over our shoulders. It was late in the evening as he finally marched us into an area located between four barracks. The corporal left us standing at attention and climbed up to the second floor of one of the barracks. After some ten minutes most of us were talking and joking and had assumed a relaxed position; some even began to smoke. The next incident that occurred will live in my memory forever. Staff Sergeant Grimes, our drill instructor (DI), made what I would consider one of the most dramatic entrées that I have ever witnessed. He began by stepping out on the second-story landing above us and just staring. After a few minutes he performed a precise left turn and proceeded down the stairs. He paused on each step and dramatically popped his heels together so loud that I'm sure you could hear them a city block away. Had this descent been filmed in Hollywood, I'm certain Sergeant Grimes would have received an Oscar for it.

Sergeant Grimes was about six feet four inches tall. His uniforms were so tailored that when he breathed, you could see his muscles ripple underneath. A part of his uniform was a swagger stick that he always carried under his right arm. A swagger stick is about the width of a broom handle with a 20mm shell casing on one end and a .50-caliber bullet on the other end. Upon reaching the bottom of the landing, Sergeant Grimes marched directly to the center of the platoon executing a precise left face, and just stared at us. By osmosis or whatever, the entire platoon came to a rigid position of attention. Sergeant Grimes then did another thing so terrorizing that I will always remember it as a significant emotional event in my life. Without uttering a word he faced left and marched to the end of the first squad. Sidestepping to the right, he stopped as he came abreast of the third Marine in that squad. With his left hand he reached out and grabbed the lapels of the Marine's uniform and picked him up about five inches off the ground. Not saying a word, Sergeant Grimes carried this Marine, who I guessed to weigh about 190 pounds, down to the end of the first squad as if he weighed nothing. Grimes then took two steps forward and sidestepped down the third squad. He stopped two Marines from me and again this time with his right hand grabbed another Marine who was about the same size and weight as the first Marine. Carrying both Marines, Grimes marched back out front to the center of the platoon. By this time both Marines in his hands were turning purple and gasping for air. Dropping his swagger stick to the ground, he suddenly swore and began banging the heads of the two Marines in his hands together. By the time he had done this five or six times there was blood and shattered teeth on both Marines. He paused for a second and shouted, "Fucking reserves!" and tossed the two battered Marines to either side. He then shouted, "Freeze! Freeze like a cold mountain of shit!" Believe me, we froze.

This was our indoctrination to boot camp. An ambulance came by later and picked up the two Marines who still had not come around. As we went to bed that night there was not a word said by anyone in the barracks. The following day Sergeant Grimes marched us down to where there was a hole in the fence surrounding the base and invited anyone to leave who wanted to. No one left, but afterward many wished that they had. Sergeant Grimes informed us that he hated to call cadence, as it was hard on his voice. He told us that we in turn were to drive our boot heels into the ground hard enough to establish a marching rhythm for the platoon. He insisted that we wear out a set of boot heels every two weeks, and believe me, we did. We learned to make our beds so tight that indeed a coin thrown anywhere on the bed would bounce. If the coin didn't bounce Sergeant Grimes would pick up the entire bed, mattress and all, and toss it out on the second-floor landing. Once our beds managed to pass one of Sergeant Grimes's inspections most of us slept on the floor for the remaining ten weeks.

Sometime during the second week Sergeant Grimes came into the barracks around 0200 in the morning and yelled, "Fire!" There was absolute pandemonium as all seventy-five of us attempted to get outside and down the stairs at the same time and form up in formation. We had been told earlier by the assistant DI that we would have exactly thirty seconds to get out of the building and into formation if Sergeant Grimes ever yelled, "Fire!" As soon as we hit the deck we formed up by squads. Sergeant Grimes stepped out on the balcony and his face turned red immediately. He ran down the stairs screaming that we were not dressed properly. The good sergeant was so mad that he gave us a right face and marched us out toward the parade ground. For the next two hours we marched up and down the parade ground, which was about six city blocks long and half as wide. Sergeant Grimes said that he would not let us come in until he could hear our heels pop on the pavement to establish our cadence. By the time we returned to the barracks everyone's heels were bloody with many blisters. We learned our lesson well, and from that miserable night on we never left the barracks without our boots.

Sergeant Grimes was probably the most perfect specimen of a Marine, or of a man, whom I have ever seen. All Marines tell tales of their boot camp training and of their DIs, but to this day I firmly believe that Sergeant Grimes was in a class all by himself. As I mentioned earlier, he stood six feet four inches tall and his body was solid muscle. He had a large "red" nose with a hook in it, and all of his cloth hats seemed to hang right on the hook. He was from Wichita, Kansas, and to my knowledge never spoke in a normal voice. You could hear him blocks away! He informed us one day that if anyone could do anything better than him, we would never have to do whatever that was again. I was very flexible while growing up and from high school football training I could really "duckwalk." This is an exercise where you waddle forward in a squatting position with your heels nearly touching your buttocks. I managed to outdistance Sergeant Grimes one day, and true to his word, we never duckwalked again.

One day a Navy judo expert came to MCRD and offered a challenge to any Marine to best him in a knife fight. Sergeant Grimes was the only Marine on base to accept the challenge. The fighting arena was packed that night with over 1,000 Marine recruits. Both contestants stepped into the ring with large bowie-type knives. The contest lasted almost thirty minutes, with Sergeant Grimes beating the Navy guy three times before he gave up. Boy, were we ever proud of Sergeant Grimes that night.

Learning to recite the history of the Marine Corps was a main part of our eleven-week training program, and Sergeant Grimes never let us forget it. Every night we serenaded Sergeant Grimes with all three verses of the "Marine Corps Hymn." Oftentimes we had to sing a verse several times before he would say good night to us. One day he marched us to the gas chambers, where we were to learn about toxic gas. We were issued gas masks and told how important they were and even more how important it was that they fit properly. Sergeant Grimes asked if everyone's mask fit, and when we responded with a "yes, sir," he marched us into the gas chamber. Taking off his mask, he began to tell us how important this particular piece of equipment was. He replaced his mask and suddenly the room was filled with tear gas. The majority of us were quick to realize that almost to a man none of our masks fit properly. Sergeant Grimes was really mad, because so many of us were crying. He then informed us that none of us would ever make a good pimple on a Marine's ass. Because so many of us were coughing, Sergeant Grimes made us all take our gas masks off. He then told us that we could not leave until we sang all three verses of the "Marine Corps Hymn" to his satisfaction. Finally, the tear gas was turned off and we were allowed to vacate the chamber. I have never seen so many red eyes in all my life. Little did we realize that the exercise was not over. After quick adjustments we were again marched back into the gas chamber. This time we were to experience what they referred to as "vomiting gas." You can guess the results. The sergeant in charge of the facility was so mad because we messed up his chamber that we had to spend the afternoon cleaning every inch of his building.

About the third week of training General Lemly came to see me. Sergeant Grimes was so upset he could hardly talk. He told us afterward that in his thirteen years in the Corps he had never seen, let alone talked to, a general officer. From the day of General Lemly's visit on, every time we went to the mess hall I had to get up on pedestal about three feet high and wait while all other Marine recruits ate. I was subsequently known for the remainder of my time in boot camp as the "general's boy."

On week nine we loaded up in trucks and headed north to Camp Matthews, for live firing and weapons training. Camp Matthews was located about twenty miles north of San Diego in Torry Pines. Again this was to be an experience that none of us would ever forget. According to Sergeant Grimes, there were no officers at Camp Matthews and the DIs were in complete control. Upon arrival we were marched to a large tent area that was to become our home for the next two weeks. We were divided up and placed in eight-man tents.

Our second day there, Sergeant Grimes told us that we would be involved in grudge fights. He formed us up and we counted off by twos. The even guys got to choose who they wanted to fight, while the odd guys got to choose how they wanted to fight. The makeup of our platoon was mostly guys from Arkansas, with six from Texas and two from California. Would you believe it that the other guy from California chose me? I told him that I would be happy to box with him. I had no idea what a grudge fight was supposed to be, but I quickly learned. We were given four-ounce gloves and told to get in the ring and go for it until one of us gave up. The other kid and I were evenly matched, and we fought for six hours. Neither one of us would give up! Sergeant Grimes became angry and told us that since neither one of us was the winner we could suffer the consequences. He said that since neither one of us had won we would both change the fire buckets on 100 tents. This was really a grinding task, as the faucets for the water buckets were a quarter-mile away. That afternoon and most of the night we carried and changed the water in 100 buckets hanging in front of 100 tents. Next we emptied the sand from the other 100 buckets and refilled them before Sergeant Grimes would let us quit.

It didn't take us but one rifle inspection to realize just how important our rifle inspections were. Sergeant Grimes would give us about ten minutes after we arrived back in the tent area from the rifle range to clean both our rifles and our bayonets. We would then be given an open ranks maneuver so Sergeant Grimes had enough room to properly inspect our rifles. He was well known throughout boot camp for his rifle inspections. A corporal would always accompany Sergeant Grimes on inspections. The corporal would carry a small box lined with velvet with various sizes of needles stuck into the velvet. Sergeant Grimes had taught us how to cinch up our rifle slings so tight that they appeared to be a part of the rifle. Sergeant Grimes would very dramatically sidestep in front of a Marine who in turn would prepare his rifle for inspection by opening the bolt and standing rigidly at port arms. Sergeant Grimes always paused and you just never knew when he was going to take your rifle. He frequently grabbed the rifle so hard that the stock would break in his hands. He broke six rifle stocks while we were at Camp Matthews.

These rifle inspections were really a show in themselves and were usually attended by a number of other DIs. Sergeant Grimes usually grabbed your rifle so fast that your eyes would blink. He then would toss the rifle vertically in the air much like a majorette's baton, catching the weapon so that he would be looking directly down the barrel. He would then flip the rifle so that it rotated three or four times horizontally and catch it so that he was looking directly into the magazine area. If he could not find any dirt, he would turn to his assistant and demand a needle. Believe me, using a needle he always found at the least a speck of dust, which would infuriate him. He would then twirl the rifle around his body and slam it back into your chest. Every move he made was dramatic and with seemingly zero effort. Some guys were able to pass rifle inspections, but I failed every one that I attempted. When you failed an inspection Sergeant Grimes would have you extend your arms out level with your eyes and with your knuckles up. He would then delicately place the rifle across the backs of your hands, and you were required to hold it up until the end of the platoon's inspection. Should you drop your weapon, you automatically joined the nightly bucket brigade. Fortunately, I never dropped a rifle.

The absolute worst inspections occurred when Sergeant Grimes decided to inspect bayonets. Almost everyone failed these inspections, especially when he used his needles. When you failed he would have you hold your right arm out and he would then insert the bayonet between your index finger and your thumb. Even though the bayonet only weighed a little more than two pounds, it became physically impossible to hold it and your arm out straight for very long. Almost everyone joined the bucket brigades after these inspections.

While at Camp Matthews we marched every day to and from the rifle ranges, a distance of about a mile and a half. So many Marines before us had marched down the same trails that they were nothing but six to eight inches of powdered dust. I always felt sorry for the feather merchants (smaller guys at the back of the platoon) who ate nothing but dust the entire two weeks. One afternoon on our way home a coalition of six guys, most of them Texans, decided to try to kill Sergeant Grimes. They waited until we arrived back into our tent area and were dismissed to prepare for a rifle inspection. When Sergeant Grimes dismissed us he always did an about face and walked off. On this day as he turned one guy stepped forward, swinging his rifle with all of his strength toward Sergeant Grimes's head. If I ever witnessed Superman in action, this was the time. By the time the event was over four Marines were taken to the field hospital with broken legs or arms while two others experienced brain concussions. No one ever talked again about trying to take care of Sergeant Grimes.

The following day, a hot one by California standards, Sergeant Grimes was again marching what was left of us back from the rifle range. As we came abreast of the camp swimming pool, he stopped us and asked if we were thirsty. Not dreaming of what he had in mind, we all shouted, "Yes, Sir!" No matter when Sergeant Grimes spoke to us the answer was always, "yes sir." He turned and, walking over to the gates of the swimming pool, shoved them open. He then gave us a column right forward march command, and we marched directly into the deep end of the swimming pool. Many guys could not swim, and by the time others of us helped them safely to the other side we had a bundle of rifles and equipment on the bottom of the pool.

Sergeant Grimes had drilled it into our heads that at any time should we ever lose or misplace our rifle or combat equipment we would then be considered "washed out" and would be sent back to another platoon. Sergeant Grimes along with the NCO who was responsible for the pool were both furious. The two sergeants had a short discussion before Sergeant Grimes marched us back to our tent area. Right after our usual weapons inspection Sergeant Grimes told us we had three minutes to change clothes and get into our swimming suits. He ordered everyone to have a water bucket in his hand when we returned to formation. He then marched us back to the swimming pool. Our job was to empty the pool (Olympic-size) with our buckets, then clean the mud and debris from the bottom. This task required all afternoon and 90 percent of the night before we finished. By popular vote, we all agreed to never admit that we were thirsty again to Sergeant Grimes.

With all of his sternness, there was a humorous side to Sergeant Grimes that we discovered while at Camp Matthews. We were required by base regulations to experience some type of entertainment during our eleven-week stay in boot camp. Sergeant Grimes marched us one night over to the outdoor movie theater. He halted us and gave us a left flank command so that we could all see the large movie screen. He then asked us if we had seen the movie, and naturally we chorused a, "Yes, sir." With nothing more said, he then marched us back to our tent area at a double-time pace to be sure that we were tired and ready for bed.

Sergeant Grimes was especially hard on me after General Lemly's visit, because he then knew why and how I had come to his platoon. He wanted to be sure that I was ready for Korea after I finished boot camp. By the time we returned to MCRD from Camp Matthews, Sergeant Grimes had almost become human. He told us many war stories about Marines and also that he had never had anything but "honor platoons" throughout his tenure at MCRD. We as a platoon were not to disappoint him, and on our final graduation inspection and parade we obtained the highest scores of the entire camp. I hated to leave boot camp and Sergeant Grimes even though I would gladly have killed him at any time during the first few weeks of training. I don't think that I ever respected anyone more than Sergeant Grimes in my entire life. Not only did he make a man out of me but, more important, a Marine! My time under his tutelage was definitely a significant emotional event in my life. He not only taught us teamwork, but he also instilled respect, character, honor, loyalty, and love of country into me so deeply that I shall never forget the lessons learned. I still get a lump in my throat just thinking about him. He was the kind of leader whom anyone would follow into combat and give their life, if necessary, to save.

5

Back to Korea

Upon graduation from boot camp I went straight to Camp Pendleton for entrance into the Advanced Combat Training Course. Here is where I learned the fine points about fighting and survival in combat under any conditions. Upon completion of this course I was ready to take on anyone anywhere and at any time. For the first time I truly felt like a real Marine. My return the second time was onboard a faster ship that only took eleven days to cross the Pacific. Upon arrival in Japan most of us were designated as replacement troops, and within twenty-four hours we were airlifted to various places in Korea. I went up north to the 5th Marine headquarters located in the mountains at a place called Hagaru-ri. Most Marines left off the ri and just referred to the place as Hagaru. The weather was not only bad; it was awful. Historians have since declared that the winter of 1950 was to be the most severe winter in recorded history for the Korean nation. The average daily temperature was thirty degrees below zero. I was certainly inclined to believe the historians.

Going back to Korea for the second time was a lot easier than the first time, as I had gained far more knowledge about the country. Foreign countries are usually mysterious to Americans, and Korea was no exception. I had studied up this time and learned that the country was basically a peninsula 575 miles long and 150 miles wide approximating the size of our state of Florida. Along the eastern coast there is a large chain of very rugged mountains that are difficult to cross under any conditions. The western part of the country is mostly flat and muddy and crisscrossed with deep and fast-moving streams. The central part of the country is hilly, with broad valleys and terraced rice paddies. In 1950, Korea was a country with very few roads and what roads did exist were like the secondary roads that existed out west in the United States in the 1930s. Their main roads were merely dirt trails full of potholes that were frequently washed out, which caused an incredible amount of problems for moving vehicles.

I discovered that in Korea road maintenance was a form of government taxation on their people. Government officials would come into a village and direct all inhabitants to turn out for work on the local roads for two weeks. Everyone, including small children, was required to break up rocks and to place them by hand in the roadbed. The roads looked good, but after the first ox cart went over them you would swear that nothing had ever been done to improve them. Whenever vehicles started using these rock roads, the roads quickly crumbled into oblivion.

In 1950 Korea was considered a remote country, with very few exports. The origin of the Korean people was mostly Chinese; however, there was a distinct amount of Japanese culture in evidence. Korea historically is what you would refer to as "the country between." It borders Chinese Manchuria and Russia in the north while the southern tip of the peninsula is only 120 miles from Japan. According to historians, Japan always considered Korea a threat to their future security. Over the centuries the Korean nation has been conquered and reconquered so many times that the true origin of the people is difficult to trace.

At the close of WW II, the U.S. government, as a part of its commitment to the North Atlantic Treaty Organization (NATO), established a small U.S. Army Group Headquarters in the capital city of Seoul. Approximately three thousand American troops were stationed in Seoul, and none of them were combat-type soldiers. According to the Cairo Declaration of 1943, the three great world powers (the United States, the Soviet Union, and England) agreed at the Yalta Conference that Korea would become a free and independent nation.

The Korean nation experienced a similar situation to our American Civil War in the 1800s during the 1940s, wherein both Korean parties agreed to separate the nation at the thirty-eighth parallel. By 1950 Russia was testing our military response on many fronts in what was called the Cold War. The Russians, according to historians, felt that the United States had basically pulled out of their commitment to assist the Korean people. The Russian policy at that time had shifted to one of limited warfare. Economically, they knew that the industrial wealth of Korea lay in the north, close to their borders. By providing the North Koreans with military equipment and supplies the Russians influenced them enough to cause them to attack South Korea.

On June 25, 1950, the (NKPA) crossed the thirty-eighth parallel in mass and the Korean War was on. At the time of the attack the ROK was small and had very little combat experience or equipment. The ROK forces quickly crumbled and fled before the might of the NKPA Soviet-made T-34 tanks.

As I reflect back, it is my personal opinion that we as a nation failed to truly understand the Soviet threat, much like we failed to understand the Japanese threat to Pearl Harbor in 1941. However, President Truman, looking at the situation, felt that the Communist assault on South Korea had to be stopped before the NKPA forces reached the southern tip of South Korea or all was lost. Again according to historians, President Truman ordered General MacArthur in Japan to attempt to stop the Communist forces using everything that he had at his disposal. It would definitely prove to become a tight race. By early August of 1950, the NKPA had achieved most of their objectives. The exhausted American forces and what was left of the dispirited ROK had established a last-ditch stronghold around the perimeter of the southern city of Pusan.

Army general Walton Walker was General MacArthur's man in charge of the NATO forces located inside the perimeter of Pusan. His forces did an outstanding job of holding off the NKPA's advance to the southern tip of the country. At the same time Walker's ragged army was holding the perimeter lines, thousands of U.S. and NATO forces, having been called to active duty, came ashore in Pusan Harbor to bolster his forces. The NATO forces broke out of the perimeter and charged north around the last week of September. Although it wasn't planned, this was the same time that General MacArthur's forces landed at Inchon in the north. During this time period the United States was rapidly mobilizing its reserve forces at home. I was a part of that mobilization, as the Marine Corps' 11th Tank Battalion on the West Coast was the first Reserve unit to be called to active duty by our president, Harry S. Truman.

My first impressions of the Korean people were ones of awe and respect because of their extreme loyalty to their country and flag. It seemed to me that they were all poor farmers, yet there was a side to them that startled me. They displayed incredible loyalty and allegiance to their flag and country, a fact that greatly impressed me. An incident that occurred during my first tour of duty comes quickly to my mind. A number of Marines, including myself, were resting on a ridgeline on our way to Suwon. We were watching an air strike on a small Korean village located in the next valley. I had never seen airplanes in action before. I was enthralled with the awesome power of the Marine F4U Corsairs as they bombed, shot rockets, and strafed the enemy troops that had sought refuge in this small village.

While the action was going on, the people of the village were running everywhere to get away from the aircraft. We watched with concern as an old man fell in the street. He wasn't able to outrun the incoming bullets from the airplanes. After the planes left, it suddenly got very still in the village. As the survivors returned, I came to realize just how different and cruel their culture could be at times. The old man in the street was lying down bleeding profusely from one of his legs, which appeared to be almost severed. As we watched, some kids and a few adults began poking sticks into the man's wounded leg in order to hear him cry out. Is this something done around the world? I don't know, but the scene reminded me of a bunch of chickens my mother had back home. If one of the chickens became injured, the rest of the flock would peck the injured chicken to death. Cruel as it was, this appeared to be a way of life for these people. In spite of what I considered to be barbaric behavior, I later developed a strong compassion for these same people.

Back at Hagaru in late November, things were happening fast and there was much confusion. I was one of fifteen to twenty new replacement troops and we were awaiting orders to go up north wherever the Corps needed us the most. We were told to stay the hell out of the administrative section and to just stand by, a thing that Marines did a lot of. Headquarters personnel were tearing things up, burning documents, and trying to load everything they could aboard the few trucks that were still in commission. Rumors were running wild at the time. It seemed that on the day that we arrived many people thought that the war was almost over and that everyone would be going home by Christmas. However, by November 26th Marines straggling in from units located north of Hagaru had other ideas. They were saying that the Chinese had entered the war and were swarming across the Yalu River in great strength. They further indicated that it wouldn't be long before they arrived in Hagaru and that all hell would break loose.

Most of the Marines straggling into Hagaru were cold, frostbitten, and exhausted from lack of sleep. These Marines were from elements of the 7th Marines that had been located north of our position near the Chosen Reservoir. Both Marine and USAF C-47s were taking off throughout the hours of daylight ferrying the sick, wounded, and dead out of Hagaru's small airstrip. While all of this confusion was going on, the weather had turned Eskimo cold, coupled with high winds and heavy snow. Everyone was miserable, and it became impossible to find a place to stay warm.

I was assigned by a lieutenant to be a part of the rear guard to protect the headquarters staff who were desperately trying to get out of Hagaru. By the time the Chinese soldiers neared Hagaru all the buildings were on fire and it was difficult to see anything. We quickly learned that the Chinese soldiers were a lot different from the NKPA soldiers. The Chinese were all dressed in the same quilted uniforms and were very organized in their military tactics. The word swarmed, as used by the Marines who came through our positions a few days before, hardly described the Chinese's actions. They seemed to come at you in suicidal waves with very little letup. Watching the oncoming Chinese, I remember thinking back on the history of some of our American Indians warriors. They often said before a battle that it was a good day to die. It was as if these Chinese soldiers were possessed with the same fanaticism to die that day. Unlike the NKPA soldiers, the Chinese always coordinated their fire support to cover their advances, and their accuracy was awesome. Fear was, apparently, not a part of their vocabulary. They displayed considerable professionalism as they came at you in small but well-organized attacks. What astounded me the most was that death didn't seem to brother them in any way, as they ran right over their fallen comrades. Their bold tactics quickly brought a new dimension to the war for our guys. Even though we felt superior as American Marines, ammunition and other supplies for us were rapidly becoming a scarce commodity. As we pulled back, there were times of doubt in many of our minds. The final aircraft had departed Hagaru earlier and the airstrip and compound were now in complete shambles. By December 6, the "rout" was on and the much-talked-about U.S. Marine Corps "Famous Retreat" to Hangnum was underway. It actually was not a retreat as far as the Marine Corps was concerned, because we were completely surrounded. The Marine Corps simply chose to attack in a southern direction.

Word filtered down from headquarters that our commander wanted us to get our asses out of "Dodge" as fast as we could move. As the departure time neared, our engineers were blowing up everything they could, and we had to move with expedience to get away from our own explosions. I remember one of our sergeants telling us to not throw anything of value away. By the time we departed Hagaru, the temperature had dropped enough that the water in our canteens froze as we walked along. Many Marines were suffering from frostbite and plagued with dysentery, and toilet paper was nonexistent. It was so cold that my BAR would frequently only shoot single shots. The corpsmen were complaining that what blood plasma they had left was impossible to use, as it, too, was frozen. The worst part about walking down that mountain road was looking up and seeing the Chinese soldiers above us on the ridgelines. It was a very uncomfortable feeling, especially when they stopped and shot at you. The only consolation was that it had to be far colder where they were than where we were at the time.

As we marched down that treacherous road, I found that I was no longer the scared young man that I had been earlier. I was still scared, but in a very different way; i.e., now at least I possessed confidence in my ability to fight and survive. Of the vehicles we had that were operational, all of them were overloaded with wounded Marines. The Chinese seemed to be concentrating their fire on these vehicles to put them out of commission. Oftentimes we would pause by a burning vehicle just to soak up a few minutes of warmth. The big problem was that you couldn't stand still for very long or a Chinese sniper would get you if their mortar shells didn't. We reached a point where the Chinese were so close that it became difficult to keep going. The ground was so hard that it was impossible to bury anything. We tied dead Marines onto vehicles that were still moving as we continued to fight and move southward.

I often thought if I ever survived, how would I describe this place to anyone so that they could believe it? There are just not enough descriptive words to cover all the emotions of the men involved. Growing up in San Diego and going up to the Laguna Mountains during the winter had not prepared me for the cold, misery, and pain that we were subjected to there in Korea. Just trying to stay alive had become a job all by itself.

Quite often we were completely surrounded by Chinese soldiers and there just wasn't a safe place to hide. Often we would huddle in the black smoke of a burning vehicle for a few moments, but we had to keep moving or suffer graver consequences. It's difficult to describe the many short moments of elation that existed and how extremely proud I was of my fellow Marines. Possibly this was where I realized how precious life was. There was no panic among our guys, using the principle of teamwork that we learned in boot camp; we just followed orders and tried to take care of one another the best we could under the circumstances. Should anyone make a mistake and stumble off the road or fall into the snow, it frequently took more effort than anyone realized to get him back upright and on the way again. Complaints about the strong winds and heavy snowfall were common; however, these conditions probably saved many lives, due to the fact that the Chinese couldn't see us.

At first I hit the ground every time a mortar round went off nearby. I quickly learned that if I was still standing after the first blast there was no reason to drop into the ice and snow. Our NCOs kept telling us to fire our rifles every fifteen minutes or so or they would freeze up on us. My feet had reached the point where I could hardly feel my toes, and my ankles hurt like the dickens with each step. I discovered a dead Marine tied on a jeep who had a pair of white cold-weather mountain boots on that were my size. I quickly removed them and placed them on my feet. It was like jumping into a hot tub, and I couldn't believe my good luck. The few K rations that we carried were impossible to eat. Not only were they frozen solid, but also it was almost out of the question to get the cans opened up. The best food that we had was frozen Tootsie Rolls from the PX at Hagaru. Trying not to sweat became a real problem, because whenever you stopped for a minute your clothes would begin to freeze to your body. Oftentimes I found myself wanting to just lie down and go to sleep, but my buddies wouldn't permit that.

42

Conditions became even worse at night, as the already-cold temperatures dropped down even lower. Suffering under these conditions, coupled with a horrible fear of the dark, was a constant companion for all of us.

That march from Hagaru to Kot'o-ri took around thirty-eight hours. The last nine miles were the worst, as Marine historians tell us that we lost 600 Marines in those nine miles. Kot'o-ri, much like Hagaru, was in complete chaos as we arrived near the airstrip. The Chinese had closed in behind us, making any movement difficult. However, we were able to keep them back to a degree, as there was one half-track vehicle still running that had a .50-caliber machine gun mounted on it. A sergeant came running over to me and told me that he needed my help. He pointed out that there were still four C-47 type aircraft on the runway at Kot'o-ri and that they needed our assistance to get off the ground. He told me to take the two privates whom he had with him and use the half-track to provide the four aircraft with ground support fire for their takeoffs. He also said that once the aircraft were airborne we were to get the hell out of there as soon as possible and to make every attempt to catch up with the rear echelon. I never forgot the look on his face as he bid us good-bye.

By the time we got the half-track in position, one of the C-47s had already started rolling down the runway. The pilot hardly got into the air before the Chinese shot the aircraft down, killing all onboard. Matters worsened as we realized that the Chinese had already secured the far end of the runway with light machine-gun and rifle fire. The black smoke from the crashed aircraft did provide us with some cover, but it was not to last for long.

One of the remaining C-47 pilots, a young lieutenant, came running over and asked us to give him a hand. I remember thinking how courageous this lieutenant was under fire. He was running toward a Marine F4-U Corsair that was parked on a nearby taxiway. The lieutenant jumped up into the cockpit about the time I arrived at the wing root. All of a sudden all six .50-caliber machine guns in the wings of the fighter went off, scaring the living daylights out of me. The lieutenant was ecstatic and told us that we needed to move the fighter over to one side of the runway as soon as possible. The four of us managed to quickly move the Corsair to one side of the runway. The lieutenant began checking one of the privates out on how to fire the guns while the other Marine and I rolled a fifty-gallon drum of gas over to the aircraft. We managed to lift the tail high enough to get the drum of gas underneath. This way all six machine guns were pointed directly down the runway on the right side while we had the half-track on the other side.

We signaled the C-47s to roll. As two of them started down the runway, we gave them all we had in terms of support fire, and it worked. The third C-47 taxied into position and suddenly stopped. The young lieutenant shouted for me to come over to the open back door of his aircraft. He insisted that I get the other two Marines and jump onboard. I told him that he was already overloaded and that if he didn't move out fast he wouldn't make it. It became one of those incredibly significant emotional moments in my life. There were tears running down the lieutenant's cheeks as he slowly raised his right hand to a full military salute. His last words to me were that if we didn't get onboard we would not make it out of there. I don't know why, but it was one of the proudest moments of my life as I slowly returned the lieutenant's salute. He ran back to the cockpit and with a roar of the engines was quickly and safely airborne. He was wagging the aircraft wings as he passed out of sight. Fate was to have a hand in this matter, as this lieutenant and I would meet again in another time, another war.

After the C-47 took off we quickly backed the half-track up to a dock and rolled as many fifty-gallon drums of avgas as we could get into the vehicle. The thought of a stray round striking one of those avgas drums never occurred to us. We didn't waste any time, as our goal was to get out of there as quickly as we could. We had no idea how far or how the conditions were south of us, but we vowed that none of us would be captured by the Chinese at Kot'o-ri even though they had us surrounded. We could see the Chinese soldiers running all over the place, and getting out of there was not as easy as we thought. The main problem was that half-track vehicles are not very fast vehicles. We were fortunate that the Chinese did not have any heavy weapons with them at the time. We managed to keep them at a tolerable distance with our .50-caliber machine gun; however, small-arms fire did occasionally ricochet off the sides of the half-track as we headed south.

44

Our first major objective was to get across the temporary spans of what remained of the bridge south of Kot'o-ri. Fortunately for us, the Marines in their haste to get out of there had not blown the temporary spans up. The temporary spans that the engineers had placed across the gorge were made of metal, and with a little ice on them driving across was extremely treacherous. The temporary spans also rocked back and forth just enough to really get our attention. We started across in low gear and held our breath until we reached the opposite side. Our biggest problem was not so much the snow as it was the ice that covered the mountain road. The road, if one could call it that, was narrow, full of bumps and large potholes, with deep precipices along the canyon side. This made it difficult for whoever was driving at the time to keep the half-track in the center of the road. For the first thirty miles or so, I don't believe we ever got out of first gear. We learned rapidly that we were not getting very good gas mileage; however, on the plus side, we were relatively safe and getting enough warmth out of the engine to make life bearable. The alternative was to walk or face death from the Chinese, so we pressed on.

Because of our slow vehicle speed we never did catch up with the column of Marines ahead of us. Our main concern was how long our gas was going to last. We blundered through several ambushes that the Chinese had set up, but the old half-track with bullets bouncing off the front and sides came through like a champ. We frequently came to places, especially down in the valleys, where adjacent roads met the one that we were on. However, I remember the sergeant telling me not to waste any time getting to Hangnum or to get off the road anywhere.

We ran out of gas about ten miles north of Hangnum and went the rest of the way on foot. Getting out of the half-track, with what little warmth it had, didn't prepare us for the brutality of the sudden bitter cold that confronted us. We could see that the city of Hangnum was on fire and burning out of control, with large clouds of black smoke destroying most of our view. As we were running down the road we met two Marine MPs in a jeep just outside a small village north of Hangnum. They had three badly wounded Marines with them and no spare room. They told us to haul ass or we wouldn't make it out. Before leaving, they explained that they were the rear guard and that it was about six miles to the harbor, where the evacuation was underway.

To the best of my knowledge we three were the last Marines to arrive in Hangnum. The chaos and destruction in the city were unbelievable, with civilians running all over the place trying to get out of town, any way they could. There were large explosions everywhere, making it all the more difficult getting through the refugees and trying to locate the harbor.

Finally arriving at the docks, we discovered that the engineers were blowing up the entire harbor; piers were on fire, and there was panic everywhere. Looking out in the harbor, we spotted a small dory-type boat that seemed to be picking up guys out of the water. I got the coxswain's attention with a long burst of automatic fire from my BAR over his head. He recognized us as Marines and made a pass close into the pier. Stopping the motor, he yelled for us to jump into the water. Even though it was the dead of winter and the jump was around eight feet to the icy water below, we didn't hesitate to follow his directions. I thought that I had experienced cold before, but as I went down into that water I wasn't sure that I would make it back to the surface. Because of my good Marine Corps training I managed to hold on to my automatic rifle; however, my hands and fingers didn't seem to want to obey my brain. I'm sure that I was screaming and yelling for help certain that I was about to go down for the last time as the dory came alongside me. Someone grabbed my arm and somehow I managed to get myself onboard.

Upon regaining my composure, I remember thanking the coxswain for picking us up, and his remark put a lump in my throat. He said that even though he was overloaded, it was Christmas Eve, and he just couldn't leave us where we were. Here again, there simply weren't enough words to somehow thank this unsung Navy hero. I never learned his name, but his deed under extreme combat conditions exemplified how important it was to be an American fighting man. The dory was incredibly overloaded, so we had to take turns getting in and out of the icy water while hanging on the sides as the coxswain slowly made his way out of the harbor. Steering was all the more difficult for him as clouds of black smoke constantly obstructed the view until we got free of the harbor entrance.

Once clear of the harbor, we discovered that the ships that were to pick us up were long gone. We discussed our situation and decided to proceed down the coast, going as far as our fuel would permit. We decided to stay within sight of land but remained far enough out so that small-arms fire could not reach us. Our goal was not to be captured by the Chinese. I guess the Chinese had more important things to do as we were not harassed or fired upon at any time. The small engine of the dory plus the close condition of the bodies onboard provided us some warmth, especially after hanging overboard for a while.

The coxswain said that he thought that there was a small Navy resupply depot somewhere down the coast, and that was our destination. I'm not sure exactly how long we motored down the coast, but someone finally spotted a large Navy LCI-type boat beached on the shore, and we immediately headed for it. A Navy ensign came down to meet us and invited us to join his detachment, and we readily agreed. After the wounded were taken care of and we were settled in, the ensign told us that the place we were at was called Chumingin. It was an aviation gas resupply depot that was supporting the First Marine Air Wing, which was located about forty miles south of our current position.

We spent the next two weeks unloading fifty-gallon barrels of avgas from the LCI. These barrels had to be manually rolled off the LCI and up a sandy beach about seventy feet before loading them onto waiting trucks. There were eight trucks that had to be loaded, and were the Navy guys ever happy for the additional help. We, too, were happy, especially to be away from the constant rifle fire from the Chinese. Now that there were extra personnel, the truck drivers requested to have the Marines ride shotgun guard in the trucks for their trip down the coast. Two times in the past week snipers had shot at the convoy as they drove south to K-18. The ensign agreed with our request, and we managed to salvage eight .30-caliber machine guns from his LCI that we were able to mount on the passenger's side of each truck. I wasn't going to go, but when I found out they had hot food and showers at K-18 I quickly volunteered for shotgun duty.

6

K-18 to Sea Duty

The forty-three-mile drive down to K-18 was uneventful, and once on the base we were free to roam until the next morning. I had never seen a fighter-type aircraft up close except for the F4-U that had been at Kot'o-ri, and I really didn't get a good look at that one. Standing out on the apron, I observed a flight of four Corsairs in the landing pattern. I waited until they had landed, and started walking down to where the airdales were parking them. *Airdales* is a term used in the Marine Corps to identify guys who work on aircraft. I guess I was as much a spectacle to the airdales as the aircraft was to me. My appearance caused them to stare at me, and as I reflect back I can understand why. My BAR was cradled in my arms, and I hadn't shaved or taken a bath in quite a while. My uniform, what was left of it, was torn in many places and fit me like a sack, as I had lost so much weight. I'm sure to them that I must have looked like the comic strip *The Mexican Bandito*. My hands were black from the oil of loading all those drums of gasoline. My steel helmet had a dent in it and was probably as dirty as I was. Also, I was wearing crossed bandoliers of ammunition for my BAR.

As I mentioned earlier, there is a lot of tradition in the Marine Corps, especially among the enlisted ranks. All Marines are basically riflemen, but some never see or use their rifles due to their job assignments. As members of the infantry our lives often depended upon the condition of our rifles. Since we literally lived with our weapons, we considered all other Marines as sort of second-class citizens. I'm quite sure that same feeling its true in any combat unit today.

As these F4-Us taxied into their parking places, the noise and power of their engines mesmerized me. These particular Corsairs all had blue-and-white checkerboards painted around their engines. I watched as the plane captains directed the pilots to their respective parking spots. They then set the chocks around the wheels, and as the engine stopped running they climbed up on the wings to assist the pilots in getting out of the aircraft. I had moved closer to one of the aircraft to get a better view when the pilot after getting out smiled and said, "How are you doing, Sergeant?"

I looked at him closely and said, "Excuse me, sir, don't I know you?"

He stopped and scrutinized me carefully, then said, "Where are you from, son?"

I replied, "Coronado."

After a few minutes of conversation, we were able to figure out where our paths had crossed before. He was a Marine Reserve pilot and had worked for the Bank of America in Coronado as an administrative assistant. He remembered me as the kid who worked at Perkins Flower Shop a few doors down from the bank. Every day I used to cut through the bank on my way to pick up the delivery truck for the flower shop, and we always smiled or waved at each other.

It was kind of like finding an old friend a thousand miles from home. He wanted to know where I got the BAR and how did I get to K-18? I told him my entire story. He insisted that I accompany him in to meet the squadron commander. I waited outside the commander's tent until the captain asked me in. The squadron commander was a Lieutenant Colonel Axtel. His first words were, "Young man, this is the home of the famous Marine Corps Checkerboard Squadron VMF-312." As dirty and haggard-looking as I was, I did my best to report to the colonel in proper military fashion. Colonel Axtel asked me what my rank was, and I told him that I had been elevated to the rank of corporal on the battlefield. He then told me that the squadron was shorthanded and wanted to know if I would like to become a member of VMF-312. I instantly replied, "Yes, sir." After hearing my story and that all of my records as far as I knew were burned up at Hagaru-ri, he told me not to worry about the paperwork. He then stuck out his hand and welcomed me explaining that I was now Sergeant Hunter and to report to the personnel tent. At that moment I transferred from Marine Corps Infantry to Marine Corps Aviation and, wow, was I excited.

I was assigned to an eight-man tent, given new uniforms, and told to report to one of the sergeants on the flight line. The sergeant informed me that I was going to become a "raggie," i.e., one who cleans and wipes down airplanes. Eventually, when I got qualified, he said, I would be assigned my own aircraft and would then become known as a plane captain. For my first job, I was given a hammer and a chisel and told to go out and clean the encrusted mud off the flaps and wheels of several aircraft that had recently landed. I never realized what joy and comfort there could be in such a picayunish job.

Due to the necessity of getting airpower into action quickly, the airstrip at K-18 was built on a shifting and sinking mud flat. The engineers had laid down a runway that looked like it was a part of a giant Erector set. The metal part was called PSP, and each piece was about ten feet long by one and a half feet wide and was full of round holes. The pieces were fitted together by hand using a tongue-and-groove method. When the aircraft landed, the weight of the plane touching down would cause mud to fly up through the holes of the PSP and cover the entire underside of the aircraft. For the first 100 feet or so of the landing it looked like the plane was water-skiing. By the time the aircraft taxied to their parking position you could count on fifty to eighty pounds of mud attached to the underside. This runway was considered primitive by our pilots, but effective for combat conditions.

Our squadron aircraft were WW II F4-U Corsair-type fighter aircraft built by the Chance-Vaught Aircraft Company. What made them unusual to look at was their inverted gull wings. In each wing there were three .50-caliber machine guns. The F4-U aircraft was powered by an R2800 Pratt & Whitney engine, which developed over 2,000 horsepower. The aircraft had good range and could carry eight five-inch rockets or four 500-pound bombs. Our aircraft were painted a dark navy blue with a three-foot-wide checkerboard band around the engine nacelles. It seemed like everything in the squadron was checkerboarded. All of the pilots had checkerboard scarves, and their helmets were checkerboarded. There was lots of spirit within our squadron, and any nonsquadron aircraft that landed or made an emergency landing at our airfield was immediately checkerboarded. We even had a small dog that had become attached to our squadron and her name was Checkers. She actually flew with one of our pilots on a number of missions lying behind his head in the cockpit.

I voluntarily extended my tour and stayed with VMF-312 through November of 1952. While I was at K-18 there was an event that I shall never forget, and it involves money. Normally I did not get into the pay line each month, as there was very little need for money. One day I decided that I needed to send some kind of souvenir home to my mother. I went to the personnel tent and spoke with the finance officer. I told him that I wanted forty dollars and would like it exchanged into Korean won. He asked me if I was crazy, and I told him no and why I wanted it. He said that I needed to come back the following day and that he would have it for me. He also said that I'd better have a wheelbarrow with me. What I didn't realize was that the exchange rate was 40,000 won to each American dollar. I wound up with three giant boxes of won, and I truly did need help to get them into the local village. However, I got my mother several beautiful Korean dresses plus a tea set, and the villagers certainly were happy with what they got.

As far as food goes, one of the things that the Marine Corps always seemed to have on hand was plenty of Spam. I had learned to absolutely hate even the smell of Spam, no matter how it was cooked. The village of P'yongt'aek was located just outside the Marine base there at K-18. Just east of P'yongt'aek was a railway junction with a number of stranded northbound trains with nowhere to go. One of these trains was carrying frozen turkeys and several carloads of beer for the holiday meals of the American troops located up north. We broke into one of the cars loaded with turkeys and brought them back to the mess hall at K-18. Needless to say, over the next few days we all enjoyed some of the best meals I have ever eaten. There was so much beer that we wound up throwing the full cans out on the nearby frozen rice paddies and using them for target practice. Just like the cowboys from the old West, I got very good at shooting beer cans from the hip with my .45 automatic.

We operated out of K-18 on the east coast of Korea for three months that winter of 1951 before receiving orders to go onboard an aircraft carrier. Life was really good to me during this time. I was promoted to the rank of staff sergeant and given a plane crew of my own. We cleared out of K-18 and were flown to an air force base in Japan. We learned that we were going to go onboard the

USS *Bataan,* a CVL small aircraft carrier that was currently in docked at Yokosuka, Japan. I'm not sure what the *CVL* stood for, but the Bataan was an aircraft carrier built over a cruiser hull. Our pilots were really concerned, as the carrier not only was small but also had a natural three-to-five-degree list to the starboard side due to the heavy super structure on that side. Another concern was the fact that of the twenty-four Marine Reserve pilots in VMF-312 only one had made a carrier landing in the past year.

We went over to an old abandoned Japanese bomber base called Itami and painted the outline of the flight deck of the *Bataan* on one of their concrete runways. For the next two weeks, our pilots spent several hours each day making practice carrier approaches and touch-and-go landings on this field. The idea was for them to learn to touch their aircraft down precisely on a spot and then try to get airborne before they ran out of painted lines. One of the officers was acting as the landing safety officer (LSO). His job was to stand beside the approach end of the painted strip and with two yellow paddles in his hands align the approaching aircraft and give them clearance to land. Oftentimes he would wave his yellow wands wildly trying to get the approaching pilot to break off his approach and go around for another try. The Corsairs usually touched down very hard, as they practiced stalling their aircraft onto the concrete. One day we lost one F4-U as the left landing gear folded up when the aircraft made an exceptionally hard landing. This accident brought us down to twenty-three operational aircraft. We were really ready to get out of there by the end of the two weeks. They bused the enlisted men down to Yokosuka and we boarded the USS *Bataan.* None of us were pleased with our new accommodations, but this was wartime, and we pressed on with our business.

We steamed southwest of Japan for two days in the Pacific Ocean before our squadron showed up and got ready to land. This first landing time was a real experience for all of us Marines. With the exception of the Navy's fire-fighting crews, Marine plane captains were the only other persons allowed on the flight deck of the carrier. Everyone according to his job assignment on the flight deck had a different color of shirt. I don't think any of us will ever forget the first official landings on the USS *Bataan,* especially our pilots.

Landing an aircraft on a ship is a very delicate and dangerous job even for pilots with many carrier landings. As the aircraft carrier increases its speed over the water for recovery operations, so do the problems associated with the taking on of aircraft increase. Depending on the conditions of the sea at the time of recovery, the flight deck of aircraft carriers will rock and roll plus often go up and down at the same time. This condition ultimately makes it all the more difficult for the pilots making their landing approaches. One additional problem for VMF-312 was the unique design of the F4-U Corsair. The cockpit was located toward the tail of the aircraft fuselage. During the final phases of the pilot's approach to the carrier it was necessary to raise the nose of the fighter to assume a landing configuration for the aircraft. When this occurred the inverted gull wings of the F4-U would blank out the LSO and oftentimes the rear end of the flight deck. It was the LSO's job to tell a pilot when one wing was low or if he was in a dangerous flight attitude. Frequently the LSO would wave off a pilot for an unsafe approach or landing. It was the pilot's responsibility to throw the power to his aircraft and execute a safe go-around. Oftentimes this led to a fatal crash, as things always happen fast when you are in an aircraft cockpit. The pilot is already under extreme stress just making the approach, and when he has to go around, the slightest distraction can be fatal, especially if he is slightly low. A successful go-around means that the pilot has to move the throttle to full military power, raise the gear and flaps, and climb all at the same time. Since the radius of the propeller blades is almost seven feet, there is zero room for error.

Onboard the carrier there are three sets of arresting cables that extend across the flight deck, and they are twenty yards apart. These arresting cables are elevated approximately six inches off the flight deck. As the pilot stalls his aircraft onto the flight deck he must engage one of these arresting cables with the tail hook of the aircraft or he will crash. To match each arresting cable there is a corresponding set of vertical barrier cables to catch the aircraft propeller should anything go wrong. There are sailors on each side of the aircraft carrier whose sole responsibility is to drop the next vertical barriers once the aircraft tail hook has engaged an arresting cable. These arresting cables are designed to catch the aircraft and to prevent it from skipping on down the flight deck and crashing into aircraft already parked on the forward part of the flight deck. One of the things that compounded our landing problems was the fact that the sailors who were manning the vertical barriers were also on their first cruise and often they failed to drop the succeeding vertical barrier in time. When this occurred, the propeller of the landing aircraft would engage the cables of the vertical barrier and lead directly to a crash.

Between attempts to land, the deck of the carrier was a sea of colored shirts. Some were pushing damaged aircraft forward or over the side of the ship and cleaning up debris while others were parking and assisting pilots out of the cockpits. During that first carrier landing, out of our twenty-three operational aircraft only the first plane made a safe landing. The next thirteen aircraft crashed either by grabbing the wrong arresting cable with their tail hooks and hitting the vertical barriers with their propellers or by sliding sideways into the catwalks that ran along both sides of the flight deck. By the time the thirteenth aircraft crashed, the captain of the *Bataan* stopped all flight operations and ordered the remaining airborne fighters to return to Japan. The captain went into a wild tirade about how terrible Marine pilots were, as they had exhausted all of the barrier cable onboard his ship. The *Bataan* now had to return to the Navy shipyard at Yokosuka in order to be refitted with more barrier cable. This wasn't exactly the best way to get started in a war, but it was reality. It quickly became obvious to our pilots that the captain cared more for his ship than he did for the Marine pilots onboard.

I never seemed to understand the complete relationship between the Navy and the Marine Corps. It was as if neither side liked the other, yet we were both fighting for the same cause. Every time we lost an aircraft, it cost the Marine Corps $1.25 in transfer fees for a replacement aircraft to be bought from the Navy. It seemed to me to be a strange thing to do, especially during wartime; however, it was again a reality. Many of the aircraft that we received from the Navy Replacement Depot in Japan had seen better flying days. The Marine pilots never complained to us; they just pressed on with the mission. These indeed were not easy times for our pilots. In addition to trying to get safely back onboard the carrier in bad seas, they had to deal with Soviet-built Mig-15 jet fighters that the Chinese, Soviets, and North Koreans were flying against them.

To provide the reader with a realistic view of combat operations that winter, we lost seventy-eight aircraft during the first three months of sea duty. One aircraft was shot down by enemy ground-placed antiaircraft guns, while the other seventy-seven were lost to carrier landings. One of our pilots, a young lieutenant, had the distinction of being the only pilot of a propeller-driven fighter air-craft in the Korean War to shoot down a Soviet Mig-15 jet fighter. The entire squadron was pumped up over this incredible aerial feat. To commemorate this event I had a Japanese artist paint the event on both ends of a Zenith Transoceanic radio that I still own today. As enlisted men and especially plane captains, we took an unbelievable amount of pride in our pilots and in our individual aircraft. The trust relationship between our pilots and plane captains was second to none. Usually the same pilot flew the same aircraft and we both had our names painted on the left side of the cockpit. A rivalry existed among many of the pilots, as they argued over who was going to fly my particular aircraft.

The call sign of our squadron aircraft was Willie Roger (WR) plus the number of that particular aircraft. WR-13 was my first air-craft, followed by WR-21 and WR-25, and I spent long hours waxing the entire plane so that it would always stand out. My aircraft experi-enced very few mechanical failures, which was another reason pilots wanted to fly WR-13.

The most dangerous part of the combat mission was always the landing phase onboard carriers. Once a plane made it safely on-board and the tail hook was released, the pilot would then taxi forward while folding the wings and being directed to a parking spot. This was always a hazardous time, as we parked the aircraft so close together, not only side by side but also nose to tail. Normally the blades of the propeller would wind up only inches from the plane in front of it. Once a craft parked and the engine shut down we wasted no time in getting the pilots out and away from the air-craft. More than once a landing aircraft had to make a go-around and I can remember on two occasions where they crashed into the aircraft parked on the forward deck. No one was killed, but it always created havoc with flight operations and lost flying machines.

On one such occasion, after parking the F4-U on the forward flight deck I was assisting the pilot, Captain Jennings, out of the cockpit when I happened to look back and froze. Coming directly toward us was a Corsair on a go-around, only instead of being up in the sky, he was just inches off the flight deck. I'm sure that the fearful look on my face must have reflected back to Captain Jennings, because we both froze momentarily. The oncoming Corsair looked and sounded like a runaway freight train bearing down on us. Things at that time happened extremely fast, yet to those of us involved everything seemed to be happening in slow motion. There was a terrible explosion as the Corsair struck the two aircraft parked directly behind us, with parts of aircraft flying all over the place. It reminded me of being inside an inferno with everything going wrong at once. I was so scared that my feet didn't seem to want to obey my brain. I remember screaming at the pilot to "get the hell out of the cockpit" before we were both consumed by fire. Somehow we both made it with neither of us getting hurt. That accident cost the squadron four aircraft.

During the first three months' tour of sea duty, I went through three aircraft. I had named my aircraft *Alice I, Alice II,* and *Alice Special,* all after the sister of one of the guys whom I had met in boot camp. The first two aircraft were both lost in landing accidents, while the third remained flying after I left the squadron. Like back on the front lines, I do not remember getting much sleep, as I spent most of my time working and polishing my personal aircraft. Some pilots were very superstitious of the number 13 and they refused to fly my aircraft, but I was extremely proud of old WR-13. To me, planes were just like automobiles: if you took good care of them, they in turn will perform well for you, and I really believed this.

Speaking of the rift between Marines and sailors, it really came to a head when we returned to port after our first combat tour of duty. We arrived in the port of Sasebo, Japan, in early March. It was the first time that I had ever been onboard a large ship trying to maneuver in a small harbor. There were no tugboats to assist the carrier, so the captain of the *Bataan* had us line the forward flight deck with six Corsairs on either side of the flight deck. When he wanted to turn the ship he would come on the radio and instruct those of us on one side of the flight deck to go to full military power until he told us to stop. It was really interesting, as we were able to turn the big carrier whichever way the captain wanted. There was never any kind of thanks to the Marines, but we felt good about our part in docking the ship.

Once we dropped anchor, everyone was excited about going on liberty. All Marines (enlisted and officers alike) were told to muster on the lower hangar deck and to stand by for inspection. While we were waiting at the position of parade rest, a whole bunch of Navy personnel went by our formation laughing as they headed for the gangplank. There were shore boats below, like taxis, that were waiting to take everyone ashore. None of us liked the situation very much as we felt that we were being treated like second-class citizens. Finally a Navy ensign accompanied by a party of sailors each with a clipboard came along and called us to attention. He informed us that he would be conducting the inspection and that if anything was wrong, our names would be placed on a clipboard and we wouldn't be allowed to go ashore. He started off inspecting our pilots, and as he stepped in front of one of our lieutenants some harsh words were exchanged between the two officers. Suddenly our lieutenant decked the ensign, and wow, the fight was on. I have never been involved in a more exciting free-for-all fight, even more exciting than emptying the dugout in a baseball game.

Within minutes there was absolute bedlam on the hangar deck. The next thing that we heard was the voice of the captain of the ship coming over the loudspeakers informing us that liberty was canceled for all Marines. This accomplished nothing other than inciting us all the more to vent our hatred for the sailors. I would guess that it was our better-disciplined training that prevailed, as we quickly secured the ship's armory. Thus we prevented the sailors from getting their hands on weapons. There were so many sailors being thrown overboard that the shore boats had to move away from the carrier to prevent injury to the falling sailors. No one was about to stop this fight, as it had been in the making for three long months. The Navy had a number of sailors who were known as masters at arms (MAs). These MAs made life thoroughly difficult for Marine enlisted men, and these were the guys whom we went after first.

To the best of my recalling ability, I think all of the MAs were thrown overboard. Finally, the captain sounded the alarm for "General Quarters" and requested assistance from the local shore patrol in Sasebo. Several shore patrol boats arrived and circled the carrier; however, we were not about to let any of the Military Police come onboard. The total fight lasted for about two hours, until the captain's voice came back over the loudspeakers announcing that if the

Marines would stop fighting they would be allowed to go ashore without an inspection. We were never to know, but I am sure that there were some harsh words exchanged between our commander and the ship's captain. After that incident we never had problems with any of the Navy personnel. We became a smooth-running team, with many of us becoming close friends.

Going onshore on first liberty was a really unusual experience in those days for U.S. Marines. We quickly discovered that the Japanese people were scared to death of U.S. Marines. It seems that they had heard so many stories of atrocities committed by the Marines in WW II that they were fearful for their lives. We were briefed to be very careful and to never threaten Japanese citizens in any way. In time, the myth of terror disappeared and the Japanese citizens began treating us as just plain human beings. I remember buying my mother a complete set of Noritake china. My problem was having to lug it all the way back to the ship in order to mail it home. That same set of dishes is in our house today.

The shore leaves were just interludes between combat tours for us. During my year with VMF-312 in 1952 we changed carriers three times. All three carriers were of the light CVL class. However, neither the USS *Baroko* nor the USS *Siscili* had a seven-degree list like the *Bataan*, which made it far easier for our pilots to get their aircraft onboard. By the time we got to the second two carriers our pilots had gained enough experience that landings accidents almost ceased to exist.

I have to come back to the USS *Bataan* for one final story. Sometime during our first combat tour we got caught in the edge of a typhoon while operating in the North Yellow Sea. The weather had gotten worse throughout the day as we cruised north, to the extent that we had to cease flying operations. We got as many aircraft as we could below into the hangar deck while those remaining on the flight deck were tied down with three-quarter-inch cables. When the waves reached forty feet in height the captain sounded "General Quarters" and all hatches (doors) were immediately sealed off. Since I had been a part of the work crew trying to secure the aircraft on the flight deck, we were the last ones to reach the safety of inside the ship. Six Marines and four sailors made it to the conning tower, where we were locked inside a small six-by-eight room for the duration of the storm. All of us were scared to death.

As the storm grew in intensity, the waves in like manner grew in height. The ship had turned, heading straight into the storm, to ease some of the strain on the vessel; however, the rocking, rolling, and creaking continued to get worse. As the waves increased in height, the bow of the carrier would plunge down into the valley of the next succeeding wave, causing the screws on the stern of the ship to come completely out of the water. This caused the screws to speed up until they went back into the water, causing an incredibly screeching noise that shook the entire ship. The noise was so awful that we were afraid that the ship would come apart and sink at any moment. There were four portholes, one on each side of this small room that we were locked in. I remember staring out the forward porthole and watching as huge waves crashed over the bow of the ship. This was the first time in my life that I realized how powerful Mother Nature could be. We were told later that some of these waves reached 100 feet in height, and I truly believed it. As these gigantic waves crashed down on the flight deck they would snap the cables and tear the aircraft off as if the aircraft were made out of paper. When the seas finally calmed down enough for us to go back out on the flight deck, we realized that we had lost six aircraft to the storm. While all this terror was going on I was too scared to get seasick. To this day, I have an incredible fear of the ocean, as well as a fear of heights.

We always had six destroyers escorting the aircraft carrier anytime that we were at sea. When the aforementioned storm struck us we had six Australian destroyers with us. I recall looking out the portholes and watching with fascination as these ships would pop out of the water as much as thirty feet in the air. You could see the entire ship with propellers turning as it slowly fell back down into the sea. The destroyer while out of the water would actually hang in the air for what seemed like ten to twenty seconds. It would then wobble back and forth while plunging back down, disappearing below the surface of the water. It would remain under the water for what seemed like minutes, and all you could see was bubbles where it had disappeared. I could never understand how the men onboard those destroyers survived situations like we were in.

7

Supernatural Powers at Work

Two times during the Korean War I was supposedly killed. In both cases I really felt like I had been. People have told me that you often see a white light just before dying, but in both cases I was too numbed to see anything.

After I was discharged from the Marine Corps in November of 1952, I returned home to Imperial Beach to spend some time with Mom and Dad. One evening while we were sitting down for dinner, Dad began to question me about several events that I had not written home about. I was astounded, as there was no way in which Dad or anyone else could have learned the details that he described to me. He said that Mom had awakened screaming in the middle of the night, having had a vision that I had been killed. She was partially right, but what Dad began to tell me was even more fascinating and scary. I knew from before that Mom always said that she had a "guardian angel" that was always near her and provided her with counsel. Her guardian angel, according to her, was an Indian. I know that Mom meditated a lot, although instead of meditation she called it being in a state of euphoria where her soul was free to roam. Dad's words actually caused the hackles on the back of my neck to rise, and I became spellbound with the details of his story.

The first incident that Dad related occurred while our battle lines were fairly stable during the first part of the Korean War. With nothing better to do I often volunteered to go out on Office of Strategic Services (OSS) missions at night. The OSS was the predecessor to our present-day CIA (Central Intelligence Agency). These night patrols behind enemy lines were always exciting and served to relieve the boredom of sitting in a cold trench or foxhole for days on end. On this particular mission we were to go behind the enemy lines for approximately eighteen miles in order to blow up several known NKPA supply dumps. We were well briefed and had all of the necessary passwords committed to memory should anything go wrong while out on patrol. This was in case we had to return to our lines by ourselves. We accomplished our goal with ease, and all twelve of us started back toward our lines. As we closed to within a half-mile of our lines we were detected by the NKPA, and all hell broke lose. As the incoming firing began, we were just beginning to climb up a trail that was traversing a ridgeline. We went from a normal walk to a double-time run in a hurry.

The NKPA troops quickly opened up on us with small mortar rounds, and they were very accurate. I was running so hard that I had no idea how close or where the enemy troops were. It was night, but there was a bright moon that failed to cover our movements. I had witnessed earlier the NKPA troops with their small leg-held mortars picking off running guys and knew how good they were. In any event, a mortar round fell between two Marines just ahead of me, killing them both. The impact of the explosion blew me off the trail and down a steep embankment. I must have rolled twenty to thirty feet down and was stunned for some time before my senses returned. As I lay there, I couldn't hear anything, but I could see the North Koreans soldiers talking to one another, so I remained perfectly still. They stripped the equipment and weapons from the dead Marines and tossed the bodies down where I was located. I waited for several hours before making a move. My ears were ringing so bad that I couldn't hear a thing as I slowly started crawling out of the crevasse.

Finding myself in no-man's-land was not a pleasant thing, as I knew the area was mined. I had determined where our lines were, but I couldn't hear the challenges from our outpost guards. I also knew that most Marines would shoot first and ask questions later, as everyone associated with the front lines was jumpy especially at night. I was fairly well concealed, so I just waited for dawn before making a move. In due time I was spotted by a Marine outpost guard and waved in. Was I ever happy to be back among friendly forces! I told the company commander that I couldn't hear him, and he gave me a tablet to make my report on. I decided then and there that I had had enough of the OSS volunteer patrols. What astounded me the most was the minute detail that Dad had gotten from Mom about this incident. It was as if someone had written the details down and forwarded them to my mother.

The first story was bad enough, and Dad could not understand why I had not written or said anything about the incident. The real reason was that it was just another day in the life of a trooper involved in combat. The second incident took place while onboard the USS *Baroko* sometime in June of 1952. We were operating in the Yellow Sea somewhere off the northwest coast of North Korea and in the process of recovering aircraft from a combat mission. Anytime an aircraft returned to the carrier with hung ordnance onboard, they had to orbit the carrier and wait for a clearance to land. The last aircraft, especially if it had hung ordnance, was always low on fuel, which caused the stress level to be even higher for the pilot. The reason for holding the aircraft up was that the Navy's Emergency Ordnance Disposal (EOD) team had to drag a large cargo net about three feet high across the flight deck. This cargo net served two purposes, i.e., to protect the aircraft that had already landed and were parked on the forward flight deck, plus the net most times would catch the hung ordnance as it skipped down the flight deck. The Navy had specific regulations and procedures for handling this type of situation. Absolutely no one was allowed on deck but the EOD team. About 98 percent of the time as the aircraft engaged the arresting cable, the hung ordnance would fly off and bounce down the flight deck and lodge in the cargo net. The minute this occurred the EOD team would be out there with their small tractor and quickly extract the hot bomb and drop it over the side of the carrier. This type of incident became such a common occurrence that we all became complacent. We were usually so busy getting the pilots out of cockpits and trying to turn the aircraft around for another flight that we very rarely left the confines of the flight deck. I have watched on numerous occasions 750- or 1,000-pound bombs bounce down the flight deck only fifteen to twenty yards away and never thought much about them.

On or about July 4, 1952, a Corsair came in with two hung five-inch rockets on one of its wings. Apparently the rear mounts holding the rockets had broken and the rockets were hanging like a letter X under the wing. Most of the plane captains were gathered near the conning tower in a bunch waiting and watching to see what would happen, and happen it did! Like when you are watching a car or aircraft wreck, everything seems to happen in slow motion. As the rockets broke free from the F4-U, they turned end over end a few times and finally struck the flight deck nose down. The force of the ensuing explosion blew a hole five feet wide in the flight deck and two to three feet wide in the hangar deck below. The blast itself blew me over to the side of the flight deck.

As I lay there I finally focused my eyes on the small railing that ran all the way around the flight deck. It was made of steel and approximately an inch and a half thick by four inches high. Just above my head, about a hand's width away, I could see that eight to ten inches of the railing was missing. I remember thinking to myself that, gee, a guy could get killed by that stuff. If the shrapnel could take out several inches of steel, what would it do to a human body? Before the day was over fourteen people had lost their lives in this incident. Here again, I couldn't get over the fact that Mom knew all about this incident, and especially the details. I laughed with both Mom and Dad, but never again was I to doubt Mom's word whenever she told me to be careful on a certain day. Often she would tell me before driving to school to look out for a particular color of car that day and I would laugh, but believe me, I looked both ways all day while driving.

Another interesting thing that occurred to me while in Korea was the loss of my hair. I lost my hair shortly after I became involved in combat. At the time, I was too frightened to even think about it. All I could think about was staying alive! Besides, other Marines were experiencing similar problems with either their hair turning white overnight or falling out like mine. During the out-processing physical at Treasure Island in 1952 two Navy dermatologists interviewed me and both agreed that the loss of my hair was due to fright and that it was a common thing. I don't know how common it was and there was nothing that I could do about it but accept it, so that's what I have done and never looked back.

I made one of those gross mistakes that you regret for a long time while I was passing through the out-processing line at Treasure Island. There was a captain seated near the end of the line and he asked me if I had anything to say before leaving the Corps. I replied, "Yes, sir, there is: if I could get anywhere near President Truman I would kill him." Needless to say, that was not the thing to say. I was pulled out of line and told to sit down in the back of the room. I subsequently spent an additional four weeks there at Treasure Island going through psychology sessions with two psychiatrists. Their job was to try to ensure that I was ready to return to the civilian world. Becoming aware of my mistake, I quickly learned to say yes to most everything they asked me. However, my reasons for hating President Truman were not exactly his fault, but I held his rationing of ammunition responsible for the deaths of a lot of Marines.

When I first arrived in Korea, I was not aware of how politics could control a war. The first thing that I became aware of politically was the so-called Rules of Engagement. Apparently it wasn't a new concept, but it was for me. From my experiences of watching John Wayne, I was always of the opinion that in a combat situation you just shot the bad guys and didn't worry about the consequences. At one point while in the Central Valley area we were told that there was an ammunition shortage. We were subsequently issued one bandolier of ammunition per rifleman per day. This equated to seventy-two rounds of ammunition for a rifleman.

When the Chinese entered the war they initially attacked in hordes, and oftentimes the odds were close to 80 to 100 or more to 1. Seventy-two rounds in a firefight would last, with luck, no more than thirty seconds. What happened was, after you fired your last round you got up and ran to the rear as fast as your feet would carry you. We lost 539 Marines during a night attack by the Chinese mostly because we ran out of ammunition. When we asked why, the answer was never clear. If it wasn't the company commander's or the battalion commander's fault, then whose fault was it? I decided that it was our commander in chief's fault. I subsequently never forgave Harry Truman for the loss of those Marines, even though later I came to realize politically that it wasn't his fault personally. The Rules of Engagement just didn't seem fair to me, particularly in a time of crisis involving American fighting men. On the positive side, I survived and I truly learned to run faster than I ever had before in my life.

I say this because while I was back in high school Coach Durland used to get so mad at me because for some reason I simply could not run a mile. Coach Durland was a former Marine who had served during WW II in the Pacific Theater, and he was a fanatic about conditioning. If you screwed up for any reason during football practice, Coach Durland had you report to the track afterward to run a mile for him. There was never a time that I could successfully make it four times around that stupid track. After Korea, Coach Durland would really have been proud of me, as I then could easily have qualified for any college track team on the West Coast.

This pretty much closes the chapters on my life during the Korea War, although there are probably many things that I have forgotten or overlooked due to the time lag between then and fifty years later. While it is true that I came home with a bitter taste in my mouth concerning politics, I never lost my faith in the Marine Corps or my country or my love of life and dedication to the American people.

8

Getting on with My Life

I came home in November of 1952 a very much confused young man with no idea of what I wanted to do or become. I asked Mom on several occasions for spiritual advice, but she refused to "read" for me or for any other member of our family. She did set up several interviews with other Spiritualist ministers, but I didn't get much out of them in terms of what I should do. All they seemed to be able to tell me was that everything would be OK. That just wasn't good enough for me. There had been too much standardization and regimentation in my life to date, and I needed something I could sink my teeth into. One of the things that I did do was go in for a battery of vocational exams given by the Veterans Administration Department there in San Diego. The results were frustrating and provided me with only three vocations, i.e., to become a cop, a farmer, or a pilot. Mom, sensing that I needed more help in terms of settling down, called my Uncle Spike. Uncle Spike owned a 39,000-acre cattle ranch located in nearby Sorrento Canyon, California. He told her to send me up to the ranch for as long as it took.

Uncle Spike was a former Marine and had served in WW II. He was a practical joker who never got tired of playing tricks on me. I eventually learned the hard way about how to stay in a saddle, but there was no doubt about who was in charge, i.e., the horse! I liked and worked close by Uncle Spike while vaccinating and caring for large animals. He convinced me that I should become a veterinary doctor for large animals. The idea appealed to me, but how to start the wheels in motion was a mystery to me. Since there was only one veterinary college in California, Uncle Spike suggested that I drive up to Davis, California, and apply for entrance.

I arrived at Davis several days later and located the school. How naïve I must have been about the civilian collegiate world then as folks in the Registrar's Office just laughed at me. They told me that they had students who had been waiting for several years to get into the veterinary school and that their qualifications were far superior to mine. The trip back to San Diego was not a pleasant one, and I bypassed Uncle Spike's ranch as I was too embarrassed to speak with him. Several days later Uncle Spike called and spoke with Mom about my visit. Mom told him that the registrar people at Davis had laughed in my face.

Two days later I received a telephone call from the Registrar's Office at Davis. Once again in my life I was to learn the significance of the philosophy "It's not what you know but who you know." What I didn't realize was that Uncle Spike was a past president of the California Cattlemen's Association and he had called the registrar at Davis on my behalf. The gentleman who called from Davis apologized for the misunderstanding that had occurred while I was up there. He informed me that the current calendar class was full. However, he said that if I would consider going to any other state college in California and taking parallel premed courses for the next two years, Davis would accept me at the beginning of my junior year. The next day I went back to the Veterans Administration and informed them that I wanted to attend college the next semester using the GI Bill. Even though my high school grades were high enough to get into any of the military academies, the Veterans Administration informed me that my test scores with them were not high enough for them to allow me to attend college. They wanted me to apply for vocational training, and I refused. I made an appointment with one of their counselors and, using my high school transcripts and my honorable time served in the Marine Corps, pleaded almost to the point of tears before he finally gave in. After he consulted with his superior they agreed that I could attend college on probation. The probation meant that I had to attain a grade-point average of 1.0 on a 4.0 (with 4.0 being the highest) scale to remain in college under the GI Bill. I readily agreed to their terms and was subsequently accepted for entrance into San Diego State College in February of 1953.

The registrar at San Diego State said that my grades were well above average from high school, but that too much time had elapsed from my graduation and I would now have to take their entrance exams. English was never one of my favorite subjects, and true to form, I failed the English portion of the entrance exam. I was informed that I would have to take their "bonehead English class" my first semester along with all of the required premed classes.

Starting college as a veteran some three years after high school placed me in a slightly different class from other incoming freshmen. Instead of being eighteen years old I was now twenty-one and far more mature than my classmates. The curriculum by itself was difficult enough to maintain; however, I managed to increase the stress level by pledging a fraternity and discovering girls and beer at the same time. Sigma Chi was good to me, and my fraternity brothers indeed saved my academic life that first semester. With a sigh of relief my scholastic average for that first semester averaged out to be a 1.0, and I was able to remain in school under the GI Bill.

Fraternity life was great at San Diego State in the early 1950s. Of the sixty-six guys living in the house, eighteen of us were veterans of the Korean War. I always enjoyed singing and I think that is what made the Sigma Chi house so special to me. Each Monday evening we had a formal coat-and-tie dinner before adjourning upstairs to the chapter room. Our business meetings were formal, quick, and efficient, as we hastened to get through them. The reason for the haste was that downstairs we had a sixteen-gallon keg of beer located in our fireplace, which was typical at that time. Each member of the house had a Sigma Chi beer mug with his name on it located on a rack that ran completely around the living room. We developed a reputation as a "singing fraternity" on campus, and with good reason. On many of those Monday nights, we sang fraternity songs into the wee hours of the morning. The result was that every year that I was there we managed to win first place in the school's Spring Sing Contest.

One of our brothers' fathers was the senior vice president for the Bank of America located in downtown San Diego. The main branch of the Bank of America had eighteen part-time messenger jobs, and they were all held by Sigma Chis. Don Allen, one of my high school classmates, had the best job of all. He was the air courier for the Bank of America and flew each night between San Diego and Los Angeles on commercial airlines. When Don graduated he sold the job to me for $175. This job was to have an impact on my life and career for the next twenty years. The way that the job worked was that the other seventeen brothers would drive out to various other locations of the Bank of America and pick up daily receipts, transactions, etc., and return them to the main branch. I would report to work at five in the evening and run everything through a photocopy machine. This was before computers, so once the documents were photocopied I then placed all of them into asbestos-lined bags and headed for the local airport. I flew five nights a week, with a four-hour layover each night at Los Angeles International Airport.

For the first six months, because of their beauty, I chased airline stewardesses every night, and did not get much academic studying accomplished. After a while the novelty wore off, and in order to stay in school I began to study. United Airlines (UAL) was nice enough to allow me to use their upstairs soundproof conference room each night to study in, and what a blessing that was. In those days there were 233 UAL stewardess working out of Los Angeles and I could call 231 of them by their first names. Airlines did not have computers during the early 1950s, and frequently the ticket agents would overbook a flight. We had worked out a neat arrangement between us, and I was always the first person to get bumped off an overloaded flight. What a deal this was! UAL would buy my dinner, put me up in a hotel of my choice, and pay me fifty-five dollars for the inconvenience. I would then take the eight o'clock flight back to San Diego the following morning. What made this so great was that I managed to schedule my classes so that I never had a class before eleven o'clock and was thus never late to class.

Life was really great in those days, as I had more money than I knew what to do with. The GI Bill paid me $110 per month, while I cleared $284 from the bank plus the bank paid gas and maintenance costs for my car. In a normal month I could always count on two to three hundred dollars extra from getting bumped by the airlines. In addition, I became a Chesterfield cigarette representative on campus and received fifty-five dollars per month for passing out Chesterfield cigarette samples to students.

Each month the Chesterfield Company provided me with two cases of L&M cigarettes, plus four cases of Chesterfield samplers to pass out. This all occurred before the threat of cancer as a result of smoking came before our media. I was a nonsmoker and the L&Ms turned out to be lifesavers for me. There were two young school-teachers living next door to the fraternity house, and they both smoked L&Ms. What made life even greater was that both teachers possessed English majors from their respective colleges. I kept them supplied with L&Ms, and they in turn wrote, corrected, and typed all of my term papers.

As I mentioned, the first semester's grades were nothing to write home about. That premed curriculum was a lot tougher than I had anticipated, with Chemistry 101, a five-unit class, almost wiping me out. I felt that for me as a potential doctor it was imperative to understand chemistry in order to be able to write prescriptions for patients. I received a grade of D in chemistry the first semester, so I repeated the class in summer school. After getting a grade of C in the class the second time I decided that maybe premed was not the career major for me. Later in life I discovered what a misconception this was, but I was happy at the time with a new major in salesmanship. Our fraternity house mother's son was a regional manager for the Cluett and Peabody (Arrow shirt) Company located in New Orleans. After an interview he offered me a job selling Arrow shirts in the New Orleans area with a starting salary of $10,000. The offer was really tempting, but I decided that my first goal was to graduate from college, so I remained in school.

One night while I was en route back to San Diego an incident occurred onboard a UAL flight that helped guide me into my future. An older female passenger experienced an epileptic fit, and the young stewardess didn't know what to do. There were only a few people on the flight, and remembering my Boy Scout training, I grabbed a spoon and held the lady's tongue down to prevent her from swallowing it. The lady recovered and after apologizing to everyone for the embarrassing situation, I told her to think nothing of it. UAL had other thoughts, as I soon discovered. Several days later a reporter from the *San Diego Tribune* came out and interviewed me. An article appeared the next day in the paper regarding my heroics in saving this lady's life on the UAL flight.

Approximately a month later when I arrived in Los Angeles one of the UAL passenger clerks told me that UAL wanted me to report upstairs as soon as I could. I had no idea what they had in mind; however, I agreed to be there as soon as I could get the bank materials signed off. Normally there was no one in the upstairs conference room except me, but on this occasion when I opened the door the room was packed with people. The president of UAL was there and he asked me to come forward. He said a few words, then presented me with my Million Mile UAL pin, plus he gave me a plaque and a Letter of Commendation for saving the lady's life onboard the recent UAL flight. In those days whenever a passenger accrued a million air miles on a specific airline, the airline usually mailed a Million Mile pin to the passenger. After the presentation the president asked me what I was going to do upon graduation from college. I remember telling him that I was not certain at the time. He then told me that the first multijet airliners were rolling off the assembly lines and that the airlines would be desperate for multijet-engine-qualified pilots. He further told me that the U.S. Air Force was the only branch of the military services that had multijet-engine pilots. He said that if I would get into the Air Force and get 300 hours of multijet-engine time, he would guarantee me a job as a copilot for UAL.

That night on the flight back to San Diego I went up to the cockpit and talked to the pilots on the way home. They informed me that it took usually thirteen to fifteen years on the average as a flight engineer before you could transition into the copilot's seat. We also discussed how great a career in flying was and how much money commercial pilots made. The next morning I found my way over to the Air Force ROTC offices on campus and into the detachment commander's office. I knew the detachment commander from a previous meeting, as he had tried unsuccessfully to recruit me into the ROTC program. The reason that he wanted me so bad was my Marine Corps experience in drilling troops. Before qualifying for the program, I first had to take a flight physical, which I passed with ease. I came into the program with the rank of cadet major. Several months later I was promoted to the rank of cadet lieutenant colonel and made a group commander.

Thursdays at school were ROTC days, and we all wore Air Force uniforms and marched for several hours during the day. It was on one of these ROTC days that I was to meet my future wife. I was indebted to one of my fraternity brothers, Andy Brown, who had saved my life on a term paper before the L&M ladies came along. Andy was a member of the San Diego State College Debate Team, and he had asked me to attend an important debate for him. On this particular Thursday, the debate team from Oxford, England, was there to debate our school's debate team. After drill practice that afternoon, I rushed over to the Little Theater only to discover that there was a line of close to 300 people waiting to get into the theater. The Little Theater had only 200 seats!

I started at the head of the line looking for someone I knew. Much to my delight there was this very good-looking girl, whom I had briefly met several weeks before at a joint exchange, standing there. Seeing that she was alone, I went up to her and crowded into line, pretending that she was holding a place for me. She played the role perfectly, and it ultimately led to my giving her my fraternity pin and later asking her father for her hand in marriage.

Once accepted into the ROTC program, I could hardly wait to get into the real Air Force. I subsequently doubled up on my class load and managed to graduate in three and a half years. On graduation day in June of 1956 fate stepped into my life again. I had an entry date in late June into pilot training; however, one of my fraternity brothers' wives was pregnant, and they needed to get on active duty so that the Air Force would pay for the cost of the childbirth. I agreed to change entry dates with them, meaning that I wouldn't be called until December of that year.

I had six months to wait, and it didn't take long before boredom set in and I decided to take a job with the Convair–General Dynamics Company as a tool dispatcher. I lied during the interview, as the company wanted me to enter one of their administrative programs. Even though I had a college diploma, I told them that I first wanted to learn the company from the ground up and being a tool dispatcher seemed the way to do it. For the next five months, I truly learned what a bureaucracy was all about. There were three classes of tool dispatchers subsequently named A, B, and C. Since I was a college graduate I was given a rating of A which meant that I had the privilege of riding a bicycle throughout the plant. I'm ashamed to say that I probably read more books while holding this job than I did the entire time I was in college. However, I did learn a lot about the aircraft-manufacturing business.

I bought my first sports car, a 1953 MG roadster, at the beginning of my sophomore year in school. What an incredible automobile that car was! I really wanted to purchase a Jaguar X-120, but the owner of the car dealership recommended that I buy an MG and learn how to drive sports cars first. I followed his advice for several months and then began to modify the MG. In order to upgrade an MG's engine there are what they call four stages that one needs to go through, and I went through them all.

72

Wescott Motors in National City had one of the best-trained foreign automobile mechanics (Wilbur Baker) in the nation in 1953. Wilbur did all of the modifications for me, and Wescott Motors agreed to sponsor me while I was racing in the California Sports Car Circuit. I never won a race but had a lot of fun competing. Eventually, I entered the time trials and ran the car on the desert flats at Muroc, California. I turned 112 mph and held the U.S. speed record for my car's class for one week in 1954, until Ken Miles turned 122 mph in his MG Flying Shingle. He still holds the speed record today for the class of cars that we were racing. I have never enjoyed driving a car as much for the pure pleasure of driving since that time. It was not uncommon in those days to drive 200 miles with the top down just for a cup of coffee. In seven months I put a little over 11,000 miles on that car.

Once a month the San Diego Sports Car Club sponsored a club rally. Rallies always required two people in a car and oftentimes two drivers would flip a coin to see who was going to get to drive and who would navigate. On one particular night a young Navy ensign who was attending his first meeting and I flipped a coin to see who was going to drive and I won. The rally was a Hare and Hound type rally, where the fastest time and distance would win the race. A lead car would take off early, and arriving at an intersection that was exactly one-quarter mile away the passenger in the lead car would throw a small bag of colored lime in the middle of the intersection. He would throw a bag of lime in another intersection a quarter-mile from there. As the driver came racing up to the intersections, he had to guess which roadway the lead car had taken from there. Should the driver guess wrong, then he just drove one-half mile in the wrong direction.

About an hour into this race we were cruising down a very narrow country back road at roughly fifty-five miles per hour in a twenty-five-miles-per-hour speed zone. I remember losing control of the MG on one of the many corners. I quickly downshifted while we were in the midst of a 360-degree spin out. Forcing the gearshift lever into first gear I quickly popped the clutch and recovered, pointing the car in the right direction as if I had done this a hundred times. Later that evening, the ensign asked me if I really had control of the car when we spun out on that mountain road. I was so macho that I lied saying, "Yes." What I didn't know was that the

73

ensign was on a medical leave from the naval hospital, as he had recently survived an airplane crash onboard an aircraft carrier. I'm certain that I undoubtedly gave him the "ride of his life," one that he probably has never forgotten.

Someone told me that there was an unwritten guarantee that you could on a level road make a U-type turn at fifty-five-miles-per-hour in an MG. For some strange reason, I believed this rumor and performed this stupid maneuver three times with a passenger in the right seat. Usually he never choose to ride with me again.

9

Active Duty

December finally arrived, and I was getting ready to travel to San Antonio, Texas, to report for active duty in the Air Force. My MG was my only means of transportation, and I was really worried about driving it so far with such a highly modified engine. Where most car engines would turn over between twelve and fifteen hundred RPMs to reach sixty-miles-per-hour, my MG would turn sixty-four hundred RPMs to arrive at the same speed. I had made arrangements for a friend, who was also going to San Antonio, to drive together with me in case something went wrong with either car. My buddy's car was a 1951 Oldsmobile that had definitely seen better days, and he was worried that it would break down somewhere en route. Dave was one of those drivers who never looked in his rearview mirror. We pulled out of El Paso, Texas, in the middle of a bad snowstorm with Dave leading the way. About eighteen miles down the road, I developed a sudden *tic-tic* sound in my engine. Thinking that it was a loose rod, I pulled over, with the impression that Dave had seen me pull off the road. He drove for four hours before he noticed that I wasn't with him. When he finally returned and located me I was practically frozen to death. We started out with me trailing on a ten-foot chain. This proved to be a useless maneuver, because my defrosters didn't work unless the engine was running and I couldn't see out the windshield. I blew my horn and flashed the headlights, and finally Dave stopped. We then cinched the two cars together and completed the final 575 miles to San Antonio.

In 1956 there was only one sports car agency in San Antonio, and lucky for me the owner was a Sigma Chi brother. I told him that I thought that I had a loose rod in the engine, and he said that they could fix it for me for cost of parts. It turned out to be a snapped crankshaft, and on a second lieutenant's pay the cost was prohibitive. Once the car was fixed, I decided to buy the cheapest

American car that I could afford, with the idea of towing the MG to my next Air Force base. I wound up with a 1951 Hudson Commodore Eight for the price of $100. It was ugly as sin, with a two-tone faded gray top and a rust-stained maroon bottom. It sat in the second lieutenant's parking lot all week, but when Saturday night came along everyone wanted to go into San Antonio in it.

Upon checking in at Lackland AFB, we were told that the pilot-training classes were currently overloaded and that we would have to remain at Lackland for three months. We were told to report to the base theater, where we would be assigned temporary jobs according to our college majors. The captain who was doing the job assignments was somewhat of a joker, and none of us appreciated his dull wit. He started by announcing a job that was going to be extremely hard, requiring long hours, and you needed a good background in drill and ceremonies. No one volunteered! Finally, an hour or so later, he informed those of us remaining in the theater that unless we volunteered for one of the jobs we would have to run the base obstacle course five times a week.

The obstacle course at Lackland AFB was world famous in the military services for being the most difficult obstacle course to complete. The reason was that they had an obstacle they called The Inverted Stairway to the Stars. This contraption consisted of four telephone poles stuck in the ground about four feet apart at the base. There were platforms about five feet apart vertically all the way to the top, which was about sixty-five or seventy feet in the air. As one climbed from one platform to the next overhead, the poles spread out. Upon reaching the top and looking down, the sight was terrifying especially if, like me, a person suffered from fear of heights. I had to roll my body over the edge of the platform and while holding on swing back and forth, hoping that I would land on the platform below.

It was at this point that I stood and told the captain that I would accept the first job that no one had volunteered for. The captain and his assistant both laughed and told me to report to the base personnel officer. Wow, what an assignment this turned out to be, and I quickly figured out why the captain had laughed at me. It seems that the Air Force was currently calling women from civilian life into the Air Force and giving them commissions and rank according to their civilian job experience. I was to become their tactical officer. I quickly became the most popular second lieutenant on the base.

At the time, I was rooming at Lackland with a good friend from San Diego State College. We both noticed that there was a large contingent of foreign officers there at Lackland, and no one had informed us as to why they were there. Being brave second lieutenants, we decided one evening to go over to the mess hall where the foreign students ate. We felt fairly uncomfortable as we proceeded through the food line, as everyone was staring at us. I said to my buddy, "There is an officer with three stars on his epaulets sitting all alone; let's go sit with him." We approached his table and asked if we could join him for dinner. The officer jumped up so fast that his chair flew over backward and crashed to the floor. Both of us came close to dropping our food trays.

It turned out that this officer was a captain in the Turkish Air Force. He had been at Lackland AFB's American Language School for two months, and we were the first Americans to speak to him on a personal basis. His name was Nevzat, and he explained that there were five Turkish officers in his class, but that four of them were third lieutenants. Nevzat told us that third lieutenants in the Turkish Air Force did not speak to captains unless they were asked to speak.

Nevzat invited us back to his Bachelors' Officers Quarters (BOQ) for a nightcap, and we accepted his offer. Nevzat had a peculiar habit that he enjoyed immensely once he opened the door to his room. He would throw his wheel-type hat at one of the bedposts on his bed. He was pretty good at this trick, hitting his target nine out of ten times. He told us that he had learned this trick while watching an American movie. This trick of Nevzat's was in the future years to save my life. It seems that in terms of drinking alcohol all Turks for some strange reason had developed a taste for American Scotch, and Nevzat was no exception. He broke out a bottle of Scotch and asked if we wanted one finger or two. I hated Scotch but didn't tell him and said that I would like just a half-finger. He shouted with glee and gave me a big bear hug, telling me that I was his kind of man! What I didn't realize was that Nevzat had only three ten-ounce water glasses in his BOQ. His intentions were to fill them up to one or two fingers from the brim. Needless to say, mine was filled to the overflowing mark. I was afraid of violating the protocol for foreign officers, so I held my breath and did my best to down the Scotch. I wound up pouring most of it down my shirtfront and into my trousers without anyone noticing in an effort to get it all down. I would not forget meeting Nevzat and that intoxicating night for many years to come.

Oftentimes during the next six weeks we would go into San Antonio for a few drinks and a night on the town. In those days and maybe now, Texas laws required you to carry your liquor bottle with you. All establishments sold only setups. We frequently went into areas of town where the girlie shows were. These were places that we were told not to go by base officials. Two times while we were in San Antonio the places we visited were raided by the local police force. The way things worked was that if the local police happened to pick up foreign officers, instead of throwing them in jail they would turn them over to units of the Military Police. These MPs would in turn just return the foreign officers back to their BOQs at Lackland with no questions asked. Should American officers be caught, they would be subjected to military discipline in the form of an Article 15, which would become a part of their permanent record. Both times that we were caught, Nevzat told us not to say a word and that he would do all of the communicating. In due time we became very close friends and vowed to stay in touch throughout the years to come.

Finally, one day the sports car agency called and told me that my MG was ready for pickup. They had installed a new crankshaft that was not dynamically balanced, and I constantly worried about driving it very far. Eventually I sold the MG to another second lieutenant who was on his way to pilot training. My roommate didn't have a car; however, we were both comfortable driving the old Hudson. When we finally got our orders we were both going to the same primary flying school in Arizona. We loaded up the old Hudson with everything we owned, plus some things for other guys going to the same place, and headed west to Tucson, Arizona.

10

Primary Flying-Training School

We reported to Marana Air Base, a civilian contract flying school located about twenty-five miles due northwest of Tucson. In keeping with my usual luck, I managed to draw the meanest instructor pilot (IP) on the base as my instructor. His name was Roy Schuman, and we called him Roy "Chewman," as he had a reputation for washing out the most pilots in the pilot-training classes. Mr. Schuman was one of those legendary pilots from the old school. He had leatherlike skin on his face and had stopped counting flying hours sometime after 15,000 hours. We learned to fly in a single-engine Cessna T-34 type aircraft. It had a 250 horsepower engine with dual cockpits, the back one being the IP's. Chewman's vocabulary was worse than those of some Marines I had known. His favorite tactic (if he thought that you had your head in the cockpit while flying) was to reach forward and beat you in the back of your head with his flight cap, at the same time calling you the vilest and lowest form of scum that he could think of. We were all Rattlesnakes; however, my call sign was Rattlesnake 94. I still have my original flight cap with the Rattlesnake 94 numbers on it.

Somehow I managed to survive Roy Chewman's flying program, and after six flying hours he soloed me out. On the day a pilot soloed upon landing, Air Force tradition said that the pilot was automatically thrown into the base swimming pool. That was one time that I didn't mind being thrown into the pool! We flew forty hours in the T-34 before transitioning into the much larger T-28. Going from a 250-horse power engine up to a 700-horse power engine was quite a jump at the time. The T-28 seemed so large when compared with the very comfortable and small T-34, and we were all hesitant to fly it. Actually, the T-28 was to become one of my favorite aircraft to fly. It was built by the North American Aviation Company and came out at the end of WW II. From what they told us, the T-28 was designed to transition pilots from propeller engines

79

to the more sophisticated jet-engine aircraft. Word came down that President Truman told the Air Force that even though the war was over they would accept all 6,000 T-28s, primarily due to the state of the nation's economy. The Air Force subsequently removed the gun ports, bomb racks, and large engines from the combat model of the T-28s. They in turn installed a much smaller 700-horse power Wright Cyclone engine with a single-bladed propeller on it. This then became the advanced aircraft for the Air Force's pilot-training schools.

Every weekend my roommate and I would load up the old Hudson and head out for San Diego. My roommate was dating a girl there, and it gave me a chance to see my girlfriend, Cynthia. Everywhere we went, we got a lot of laughs from people about the old Hudson, but it never failed us. It would peak out around seventy-five miles per hour on a good day on level ground. We always held our breath when departing El Centro and starting the climb up the Alpine Pass toward San Diego. Quite often we were down to a maximum of fifteen to twenty-miles-per-hour by the time we reached the top of the pass, and both praying that the car would not stop. We broke a fan belt one weekend about thirty miles east of Yuma, Arizona. The only thing we could find was an old piece of manila rope, which we tied around the crankshaft and water pump. Believe it or not, we made it into Yuma on that piece of rope. One weekend while I was home, Dad ran a compression check on the Hudson's engine. The pressure on the cylinders varied from a low of 20 psi to a high of 80 psi. A normal engine would have 120 psi on all cylinders.

Once we moved up to the T-28, we found ourselves flying normally once a day, while the remainder of the time was spent in classes learning about weather, navigation, and engine systems. Evenings were spent socializing (drinking) and memorizing emergency procedures checklists. Drinking was a common experience, it seemed, for everyone. Most guys said that it helped to control their jitters and fears of flying. A day didn't go by that one of us wouldn't do something stupid that would scare the living hell out of him while flying. I remember one time that six of us to offset our jitters went down into Mexico to the town of Nogales for a weekend of fun. We found ourselves the first night in a sporty cantina raising hell and trying to drink all of their tequila. That same night some really nice students from the University of Mexico joined us and taught us how to really drink tequila. We, as Americans, were in the habit of licking our hands and then pouring salt on the licked spots. You then quickly chugged a shot of tequila and chased it with a piece of lime.

Those Mexican students introduced us to a brand of Mexican tequila known as Sin Revel. It came in both dark and light colors. The interesting thing was that there was a large tomato worm inside each bottle. According to our hosts, the idea was to drink all of the tequila, so that you could suck the worm out and consume it. By the time you reached the worm, you were in a state where you didn't care what was in the bottle. We brought back several cases of Sin Revel to Marana, and I drank so much of it that I'm not sure how I managed to remain sober enough to graduate from the program.

Marana Air Base was a great place to start my flying career; however, halfway through our T-28 checkout the Air Force decided to close the base down for economic reasons. We were given a choice of going to several contract flying schools to complete our training. Most of the married guys chose to continue training in the multien-gine B-25 type aircraft, while the single guys went to Moore Air Base in McAllen, Texas, and stayed in single-engine T-28s. Cynthia and I had already planned on getting married on June 22nd, and now due to official Air Force orders we had to move the wedding back a week to the fifteenth. I remember her mother wasn't too happy with the news, as all of the invitations were already printed. Mrs. Cook was very resourceful and somehow managed to get the date changed at the church and to get cards printed up to go into the invitations announcing the change in dates.

One of the things that I always admired about Cynthia's father was that after I asked him for her hand he insisted that she remain in college until she graduated. After the wedding I was fixing to drive the old Hudson from San Diego to Texas when Mr. Cook suggested that I take Cynthia's new Plymouth instead. I hated to leave the Hudson with her, but she only had a little distance to go to school, while I had to go all the way to Texas. The Hudson looked so awful that Cynthia's mother insisted that she park the car a block away from their house. Shortly after I left, Cynthia informed me that the Hudson's engine got hot one day and she couldn't get the hood open. So she took a garden hose and ran water over the front of the radiator. She actually drove that car six months with little to no water in the radiator, and it never failed her. It pained me to finally sell the old Hudson for twenty-five dollars to a man who owned a gas station there in San Diego.

After I got settled in at Moore Air Base, in McAllen, Texas, flying really became fun. The Navy had a pilot-training base located a short distance away in Corpus Christi, and we spent a lot of time and fun mixing it up with the Navy pilots. We didn't dogfight with them too long, because they could get more speed out of their T-28s with their 1100-horse power engines, as opposed to our old 700-horse power engines. The reason for their larger engine was because they had to practice carrier-type landings and needed the extra power.

Most pilot-training squadrons are made up of outstanding young college graduates. Usually all of them make it through graduation; however, some were washed out for any number of reasons. It seems that all squadrons had at least one class clown, and ours was no exception. We had a young lieutenant by the name of Chester J. Chester, a Stanford graduate, who was the brunt of many jokes each day. Chester didn't have many friends simply because somewhere in his past his social skills seemed to have failed him. Whenever Chester spoke to anyone, he got within three to four inches of your face and you found yourself continually backing up. This unusual habit of Chester's caused many funny things to happen to people, such as backing up into the swimming pool, falling over potted plants, or backing into the squadron commander's wife at parties.

Everything Chester did he did as if he were a robot. One of the most comical events that happened occurred during a daily flying schedule. Each flight instructor had three students assigned to him for flying training. While one student would be out flying, the other two would be waiting their turn inside the flight study room. Once the aircraft landed and taxied in, we were to be in place on the flight line with our parachutes on and ready to exchange seats with the students in the front seats while the IPs held the brakes in the backseats. Somehow Chester lost track of time and was sitting at his table studying when someone yelled that his IP was waiting for him on the flight line. Chester was so startled, he jumped up, turning the table over in the process, and ran for the parachute rack. He grabbed a parachute and, sticking his arm out like he was going to straight-arm someone, hit the double doors with such a jolt that the D ring on the parachute caught on the door handle. The parachute began to unfold, and Chester, being unaware of the dilemma, continued to run until he came to the end of the parachute lines. Chester subsequently did a complete 360-degree turn in the air and hit the ground so hard that he broke his leg.

At the time, we were laughing so hard that we didn't realize the extent of his injury. Chester kept crawling through the grass toward the flight line dragging his parachute along with him. It took several minutes to calm Chester down and get an ambulance to come and pick him up. He was washed back two classes while his leg healed. We later learned that during his final check ride in a T-33 jet, while he was taxiing the aircraft out, for some strange reason he retracted the gear. He then added more power to the engine as the landing gear began to retract. The aircraft continued sliding down the taxiway on its belly until the IP could get the engine cut off. Chester was eventually washed out of pilot training as a result of this incident.

Most of us had become very cocky by now, and we all thought that we were the greatest gift to the Air Force as future pilots. We painted our helmets various colors to display our machismo and proceeded to enjoy the freedom of flying. In South Texas there were always afternoon clouds in the local flying area, and we were told to stay away from them. These daily cloud formations were absolutely beautiful, as they grew in intensity throughout the day.

One day I could no longer stand it, and while out on a solo flight I selected a rather large fluffy cloud and turned toward it. Shoving the throttle to the full open position, I entered the cloud in horizontal flight at about a two-thousand-foot altitude. Did I ever learn a lesson that still makes me wonder why I am here today! I can't remember exactly what happened, as it happened so fast. The turbulence was so severe inside the cloud that I lost complete control of my aircraft and I wasn't sure which way I was going. When I broke out of the cloud I was pointed straight down toward the ground with the throttle wide open. There was not a lot of space between me and the ground to recover in. I know that I came close to pulling the wings off that old T-28 as I bottomed out, because my altitude was lower than the surrounding power lines.

I had an incredible civilian flight instructor while there at Moore Air Base whom we called Uncle Orris. He told me that I was one of the best "stick and rudder" students that he had seen in a long time. I later graduated from Moore as the top acrobatic pilot in my class.

11

Basic Flying-Training School

After several months at Moore Air Base, we received orders assigning us to the 3640th Pilot Training Wing at Laredo, Texas, for the Basic Flying Training School. There wasn't a lot to say about Laredo, Texas, in 1957. It was located about 150 miles southwest of San Antonio right on the Mexican border. Most of us considered the town of Laredo the armpit of the earth, as the temperature was fiery hot and there was nothing to do in the town. The highlight of my life was when Cynthia decided to leave San Diego for the summer and be with me. Right after our honeymoon, she had returned to San Diego to finish up her degree at San Diego State as per her father's request. What a time I had trying to locate a suitable place for us to live. I eventually did find a small upstairs apartment that was located in a neighborhood where no one spoke English. I have often thought what a courageous and determined person Cynthia was to have agreed to live in a situation like this. When the Greyhound bus arrived in Laredo, Texas, Cynthia was the only female onboard, and during her ride she experienced many examples firsthand of the south's racial prejudices.

[In the words of my wife, the trip from San Diego to Loredo on the Greyhound bus certainly was an eye-opener for her. All of the San Diego school systems were multi-racial, so she had not been exposed to the segregation that existed in the South.

When she left San Diego, she sat across from two black sailors who had to take the same bus to Texas. Cynthia said that the bus driver had asked the two black sailors to sit up close to him so that he could insure that they would be okay. They traveled through Arizona pretty much without incident, although some passengers did ask why the black sailors were sitting in the front of the bus. At the café on the Arizona-New Mexico border, when they stopped for lunch, the bus driver said he would appreciate it if the two sailors would eat with him as this was a rough town and some racial incidents had occurred. A few bus stops later, another bus driver asked if he could bring hamburgers back to the bus for the sailors as this was the first of the divided restaurants. He told the sailors that it was just understood that blacks customary ate in a certain area.

As they neared Texas, the restaurants were clearly divided with signs that said "white section" and "colored section" only. She said that the drinking fountains and bathrooms also had signs indicating the same thing. To the credit of the Greyhound bus drivers, the two sailors remained next to them on the bus for the remainder of their trip.

In those days, the military leased the schools that the base children attended, so all of the dependents could attend the same schools. We were later stationed in Little Rock, Arkansas in 1958 and witnessed the confrontation between Governor Faubus and the black children attempting to enter Little Rock High School.]

Pilot training in single engine T-33 jet fighters was considerably different from flying propeller-driven type aircraft. With a propeller you have instant power when you slam the throttle forward. With a jet engine, even though you can slam the throttle full forward, it takes a lot of time for the engine to respond and reach full power, and a lot of things can happen while the engine is winding up. Like in primary training, we flew once or twice a day, while spending the remaining hours in classes learning about jet engines. We concentrated far more on aircraft emergency procedures, as we were now flying at far greater speeds and without the instant power we had to be quicker with our decisions.

Once again, we were assigned three students to a table, only this time we had Air Force officers as IPs. We wound up with one extra student in our section, and somehow I got caught in the cycle of always being the extra guy. By this, I mean that I flew with my primary IP on my dollar ride and never saw him again until eighteen rides later. There were both good and bad things about this situation. On the good side, I became very proficient in terms of aerobatics-type flying. On the bad side, I knew nothing about instrument-type flying, which eventually caught up with me.

Before Cynthia arrived, I was one of three guys to a room in the BOQ. Fritz, Kay, and I had developed a very close relationship and respect for one another. We spent most of our evenings drinking beer and going over "Bold Face" emergency procedures for the T-33. It seems that the most critical things in flying aircraft always occur close to the ground, especially during takeoffs and landings. For some reason, each of us differed on exactly what we would do during takeoff should the engine fail. When we took off to the south, shortly after leaving the runway there was a large lake directly ahead of us. We constantly argued about what exactly we would do should we encounter a takeoff emergency to the south. Kay, who had the most flight experience, said that he would attempt to bend the aircraft around back toward the runway and bail out. Fritz felt that he would try to extend his glide until past the lake, then bail out. I was more in favor of crash-landing on the lake and taking my chances in the water. The indecision by the three of us later cost Kay his life.

Kay's death caught us all off-guard and we just were not ready for it to happen. We had reached the point in our training where we were supposed to take off a couple hours before dark, burn our fuel down, and log three night solo landings. Maintenance had somehow gotten the wrong fuel load in our aircraft, and all tanks were full. A jet engine burns an incredible amount of fuel when flying at low altitudes, so our instructors told us to take off and burn the fuel out of our wing tanks first. We were to remain in an extended flight pattern at 1200 feet north and south of the base until we burned all the fuel out of our wing tanks and were then light enough for landings. On a normal mission we always burned fuel out of the internal main tank, then transferred fuel from the tip tanks to the main tank. That evening there were eighteen of us in the base traffic pattern. As we were flying around, we couldn't talk to one another, since we were all on the same command frequency. It was very quiet when all of a sudden someone said, "Partial engine failure." That message got everyone's attention, and the instructor in the ground control unit immediately asked the pilot of the aircraft with partial engine failure to identify himself and to give his flight position. About twenty seconds elapsed, and the next thing we heard was, "Flameout."

I did not see the actual crash, but you could see the burning wreckage for miles from the base. It didn't take the flying safety people long after the crash to figure out what happened. Apparently, Kay was so used to using a normal fuel sequence that he had not turned his wing tanks on and burned fuel only out of the main internal tank. When the main tank was running out of fuel, he experienced a partial engine failure. Within seconds after the tank ran dry, the engine quit completely. Under normal flight conditions, should a pilot experience a flameout it usually takes about ten seconds to get the engine restarted. Again apparently unaware that he still had full wing tanks, Kay attempted to bend the aircraft around in an effort to try to land on the runway. The problem was, the extra weight in the wings' tanks caused the aircraft to instantly stall when he tried to turn the aircraft back to the runway. At such a low altitude there was no possible way he could recover the aircraft, and he was subsequently killed. The loss of Kay affected the entire class. He had the most flying hours of anyone in the class and at twenty-two was truly an outstanding person and friend to all of us.

Two of the students at Fritz's table had washed out, leaving just Fritz to fly with his flight instructor. His flight instructor's call sign was Blizzard, and we were all envious of the things he allowed Fritz to do while in the air. One day I was asked to join Blizzard's flight of two aircraft, and I was really excited to be able to fly with the two of them. During the preflight briefing I failed to mention to Blizzard that I had a bad head cold. I knew that if he found out he would not let me fly and would probably have me grounded until I got well. Here again, you sometimes learn lessons the hard way as I most certainly did in this situation. We took off, climbed to 20,000 feet, and leveled off. Blizzard knew that Fritz and I were roommates and excellent student pilots. He gave us the signal to move into a trail flight position, and once we were there the rat race was on. Blizzard immediately rolled his aircraft inverted and with full throttle dived straight for the ground with us in a tight formation directly behind him.

The T-33 cockpit is not pressurized inside like commercial airliners are, and things started happening to me fast. The pressure built up so rapidly in my blocked sinus that I initially grayed out. I immediately pulled out of the dive and was having difficulty breathing. I discovered that my oxygen mask was filled with blood as I tore it off my face. Upon regaining my eyesight and control of the aircraft, I called the control tower and declared an emergency, requesting an immediate landing. I told the tower that I thought that I had broken a blood vessel in my head and was having difficulty breathing. By the time that I got the aircraft safely stopped on the ground the entire front of my flight suit was soaked in blood. An Air Force ambulance met my aircraft as I pulled into a parking place. The flight surgeon jumped up on the wing of the aircraft and began helping me to unbuckle. He was really mad and told me that they would probably kick me out of the program for flying with a head cold, as it appeared that I had ruptured both my sinus cavities. We had been told during an earlier briefing by a flight surgeon not to fly with a head cold, and I had ignored the advice. Because of my standing in the class the squadron commander didn't wash me out, but he certainly made an example out of me and scared the hell out of everyone else. From that date forward I never flew whenever I had a head cold.

I never got a chance to fly with Blizzard again, but on many occasions Fritz and I would meet up and terrorize the local inhabitants around Laredo. There was a large lake located about ten miles south of Laredo called Zapata. One of our favorite things to do was catch fishermen in small boats and buzz them. Many times, as we looked back after our buzz job, we could see both occupants of the boat in the water. It never occurred to either of us at the time that the boat occupants might not be able to swim.

Fritz came in one evening very excited and told me what he and Blizzard had done that day and did I have the guts to try it tomorrow? What a stupid dare that was, and again, it almost cost me my life. It was a strange feeling that I had like someone was looking out for me, because I did so many dumb things and shouldn't be alive today to even speak of them. The following story is an example of what I am talking about.

There were lots of hay fields located in and around Laredo, and all of them had fire trails cut through them for fire prevention. Fritz informed me that a T-33 with its flying wing tanks would just fit perfectly inside the cut fire trail. Needless to say, several hours later we were both zooming down these fire trails just inches off the ground flying in excess of 400 mph and having the time of our lives.

Fritz was right that if you leveled off about a foot above the ground you could see the wheat stalks zip by your wing tanks in your peripheral vision. This type of flying necessitated a lot of concentration and manual skill to stay ahead of the aircraft so close to the ground.

As I was zipping down one of these fire trails, I noticed out ahead of me a farmhouse with a lot of people standing around in the yard. I decided to put on an air show for them. As I sped toward them I pulled up, and I rolled the aircraft inverted as I passed over them. What happened next has lived with me in the form of a nightmare ever since. This was the first time that I had been upside down in an aircraft so close to the ground. What I did initially was pull the stick back, thinking that I would zoom up; however, as the nose came down I realized in a nanosecond that I was inverted. When upside down, the flight controls are reversed, i.e., back is down while forward is up! What a shock when the realization hit me. To this day I do not know how I recovered from an almost certain crash. I never went down a fire trail again, nor did I brag to anyone else about doing such a stupid thing.

Other than Kay, Fritz was probably the sharpest pilot I ever knew. He and the aircraft he was flying always seemed to be one. During the Basic Flying Program we flew a lot of solo formations and aerobatics together, and Fritz was the smoothest on the flight controls of anyone I ever flew with. He later went to Nellis AFB as an aide-de-camp to a general officer. Fritz and I had flown a couple times down inside the Grand Canyon in T-33s, and the flights were always spectacular and exciting as we zipped around the canyon walls. Later on a training mission in a T-33 while flying down inside the same canyon Fritz hit a cable that was strung across the canyon. The impact of hitting the cable tore clear into the wing spar and caused the tip tank to turn thirty degrees off the wing. He recovered from the impact and flew a very crippled aircraft back to Nellis and effected a safe landing. Fritz had such an outstanding career going it was indeed a shame that he elected to leave the Air Force several years later.

Time was moving right along for us during the basic flying phrase of our training, and before we knew it we were going up for our ninety-hour flight instrument checks. We first needed to have a check ride in the old stationary Link Trainer, a relic from the dinosaur days. The Link Trainer reminded me of a contraption that must have been invented alongside the Model T automobile. It was an elongated black box located on top of a pedestal that enabled the trainer to go up, down, and around in circles. If you ever got a case of claustrophobia this was the place to get it. There was no air conditioner, and once you were strapped in, it became a real sweat-box. On my initial check ride I received my first "Pink Slip" for an unsatisfactory flight performance, and I had to report to the squadron commander the next day. For once he listened to me as I told him that I had received absolutely no instrument training as a result of having flown with so many different instructor pilots. He decided that he would give me an additional ten hours of instrument flight training and all with the same instructor.

Our final flight exam before receiving our wings was called a 60-4 Instrument Flight Check. By the time I completed the additional ten hours of instrument training, most everyone else was finished with the program and signed off. The Base Training Section had scheduled me for a Saturday morning flight, as the following Monday was graduation day for my class. To increase my anxiety I discovered that I was scheduled to fly with an IP from the Base Standardization Evaluation Section who was known for washing out more students than anyone else.

I arrived Saturday morning with butterflies in my stomach in anticipation of what was to come. The IP, who was a captain, didn't have anything to say to me during the preflight portion of the flight, which increased my nervous condition all the more. The takeoff, climb-out, and level-off were probably the only normal things that happened on that flight. I was in the backseat of the T-33 with a canvas hood pulled over the inside top of the canopy so that I couldn't see out. The IP told me to get a clearance on the radio and to proceed to Catulla, Texas. I was to request a clearance into the holding pattern at 20,000 feet, followed by a penetration and low approach to the Catulla VOR navigational fix. I accomplished all of this while hyperventilating and sweating profusely at the same time. Following the low approach, we were to climb back on a specific heading until we reached 20,000 feet. As I leveled off at 20,000 feet, the IP told me to come out from under the canvas hood and relax. He also told me that I had failed the instrument check ride.

I felt lower than a snake in that I had never failed anything before in my life and I had no idea what would become of my Air Force career. There was no way that I could relax under the conditions of failure, so thinking that this was my last flight, I asked the IP if I could fly a little aerobatics to relieve the tension. He concurred and said that he would clear me away from other aircraft that might be in the vicinity. I proceeded to do a four-point roll, then a six-point roll, followed by an eight-point roll without losing a foot of altitude. The IP for the first time became almost human and asked me how I had accomplished the perfect rolls. So for the next hour or so I became the IP and talked him through the rolls.

We were both enjoying the maneuvers when suddenly the IP said, "My God, we are running low on fuel." The IP took over the flying and selected a heading that would take us by the shortest route back to Laredo. We were in such a hurry to get back that the IP decided there wasn't enough time to get into a holding pattern and make a normal instrument penetration. He told me not to put the hood up and said that I could fly the aircraft and that he would give me headings, et cetera, to arrive over the end of the runway at the proper altitude and airspeed. By the time we rolled out on final approach we had a yellow low-fuel light illuminated on the instrument panel. The IP took over at this point and made the quickest descent and landing that I have ever seen. Once on the ground he smiled for the first time and informed me that I had passed the flight check. The next day I discovered that I had received the highest T score of anyone in the class on my 60-4 Flight Exam.

The squadron commander called me in Monday morning and had what he called a little heart-to-heart talk with me. He informed me of my high T score on my check ride and told me how lucky he thought I was. He knew exactly what had happened and was just trying to get me to admit what I had done, and I did. He told me that class assignments were in and that he was sending me to Daylight Fighters. He said that if he sent me anyplace else I would probably kill myself and whoever else was flying with me. I wanted to jump and shout, as this was the type of assignment that everyone wanted. Class assignments were decided by the overall evaluation of each student, and we were rank-ordered on a list according to how many points we had. The top pilots in the class always took the daylight fighter assignments, while the next bunch had to select from all-weather fighters. After the all-weather fighter assignments came the multiengine assignments, and finally the bottom guys were stuck with SAC assignments into the backseats of B-47 bombers. There were only six assignments to F-86F daylight fighters, and I had one of them. The squadron commander swore me to secrecy until the assignments were posted the next day for the entire class. The F-86s were a part of the Air Force's Advanced Gunnery School, which was located at Williams AFB just outside Phoenix, Arizona.

12

Advanced Gunnery School

Cynthia finished up and graduated from San Diego State early, so we rented our first real home in Chandler, Arizona. Williams AFB was about ten miles due east from Chandler and was a very easy drive. Checkout in the F-86 was unlike anything else that I have ever done. There were no two-place models of the F-86, so for your first solo ride you were all alone. On my initial checkout, the IP climbed up on the wing of the aircraft and went through the start-engine part of the checklist. As soon as I had my engine running the IP ran over to his aircraft, and very soon we taxied out to the end of the runway. The tower cleared us for takeoff, and wow, what power the F-86 had when compared to the T-33 as we released brakes and started the takeoff roll. Was I nervous? No question about that! I got the gear and flaps up after takeoff and continued to climb as per the instructions that I received from the IP. The more I flew, the more confidence I gained in handling the aircraft. The IP seemed pleased with my flight performance and suggested that I join up on his right wing for a little formation flying. We accomplished some easy flight maneuvers, and finally satisfied, he told me to go to the trail position. In fighters, the trail position is where one aircraft is in formation underneath the other aircraft and approximately three to four feet behind it.

Using this formation, we flew more difficult flight maneuvers, including aerial acrobatics. I was trying as hard as I could to maintain my position below and behind the IP's aircraft so that he would think that I was a shit-hot fighter pilot. All of a sudden I saw his aircraft begin to fall over backward, barely missing my aircraft, and he said, "Two, check your airspeed?" Glancing down inside the cockpit, I discovered that the airspeed indicator was reading 0. At this point, the aircraft that I was flying flipped over and literally fell out of the sky, accelerating into a tight spin. I recovered from the first spin and because I overcontrolled the aircraft went right into a second spin in the opposite direction. The IP yelled, "Let everything go!" and I did. I quickly discovered that the F-86 had marvelous flight characteristics, as it brought itself out of the second spin in a short time. Immediately I developed a love affair with this aircraft that I had never experienced before with an aircraft.

On our second mission we were given permission to enter a training area where we could break the sound barrier. Breaking the sound barrier (756 mph) in 1958 was really a big thing, and we were all excited about it. We had heard rumors about the terrible things that would happen to the aircraft as you approached Mach one, and I found myself concentrating so hard that I was hyperventilating. I had climbed up to 44,000 feet to be sure that I would have enough altitude to recover, as I wasn't sure how much altitude I would lose going that fast. Flipping the aircraft over, I pulled the nose of the aircraft vertically to the straight down position with the throttle wide open. The Mach needle seemed to take forever to start moving, and I was splitting my time between watching the ground come up and watching the airspeed. I was disappointed when the Mach needle slipped through Mach one, as nothing unusual happened. Later I realized that the instructors had been playing games with the students, trying to get them psyched up about being able to control the aircraft. The only problem I had was having my hands full trying to pull the aircraft out of the dive without hitting the ground. I know that I pulled over six gees because I blacked out for several seconds during the pullout. Once I was back on the ground that afternoon, the factory representatives from North American Aviation Company presented each of us a Mach Buster's pin. I wore that pin with pride for many years, as there were not too many aircraft at the time that could break the sound barrier.

We flew all sorts of missions in the F-86 of which air combat maneuvers (ACM), or rat racing, as we fondly called it, was my favorite. I qualified in every phase of training except dive-bombing. For some reason, even though the target circle was probably over 100 feet wide, I could not seem to get a stupid bomb to land inside the rings. My specialty quickly became air-to-air gunnery, and I became very good at it. Only two of us in the entire class of some eighty-four students actually qualified in air-to-air gunnery. Our base squadron operations officer was the current "Top Gun" in the Air Force. He challenged me one day to a shoot-off using all six machine guns in the F-86. Normally the ground crews only loaded two of the six machine guns. He was using green-tipped bullets in his aircraft, while I had purple-tipped bullets in mine. Between the students and the instructors, especially in our flight section, a lot of betting was in progress.

We took off together and climbed to 5,000 feet and turned toward the gunnery range. About ten minutes later we established contact with the T-33 that was towing the airborne target. The airborne target was a large rectangular sheet of canvas approximately ten feet high by ten yards in length. When over the target range we climbed up to 10,000 feet and got into position above and about a half-mile out and behind the target ship. The pilot of the T-33 when he was ready would clear us in for a hot pass. We would then execute a wingover maneuver diving in a giant S-type pattern. You had approximately three-tenths of a second to fire your guns as you flew by your target. After four passes we returned to the base and awaited the landing of the target ship. What a thrill it was after they finished counting the colored holes on the target. The major had fired an 86 percent hit rate while I had a 94 percent hit rate. We all drank lots of free beer that afternoon. The next day the squadron commander asked me if I would like to remain at Williams and become one of his instructor pilots in the F-86 program. I was in Hog Heaven for one of the shortest periods in my life.

Now that Cynthia and I were finally living together, she informed me one evening that she had never seen me fly. I told her that we were coming up for a night round-robin flight in two days and that I would fly over the house for her. Since this was a solo night round-robin flight around the state of Arizona, we were briefed not to buzz any towns or we might lose our wings. The briefing officer also told us that there would be an IP in the Mobile Control Unit with field glasses following our departure to ensure that none of us buzzed nearby Chandler. We took off just prior to sunset, and I had not told any of my classmates what I intended to do.

After takeoff I extended my climb out until reaching 18,000 feet. I figured that I was far enough away that the IP in the Mobile Control Unit could no longer see me. We had taken off to the west, and were flying under visual flight rules (VFR), so it was easy to turn back and locate the town of Chandler. On the first pass I was traveling so fast that I couldn't find our house. Pulling up into a large loop, I topped out at 10,000 feet and prepared for a second pass. This time I looked down, located the high school, and counted three blocks over and three houses down from the corner. That was a buzz job that I shall never forget! I went over the house so low that it later cost me eighty-four dollars to repair the shingles that I had torn off the roof, but Cynthia did see me fly, and she never asked again.

The next morning we pilots were called into a special meeting with the base commander presiding. The mayor of Chandler was with him. I don't think to this day that I have ever seen a full colonel so mad. He told us that seven F-86 pilots had disobeyed orders and buzzed the town of Chandler last night and that they were going to take action against the pilots in question. He went on raving that one of us had been so stupid that he buzzed the town twice, giving the citizens of Chandler the red and yellow colors of the aircraft's tail section. The colonel informed us before he stomped out that he was going to pull the wings of all the pilots involved. What was really funny was that twenty minutes later there were seven second lieutenants out on the flight line looking to see what tail colors were on the planes that they had flown the previous night. I was so scared that I didn't confess my actions to anyone.

Cynthia's favorite story of me while stationed at Willie was how I got lost over Phoenix one night while on a student cross-country flight. I never thought it was so funny, but she sure got her two cents' worth out of the story. We had taken off and were again on a basic flight around the state of Arizona. Sometime during the final leg of my cross-country I maneuvered away from a giant thunderstorm that was in my flight path and in the process of trying to locate myself became disoriented. I flew around awhile trying to figure out what to do, as I sure didn't want to declare an in-flight emergency, as it would be too embarrassing. I switched radio channels and went to the ground mobile control frequency at Williams AFB. They immediately answered my call and asked me what I could see. I explained everything to the best of my ability as to what I was looking at, and I'm sure that my voice level had gone up several octaves while in the process. The IP in the Mobile Control Unit using a very calm voice told me to cancel my instrument flight plan

(IFR) with Phoenix Center and request a VFR flight plan and return to his frequency. Once back on Mobile Control frequency I was instructed to descend on an easterly heading and that Williams AFB was directly in front of me. Did I ever feel foolish over that flight? There were many laughs in the ensuing squadron parties about my getting lost while over the largest city in the state of Arizona.

As a young fighter pilot, I had a lot to learn. I was starting to figure out what my squadron commander meant while back in basic training about his not wanting to send me to a program where I would have to fly on instruments. I still didn't have the big picture about survival in the skies. I remember being out on a daylight cross-country flight while under an IFR flight plan and heading south down the eastern side of the state. I was flying at 34,000 feet and minding my own business. Looking ahead, I noticed large thunderstorms building up above my altitude directly in my flight path. I called Phoenix Center explaining the problem and requested a higher altitude. They cleared me to climb to and level off at 38,000 feet. The closer I got to the thunderstorms the quicker I realized that 38,000 feet wasn't high enough. The first stupid mistake I made was to cancel my IFR flight plan. My reasoning was that under VFR flight rules I could deviate around the thunderstorms. Upon receiving the VFR clearance I immediately began to climb to 46,000 feet, thinking that I could fly higher than the tops of the thunderstorms. What a mistake that turned out to be. I was very near the operational ceiling height of the F-86, and suddenly the aircraft got very sloppy on the flight controls. I couldn't get any more altitude out of that old 86, and upon my entering the clouds the weather suddenly got extremely violent, the aircraft stalled, and I found myself quickly in a tailspin. I recovered from the spin but kept the aircraft in a dive down to 14,000 feet. I popped out of the thunderstorm and immediately picked up a heading to the west. Eventually I was able to pick up the Williams AFB radio beacon and found my way home. What I didn't take into consideration at the time of the incident was that the tops of the mountains below my flight plan were close to 14,000 feet. I still sometimes shake when I think of how stupid I was in those early days of flying.

One of the highlights of being stationed at Williams during that time period was being able to fly in a Hollywood movie. MGM was filming *Fate Is the Hunter*, with Robert Mitchum as the star. This was a story about Air Force major James McConnell who not only was an ace but also received the Congressional Medal of Honor for a combat flight flown during the Korean War. For our part, we got to go out for several weeks and chase F-84 fighter jocks that were flying out of Luke AFB, located on the western side of Phoenix. The F-84 jets were painted light blue with bright red stars on their tails to indicate that they were North Korean fighter aircraft. While the filming of this movie was going on, Bob Hoover, a pilot of international fame, arrived at Williams to put on an air show for the student classes going through Advanced Gunnery School. I have never been as impressed with anyone as I was with Mr. Hoover. Base Maintenance had cleaned and waxed the base commander's F-86 for Mr. Hoover to use in his air show. I was standing there when he said that he didn't want to fly the base commander's aircraft. He proceeded to walk down the flight line and said, "I'll take that aircraft." His show was incredible. Just as he lifted off the ground during his takeoff, he rolled the F-86 with the gear and flaps still down. He couldn't have been more than thirty to forty feet in the air at the time. Later he landed the aircraft out of what he called a Falling Leaf type maneuver. He started the maneuver at 10,000 feet right over the field. He just swung the aircraft back and forth through air like a falling leaf, eventually touching down one wheel as he came across the runway. I still haven't figured out how he accomplished this feat without killing himself. After Mr. Hoover left, we heard that two instructor pilots killed themselves trying to duplicate his rolling the F-86 while on takeoff roll.

About the time the Advanced Gunnery School program was winding down, some bright staff officer in the chief of staff's office managed to sell General LeMay on what he thought was a good idea. Strategic Air Command (SAC) was having flying safety problems. The six-engine jet B-47 bomber with its unique bicycle-type landing gear currently held the world's flying safety record for the most aircraft lost in flying-training accidents. What this staff officer told General LeMay was that SAC was receiving their pilots from the bottom one-third of the classes graduating from the Air Force's Pilot Training Programs. This same officer suggested to the general that since SAC currently had the highest priority in the Air Force, they freeze the next six classes from both of the Air Force's advanced gunnery schools. He also decided to take the bottom ten instructor pilots from each gunnery school. This officer later proved to be correct in his analysis, but he sure destroyed a lot of good fighter pilots' careers. Feelings were so strong among the single-engine guys that when the orders came down, eight fighter pilots resigned their wings rather than fly for SAC.

From my earlier college days, while working as an air courier for the Bank of America, I flew five nights a week between San Diego and Los Angeles. I remember the president of UAL telling me that if I would get 300 hours of multijet time, he would guarantee me a job as a copilot. Realizing that I had no control over my flying future at that point, I figured it was just fate telling me what to do. I knew that SAC B-47s flew long airborne missions, so it shouldn't take me very long to obtain the 300 hours of flying time and get out of the Air Force. With this in mind I kept quiet, because I was the number-one student in my class and I got to select the SAC base of my choice. Cynthia and I picked March AFB, California, since it was close to both our parents' homes, and suddenly SAC didn't look so bad.

From Williams AFB Cynthia went back to San Diego while I went to the Air Force's Advanced Survival School located at Stead AFB in Reno, Nevada. While at Stead, I received probably some of the best training that I ever received while in the Air Force. The school was tough, and yet you either completed it or received a Letter of Reprimand and were returned to your base. If you failed the survival course you were taken off flying status until you came back later and successfully completed the school. The worst part of the course was having to eat live grasshoppers, grubs, and other assorted bugs. Grubworms I hated the most, simply because they were dirty and looked so awful. The fifty-mile trek through the Grand Truckee Mountains while trying to evade mock Russian Guards was probably the most fun. It reminded me a lot of my experiences in the Marine Corps during the Korean War, only this time it was pleasurable.

13

Strategic Air Command

Upon graduation from the Survival School, the entire SAC class headed for the B-47 Ground Training School located at McConnell AFB in Wichita, Kansas. The B-47 school teaching staff at McConnell was quite concerned about our arrival, and believe me they had good reason to be concerned. On the opening day of classes one of our classmates had obtained a box of the largest and most disgusting-tasting and worst-smelling cigars that I have ever seen. Arriving in class each morning, the entire class lit up these awful-smelling cigars and of course blew the smoke to the front of the room. Only the copilots and navigators had to take the B-47 ground school, and we were quickly paired off as members of our future B-47 crew. I have to admit I have never been to a school quite like this one as there was an incredible amount of information to learn. The B-47 is a very large airplane with numerous systems, both electrical and hydraulic, and there was what seemed like endless tests on each component of the aircraft. In addition, we went on temporary duty (TDY) to Texas for two weeks to the Nuclear Weapons Training School in Houston, Texas. We also spent a lot of time learning about navigating using sextants and the International Star Charts. Actually, learning about all the navigational stars in the sky was really interesting, and I have never forgotten the information that I learned there at McConnell.

Cynthia and I had rented a small apartment in Wichita and were having a great time. We experienced our first blizzard together. I'll never forget that Cynthia insisted that I barbecue one evening during the worst of the blizzard conditions. I put a large packing crate over myself and the barbecue and had at it. When you are young, you'll do most anything. Our first daughter, Jane Jennifer, was born on December 31, 1958, in the McConnell AFB Hospital. What a beautiful girl she was (and still is today).

The navigator that I was teamed up with was a Lt. Col. Ernie Perez. I was so rank-conscious that I had difficulty with Ernie, as he insisted on having me call him just plain Ernie and not Colonel. We eventually became very close and worked together well. Upon completion of the B-47 ground school we both headed south to Little Rock AFB, Arkansas, for the flying phase of our training.

On our first day of duty at Little Rock AFB, we were ushered into a large theater-type building where the wing commander was to introduce new crews. Word had arrived ahead of us that the entire class of incoming ex–fighter pilot copilots was filled with misfits. Upon entering the theater the navigators and copilots were told to sit in the backseats while the new upgrading aircraft commanders were seated in the first two rows of seats. The wing commander proceeded to call the new aircraft commander's name, which base he was from, and how many hours over 2,000 that he had in the B-47 and then invited him up to the center of the stage. The wing commander next called the copilot and navigator up to the stage, where we were supposed to report in a military manner. As I approached my new aircraft commander (AC), Captain Luke, he stuck out his hand and said, "Anything over thirty degrees scares me." I knew that he was joking, but in front of the microphone and the entire audience I told him to go screw himself! It brought the house down, but it definitely was not the best way to get started in SAC, and the wing commander was quick to remind me of this.

Several days later we spent a half-day briefing for our first mission. The mission was approximately seven hours in duration and designed to provide air-to-air refueling training plus numerous touch-and-go landings for the two new upgrading aircraft commanders. They also assigned two copilots to the mission but left the navigators at home. The model of B-47 that we were to fly that day was a RB-47. The R stood for reconnaissance, which meant that the entire front of the nose of the aircraft was glass panels. One copilot was to sit in the navigator's seat, while the other was to strap himself into the fifth man's seat, which was located beneath, and to the left of the AC. From this fifth man's position you could see absolutely nothing, and there were no lights to assist you. Since I was asked to sit in the fifth man's seat, I made the mistake of asking the IP what the copilot's portion of the mission was to be during this seven-hour flight. His response was that we were "supposed to listen to

SAC talk." I couldn't believe what he said, because at the time I was too intimidated to believe what he said. Following the flight, the next day, I requested permission to speak with the squadron commander. I told him exactly what I thought of this first flight and that if SAC treated their combat crews this way, then I wanted no part of the B-47 program. I told him he could have my wings if he wanted them. So for the next two months I caught every "shit" detail there was in the squadron. I wound up painting all of the strips on the squadron's parking lot, painting the operations and briefing rooms, and updating all of the squadrons' books.

One of those details that I have regretted ever since occurred one day when the squadron commander told me to go out to the main gate of the base and pick up the guest speaker for the noncommissioned officers' graduation program. I picked up a very elderly retired colonel in civilian clothing and, as per my instructions, took him to the base officers' club for lunch. We spent an hour talking about fishing and weather. The gentlemen's name was Benjamin Foulois, which at the time meant absolutely nothing to me. I was such an attitude case and just dumb enough not to realize what a historic celebrity I had with me. Later I found out that he held the number-one certificate for flying proficiency in the United States and that he had signed off both the Wright brothers' flight certificates in 1911 when they first learned to fly. I was upset for days afterward when I realized what a famous person he was and that I had let him slip right through my fingers.

The end of the B-47 flying course arrived none too soon, and each crew member in the training program was required to pass a 60-4 Flight Examination. When I went up for my check ride, I had exactly four hours' total time in the B-47, as the other copilot and I had to split the time on the first mission we flew. Since all of my flying time had been in the fifth man's seat, needless to say, I busted the check ride big-time. The result was that our crew was the first and only crew in that training wing to complete the combat crew-upgrading program with a non-combat-ready status.

14

March AFB

Our reputation certainly preceded us to March AFB, and the squadron commander of the 141st Bomb Squadron could hardly wait to get his hands on me. He not only read me the riot act but also told me that if I didn't get my act together he would see that I received an Undesirable Discharge (AFR 39-12) from the U.S. Air Force. He further said that in all of his years in SAC no one, absolutely no one, had ever received the type of flying scores that I had from the training wing at Little Rock. He was embarrassed that I had been assigned to his squadron and said that he had never met anyone with an attitude like mine. The more he talked, the madder he got, and finally he told me that I was a disgrace to his squadron and for me to get the hell out of his office. I got out of there in a hurry and tried my best to avoid him whenever I could. Luke and Ernie were my only two friends, and they did their best to help me to get ready to pass the copilots' upgrading program for the 320th Bombardment Wing there at March AFB. We flew every other day for the first two weeks in order to get me ready for my Standardization Evaluation Test, which I did manage to pass with extremely high scores.

In between flying days, I again caught every rotten detail that the squadron commander could come up with. No one in the squadron seemed to like me, especially the other copilots, as they were all aware of my fighter pilot's type background.

One Thursday afternoon, I was called into the squadron commander's office and told that the next morning I was to report to the base officers' club as a part of the squadron's decorations committee. It seems that the 141st Bomb Squadron's Wives Club was hosting a party that night and six second lieutenants were assigned to decorate the club for the party. We spent most of the day blowing up balloons and pasting decorations on the walls of the club room that we were using. Toward the end of the day the squadron operations officer, a lieutenant colonel, came in to see how we were doing.

The colonel bought four pitchers of beer and called the six of us over to sit and relax for a few minutes. He sat down and introduced himself, as he knew that several of us were new to the squadron. However, when I introduced myself he already knew about me and made no bones about his dislike for me. I ignored his treatment of me and turned to drinking the beer. Sometime during the next several minutes, one of the lieutenants, whom I considered a dumbhead, asked the colonel to describe the merit badges that he was currently wearing on his uniform. I guess it was my Marine Corps background coming to the surface, but I couldn't believe what this idiot lieutenant had asked the colonel to do. It just wasn't proper military protocol to do something like this. I think the colonel was embarrassed at first and then realized the bad manners of the lieutenant, but he did proceed to try to explain what each of his ribbons was for. When the colonel got to his top ribbon, which was the Distinguished Flying Cross (DFC), the same lieutenant asked him to explain how he got it. I knew that the colonel was embarrassed as he paused for several minutes before he began his story.

He told us that the DFC was the fourth-highest medal for heroism in our nation and that he received it for a flight that he flew during the Korean War. Before getting started with his story he drained his glass of beer and refilled it. He told us that he was involved in flying C-47 Gooney Birds during the worst winter on record in Korea. He said that the Marines were evacuating their forces from the Chosen Reservoir up on the thirty-eighth Parallel and that he was involved in flying out the dead and wounded Marines from several different in-country sites. He described how difficult it was flying in and out of such small airstrips, especially in inclement weather and with people shooting at you.

At first I was bored with the story; however, the second he mentioned flying out of Kot'or-i I became very attentive. He was talking about being one of the last Gooney Birds to get out of Kot'or-i when I stood up with a glass of beer in my hand and proposed a toast to the colonel. He looked at me with hostile eyes, as I know he was irritated with the other second lieutenant and surely knew about the squadron commanders' feelings about me. My toast was, "To the Marines left behind." The colonel was so mad that he almost got up and left. I looked at him and said, "Please, sir, I would like to finish your story." Before the colonel could say anything I picked up his story. I began to describe how three very young Marines, a corporal and two privates, were left behind. Their mission was to provide ground firepower for the last four Gooney Birds, enabling them to get off the ground at Kot'or-i. As I was completing the story, it got extremely quiet at the table, as those at the table couldn't believe what I was doing.

The colonel stood up, came over to me, and placed his arms around my shoulders. He said, "You were the corporal that I left behind and gave up for dead at Kot'or-i in 1950, weren't you?"

I replied, "Yes, sir."

There were tears in both of our eyes during that very emotional moment, and for a while neither one of us could speak. For a few minutes he had lost his voice, and I didn't know what to say. He finally stood back and told me that he wanted me to meet his wife that evening and that he wanted me to report to his office first thing Monday morning.

Well, the colonel and I met on Monday, and I explained exactly what had happened both at Williams AFB and at Little Rock. I told him that there was really nothing wrong with my attitude; it was just that I had a difficult time of trying to "listen to SAC talk" for seven hours while strapped into the fifth man's seat on that RB-47. He was the first senior officer to actually listen to my side of the story, and he agreed with my feelings. He told me that I was stuck in SAC for the time being and that we needed to turn my flying career around. I never before had a mentor like this, and what a pleasure it became to work under him. I mentioned that I was behind my classmates by about three to four hundred flying hours. He told me that there were three B-47 squadrons in the wing and that there was ample opportunity to build up my flying hours so long as I didn't care which squadron I flew with. He said that there was still a shortage of copilots in the wing and other squadrons would be happy to have me fly with them. I told him that I would not let him down and that I would fly as often as he could schedule me. For the next three months I flew three to four times a week, with any squadron that needed me.

Before going on, I need to describe some of the unusual flight characteristics of the Boeing six-engine B-47 jet bomber. On the negative side, the aircraft was one of those flying machines known to Air Force pilots as an "unforgiving-type aircraft." By that, I mean if you made even a small mistake while flying, the aircraft would kill you. As an example, most of the aircraft of the 1950s had a landing gear in each wing plus either a nose- or tail wheel. This arrangement of three landing gears on most aircraft enabled pilots to recover from unusual attitudes close to the ground and effect many safe landings. The B-47, however, had a tandem-type gear arrangement of its two main landing gears directly under the fuselage, much like a common two-wheeled bicycle. There was a small outrigger-type landing gear located inside the double engine nacelles, but it didn't provide you with much stability. Another of the basic problems was that the aircraft was designed to be a medium-heavy six-engine jet bomber. The power of the six jet engines was not a problem once you got them up to full power, but the operating weight of the aircraft was. The B-47 was designed to fly at 125,000 pounds. We were operating them on a daily basis at 193,000 to 198,000 pounds, and our B-47s while on alert status weighed in excess of 223,000 pounds which necessitated using rocket-assisted power for takeoff (JATO).

The JATO rack was a large half moon device that fitted onto the rear underside of the B-47's fuselage. It held thirty rocket bottles in three rows with ten bottles in each row. Each rocket bottle when fired provided an additional 1,000 pounds of thrust during the take-off roll. That was a lot of instantaneous power, i.e., 30,000 pounds all at once, and sometimes it did strange things to the aircraft. As a result there were a lot of problems associated with these JATO racks especially if you were a follow-on aircraft during the fifteen-second takeoff intervals. All aircraft using JATO racks for training purposes weighed around 198,000 pounds during takeoff. The min-ute the first aircraft down the runway fired the water on all six engines to achieve approximately 15 percent more engine power, there was so much black smoke on the runway that the succeeding aircraft went on instrument flight conditions for their takeoffs. To compound that problem, the JATO was supposed to be fired when the aircraft reached 131 knots of airspeed during takeoff. Usually the pilot had to guess the airspeed, as the airspeed indicator was bouncing around so much that it was impossible to read accurately.

During the takeoff roll of a B-47, the aircraft commander was always too busy with the flight controls to do anything else but get the aircraft safely airborne. Therefore, it was the copilot's duty to fire the JATO. In the back cockpit there were three circuit breakers located on the right rear instrument panel slightly behind the copilot's seat that when pushed in actually fired the JATO. The JATO circuit breakers had little red plastic tabs over them to prevent accidental firing by someone inadvertently striking them. Therefore, during the takeoff roll the copilot had to gently remove the plastic tabs and get ready to push the circuit breakers in at the AC's command. What happened so often, and it was both humorous and not so humorous in many cases, was that the copilot would push in one circuit breaker at a time instead of all three at once. If you were alongside the runway during one of these JATO missions you could easily see what was happening to the aircraft as the copilot fired the JATO. Should the copilot push the circuit breakers in one at a time, the tail of the B-47 would jump up, pushing the nose down each time the copilot pushed a circuit breaker in. Sometimes there was not enough up elevator left for the AC, resulting in a nose-down crash.

Another unusual design feature of the B-47 due to its heavy landing weight was in the approach chute. This was a small parachute located in the tail section of the B-47 that the AC deployed oftentimes during the downwind leg of the traffic pattern. The idea was to assist in the stabilization of the aircraft by providing the AC with a higher power setting during the landing phase of flight. What generally happened was that if the AC got too low on airspeed before the actual touchdown, the aircraft would slam down on the forward main gear. The resulting action was that the forward main gear would hydraulically compress and subsequently bounce the aircraft back into the sky. At this point the B-47 was usually out of control, causing the AC to panic somewhat. The AC had two options when this happened. He could throw the power to the aircraft and hope to make a successful go-around (this was not easy, as it took thirteen seconds for the jet engines to reach full power), or he could deploy the brake chute. Deployment of the brake chute at the wrong time often resulted in a porpoising type maneuver, as the aircraft bounced up and down going down the runway, which in 90 percent of the cases ended in a fatal crash. Pilots had the option of either using the approach chute or not using it. Most pilots would use the approach chute for two or three months, then experience a bad landing, and then would not use it again for a period of time.

The brake chute was a large parachute that was packed, loaded, and locked into the tail section of the B-47 by only the aircraft commander. Upon landing, the AC would deploy the brake chute after the aircraft was settled successfully on the ground. Should the brake chute fail to deploy on landing, in most cases it would be impossible to stop the B-47 on the remaining runway. All B-47 pilots very definitely earned their flight pay by just getting the machine safely on the ground. Normal training missions were of such long duration that SAC started issuing the drug Dexedrine to ACs. They were required to take the drug two hours prior to landings. Most of us saved the Dexedrine and used it whenever we drove home during holidays.

There were a lot of things that could kill a pilot quickly while flying a B-47. The pilots first had to always respect the B-47 and never let themselves get complacent even for a second. Complacency in a B-47 kills quickly! In the 1500 flying hours that I accumulated in the B-47, I learned to really appreciate what the Boeing Aircraft Company had created in this flying machine. The aircraft had plenty of power once it got successfully off the ground. When airborne, it could easily reach aileron reversal speed of 442 mph of indicated airspeed. What this meant was that the pilot could turn the flight controls to the left and the aircraft would turn to the right due to the bending of the wings. Should you let the airspeed accelerate to 446 mph, you could still turn the flight controls, but nothing would happen. B-47 pilots called this phenomenon "total aileron and elevator ineffectiveness," and should the pilot allow it to continue for very long, he was history. In spite of all of these unusual features, the B-47, when flown properly, was a workhorse and a good flying machine.

15

The Saga of China 64

In keeping up with my attempt to build up my flying time, on October 27, 1959, I volunteered to fly a mission with a crew from the 443d Bomb Squadron whose copilot was ill. This particular flight was to become one that I shall never forget. The flight not only made SAC history but also became one of the most terrifying flying experiences of my early flying career. It definitely made a true believer out of me about the incredible sensitivity and power of the B-47 aircraft when treated with respect. The flight was later headlined in the March 1960 issue of the *Air Force Flying Safety Magazine.* After a Letter of Commendation from the squadron commander of the 443d Bomb Squadron plus one from the wing commander, I went from the lowest form of humanity according to my squadron commander, to the top copilot in the wing. My status after this mission was such that later in the year when higher headquarters deactivated the 320th Bomb Wing at March AFB, I was given the first choice of assignments over all other copilots in the wing. Thus ensues the saga of "China 64."

On October 26, 1959, I reported to the 443d Bomb Squadron, where I was scheduled to fly as a copilot with Crew E-11. I chuckled to myself when I saw the aircraft call sign that we were going to use for the mission, i.e., China 64. SAC as a command changed the call signs of their bombers in each bomb wing usually on a monthly basis but sometimes even on a daily basis. What made this call sign so unusual was that while we were on alert status our targets were in either China or Russia. I thought to myself, *Is this a bad omen? Are we the targets?*

The AC from the 443d was a senior major with command pilot's wings and had over 3,500 hours of flying time in the B-47. Most training missions in 1959 in SAC required a heavyweight takeoff for training purposes for the combat crews. Missions usually included in-flight refueling, radar bombing, and night celestial navigation legs and lasted anywhere between seven and nine hours. Thus with all of the math and research involved in mission planning, it required the better part of a day to complete all of the paperwork and have it signed off. When I reported in for the mission planning that morning, the AC told me that his navigator was not going to be there and that he was counting on me to complete most of the mission planning. I was really upset with this information, as it was critical that the navigator and copilot work together, especially on the night celestial navigation portion of the mission. The navigator usually selected a point in space, and then the copilot, going into the Star Charts, computed the logarithm for each of the three stars that he would shoot on that fix. The AC said that we could compute the information while flying, but I knew this to be almost impossible, as there was not enough room for the copilot to research the logarithms inside the cockpit. I was subsequently pissed off with the AC's approach, as everything depended on the precision and exactness of proper mission planning and my workload for this mission was going to be tremendous.

At the conclusion of the day's mission planning, the AC told me to meet him at the Personnel Equipment (PE) Shop the next day around thirteen hundred hours. The navigator and I arrived first and while getting acquainted gathered all of the required PE for the flight. This amounted to several hundred pounds of assorted PE gear for the three-man crew. Some time later the AC appeared and he seemed to be very upset. His face was almost white, and he was extremely nervous. He told us that a member of SAC's SSG Team was going to fly with us and that we needed extra equipment for him. In my innocence in SAC, I had no idea what SSG was or even what it stood for. Before leaving the PE section, I made a detour into my own squadron and, locating my AC, asked him what SSG was. He informed me that SSG stood for the Strategic Standardization Evaluation Group located in Barksdale, Alabama. He further volunteered the information that these SSG people were highly feared by all SAC crews. SSG operations were classified, and if one of the crew members violated any of SAC's policies both before and during the flight the entire crew would lose their combat flying status and most likely be grounded with administrative discipline. He also told me that the entire crew would be subjected to six to eight hours of examinations after the flight regardless of the outcome of the evaluation. *What rotten luck*! I thought to myself. After such a shaky start in the squadron, I sure didn't need this to happen to me. Not only was the paperwork workload a heavy one without the navigator's help, but I was the junior copilot in the 320th Bombardment Wing and with very little flying time in the B-47.

In those days it was standard procedure for the combat crews to arrive at the aircraft four hours prior to takeoff. The navigator and I laid all of the PE equipment out on the ground in front of the aircraft and then assumed a position of parade rest while the AC read from the preflight checklist. The SSG captain in his black flight suit stood to the side with a notebook and never said a word. Once the preflight portion of the checklist was completed, the navigator and copilot had to load and properly store all of the PE equipment onboard the aircraft. This was no easy job, as you had to manhandle everything up a thirteen-foot ladder just to reach the cockpit. While we were loading the PE equipment, the AC made his walk around accompanied by the SSG captain silently evaluating every action made by the AC. The most critical thing on the walk around was the manual installation and hook-up of the brake chute by the AC. The reason that only the AC could accomplish this important task was that the brake chute could easily be hooked up backward and if it were, the chute would fail to deploy during the landing phase.

With everything in order we started all six engines thirty minutes before our takeoff and called the tower for taxi instructions. We were a part of a cell of three B-47s and scheduled as number two for takeoff. The cell leader taxied into position, received his clearance, and proceeded to take off. We were then cleared by the tower into the number-one position and told to hold prior to release. Sitting there, we completed the pre-takeoff checklist and got ready to roll. After release by the tower, everything was going fine during the takeoff roll until we reached an airspeed of about ninety knots. Suddenly the AC shouted, "Abort-Abort." He quickly pulled all six engines to idle power and deployed the brake chute. He did not call for any Emergency Procedures Checklist, nor did he tell anybody what was wrong. As we continued to career down the runway the tower called and told us that we had a failure on our brake chute deployment and that our brakes were all smoking. Trying to

112

stop a 198,000-pound monster that is moving down the runway at or near 100 mph is not easy even when everything is going right. In this case, the AC managed to bring the aircraft to a complete stop on the overrun portion of the runway. We were immediately surrounded by a host of fire trucks, as our brakes were now on fire. Finally, the fire marshal told us that the fires on our brakes were out and that we were cleared to taxi back to our parking area. Only then did the AC tell us why he had aborted the takeoff. He said that he had lost oil pressure on number four engine and as a result elected to abort the takeoff. He failed to mention that the brake chute had failed to deploy which was why we needed the entire runway plus use of the overrun to stop the aircraft.

After parking and deplaning, the SSG captain called us together and told the AC that he had failed the flight. The captain's reason was improper use of Emergency Flight Procedures Checklists. And in addition, the fact that the AC had hooked up the brake chute backward during the initial walk around, causing it to fall out onto the ground when we needed it the most. The operations officer told us to wait around while the maintenance people looked over the number-four engine. Three hours later, the maintenance personnel informed us that a fuse had blown on the number-four engine oil pressure gage. Maintenance personnel replaced the blown fuse, ran the engine up, and told us that we were cleared to continue the mission just as quickly as they could refuel the aircraft. The squadron operations officer told us that even though we had already received an "unsatisfactory" on the mission we should try to salvage as much as we could out of the original mission.

As soon as we had all six engines started and in the green, we again contacted the tower for taxi and takeoff instructions. During our taxi out we had to refile our original flight plan with Air Traffic Control (ATC). We completed all checklist items and were cleared onto Runway 310 for takeoff. At about the same point during the takeoff roll, the AC informed us that he had again lost oil pressure on number-four engine but was going to continue the takeoff.

We broke ground and the AC started a left-hand thirty-degree climbing turn. As soon as he rolled out on a southern heading he turned the aircraft over to me and requested that the navigator read the Emergency Engine Shutdown Procedures Checklist. My initial reaction was one of immediate distrust of the AC, as in most cases

113

the pilots usually handled any in-flight emergency together while the navigator kept us clear of any hazards. I thought to myself, *Why is this guy avoiding communications with me, especially at a time like this?*

This was the first time that I had ever actually flown the B-47, and due to the heavy weight condition I found it somewhat sluggish to fly and rather slow to climb. While concentrating on my heading and flight conditions, I was monitoring the conversation between the AC and the navigator. While reading the checklist, the navigator told the AC to pull the fire button on number four engine and then to stopcock the throttle. In both positions in the cockpit there are six large engine fire-warning lights located on the forward front of the instrument panels. According to the B-47's Dash-1, should one of these lights come on during flight, you had three seconds to shut down the engine before it blew up. By pulling the individual engine fire-warning light out you would automatically shut off the fuel and ignition to that engine, causing it to stop. I watched as the engine fire-warning light came on for the number four engine. Then, before I could say anything, the AC pulled the number five engine throttle instead of the number four throttle into the shutoff position. We were just clearing 5,000-foot altitude, and in our heavy-weight flight condition the loss of two engines on the same wing was almost catastrophic. I remember tersely swearing at the AC as I had my hands instantly full of a shuddering and unstable aircraft. It required both full left rudder and full opposite aileron just to keep the wings level. While all of this was going on I stopped trying to climb and called ATC, explaining that we were in the process of an in-flight emergency. I requested permission from them to level off at 5,000 feet until we could clear the emergency. At the same time that this was going on, the AC was shouting at the navigator, telling him that it was his fault before he finally realized that he had made the error. Meanwhile, the SSG captain, sitting in the fourth-man seat located in the aisle just below my feet, was writing so fast you could almost see the smoke coming off his pencil. He was adding yet another unsatisfactory check to the already-growing number of screw-ups on this flight.

The AC then accomplished another no-no as he restarted the number five engine without calling for the proper checklist. We eventually got things under control and received a new clearance from ATC to climb and continue our mission.

One of the first things that we were supposed to do after reaching our proper altitude was receive an off-load of fuel from an already-airborne KC-135 tanker aircraft. As we were moving into position behind the tanker, the SSG captain reminded the AC that he was not supposed to try to refuel unless he had all six engines operating. The AC because of his vast experience in the B-47 decided to ignore the SSG captain and attempted to go ahead with the refueling.

The AC did everything possible trying to get a hookup on the flying boom, but with only five engines operating he was unable to do so. After fifteen unsuccessful minutes of trying to obtain a hookup, the AC finally requested the KC-135 to descend. It was the AC's hope that this would give him a little more speed to play with. The tanker pilot said that they were unable to accommodate a descent due to the restrictions in their block-assigned altitude by ATC. It was at this point that our AC decided to call off the refueling part of the mission. Looking down, I noticed that the SSG captain was again writing furiously in his notebook.

After exiting the refueling track, we turned out over the Pacific Ocean to try to complete our night celestial navigation portion of the mission. Timing for a celestial navigation leg is critical; otherwise the information received is useless. In order to properly fly a celestial leg, the copilot and navigator must select what three stars to shoot and the timing has to be exact. Once the copilot determines the stars he wants to shoot that lie along the aircraft's flight path, then the copilot must go into the International Star Charts and locate the logarithm of each star for that moment in time using Greenwich Mean Time. The copilot then inserts a sextant into the top of his canopy and sets the proper logarithm coordinates for the first shot. The copilot then waits for a time hack from the navigator before actually shooting the star. Once the time hack is given, the copilot begins to shoot each star for a three-minute time period. During the shooting time, the copilot continually adjusts the coordinates inside the sextant to keep the star in the center of the sextant's sights. At the conclusion of the shot, the copilot gives the navigator the final coordinates from the sextant. While all of the shooting is going on, the AC's job is to constantly monitor the aircraft's heading while flying on autopilot. Holding the aircraft on the exact heading and altitude is critical especially during the shooting time; otherwise the shot is useless. As a result of the delayed takeoff by three hours, the navigator in addition had his hands full trying to compute all of the precomputations on the stars we were now going to use.

I was experiencing difficulty with the sextant while shooting the first star when I happened to look at the instrument panel and realized that the AC had allowed the aircraft heading to wander twelve degrees off the proper heading. I immediately called this to the attention of both the navigator and the AC. The AC's comment was that the circuit breaker for the autopilot had popped out on his side instrument panel. The AC then disengaged the autopilot and told us that he would hand-fly the aircraft for the next two shots. Both shots became useless, as the AC was unable to hold the aircraft on its heading during the star-shooting time. This now necessitated aborting the celestial navigation portion of the flight plan. The AC now made the comment that he felt that there was something wrong with the electrical trim tabs and that was the main reason that he was unable to hold the aircraft on a proper heading. The original flight plan also called for several radar bomb release times with Los Angeles's Radar Bomb Plot. However, we were so far out over the Pacific Ocean we were unable to obtain enough speed by using only five engines to make our bomb release times. We discussed all of the problems that we were having with the aircraft and decided that we should just head back to March AFB. Remaining at altitude, we headed back to March AFB and contacted the 320th Bomb Wing's Command Post making them aware of our flight problems. The Command Post advised us that March AFB had now gone below landing minimums due to fog and advised us to proceed to Davis-Monthon (DM) AFB in Arizona for landing. They told us that they would advise Davis-Monthon that we were inbound to their station and requested an estimated time of arrival (ETA) from us.

The flight to Arizona was uneventful and we arrived over their navigation beacon exactly on our ETA at 20,000 feet. The AC called Davis-Monthon Approach Control and received permission to start a descent to traffic pattern altitude. The AC, without calling for a Pre-Descent Checklist, departed 20,000 feet toward and began the penetration. The SSG captain who was monitoring everything tapped me on the leg, giving me a note that said that he had to get into my seat to evaluate the approach and landing by the AC. I quickly unstrapped from my parachute and exchanged seats with him. SAC regulations require the AC to call for each checklist as needed for whatever flight condition you are in. The AC made a normal penetration and low approach; however, he forgot to call for the Before Landing Checklist. The SSG captain allowed him to continue his approach until just before reaching touchdown on the runway. At this point the SSG evaluator slammed all five engines to 100 percent, and told the AC to execute a go-around. The AC had forgotten to put the flaps down and had not computed either an approach speed or a landing speed. As the AC started his go-around he called for the flaps and suddenly realized that they were already up. The SSG evaluator responded by informing him that he had failed to call for the flaps to come down and, further, failed to call for any of the mandatory checklists. He further informed the AC that this was another bust item on the flight. At that point it got very quiet inside the cockpit.

We eventually got the aircraft safely on the ground and were directed to a parking place on the DM ramp. During the hour or so it took to debrief the flight we explained to the ground maintenance people all of our write-ups. The AC told the maintenance personnel to put a partial fuel load on the aircraft, as it was just a short flight back to March AFB. SAC and the 320th Bomb Wing policy both required a minimum of twelve hours' crew rest on the ground before a flight crew could fly again. The AC informed the DM people that he intended to be airborne in exactly twelve hours. Once this decision was made next came the hassle of trying to find beds in the Base Officers Quarters (BOQ) at five-thirty in the morning. It was around 6:30 A.M. before any of us got into bed, and it quickly became apparent that sleep was going to be next to impossible. All of us were already suffering from a high state of anxiety as a result of so many things having gone wrong with the original flight. Reaching our assigned rooms we discovered that there were around sixty to eighty Marine officers in the same BOQ who were just getting up and the noise level was unbelievably loud. Unable to sleep, all of us were up by eleven o'clock. We had breakfast and caught a taxi to base operations, where we prepared a flight plan to get us back to March AFB. The base operations officer told us that our aircraft was fixed; however, Maintenance Control had screwed up and put a heavyweight fuel load on the aircraft. The AC was really upset by this, but there was absolutely nothing that we could do but take off and try to burn a lot of fuel off prior to reaching March AFB. Being anxious to get out of DM, we quickly computed the takeoff data and headed out for the preflight check of the aircraft. The AC decided that we would fly to the California Thermal VOR fix at 20,000 feet in an effort to burn off enough fuel to be able to land the B-47 once we arrived there. The SSG captain informed the crew that the evaluation was over and that he would just be a passenger on the way home.

The takeoff, twelve hours and ten minutes after landing, was normal, but once again on climb out, the number four engine oil pressure gauge became inoperative. This time the AC called for the proper checklist from the copilot, and the number four engine was shut down properly. Since there was no mission involved other than to just return to March AFB, I requested permission from the AC to hand-fly the aircraft back the Thermal VOR, and the AC concurred.

Shortly after takeoff we received clearance from Los Angeles Center to proceed directly from DM to the Thermal, California, VOR at 20,000 feet. Upon arrival, we were to enter a standard holding pattern and call for further clearance. Somewhere around the ninth circuit of the holding pattern, out of my peripheral vision I noticed the outrigger gear located in the wings coming down. Sometimes pilots lowered these outrigger gears in an effort to create more drag on the aircraft when they wanted to burn off fuel, but they usually informed everyone. I assumed that the AC had put the gear down without saying anything to me, as he was a man of very few words by now. Within two minutes of noticing that the outriggers were down, the cockpit suddenly filled with smoke, causing us all to go on 100 percent oxygen. Fire onboard an aircraft is always critical, and while I continued to fly the aircraft the navigator read the Emergency Flight Procedure Checklist to the AC for the removal of smoke from the cockpit. Once we were able to breathe normally, I asked the AC if he had put the outrigger gear down. He said no, he couldn't put them down from his position. Looking out, he took control of the aircraft and asked me to recycle the outrigger gear. The outrigger gear came up normally, and just as soon as I placed the switch in the neutral position the gear immediately started back down. The cockpit once again filled up with smoke. This really got our attention, as fire was prevalent on everyone's mind, especially if the fire was located somewhere in one of the wings.

By the time the smoke dissipated enough so that we could see again, the anxiety level had gone up again for all of us. The AC now called the CP at March and informed them of our current situation. No one in the CP had ever heard of this type of a problem with a B-47, so the CP called the Boeing Company in Seattle, Washington. We waited for what seemed like an hour before the Boeing people made their minds up as to what the problem was. Finally, they told us to place the main gear handle into the down and locked position. Once the gear all showed down and locked, they asked for the copilot to pull the circuit breakers on all of the landing gear. By the time we got through talking to the Boeing engineers and other experts from SAC headquarters, we had spent almost four hours in the holding pattern. Our fuel situation was now becoming another major consideration. We needed to perform a penetration and get the aircraft on the ground as soon as possible.

We exited the holding pattern at Thermal and contacted Los Angeles Center for a new clearance, explaining that we needed to get the aircraft on the ground immediately. Los Angeles Center told us that the current March AFB ceiling was 2300 feet with broken clouds. The center also informed us that there was a solid 3000-foot overcast above the 2300 feet and that the tops of the clouds were 6500 feet. We knew from experience while flying in and out of March AFB that the weather would deteriorate rapidly, so the AC requested an immediate penetration. Los Angeles Center cleared us to enter the holding pattern again, and once stabilized in the pattern we were cleared for a penetration at 1818 hours. The AC had taken over control of the aircraft, and he arrived over the penetration fix exactly on time. We then switched to the Approach Control frequency, and the AC told Approach Control that we were departing 20,000. We received a "Roger" from them, which the AC interpreted as his clearance to penetrate. Radio reception over Thermal VOR was often garbled at times due to interference from the Navy and San Diego Approach Control, which were operating close to the same Air Force radio frequencies. This problem merely added to the confusion that we were already experiencing.

Unfortunately, March Approach Control had only acknowledged China 64's radio call and had not given us a clearance to

119

penetrate. We were near 15,000 feet when March Approach Control realized that we had left 20,000 feet. They told us to immediately climb back to 20,000 feet and to contact Los Angeles Center before entering the Thermal holding pattern. It was at this point that things really started to go bad. The AC was mad as a hornet and racked the aircraft around in a tight turn, causing it to shudder just below stalling speed. There are certain standard Air Force procedures for entering a holding pattern, and the AC violated all of them. This immediately got the attention of the SSG evaluator who was sitting in the aisle. He quickly told the AC that this was another "bust" and that he'd better watch what he was doing. Many unpleasant words were shouted back and forth between the SSG evaluator and the AC. Finally, the AC told the SSG evaluator, to shut the fuck up and to mind his own business. It got very quiet again inside the cockpit after that. Finally, thirteen minutes later, we were officially cleared to penetrate from the Thermal VOR.

Departing 20,000 feet we hit the Stardust Radio Intersection right on the money and started a right-hand turn to a heading of 314 degrees. As a result of already having our gear down and locked, the forward landing lights were automatically on. This caused an eerie feeling in the cockpit as the landing lights bounced off the clouds that lay ahead of us. I called, "Departing the Stardust Intersection at eight thousand feet!" March Approach Control told us to continue the approach and call when over the Bachelor Fan Marker at 6000 feet. During our descent we entered the clouds somewhere between 7000 and 6000 feet. At this point things deteriorated rapidly. It was bad enough being inside the clouds with the landing light on; however, this problem worsened, as the rotating anticollision lights were now reflecting off our canopy. There was so much static on the command radios that we requested and received an alternate frequency. When we arrived at the Bachelor Fan Marker, ATC cleared us to descend to 3700 feet and told us to turn immediately left back to 315 degrees.

As the aircraft was passing through 3200 feet, I asked the AC what he was doing, as I knew that he had flown this very same approach at least a hundred times before. He replied that he understood that we had been cleared down to 3200 feet. While responding to me he continued to descend and started turning right instead of left as Approach Control was requesting him to do.

By this time, communications became next to impossible, as the navigator, the evaluator, and I were all yelling at the same time trying to get the AC to turn back to the left. Somewhere in the process we lost communications with March Approach Control. I argued with the AC for a few seconds and then told him that I was taking control of the aircraft. He began fighting me for control of the aircraft, and there ensued absolute chaos in the cockpit. We were now at 2900 feet, and the navigator was screaming over the interphone that all he had on the radar set was mountains and began yelling, "Pull up, Ace! Pull up!" I jammed all five engine throttles to 100 percent and, not thinking, placed the main gear handle into the up position. The gear warning horn and the light inside the gear handle came on immediately, adding even more to the confusion. I quickly realized that the gear wouldn't come up, as we had pulled the circuit breakers prior to leaving Thermal VOR. I also couldn't let go of the flight controls and return the gear handle to the neutral position, because the AC was still fighting me for control of the aircraft. The AC was jerking the flight controls left and right and up and down, trying to get me off the controls. Fortunately, I was larger and stronger than he was and was able to overpower him. At one point he pulled the throttles back to the idle detent position and managed to pull the nose of the aircraft up before I could overcontrol him. I quickly got the throttle back to 100 percent; however, our airspeed had now dropped to six knots below best flare speed. As all B-47 pilots know, this situation definitely placed our aircraft on the "back side of the infamous power curve."

Things had gone absolutely critical now! I managed to jam my right foot against the throttle quadrant so the AC couldn't pull the throttles off again. At the same time, I was still trying to keep the wings level. I knew that we were but a heartbeat away from stalling and falling out of the sky. At one point we flew right between two mountain peaks, with the right wing missing the ground by less than ten feet. This scared the daylights out of me, and I seriously considered bailing at that second. Somehow, even though it wasn't my crew, I felt an obligation to stay with the aircraft and attempt to gain enough altitude so that the navigator could bail out. In a B-47 emergency, both pilots' seats eject upward while the navigator's seat ejects downward. By now my right foot was really getting cramped, but I was too busy to think about it. I had put the flaps partially down when we suddenly dropped to six knots below best flare in an attempt to keep a little lift on the wings. I had started a very shallow turn back to the left, as we were now almost seventy-five degrees to the right of our landing heading and headed straight for the 12,000-foot-high San Bernardino Mountains. As the airspeed was building, I slowly began to very gradually milk the flaps up. My goal was to get the aircraft back above best flare speed. The aircraft was both staggering and shuddering badly, and only the Lord knows what kept it in the air! I was so scared that all I wanted to do was just get enough altitude so that everyone could safely bail out. While all of this activity was going on the SSG evaluator had unstrapped himself and was fighting with the AC trying to get him out of his seat. The AC had completely lost control of himself. Not only was he screaming, but he was also trying to stomp on the evaluator's hands with his booted feet while at the same time jerking the flight controls one way or another.

Eventually, we broke out of the clouds at 13,000 feet. Once in the clear, things suddenly became very quiet inside the aircraft. When my breathing returned to normal I called Los Angeles Center and declared an in-flight emergency. As we passed over Lake Arrowhead, I could see Edwards AFB off to the north. I requested an immediate descent from Los Angeles Center with a full stop landing at Edwards AFB. I already knew that there were fourteen miles of runway at Edwards AFB and the weather was clear. I'm sure that the controller I was speaking with in Los Angeles Center realized that my voice was several octaves above normal. In his most professional and calm voice he cleared China 64 from our current position to descend directly to Edwards AFB. I told Los Angeles Center that I needed to go back to our Command Post radio frequency for a few minutes and explain to them what our intentions were. The Command Post said that Approach Control had lost radar contact with us on their radar screen eleven miles out and seventy-five degrees off-course. They assumed that we had crashed somewhere in the San Bernardino Mountains. The Command Post controller demanded that we return to Thermal VOR and make another penetration. I told them that I was leaving their frequency and had already received instructions from Los Angeles Center to land at Edwards

AFB. I asked them to send a vehicle for us and said that we would call them once we were on the ground with a full report.

As we were descending toward Edwards, the AC broke down and started crying and began apologizing for his actions. It was a very delicate time inside the aircraft, as no one felt like talking. I had never landed a B-47 and was scared stiff, as forward vision is very difficult from the copilot's position. Once established under Edwards Approach Control I briefly explained what had happened and told them that we needed an ambulance to meet the aircraft. It suddenly became a no-nonsense approach, because we now had twelve low-level amber lights burning on our fuel control panel. This equated to somewhere between four to ten minutes of flying time before the engines quit. This meant that we could not make a go-around and that we had only one chance to get the aircraft safely on the ground. Normally a B-47 fly's final approach at around 140 knots indicated airspeed; however, we were so light that we got down to 110 knots before finally touching the ground.

It got very quiet as we rolled down the desert runway as the five engines began to flame out. We finally rolled to a stop and were met by a host of emergency vehicles. I don't remember turning off all the switches, but it seemed to take forever to get out of the aircraft. The Air Force medics who came onboard the aircraft managed to safely get the AC out of the aircraft. Once on the ground they placed the AC in a straightjacket before they departed. The base operations officer said that they would take care of our aircraft and have it refueled and ready for a takeoff that afternoon. I told the base operations officer that our crew would not be flying the aircraft back to March AFB. I mentioned that our crew would like to wait in base operations, as I had already called for a vehicle to return us to March AFB. I also told him to have Maintenance place a light fuel load on the aircraft, as another crew would be flying China 64 straight back to March AFB. He smiled and said that he understood.

Except for the very important fact that we did not crash, this would have been one of those unexplainable aircraft accidents. An investigator's report would have read: "A SAC Senior Combat Crew out of March AFB was recently lost. The crew was commanded by an Aircraft Commander with over 3500 hours in a B-47. The AC for no apparent reason had gotten lost during an instrument approach that he had flown at least 100 times before and crashed into the San Bernardino Mountains 13 miles east of March AFB.''

It took a long time before we heard any analysis concerning this ''almost fatal'' accident. At first it was believed that the primary cause was a severe and incapacitating case of vertigo on the part of the AC. Shortly after we landed at Edwards, SAC flew the AC back to the Medical Flight Research Center at Brooks AFB in Texas for analysis. Several months later we were informed that the AC was the first pilot to experience a case of ''spacial disorientation'' and actually live through it. The Air Force was really concerned about this relatively new phenomenon, as they were getting ready to send astronauts into space and were worried about how they would handle spacial disorientation. Many pilots who experienced cases of vertigo while flying are alive today simply because they were able to believe their instruments instead of the conditions around them. According to the After Accident Report by the medics, a pilot suffering from spacial disorientation did not have the ability or capacity to correctly interpret his flight instruments; subsequently the results were almost always fatal. We never again saw the AC after this incident at March AFB.

I learned a lot about myself during this flight. In my entire military career up to this point I had always been particularly conscious of military rank. I learned from this incident not to always trust what a senior officer told me. That survival, especially when flying, often depends upon taking the ''bull by the horns'' when it becomes necessary, that is, if you chose to survive. I was definitely intimidated by the senior majors' rank, yet the will to live finally overpowered my thoughts, causing me to take the action that saved our lives. Thus ended the saga of China 64.

16

The Effects of the Cold War on SAC

The Cold War between the United States and the Soviet Union had a significant impact on SAC and their combat aircrews throughout its duration. General LeMay in 1948 was given a carte blanche order by Congress to prepare for war. He was to have his forces ready at the drop of a hat to conduct intercontinental nuclear warfare. SAC went through an incredible buildup during the decade of the 1950s. General LeMays's standing orders to his command was to consider themselves at war twenty-four hours of every day. Hard-core training became a way of life for all SAC crews, and the flying-training accident rate was out of sight. During the late 1950s and early 1960s SAC combat crews all over the world were on alert twenty-four hours a day. Squadron crews from the 441st Bomb Squadron spent fourteen days per month locked up in an alert facility in two seven-day increments. We were carrying nuclear bombs so powerful that even we did not know the total destructive power of these weapons. To give the reader an idea of the size of the weapons we were carrying, one must first understand the measurements of the bomb bay in the B-47. The bomb bay was twenty feet long by eight feet high by eight feet wide. When the loading crews loaded a Mark 39 thermonuclear weapon into the bomb bay of a B-47, the fit was so tight that a person would have difficulty getting his hand between the weapon and the skin of the aircraft.

Our early original missions called for high-altitude bomb releases when over enemy target areas. However, by 1958 the technology of the Soviet military air defenses was sophisticated enough that our loss rates would not be acceptable. Therefore, we had to come up with an alternative method of releasing these weapons without getting ourselves blown out of the sky. SAC had assigned the 441st Bomb Squadron to test a new method of low-angle delivery for nuclear weapons. Two senior crews were selected for the project, with both having ex-fighter copilots on them. As a result of my experience on the China 64 mission, plus my fighter aircraft background, I was selected as one of the copilots. In the U.S. Air Force multiengine-type pilots were forbidden to perform acrobatic maneuvers such as aileron rolls and loops, as the aircraft were not stressed for that type of flight. The maneuver that SAC selected to use was called an Immelmann, named after the famous WW I German ace Max Immelmann. It amounted to coming in right on the deck as low and as fast as the pilot could fly to a predetermined point. Upon arrival at this point with the bomb bay doors open, the AC would pull the aircraft straight up into a loop. The second the time expired and the AC reached a four-G pull-up, the bomb would release automatically and arc toward the target. The aircraft itself would continue on over the top of the loop. Once the nose of the aircraft was pointed down, the AC would roll the aircraft upright and continue to accelerate away from the bomb blast. We later identified this maneuver as a "Low-Altitude Bomb System" and shortened it to LABS the acronym.

The AC whom I was to fly the LABS maneuvers with was really an old-time aircraft commander in the 441st Bomb Squadron. He both walked and talked like a cowboy, and everyone called him Hoss! He was a lieutenant colonel and, as I quickly learned, was an outstanding B-47 pilot. In just a few missions he taught me things about the B-47 that I never dreamed possible. The knowledge that I learned from Hoss was to save my life on several occasions in my future SAC career. SAC never allowed other combat crews to train using this maneuver because it was simply too dangerous. It did, however, remain in SAC's SIOP war plan as the only safe way to deliver nuclear weapons over Soviet soil.

During those Cold War years there was an ample amount of protestors scattered around the country, and they were forever carrying banners proclaiming: BAN THE BOMB. I remember an incident that still makes me chuckle today just thinking of it. Our crew was going on alert one Monday morning, and for some reason everyone was in a particularly good mood. While Ernie and I were getting all of our crew's personnel equipment loaded onboard the alert aircraft, Captain Luke, our AC, was inspecting the bomb bay. At the time we were still carrying Mark 39 thermonuclear bombs that weighed in excess of 10,000 pounds per bomb. Luke was always somewhat of a joker, and with a grease pencil he wrote: BAN THE BOMB on the lower exterior of the weapon in our bomb bay. During our preflight as we inspected the bomb bay, we all got a great laugh at the informal pun. Several weeks later some AC had submitted a formal incident report, and a team from SAC headquarters came out to March AFB and interrogated every combat crew that had gone on alert in that particular B-47 for the past month. When no one volunteered any information, the SAC team got so mad that they took samples of everyone's handwriting; however, they never located the culprit.

The year 1959 saw me flying all over the world. Our alert schedule was grueling enough, but when it was combined with our flying schedule we had very little time with our families. Right after the usual second seven days on alert and seven off, we would reflex somewhere in the world to a secret foreign base for fifty-nine days. SAC always played the game to the hilt, for if we remained for sixty days, then each crew member would have received more station allowance monies. While in one of these secret foreign bases, we pulled fourteen days on alert, got seven off, then fourteen more on alert, and then were given ten days off. After the ten days off, we went back on alert for fourteen days and then headed for home. During this ten-day Rest and Recuperation (R&R) cycle we had an Air Force C-54 transport aircraft that would take the crews that were off alert status anywhere in Europe that they wanted to go. Usually two crews were off at the same time, and we always voted as to where we wanted to go. I managed to see a lot of both Europe and the Orient during these R&R times.

In late 1959, whether it was due to the extremely high cost of maintaining such a large combat force or a decline in the international Cold War, SAC decided to start downsizing their strategic bomber forces both in Europe and in the United States. The 320th Bomb Wing at March AFB was one of the first bomb wings selected to be deactivated. Most of the senior aircraft commanders received assignments to B-52s, while only six copilot slots came down. For a copilot to be considered for B-52s, he had to have in excess of 2,000 hours in the B-47. As a result of the China 64 flight, the wing commander had raised me to the number-one position of all copilots on the base. Therefore, I had my choices of one of the B-52 slots even though I had accumulated barely 500 total flying hours.

I wasn't too popular with the other copilots, but that was life and I couldn't do anything about it. Cynthia and I selected Columbus, Mississippi, as our next duty assignment. Fate was to step into my life once more before I could really think about it. One of the senior Stanboard copilots, who was a very good friend of mine, and his wife were both from Columbus, Mississippi, and they talked me into swapping assignments. It meant that we would be going to Little Rock, Arkansas, instead and I would be remaining in B-47 aircraft. The thought of Little Rock wasn't too bad, as one of my former fighter pilot buddies was stationed there. Also, by now the B-47 was looking pretty good to me. There were two other factors that helped influence our decision. One, I had lots of relatives from my mother's side of the family located in the northwest coroner of Arkansas. And two, Little Rock AFB was just opening up their brand-new Capeheart Housing area and because I was a combat crew member we qualified for a new house immediately. There was no question that I would upgrade to an aircraft commander faster in the B-47 than in the B-52. We were subsequently assigned to the 384th Bomb Wing and to the 545th Bomb Squadron at Little Rock. This time my reputation preceded me to Little Rock, only instead of being bad, it was good.

17

On to Little Rock

Once I got settled into the 545th Bomb Squadron at Little Rock, I met a senior AC who had been assigned as the project officer for the new Electric Counter Measures (ECM) Program for the 8th Air Force. I had been exposed to the ECM program while at March AFB and was really interested in helping Major Lewis set up a program for the 384th Bomb Wing at Little Rock. Together we established an ECM program that soon became the standard ECM program for all of the 8th Air Force. Two years after I met Major Lewis, he was promoted below the zone to the rank of full colonel. Shortly thereafter, he was offered the position of wing commander of SAC's secret Triple Nickel (555th) B-47 wing located at Forbes AFB in Kansas. Before he left, Colonel Lewis offered to take me with him to Forbes or see to it that I received one of the ACs upgrading slots for the 384th there at Little Rock. We didn't want to leave Arkansas and I very much wanted to become an aircraft commander, so we thanked Colonel Lewis and remained at Little Rock.

Being the only first lieutenant in the 8th Air Force to be selected for upgrading, I was pretty pleased with myself. We bundled up the kids and two dogs and headed north for three months to attend the Aircraft Commanders Upgrading Course at Wichita, Kansas. Having been located there once before, we knew right where we wanted to live, but we were not so lucky the second time. We did locate a duplex apartment just west of the base. However, it was located right under the base flight pattern. Living under the traffic pattern there at McConnell AFB provided some interesting observations, particularly during the wintertime. We quickly got used to aircraft noise level and didn't pay too much attention to all of the aircraft that flew around in the daily flight pattern. The owner of the duplex that we rented wasn't very happy, as we were only going to be there for three months. He informed us that we had to be out of the house exactly on the ninetieth day.

Strange things sometimes happen, and this next incident was to be one of them. One day as we were watching a B-47 in the traffic pattern, the canopy suddenly blew off the aircraft. This unusual situation really got the entire base's attention. I did not know the particular pilot, but somehow shortly after takeoff either the pilot or the copilot inadvertently pulled up the right-hand handle of the ejection seat. This maneuver automatically bottomed both pilots' ejection seats and blew the canopy off the aircraft. It was snowing lightly at the time and the outside air temperature was way below zero.

This situation placed the aircrew in a very critical flying position. Because of their heavy fuel load on board the aircraft, they had to remain in the traffic pattern in order to burn off enough fuel to safely land. We watched for several hours as the B-47 flew in a large rectangular pattern around the base. The flight crew eventually did get the aircraft on the ground, but all crew members suffered from severe frostbite. The bottom line of the story is that this crew was very lucky to have survived this flight.

At the end of the three months' course I was one of the last ACs in the class to be scheduled for my final check ride. We were a little upset as my final check ride was scheduled for the same day that we had to be out of our apartment, plus the check ride was to be in excess of seven hours. We cleaned the house and checked out with the landlord around 10:00 A.M., and headed for the base. I left Cynthia with the kids and dogs and headed for the squadron to prepare for the mission. I told her that I would meet her at 11:30 P.M. at base operations. I know that Cynthia and the kids went to the Base Theater that afternoon while the dogs enjoyed the inside of my Jeep.

This check ride mission was hampered by bad weather from the start to the finish as the longer we flew the worse the weather got. We were shooting low approaches to the field at 11:00 when the tower informed us that we needed to land shortly, before they had to close the field due to too much snow on the runway. On the final go-around we shortened the traffic pattern, and we were the last B-47 to land that evening. As we taxied in, the instructor pilot, who knew that my family was waiting for me in base ops, told me that I had passed with flying colors and was free to go as soon as we parked the aircraft. Arriving at base operations, I quickly secured the old 1942 jeep to the rear end of our 1957 Dodge and we took off for Arkansas. Part of the excitement that evening was the fact that upon completion of the upgrade program I commanded the only all-lieutenant combat crew in B-47s in SAC.

We left the base ops parking lot around midnight with the kids bundled up in the backseat while the two beagles rode inside the jeep we were pulling. As tired as I was after a seven-hour flight, I decided to drive until we were outside the town limits of Wichita. Pulling over, I told Cynthia, who was going to drive for the next four hours, to just stay on State Highway 35 going south until she came to Oklahoma. Ninety percent of all roads in both Kansas and Oklahoma run north and south and east and west. This makes it very difficult to get lost in these two states. I further told Cynthia when she came to Oklahoma State Highway 64, which ran east and west, to turn left and head for Arkansas. I will never forget the feeling when I woke up four hours later and looking out the window saw a road sign indicating that we were coming into Enid, Oklahoma, instead of Little Rock, Arkansas. Cynthia had turned right when she ran into Highway 64 instead of left and we ended up in the southwestern part of Oklahoma! I guess it is things like that that have a tendency to strengthen marriages, as we have developed many memories and enjoyed a lot of laughs over incidents like this over the years.

When we arrived back at Little Rock, everyone was looking at our crew, as it was so unusual to see an all-lieutenant combat crew in SAC. There are three types of combat crews in SAC wings: R, E, and S. R was the lowest and stood for "Ready." E stood for "Lead," while S stood for "Select crew." Coming back from McConnell, we were a non-combat-ready crew; however, we received a Stanboard Evaluation on our first flight and were immediately raised to an R crew. We rose from the 88th combat crew in the wing from R status to that of a Select status in a year and a half. Ninety percent of the credit for our quick upgrade went to our outstanding navigator, Ed Lamm. Ed's radar bombing combined with his and our copilot's celestial navigation legs was incredible. On nine out of ten radar bomb drops, Ed received perfect scores or in Air Force language, "shacks" for ground zero scored radar hits.

Although most pilots have a tendency to ignore their navigators socially, Ed and I became very close and chummed around together no matter where we went. Several years after I left SAC, Ed was accepted into Pilot Training. He graduated at the top of his class and later became an aircraft commander on a KC-135 Tanker aircraft. Prior to my leaving the 384th, on many occasions I put Ed in the backseat of the B-47 and let him shoot occasional landings. Ed got very good after a while, although we couldn't tell anyone about his landings. Ed and I did a lot of crazy things together especially while on R&R leave from overseas alert bases. During one of our reflex deployments we landed at Greenem-Common Air Base in England. After the usual fourteen days of lock-up, we decided to take one of the then-famous British subway trains into London. Our goal was to watch the Changing of the Guard at Buckingham Palace. London was only a twenty-five-minute ride from Greenem-Common according to the train schedules.

Normally, Ed and I could get along language-wise just about anywhere in the world. England became our downfall! We absolutely could not understand the Cockney accent of many of the British people, plus they spoke so fast, the words just sort of ran together. The twenty-five-minute subway ride to London turned into more like a six-plus-hour ride. I'm sure that we saw most of London from every possible street that the subway trains ran on, and who knows how much of England we saw during those six hours? We eventually arrived in downtown London proper; however, by that time we were too inebriated to locate the palace and wound up spending the night in a hotel room. We never did get to see the Changing of the Guard, but we learned a lot about English pubs. They all seemed to be named after some royal person or had animal names like the Rat and Poke Club. Another disgusting thing for us was that all of their beers were served at room temperature. From our hotel we were able the next day to get back to Greenem-Common without further incident.

We completed fifty-eight days of temporary duty at Greenem-Common, and prepared to depart England for home on the 59th day. Ed had spent all of his savings and purchased a large German Telefunkin radio console. We took a lot of time getting this monstrous box loaded and strapped down on a pallet in our bomb bay with our flight bags stowed around it. Once we were loaded and on our way, the flight home was about as normal as any long-distance flight in a B-47 could be. We had a significant number of aircraft write-ups, but most important, we still had all six engines running. However, our luck ran out around two hundred miles off the Florida coast, as the thunderstorms became more numerous, with the tops in excess of 70,000 feet. At the prescribed point out over the Atlantic we made our mandatory position report upon crossing the Atlantic Air Defense Identification Zone (ADIZ) to Birmingham Center. Failure to make this call will get Air Defense fighters on you in a hurry. Birmingham advised us to contact our Command Post using our High Frequency (HF) long-distance radio as soon as we could. When we established contact with our Command Post, they informed us that Little Rock AFB was below current weather minimums and that we were to divert and land at Columbus AFB in Mississippi.

Columbus AFB was not only a SAC base but also home to one of the most notorious components of the U.S. Customs Bureau at the time. Ed was absolutely panic-stricken, as he would have to declare the Telefunkin and none of us had enough money to pay the duty taxes on it. On most SAC bases you could defer customs until you reached your home base, but not at Columbus. We landed uneventfully at Columbus in a driving rainstorm around 0200 hours in the morning. Instead of an Air Force crew chief meeting and parking the aircraft, there was a U.S. Customs agent handling the wands. He placed the chocks around our tires, and even before we got the engines shut down the agent was up the thirteen-foot ladder identifying himself. He informed us that he would be making a complete and thorough inspection of our aircraft.

Word had gotten out in the Customs Bureau that B-47 crews in particular were smuggling a lot of illegal booze back to the States in secret hiding places in the B-47s. This agent was not in the least bit friendly and wanted to know exactly what we had to declare. I thought to myself, *What an idiot this guy is*, and wondered how many more were like him there at Columbus. Initially, he was interested only in whatever type of food that we may have onboard. I informed him that the only food that we had was in the leftover flight lunches, and he insisted on confiscating the lunch boxes immediately. I remember his mannerisms as being very gruff, and he didn't seem to want to believe anything that I said.

He insisted that I climb down from the cockpit and accompany him on his inspection around the aircraft. It was raining like you

133

couldn't believe, but this didn't seem to slow this agent down at all. The agent dragged a small ladder over to the left wing and, using a screwdriver, proceeded to pull the panels on all the inspection plates located on the underside of that wing. He checked the other wing, too, and having located nothing, he insisted on going through the inside of the aircraft. I was beginning to think that this guy was a psycho. Ed climbed up the ladder behind us and was holding a flashlight so that the agent could see his way down the crawlway to the bomb bay. The agent screamed at Ed and told me to have my crew stand by outside the aircraft. I rapidly informed him that this was not possible. I told him that I was the aircraft commander and that I would make the decisions as to who could be inside the air-craft. I further informed the agent that we had "Top-secret" things onboard the aircraft that were none of his business and that he could not see them.

This last statement pissed him off but sobered him up right away. He agreed to have the crew come in out of the rain and accompany him on the inspection. I asked Ed to go back and turn the aircraft power on long enough to open the bomb bay doors, which would give us a little more light. Following the inspector into the bomb bay, I turned on the internal bomb bay lights. I watched with bated breath as the customs agent crawled right out on top of Ed's Telefunkin. The agent was mumbling to himself as he reached down to look through each of the flight bags that were stacked around the Telefunkin. He was using the top of the Telefunkin box as a table to inspect each bag. The box that the Telefunkin was in had *Telefunkin* stenciled in ten-inch letters on all sides of it.

Ed and Bob had climbed down out of the aircraft and were now inside the bomb bay while standing on the ground. I remember glancing down at Ed as he peered up at the inspector. Ed never said a word but had a sickly smile on his face. I made the mistake of laughing at the funny expression on Ed's face. The agent instantly wanted to know what was so funny. I told him that the navigator had just passed gas and, being so tired after such a long flight, I couldn't help but laugh. We had been in the air for over nine hours and all of us were truly tired.

The agent, having completed his search and found nothing but our discarded flight lunches to confiscate, then offered us a ride to the base operations building. He told me during the ride in that we had one of the cleanest B-47s that he had ever searched and inspected. I thanked him for being so professional and for giving us a ride. We parted at base ops and I told him that I hoped that we would see him again. The base ops officer apologized to us, telling us that the transient ground crew had been tied up with a B-52 problem and couldn't meet us. He told us that the customs agent had agreed to park us so that we wouldn't have to wait so long. We got our required crew rest and left Columbus as quickly as we could. I remain in touch with Ed at Christmas, and despite the forty years since it happened we are still laughing about this incident.

18

Morocco

In early 1961 the 384th Bomb Wing out of Little Rock AFB was staging B-47s on reflex operations to three secret bases located in North Africa (this is now unclassified information). On one of our reflex tours Ed and I met the deputy base commander at Sidi Slamein. He turned out to be a Sigma Chi fraternity brother of mine, and during our conversation we somehow got on the subject of skiing. He told us about an incredible ski area that was located about four hundred miles from Sidi Slamein up north in the Atlas Mountains. We worked out a schedule that was coordinated with his leave so that when we returned to Sidi Slamein on our next reflex tour, we would be able to use his staff car for ten days to go skiing.

Several months later Ed and I arrived at Sidi Slamein with our skis in the bomb bay of our B-47. We could hardly wait for our ten days off, as both Ed and I were avid snow skiers. At the end of our seven-day alert cycle we picked up the deputy's 1959 Ford station wagon and prepared to drive north to the Atlas Mountains. The transportation guys were great and since there were no gas stations en route they provided us with ten five-gallon jerricans of gasoline plus two spare tires. We had a WW II map of the area and enough canned food to last us a week. There were very few towns along our route, and the only stop we made was in the ancient town of Marrakech. While there, we accidentally ran into the British consul who was out having his afternoon tea in one of the local restaurants. He was delighted to meet us and offered to show us around the city. What astounded us the most was that the Marrakech of 1961 was just like the Marrakech of 2,000 years before. It was definitely like going back in time. The snake charmers, sword swallowers, belly dancers, and camel caravans coming and going into the vast deserts just fascinated us.

The consul's directions were excellent, and even though there were no street signs we managed to locate the correct road out of town headed toward the Atlas Mountains. We called it a road, but it was not paved and was full of potholes; a better description would have been "a trail leading to who knows where." As we drove to the east we could see Okomidin Mountain, which looked much like Mount Rainer in Washington State. It was 12,000 feet above sea level and stuck out like a sore thumb. About fifty miles east of Marrakech we ran into a very unusual situation. The road came right up to the base of a cliff that was about three to six hundred feet high. There was a large sign in Arabic at the base of the cliff that we couldn't read. We discovered later that it said "proceed at your own risk." We quickly discovered why.

As we studied the road up the cliff, it looked scary as hell. It traversed the cliff much like a skier would descend a cliff. The road that was cut into the sandstone cliff was only two feet wider than our station wagon. At the base of the cliff there was a long rope hanging down from the top of the cliff with a red can on one end and a green one on the other end, which we stupidly ignored. As we were being professional Air Force officers, how were we supposed to know that this meant that it was a one-way road up or down? Like idiots we started up and came to the first turn around sixty feet up the base of the cliff and discovered that we could not make it around the first corner.

Ed wasn't really very happy sitting on the outside during the first traverse. He informed me in plain language that if I would just stop the car he would walk up the rest of the way. We were really in a predicament, as we couldn't back down and the only way that we could get around the corners was to inch back and forth until we could actually make the corner. While we were doing this, the rear end of the station wagon hung out over the cliff. At each corner Ed would advise me as to exactly how many inches I could back up. We somehow finally made it to the top. I didn't want to admit my fear, but I told Ed that it would be his responsibility to get the car back down the cliff whenever we returned.

The country was absolutely beautiful from the top of the cliff up to the ski resort. Snowplows had cleared the road and it took us just a little over an hour to make it to the resort. We pulled up in front of a large three-story chalet-type building and went inside.

There was an elderly lady at the desk who smiled and said something to us in a language that we had not heard before. The interpreter back at Sidi had made the reservations for us, and we were not sure if we were in the right place. We took out a lot of money and, like so many other places in the world, went through the "pointy talkie" pantomime. It was soon obvious to us that the lady was not in a good mood, as her voice was getting louder and louder by the minute.

We motioned for her to follow us outside, where we could point to the small chalets that were scattered around the hillside. The deputy base commander back at Sidi had told us to be sure to rent one of the small chalets and to not stay in the main lodge. The lady really got mad, and I'm sure she thought that we must be perfect examples of "the Ugly Americans." She went back inside, and as we entered she slapped a key down on the desk and with her hand motioned us to get out of there. We got in the car and started to drive up the hill but didn't get very far. It didn't take us long to realize that we had to put chains on the station wagon if we planned to make it up the hill. Fortunately the key had a number (19) on it and we proceeded to wind our way around the hill until we located chalet number 19. The place wasn't much by American standards, but it did have a fireplace and lots of wood. The beds that were scattered around looked like bunks from an old military academy, i.e., small mattresses, iron frames with wire springs. We didn't really care, as sleeping wasn't one of our highest priorities.

Once settled in, we decided that we needed to go down to the main chalet, as we hadn't eaten all day. Ed and I went into the dining room, and a cute waitress came over and seated us at a large table. The waitress began speaking to us in the same language that the lady at the front desk had used on us. Since we couldn't figure out what she was saying, we both gave up and just agreed with whatever she said. The next thing that happened was that she brought a very large lazy Suzan with an incredible array of salads on it. Being confused by the language, we didn't ask any further questions and just dug in. We actually ate everything off the lazy suzan and were about to go to the bar when the waitress arrived back with another course of food. Before the meal was over we discovered that we were the victims of a seven-course dinner. Ed and I never forgot that experience, and neither one of us could eat for several days after.

The next morning we hustled up to the main ski lift ready to tackle the world. The first thing that we discovered was that the ski lifts were operated by Arabs and they wouldn't accept anything but Arabic money. This caused an hour's delay by the time we got back down to the main lodge and exchanged some of our Moroccan durhams for Arabic coins. The lift operator was delighted to extract whatever money he needed, and probably some extra to boot! Ed and I subsequently took off for what turned out to be an absolutely outstanding day on the slopes. The snow was incredible, with eight to ten inches of new powder. It was the kind of fluffy powder that reminded one of talcum powder. From the top of Okomidin Mountain looking west we could see the entire outline of Morocco, the towns of Casablanca, Rabat, and Tangier. Looking north, we could see across the Mediterranean Sea, the Rock of Gibraltar, and much of southern Spain. To the east lay the empty Sahara Desert.

Somewhere on the slope that day, we encountered a young lady from Rabat who spoke English. What a godsend she turned out to be. The three of us skied down to the main lodge for lunch, where this very nice young lady introduced us formally to the lady who ran the lodge. It turned out that everyone was speaking French to us and, as hard as it was to believe, neither Ed nor I had ever heard that language before. What the woman in charge of the hotel had been trying to tell us was that there was no hot water in the chalets and that was why she was trying to get us to stay in the main lodge. We apologized for our poor behavior, and she said that they couldn't stop laughing about our meal the previous evening.

Our interpreter also told the women that we were pilots in the American Air Force. She informed us that her husband had been a fighter pilot during WW I and had flown with France's famous Lafayette Escadrille Squadron. That evening we brought four bottles of I.W. Harper down and presented them to her husband. The next morning we were moved at her husband's orders to another chalet. This one contained sixteen young women from Rabat and us! Ed and I both partied and skied hard for the next several days. They were all great skiers, and we had a ball.

Our week ended with a guide taking Ed and me plus eighteen other skiers on a twenty-mile ski trip down the back side of Okomidin. The trip down the hill was fantastically challenging, beautiful, and awesome. At the bottom of the run there was an old bus (about

139

a 1930 edition of something foreign with an Arab driver) waiting for us. The ride back up the hill to the ski area was one that none of us will ever forget. The driver had only two positions on the bus's throttle, i.e., full on, and full off. It seemed that we went around all corners on only two wheels with everyone yelling for more speed. I'm certain that this driver was related somehow to the world-famous Formula One race driver Mario Andretti!

19

Covert Training

An unusual incident occurred in late 1962 at Little Rock AFB. Our neighbor several doors down was a young second lieutenant personnel-type officer. Warner called me one day and told me that he had some exciting news on his desk that I needed to see. He told me that the information held a classification that I was cleared for and that he would leave the information on the top of his desk as he left for lunch that day.

When I arrived in his office his NCOIC was working on files at his own desk. I casually sat on the corner of Lieutenant Warner's desk and talked trivia with the sergeant. At that time in history, SAC crew members were not allowed to see other Air Force assignments of opportunity. I casually picked up the document, removing the Secret Cover, and began reading it. The sergeant quickly told me that I was viewing a document that I shouldn't be looking at. I laughed and told him that I was cleared above top-secret and that he didn't need to worry about it. The document called for all Air Force pilots with an Air Force designator of 1115Z (career fighter pilot) to apply. I spent the next thirty minutes filling out the requested information and then asked the sergeant to forward the application on through channels to Air Force.

About four months went by, and it was now late 1962. By this time I had forgotten all about the volunteer application that I had made. As I was coming home from a training mission one day while on final approach for a landing, Little Rock Approach Control told me to contact the 384th Command Post immediately. Once in radio contact, the controller in the Command Post told me to report to the wing commander's office as soon as we got on the ground. This was a very unusual situation, as you did not get called to wing headquarters unless there was something wrong. I asked both the navigator and copilot if they had done anything that I was not aware of, and both pleaded innocence.

I reported to the wing commander's office in my smelly flying suit after having flown for seven and a half hours and was given a cup of coffee and introduced to a Major somebody. For the next forty-five minutes the three of us talked about fishing, football, and flying. At the time Lance Allworth was an All-American running back for the University of Arkansas's football team. We spent several minutes talking about Lance Allworth. At the time if there were fourteen pages in the *Arkansas Gazette* newspaper Lance's picture would be on thirteen of them. Some of the things that this major talked about between football and fishing didn't seem to make sense at the time. I remember him suggesting things such as: would I like to fly WW II fighter-type aircraft? Who in their right mind wouldn't want to do that! Next he wanted to know if I would be concerned about flying these same fighter aircraft in foreign countries? I remember telling the good major that given the chance I would be absolutely excited to fly a WW II fighter, wherever and whenever the Air Force wanted me to go. He further asked me if wearing civilian clothes and flying combat missions concerned me. I told him that after two years in Korea nothing about combat scared me.

In any event, after forty-five minutes and five cups of coffee the wing commander thanked me for coming in and dismissed me. What I didn't realize was that this had been a covert interview by a major from the CIA. At the time, I didn't know what the word *covert* meant. I later learned that the IBM company had been using this type of interview for several years to select their administrators. I returned to the squadron area and finished up the paperwork with my crew. Both Ed and Bob asked me what the meeting was all about, and I told them that I thought that it was a public relations (PR) stunt for the wing commander and thought nothing more about it. Several months passed by and I subsequently forgot all about the meeting with the strange major in the wing commander's office.

Five or six more months had passed by, and due to the stress placed on SAC combat crews for combat perfection, I had completely forgotten about even processing the volunteer application in the good lieutenant's office. During this time our all-lieutenant crew had moved from the lowest combat crew designator, N for non-combat-ready, to an R, which stood for ready status, and subsequently on up to an S for select crew. We were about four hours into our flying training mission and several thousand miles from

Little Rock when the 384th Command Post contacted us using our HF radio. The Command Post informed me that I was to report to the wing commander's office immediately upon landing. By this time the wing commander and I were on very good terms, as I was his only lieutenant AC. Our crew had only recently been upgraded to Select status (thanks to my navigator's outstanding bombing scores), and in addition we were the only all-lieutenant combat crew in the 8th Air Force. After landing I left the squadron area and headed for the wing commander's office, this time not worrying about anything being wrong. I knew that the captain's promotion list was on base and thought that possibly this was what this meeting was all about.

Indeed, the wing commander greeted me outside his office as Captain Hunter and asked me to accompany him into his office. He went immediately to his wall safe and spun the dials. He pulled a manila folder out of the safe and said, "You need to open these orders in my presence." We both signed the cover sheet and I broke the outer seal on the manila folder. Inside was a set of orders from the Defense Intelligence Agency (DIA) referring me to the CIA for further assignment. Years later we discovered that a number of Air Force pilots had received copies of these mysterious and unusual orders at the same time that I did. I read the orders all the way through and then handed them to the wing commander. He remarked that he had never seen anything like what he was holding in his hand in his entire military career.

According to the secret orders, I was to depart Little Rock AFB within twenty-four hours. Included with the orders was a voucher for a seat on any civilian airline to Wichita, Kansas, plus a key to a locker located in the local Wichita train station. I was informed that there would be further instructions on the orders that were located in the train locker. Located at the end of the DOD orders was an address in Washington, D.C., that both my wife and I could use for correspondence purposes. I was also informed that all mail would be subject to censorship. Colonel Hogan told me that he would cut orders immediately relieving me as an AC in the 384th BW and that I was to tell absolutely no one where I was going. He also said that I would not have to go through the usual base clearing process, that he would personally clear me.

Cynthia was used to the many "secret" SAC flying assignments utilized in our reflex deployments around the world, so she paid little attention when I informed her that I would be leaving the next day. Usually notification of an impending reflex assignment would come in the form of a telephone call from the Command Post late at night. The Command Post operator would just say either "Red" or "Green" alert. The procedure was to report to your squadron ASAP. Red meant that you were going somewhere in the world where it was hot, and converse for green. As a result, all SAC combat crew members kept two suitcases packed at all times. In this particular case I was forced to pack a small amount of clothes for both places. I called UAL and confirmed a seat for Wichita the next morning. Cynthia did not question my destination; she just told me to write to her as soon as I arrived wherever I was going. What a marvelous Air Force wife she was! Several years before, we had worked out our personal correspondence code using relatives, dogs, cats, and kids' names to denote areas of the world where I was. Our code proved to be very effective.

Arriving in Wichita the next day, I caught a taxi to the train depot and went searching for the designated locker. Upon opening the next set of orders I found a train ticket to Springfield, Missouri. This time I was given a key to a locker located inside the Greyhound bus terminal in Springfield. I was tired, but the excitement was really starting to build. To my knowledge things like this only happened to comic characters such as Steve Canyon or Terry and the Pirates. Later that same day I boarded a Greyhound bus for Fort Walton Beach, Florida. I had no idea where Fort Walton Beach, Florida, was, and I really didn't care. I began to wonder if I was still in the Air Force.

Sometime during 1967 I happened to read a book by author Orr Kelly titled *From a Dark Sky*. What an eye-opener this was for me. What I didn't realize was at the time I wasn't the only one who had received these mysterious orders. I also discovered in Mr. Kelly's book that 40 percent of those pilots who received similar interviews around the Air Force did not make it into the secret program.

Stepping off the bus upon arrival in Fort Walton Beach, I was met by an NCO who wanted to know if I was Captain Hunter. He told me to get my luggage and meet him by the jeep that was parked out front of the Greyhound depot. I asked the NCO where we were

144

going, and his reply was, "Eglin Number Twenty-three for processing." I wondered what and where Eglin #23 was but was hesitant to ask, as the NCO wasn't the real friendly type. He did welcome me to the "Agency" and said that after several days of testing we would be transferred to Eglin #9, located at Hurlburt Field.

During the next few days I felt like I was back in the Marine Corps. We were assigned to specific barracks and formed up into three companies. I was assigned to the T-28 company. We were then put through several days of psychological testing. Some members of the company were washed out during this psychological testing phase and sent back to their original Air Force bases. Those who had not attended the Air Force's Survival School at Stead AFB in Nevada were sent immediately to complete that three-week course. The remaining people were assigned to the 4400th Combat Crew Training Squadron of the Air Force's Special Operations Command. The next day we were introduced into the Special Ops rigorous commando training program. We were up every day at 0300 hours and fell out for a ten-mile morning run. Returning back to camp from the run, we had breakfast and then started the day's physical exercise programs in individual martial arts training. At the culmination of the program, those who passed received the equivalent of Black Belts in the Korean art of Rangori judo.

The afternoons were spent checking out and flying interdiction missions in a number of different WW II type fighter aircraft, the most prevalent of which was the modified T-28D. We were told that we would be flying the modified T-28 in combat, but we could check out in the other fighters on the flight line if we so desired. No one asked where the Agency had procured the different fighter-type aircraft; we just flew them and enjoyed the flying immensely. After two and a half months, we were called into a large briefing room for a mandatory briefing. The intelligence officer who conducted the briefing had an unusual sense of humor. He passed around a large jar, which contained yellowish pills. He told us each to take one pill and to place it in our mouths. He said that it would only take a few minutes after we swallowed the pills (M&M covered peanuts) and we would forget where we were and everything that had happened to us in the past two and a half months. He further said that we were all going to return to our former bases as if nothing had happened. We could tell absolutely no one what we had been doing or where we had been located.

The following day was sad indeed as we said our good-byes. Many of us had become close to one another especially during the accelerated portion of our special training, and the thought of going back to SAC and B-47s was deplorable. SAC's Cold War mission was extremely hard on family life what with the amount of alert we had to pull. At the time I didn't care for the idea of SAC's suicide missions and I didn't care for the type of people who became "SACimsized" by the command.

Arriving back at Little Rock AFB, I reported directly to the wing commander. Colonel Hogan informed me that my old crew had received spot promotions from SAC, but because I had left the wing the promotion didn't apply to me. SAC was the only command in the Air Force at that time that had the option of rewarding their crews with spot promotions for outstanding work. I was subsequently assigned to another crew as their AC. It was hard getting back into the SAC society, and the days ahead were not easy ones. The Cold War reached its critical stage during 1962–63, and the courage of SAC's combat crews played a significant role in the eventual outcome.

20

High Speed Taxi Test

Early in March of 1962 my new crew and I were airborne on our way to Morone Air Base in Spain for another 59 days of reflex alert duty. After landing we debriefed the mission and then proceeded to get our usual crew rest. The next morning we reported for eight hours of new target study, culminated with the usual nuclear weapons exams. Prior to reporting to the alert facility another AC told me that the particular aircraft that we were scheduled to preflight had a steering problem upon landing. Arriving at the aircraft maintenance personnel met us and wanted us to perform a high-speed taxi test to insure that the steering mechanism was OK before placing the aircraft on alert.

I had never heard of performing a high-speed taxi test, and there was no literature in the B-47 Dash-1 handbook regarding this type of maneuver. Fortunately for me the Chief of Standardization from Little Rock AFB was on station for two weeks of TDY duty. I called him and told him that I was told to perform a high-speed taxi test and that I wasn't sure exactly what this entailed. He told me to taxi the aircraft out to the end of the runway and to run the engines up to 100%, arm and fire the water injection system then to accelerate to 70 knots. While all of this was going on I was supposed to maneuver the aircraft back and forth while accelerating down the runway to ensure that the steering mechanism was working properly.

If you could imagine yourself driving a large D-12 Caterpillar tractor down a hill and having the brakes go out while trying to steer and stop it, then this would give you a feeling for what happened to us next. First of all, we were taxiing a B-47 that was fully loaded for alert duty. This meant that the aircraft weighed in excess of 222,000 pounds, which included a 10,000-pound thermonuclear bomb in the bomb bay. At the moment, no one considered the danger of a nuclear incident involving fire and possible detonation, so we proceeded down the runway.

Morone Air Base, like most SAC bases, had a 13,000-foot runway to accommodate both B-47s and B-52 type aircraft. As we started decelerating down the runway I quickly noticed that the aircraft wasn't slowing down like it should under normal conditions. I alerted both the navigator and copilot and slowly began to apply more brake pressure to the main wheels. We could feel the antiskid action working as the brakes released and caught over and over. Deploying the brake chute at the same time didn't seem to slow us down much, either. While passing the 8,000-foot marker I realized that we had only 4,000 feet to go and immediately began pushing harder on the brake pedals, eventually going into what we called the "emergency braking" mode. The control tower called and informed me that our brakes were smoking badly and that it appeared that we might have a tire on fire. From the front cockpit I felt both forward main tires blow as we continued on down the runway on what was left of our wheels. The aircraft was shaking badly and the rumbling noises inside were loud and extremely frightening as we approached the end of the runway. I know that as the situation got worse I was screaming at the tower to get the fire trucks after us.

What I didn't realize was that the control tower had already alerted every fire truck on the base and that they were all chasing our aircraft as it careened down what was left of the runway. I remember seeing the end of the runway arrive and thinking that this was a hell of a way to go out, as the aircraft was totally out of control. At this point everything seemed to be happening in slow motion. Stuff was flying all around inside the cockpit and the aircraft still did not seem to be slowing down. Because of the possibility of fire I alerted the crew and blew the canopy off the aircraft, which increased the noise intensity drastically. I was so scared that I totally forgot about the nuclear bomb in the bomb bay and could only think about the thousands of gallons of high-test fuel that surrounded us. The noise of the canopy leaving the aircraft caused the navigator to leave his seat and crawl back into the aisle just below my feet. He was trying to open the lower crew exit door, but the aircraft was shaking too violently for him to accomplish this.

The screeching and wild vibrations ceased as we slowly slid off the runway's overrun and into the deep mud beyond. The aircraft rotated ninety degrees as the front main gear sank in the mud and we finally came to a complete stop. I remember stopcocking the throttles and pulling the engine fire buttons to stop the flow of fuel to the engines. At the same time both the navigator and copilot were already out of the hatch and running for their lives. It's funny how things pop into your mind, especially when under intense stress. It was normally thirteen feet from the escape hatch to the ground. However, the aircraft had sunk so deep in the mud by the time I managed to get myself out of the ejection seat that it was only a few feet from the bottom of the aircraft to the ground.

The fire department's P-2 fire trucks sprayed enough foam on what was left of the main gears that you could not see the bottom of the aircraft. Any incident worldwide involving a nuclear weapon requires a special report called a Broken Arrow. This particular incident really got the attention of SAC headquarters due to the size of the nuclear weapon that we had onboard. SAC later sent a special investigation team to Spain to study the situation in more detail. Our intelligence officers told us that had the weapon cooked off, most of northeastern Spain and part of western France would have been pulverized into a wasteland covered with a "hot" nuclear fall-out. SAC initiated an Article 15 (disciplinary punishment) on the chief of standardization for the 384th Bomb Wing, while the rest of us got off with a slapped hand and a good ass chewing. The fear didn't hit us at first, but as the impact of the incident wound down I don't think that any of us will ever forget the consequences that could have evolved out of this greenhorn mistake. SAC sent out an "Operational Immediate" message throughout the command that would prohibit all future high-speed taxi tests on their bomber fleet.

One of the things that came to mind after this incident was that SAC, like many other large organizations, was so quality control–minded that they sometimes didn't see the forest for the trees. The 384th Maintenance Control Section, like most other maintenance sections in SAC, in trying to keep from getting write-up pressure from higher headquarters oftentimes would send their "hangar queens" overseas to forward reflex bases. Once there these hangar queens would often sit on the ground on alert status for up to three months before they would be rotated back to the parent bomb wing. (*Hangar queen* is an Air Force term that is given to an aircraft that experiences mechanical problems whenever it flies. Like a "lemon"-type automobile, a hangar queen usually spends more time on the ground than in the air.) This procedure didn't make a lot of sense to the aircrews, as we all knew that any aircraft that sits on the ground too long will ultimately experience any number of problems whenever it flies again. It was not uncommon when flying one of these hangar queens back to the States to accumulate more than thirty-five to forty maintenance write-ups. Sometimes there would be so many write-ups that the aircraft would wind up crashing and killing the aircrews.

21

Class 26 Action

When an Air Force aircraft of any type has crash-landed and/or broken apart beyond fixing we refer to that incident as the "Class 26-ing" of an aircraft. This then sets the stage for my next story, which occurred on June 25, 1962 (as you will note later in this book, the date June 25, is not a particularly good date for the author). As we attended the prerotational flight briefing the day before we departed Nourasseur Air Base in North Africa, we learned that we as a crew would be flying one of the wing's worst hangar queens back to Little Rock. The aircraft commander who had flown the aircraft over to Nourassuer from Little Rock several months before was attending the briefing. He told me that they had experienced some gear problems getting the forward main gear to come up and lock as they departed Little Rock. He further explained that the squadron commander was acting as his copilot during takeoff and that they had recycled the main gear nine times before it came up and locked into position. He told me that they didn't write it up since the write-up violated SAC regulations; otherwise the flight was uneventful.

As we taxied out of the alert facility parking lot I mentioned the problem to my copilot and told him to be sure that he got the gear handle solidly in the "up detent" when I called for the gear up after takeoff. We were the number-three aircraft in a flight of three B-47s, which was called a cell. Anytime we had a flight of two or more B-47s departing the base, a member of the 384th Bomb Wing's Standardization Evaluation Section (Stan-Eval) was required to be in the control tower to monitor the takeoffs. On this particular day, unknown to me, the chief of the Stand-Eval Section was in the tower.

Sure enough, as we broke ground and I called for gear up, the forward main gear indicated not up and locked. I immediately

151

slowed the aircraft down and contacted the cell leader and explained the problem. I told him that we would be off-frequency for a few minutes while we attempted to correct the problem. According to the B-47 Dash-1, we could legally recycle the main gear one time. As we reached the gear-lowering speed of the aircraft, I told the copilot to go ahead and recycle the gear. Again, the forward main gear came up, then went *clunk* refusing to indicate up and locked. By this time we were more than four miles from the base and we wanted to get home badly, so I told the copilot to take control of the aircraft and that I would recycle the gear one more time from the front cockpit. This time we were successful, as the gear finally indicated up and locked.

I informed the tower that our gear was up and locked and that we were going back to our climb-out radio frequency. Contacting the cell leader, I told him that our gear was up and locked and that we were climbing on-course to join the formation. As we pulled into position and checked in with the cell leader, who was a former Stan-Eval copilot, he asked me if I had filed a Flight Hazardous Report with Nourasseur Tower regarding my gear problem. I told him that I figured that we were far enough from the base that they could not see us and that no, I had not filed a report, but that I would write the problem up after we landed at Little Rock. He mentioned that was a violation of SAC regulations and, since the chief of Stand-Eval himself was in the tower monitoring the takeoffs with binoculars, he would most likely file a Flight Hazardous Report on me. The three of us onboard talked it over and decided to press on anyway. Later I discovered that the cell leader was correct and that the chief of Stan-Eval had indeed filed a report on me. Even though the cell leader sounded serious and wanted us to turn back, I wasn't too worried, because I knew that the report had to go through my squadron commander, and to put it bluntly, "I had him by the balls," since he had recycled the same gear nine times.

Sometime after catching up and joining the formation at 34,000 feet, we noticed that it was getting very cold inside the aircraft. After a quick scan of the instrument panels, we discovered that the automatic heat control on the cabin air-conditioning system was inoperative. We solved the problem by using the copilot's manual switch to override the system, eventually getting heat. Our problem for the next seven hours was one of recycling the system manually from "full on" to "full off." In the full off position we waited until ice formed inside the cockpit before we manually turned the heat on and started to sweat. It wasn't the best solution, but it worked.

Several hours out, our cell leader contacted the lead tanker of the airborne KC-135s to set up our first in-flight refueling. The entire process was normal with each B-47 taking approximately forty minutes on the "boom" to receive our on-load. Breaking away from the tankers, we climbed in formation back to our cruising altitude. During the level-off checklist, I discovered that my forward main fuel gauge was inoperative. According to the Dash-1, this was a highly critical situation for the B-47. We did everything that we could think of, including pulling and resetting all of the fuel pump circuit breakers as described by the Dash-1.

According to what we had learned while in B-47 ground school, this constituted one of the worst airborne emergencies that you could encounter in a B-47. The B-47 by nature was a critical maze of gas tanks and fuel lines. Should any one of the three main fuel tanks get the least out of sync, due to improper fuel management, the pilot could experience a real airborne problem with the center of gravity while flying the aircraft. It was the copilot's responsibility to manage the fuel distribution while in flight. I told the copilot that while we still had electrical power, he should start transferring as much fuel as possible from the auxiliary tanks to the three main tanks. Should we experience a complete electrical failure, this would prevent trapped fuel in the wing auxiliary tanks and allow us to keep the engines running using a gravity flow of fuel even if we lost all fuel pumps. While all of this was going on, I told the copilot that we would both monitor the aircraft trim wheel every ten minutes to ensure that the trim was as close to a 0 reading as we could get it.

We had many little annoying things go wrong with the aircraft over the next several hours, but nothing that was detrimental to safe flying. About the time that we reached the point for our next in-flight refueling, the weather started turning bad at our altitude and it was quickly getting dark. Our cell leader established radio contact with the cell of KC-135s, and we discovered that there was only one KC-135 for the three of us. By the time that the lead aircraft made his hookup with the tanker at 34,000 feet we were all going in and out of cloud formations. Our cell leader requested an en route descent from the tanker down to 20,000 feet, hoping that somewhere in between we would break out of the instrument flying conditions. The number-two B-47 explained that he had lost his airborne radar and that he was going to pull in as close to the leader as he could get. Flying conditions were horrible and necessitated that both of us close up the formation as tight as possible to try to maintain visual contact with each other. The tanker commander apologized and said that the second KC-135 had ground-aborted, but that he would give us as much fuel as he could.

Our cell leader decided that because of the problems the number-two B-47 was having, he and the number-two aircraft would get the lion's share of the tanker's off-load of fuel. I didn't get a chance to explain our problems to the cell leader, as things were happening too fast. Flying instruments and trying to just keep the formation in sight were difficult enough at the time. We went into a bad cloud and I pulled the power back and asked the navigator to locate the formation for me. Flying formation was always easy for me, but night weather formation flying in B-47s placed a strain on everyone. In fighter-type aircraft, you could usually tuck your aircraft in real close to less than six inches from whomever you were flying wing on and the weather didn't brother you too much. Flying a swept-winged bomber was another story, as you could not take the chance of getting too close and overlapping the wings. Also, when you add nighttime and weather flying to the formula, you are approaching a possible airborne disaster.

Leveling off at 20,000, I watched the number-two B-47 break away from the tanker and I proceeded to pull into position. The tanker pilot informed me that he could only give me a token off-load, as the other two B-47s had used up most of his fuel and his home base was now below minimums. He explained that he had to have enough fuel onboard to make it to his alternate base. Due to my unknown status of usable fuel, I used a SAC secret airborne code word informing the tanker that I needed more fuel than he was willing to give me. I quickly explained my fuel tank problems and he, recognizing the crisis, agreed to split what fuel he had left with just enough emergency fuel for him to land at a closer alternate base. I then realized the predicament that one of us was probably going to run out of fuel and have to make a crash landing. I knew that the tanker crew did not have ejection seats, so I told him to give us what fuel he could and thanked him.

We got our token off-load and backed off below and away from the tanker. I then asked the navigator for a heading to try to locate and catch up with the other two B-47s ahead of us. While waiting for Ed to respond, I attempted to call the cell leader. It didn't take but a moment before I realized that our command radio had failed and that we were unable to transmit using the UHF radio. I asked the copilot to try his command button, and it, too, was dead. We could hear the cell leader at the time talking to the number-two B-47, telling him to turn left, right, et cetera, to keep from plowing into a thunderstorm.

Our situation was deteriorating rapidly. We could not transmit to anyone on the command frequencies, and Ed had just informed me that our radar had just quit functioning. We were climbing in and out of clouds going through 24,000 feet on our way back to our assigned altitude of 37,000 feet. It had suddenly become a very scary situation. We were, by best guesswork, approximately 250 miles out from landfall over the Atlantic Ocean. The thunderstorms around us were topping out above 70,000 feet, and I certainly didn't want to drive into one of those monsters. I was watching the intensity of the lightning ahead of us and trying to adjust our course away from areas where it appeared to be the worst.

Just before reaching our cruising altitude we entered a thunderstorm and the aircraft stalled abruptly, causing us to drop several thousand feet before getting the aircraft under control again. Once the craft was level and under control I began a slow climb back to altitude, and the aircraft stalled again. Normally, like with power controls in a car, you have a positive feel in the aircraft controls, and suddenly I had nothing. My first reaction as we stalled a third time was, "My God"; the cable running back to the elevator had broken. The flight controls had become so sensitive that with almost 0 pressure either way, the column would flop from full nose-up to the full nose-down position. I had never heard of or experienced anything like this in an aircraft, and the fear factor had full control of me.

In an effort to provide us with some time to try to figure out what was wrong, I placed the aircraft on autopilot. The second that the autopilot took control the stalls became increasingly violent, and I rapidly shut it off. I asked the copilot if his control column was engaged, and he responded, "Yes." I told him to hold the controls tight while I attempted to move them from the front cockpit. This maneuver also failed, as we were both experiencing the same flight control problem. I then told the copilot that I would manually fly the aircraft while he and the navigator went through the entire Emergency Procedures Section of the B-47 Dash-1 to see if we could come up with a clue. There was ice forming again inside the cockpit, as we hadn't had time to manually warm it up. At the same time, I was sweating profusely and trying not to even breathe on the control column for fear of creating more stalls.

We were being peppered with heavy rain and hailstones, plus green Saint Elmo's fire was running all over the cockpit. This Saint Elmo's fire phenomenon in itself was enough to scare you, especially when it jumped off the canopy railing onto your flying suit and ran down your arm. In addition, the lightning flashes were so close that they caused momentary blindness. Without warning we hit a violent updraft, and the nose of the aircraft shot straight up and continued over until we were inverted. The aircraft was in a complete stall and began to spin downward. When the aircraft went inverted, everything that wasn't tied down inside the aircraft flew down and scattered all over the cockpit. This only added to the pandemonium that already existed inside the airplane.

Everyone was trying to talk at once, and I finally yelled, "Hang on! I'm going to try and roll this baby over and see if I can get the nose down!" Being inverted, I wasn't sure which way we were spinning initially. Somewhere between thirty and twenty thousand feet I managed to get the aircraft right side up. As soon as I had the aircraft right side up, I placed the throttles in the idle position and applied full opposite rudder to the way we were spinning. This was not an easy trick, as I had milk cartons and God only knows what else flying all over the cockpit. Slowly the flight controls responded and the spin slowed down, although the nose of the aircraft was pointed almost straight down.

The airspeed indicator was fluctuating so badly that it was impossible to determine our correct airspeed. I remember glancing at the altimeter as we passed through 14,000 feet. There was a SAC regulation that said that if you were in a spin and out of control the crew should bail out at 10,000 feet. I knew even though it was completely dark outside that there was nothing but water below us, so I told both the navigator and the copilot to hang on for a while longer. We eventually bottomed out at 4,000 feet. I continued the descent on down to 2,000 feet, until we were completely out of the clouds and leveled off. I slowly turned the aircraft to a westerly heading, and probably five minutes elapsed before anyone could talk.

When I could finally speak, I told the copilot that I thought that the artificial feel system in the aircraft had malfunctioned. I remembered recently reading about a B-47 that had crashed in Kansas and the flying safety people had determined that the cause of the crash was due to a fire caused by the artificial feel system heater. Subsequently SAC sent out a message to all units telling them to deactivate the artificial feel system heaters immediately. This was a typical maneuver by SAC headquarters after every B-47 crash until they finally found the exact cause of the crash. The aircraft controls were still hypersensitive, but I was sure that I had figured out that the artificial feel system had frozen over, thus eliminating our normal power controls. An aircraft responds just the opposite of a car with power controls. When you lose power control in your automobile the steering wheel becomes very difficult to turn, whereas in an aircraft under the same circumstances the flight controls become hypersensitive. I told the crew that we would remain on a westerly heading as long as the aircraft would fly until we reached landfall. I did not want to even consider bailing out while over the Atlantic Ocean. Everyone agreed with my decision.

At lower altitudes you burn a tremendous amount of fuel in any jet-engined aircraft. The weather around us was improving somewhat, so I told the crew that I was going to start a slow and gentle climb back to our original assigned altitude. The weather continually got smoother even though we remained in IFR flight conditions. Eventually we arrived back at our assigned altitude. There were still a lot of thunderstorms around, but we were able to see most of them and alter our course around them. Even though we couldn't transmit on the command UHF radio, our receivers were still working and I heard someone talking to Birmingham Center. I asked the navigator to get out of his ejection seat and come back to where we had an emergency parachute stowed. I wanted Ed to get the emergency handheld radio out of the parachute pack.

Ed handed the radio to me and I extended the small antennas as far as I could in the cockpit and called Birmingham Center on Guard Frequency, declaring an emergency. Birmingham Center responded immediately. I quickly explained our flight problems to Birmingham Center and requested flight following, telling the center that it was critical that we stay away from thunderstorms. I told them that I was using a handheld survival-type radio and that I couldn't talk and fly at the same time, but that I could hear them on our UHF radio.

Birmingham Center positively identified us and proceeded to give us flight vectors. Out in front of us I could see another line of thunderstorms across our flight path, and as Birmingham Center was getting weaker by the minute I began to worry about our current heading. I began watching the tops of the cumulonimbus clouds and tried to pick a flight path that would not get us into another thunderstorm. Once through the line of thunderstorms, we broke out and could see with unlimited visibility. By using our VOR and TACAN type navigation equipment, we were able to locate ourselves.

Arriving over Memphis, Tennessee, I had Ed again hand me the survival radio and was able to contact Memphis Center. I quickly explained our problems, and since we were only a little over 100 miles out from Little Rock, I requested an immediate descent to Little Rock AFB. They cleared us to descend straight ahead and to contact Little Rock Approach Control when we could. We departed 37,000 feet as quickly as we could; however, a new problem presented itself in the form of twelve illuminated amber low-level fuel warning lights on our fuel panel. I told the copilot to "gang-load" all of the fuel to the main tanks and for everyone to start praying.

As we descended below 7000 feet, the power controls began to fluctuate back in and out. I felt good that I had correctly guessed what had been wrong. By the time we had descended to 1500-foot altitude the temperature was high enough that all of the ice had melted off the aircraft, and the flight controls seemed to be functioning normally. The ground controller who was providing us with flight vectors told us to immediately contact the Little Rock Command Post and to return to his frequency as soon as possible. In order to accomplish this I had to have Ed again unstrap and climb back and hand the URC survival radio to me. When I established contact with the Command Post, they wanted us to make a low approach, as they were launching a KC-135 that was on emergency takeoff status. They wanted us to hook up with the tanker and to obtain enough fuel for them to fully analyze our current flight problems. I informed them that I had twelve amber low-level fuel lights on and that I was coming in for a full stop landing. I threw the URC radio down and continued the approach. Too many things had gone wrong and were currently going wrong, and I wanted to get this beast on the ground as soon as possible.

Knowing that we were extremely light and would float a long ways at about one hundred feet in the air I had rolled the elevator trim wheel to the full up position for landing. This had been a normal way for me to land a B-47, by slowly letting the aircraft sink gently down onto the runway. We had passed the end of the runway when without warning a piece of melting ice apparently had stuck in the artificial system relief valve. Abruptly, with 3,400 pounds of hydraulic pressure behind it, the control column slammed back into my chest. The nose of the aircraft violently pitched up beyond sixty degrees while the aircraft began to shudder and stall. I slammed all six throttles to 100 percent and tried to maintain directional control by using the rudder as the aircraft came crashing down. I knew for certain, as the saying goes, that we were in deep shit. From constant training it flashed through my mind that it took thirteen seconds for the B-47s' engines to go from idle power to reach full power. When a pilot flies something in excess of 130,000 pounds that has stalled that close to the ground, he is without doubt close to rubbing noses with his maker. The aircraft fell back, violently colliding with the runway. There was a loud bang as it struck the concrete.

I immediately moved all six throttles to idle as we bounced back into the air. When we touched down again I deployed the large brake chute. The aircraft made no effort this time to bounce back into the sky, for which I was eternally grateful. I had three fire-warning lights illuminated on the right side of the instrument panel, and as soon as I could I closed all throttles to the off detent as we progressed down the runway. Directional control of the aircraft was getting tougher the farther down the runway we went. As we slowed down it became increasingly more difficult to keep the aircraft on what was left of the runway. Somewhere near the 11,000-foot marker, with only 2,000 feet to go, I lost control, and the aircraft ground looped to the right in a complete 360-degree turn before coming to a complete stop. At the time I was unaware that the rear mounts on engines four and five had broken off the right wing when we first impacted the ground. Also, I was unaware that the right wing main spar had cracked and raw jet fuel was running down the outside of the fuselage.

The aircraft came to a final halt in a complete cloud of dust and flying debris. There were heavy fuel fumes in the cockpit, so I screamed at Ed and Bob to get the hell out of the aircraft without touching anything electrical. It was only then that I noticed the ten or twelve base fire trucks surrounding us and people running all over the place. I remember manually opening the canopy because of the heat inside the cockpit and sliding it back. I felt like a balloon that had suddenly lost all of its air. I was sitting in the ejection seat drinking in great gulps of fresh air when suddenly the squadron commander's face appeared by the open canopy. He had climbed up an outside ladder when he realized that I hadn't moved from my seat. He casually handed me a cold beer and suggested that I unstrap and get the hell out of the aircraft, as the fire trucks were blowing white foam all over the aircraft fuselage and wings.

During the flight debriefing, we wrote up a Flight Hazardous Report which was forwarded to SAC headquarters. Several days later a team from SAC headquarters arrived and conducted a detailed investigation into the accident. The ensuing report cleared our crew of any improper flight procedures. The aircraft was a complete wreck and would never fly again. Our local maintenance shop determined, after studying the reports and what fuel was left in the aircraft, that it was a good thing that we didn't try to make a go-around during our approach to the field. Had we attempted this we would have run out of fuel and crashed somewhere in the flight pattern.

During the debriefing we agreed to not say anything about how far we dropped during the spin, as I had violated SAC regulations by descending below 10,000 feet without bailing out. This was one of those cases where we were able to walk away from a harrowing experience and live to talk about it. I did feel bad about Class 26-ing one of SAC's B-47s.

22

The Thirteen Days of October 1962

By the middle of October 1962, the entire world was rapidly approaching a real Armageddon. Both the Soviet Union and the United States were building larger nuclear weapons and placing many of them on missiles, and there seemed to be no end to the nuclear weapons race. The Bay of Pigs incident in 1961 had only increased the international tension between the two superpowers. On October 17, 1962, during a normal U-2 reconnaissance overflight of Cuba our intelligence agencies determined that the Cubans were building missile launch sites using large Soviet-made missiles. These missile launch sites were only ninety miles off the southern coast of the United States. President Kennedy, his immediate staff, the JCS, the CIA, and the Pentagon staffs were all placed on the highest alert status. All over SAC, flying-training missions were curtailed and our standby alert force was increased in number. It seemed to the alert crews that each day presented some new international crisis that had a significant impact upon our strategic forces. On or about October 21st our nation exploded a large hydrogen bomb on a Pacific Ocean atoll, causing all the more international tension. Each day during our mandatory combat crew briefings new red flags would appear on the large world chart that covered the entire wall behind the morning briefing stage. Our intelligence officers during their briefings always seemed to delight in scaring the hell out of the flight crews. Our individual tension and adrenaline were already so high that very few people were even talking. We felt that when the next alert klaxon sounded we would be leaving our families and America and going on to be part of a holocaust that would leave few human beings alive when it was over.

SAC's highest war plan was called the Single Integrated Operational Plan (SIOP), and there were five stages of defense conditions within it, called DEFCONS. They went from DEFCON FIVE, the lowest state of readiness, up to DEFCON ONE, which meant all-out war. Historically, SAC combat crews had never been involved in any DEFCON higher than a four. On October 21, 1962, the 384th Bomb Wing went straight from DEFCON FIVE to DEFCON THREE. Initially, there was lots of panic and confusion on the base until the professionalism factor kicked in. I was really proud of the families and base personnel during that time. People on military leave were recalled immediately, and no further leaves of any kind were approved. Combat crews were restricted to the base and told to report to their individual bomb squadrons immediately. Civilian personnel were told to leave the base and go home until recalled by their supervisors.

I remember telling Cynthia before I left home that if she should see a bunch of B-47s taking off in fifteen-second intervals she should immediately gather the kids and dogs in the car and take off for Green Forest, Arkansas, the home of my aunt and uncle. The base put out a bulletin to the effect that if all the combat crews left the base, their families should head north immediately. Head north to where? was the big question for most of the families. We thought that it was funny, but thereafter just *head north* became a term used by us as to how to face any future emergency that was thrust upon us by the military.

Back to Green Forest, as this was our family's northern destination in time of war. Green Forest was located about seventy-five miles northwest of Little Rock, close to the Missouri border. My Uncle Everet and Aunt Ruby owned a small farm a few miles outside of town, and there were a number of fairly large caves on their property. Upon arrival Cynthia was to convince Everet and Ruby that a nuclear war was imminent for the country. She was to tell them that they needed to gather all the food, medicine, blankets, and water that they could carry and get into one of the caves as soon as possible. I also told her that according to our war plans everyone should stay underground for a minimum of eighteen days. At the end of eighteen days one or more persons could come outside for no more then thirty minutes. Each day after that they could extend the outside time by thirty additional minutes. Last, I told her that if I should survive the world holocaust, I would eventually work my way back to Arkansas and search for them. This all sounded kind of terrible, but it was the real world in 1962.

As soon as all the combat crews reported in, the squadron commander conducted a classified briefing for the 545th Bomb Squadron. He told us that the classified name of our impending deployment was Operations Clutch Pedal. We were to take off fully loaded with a nuclear weapon and proceed to a specified place and altitude where we were to set up a holding pattern. We would then orbit the holding pattern and wait for receipt of a classified message from SAC headquarters. This message required authentication from all three crew members to properly validate it. We were then to proceed from our current position directly to Memphis International Airport. To prevent the Soviet missiles from wiping out our entire strategic force, B-47s were to disperse to civilian air terminals all over the country. We were one of six B-47s to land at Memphis International Airport.

Upon arrival at the airport we positioned and refueled the six B-47s just off one end of their main runway. The airport wasn't too happy with us tying up one end of their runway, but they were unable to do anything about it. We had no more landed and gotten pre-positioned when we received a message from SAC headquarters notifying us that we were now upgraded to DEFCON TWO. We sat in the cockpit for six straight hours with the engines running, awaiting departure orders. There wasn't much talking, as the navigator was busy planning our route to the target while the copilot worked on the fuel charts. We were to reach our target with bombs away at dry tanks. Carrying a twenty-megaton-plus weapon didn't seem to faze the crew as far as survival was concerned. In actuality, we were so entrenched with honor and professionalism that none of us thought about the fact that we might not survive the mission. At the end of the first six-hour shift we shut the engines down and refueled the aircraft. Four hours into the second six-hour shift we received an Ops Immediate message indicating that we could shut down the engines, but the crews had to remain in the cockpits. We thus sat there for the next twelve hours on cockpit alert. The ground crews had shuffled back and forth between the crews and the local Holiday Inn, bringing us sandwiches and soft drinks. Eventually a support aircraft arrived with enough personnel and they made arrangements to relieve and feed the six aircrews.

The next day, three crews were allowed to go to the Holiday Inn to eat while the remaining three crews stayed in their cockpits.

We followed this schedule for the next three days. An incident occurred the second day while we were eating breakfast in the Holiday Inn that I shall never forget. As I mentioned earlier, SAC headquarters would not allow combat crews to see regular Air Force assignments that arrived on their bases. The only way out of SAC at that time, according to the old heads, was to drive a B-47 into a mountain or die of old age.

We had a young AC with one of the crews who was so SACimized that no one wanted to be around him. He entered the Holiday Inn that morning with a loaded .38-caliber pistol in the lower pocket of his flying suit. By the time his crew arrived for breakfast, the dining room was full of civilians who were all trying to find out what was going on. While the AC was moving around, the .38 fell out of his pocket, hit the floor, and discharged among the crowd. No one was hurt, but it sure cleared the restaurant out in a hurry. The rest of us couldn't believe that he was carrying a loaded and cocked pistol in his pocket. Several months later this young AC received an assignment, outside of SAC to become an instructor at the Air Force Academy. The saying "screw up and move up" took on a new meaning for all of us.

We were all getting tired of this very grueling schedule, but just thinking of our buddies who were flying the B-52s made life a little easier for all of us. The B-52s had been launched at the same time we were. The difference was that they proceeded out over the Atlantic Ocean to a point that we called the "H" Hour Control Line (HHCL). Upon arrival at this point, they commenced to set up race track flight patterns and subsequently flew in circles for twenty-four hours at a time. Thinking of their schedule suddenly made our schedule look much better. The whole idea of this Operation Clutch Pedal was to disperse our B-47 nuclear strike force so that incoming Soviet missiles would not destroy our aircraft that were back on the ground at the various SAC bases. Under this operational plan our strategic B-52 force had completely surrounded Russia at the HHCL and were just waiting for the "Go Code" to proceed to their assigned targets. The Soviets were also aware of the orbiting B-52s and were very much alarmed by their presence.

History indicates that on October 26, 1962 (the thirteenth day), President Kennedy received a message from Premier Nikita Khrushchev, who quickly agreed to remove all of the strategic Soviet nuclear missiles from Cuba if we would withdraw our strategic forces. Our DEFCON status was quietly reduced to DEFCON THREE, and everyone returned to their original bases. The tension remained high on all SAC bases, as there were still a number of Soviet nuclear bombers on airfields in Cuba. Fidel Castro informed the United States that the Cuban government had purchased these bombers and that he now owned them. President Kennedy was not to be fooled by Castro and he quickly brought enough pressure on Mr. Khrushchev that he agreed to remove the Soviet bombers ASAP. In late December President Kennedy in addition brought enough pressure on Fidel Castro that he agreed to release over 1,100 American and foreign national prisoners that had been captured by Cuban forces during the Bay of Pigs invasion.

23

Special Air Operations

Somewhere in early June of 1963 I received a telephone call one day from Florida. It was the squadron commander of the 6th Fighter Squadron on the line. He wanted to know if I would like to get back into the same outfit that I had trained with a few months before at Eglin #9. I couldn't get "yes" out of my mouth quick enough. He told me that he would contact the wing commander of the 384th Bomb Wing with verbal orders and that I should start out-processing as soon as possible. What a whirlwind of activities this caused for the family. I can never remember out-processing a base so fast. We were loaded into the car and on our way to Fort Walton Beach, Florida, the next day.

This time I was to report directly to Hurlburt Field, Eglin Auxiliary #9, which was the new home of the Air Forces Special Operations Command, and the birth of the First Air Commando Squadron. As a apart of the 4400th Combat Crew Training Squadron Composite, I was to report to the 6th Fighter Squadron. What a thrill this was for me, and I quickly thanked the squadron commander for requesting my return. I was informed that we would be training for two and a half months in modified T-28s this time and that the program was definitely on the "green for go."

Upon arriving in Fort Walton Beach, we rented a small cottage next to large canal that ran out to the ocean. This place was complete with mosquitoes and an unusual assortment of spiders, plus every other imaginable type of bug in existence.

Rechecking into the 6th Fighter Squadron was one of the most exciting things that I have ever done. I felt that I was finally home, i.e., after accumulating some fifteen hundred hours in multiengine jet aircraft. Here I was going to be in fighters and all by myself! With the exception of the squadron commander, all of the personnel were new to the squadron. I quickly made a bunch of new friends, and got right into the program. Other than flying the modified T-28-D fighters, the rest of the program was very similar to the one that I had completed while involved in the original Jungle Jim Program. This new program was called Operation Farm Gate.

I soon discovered that Eglin AFB was one of the largest bases in the Air Force. There were twenty-three separate bases located within the confines of Eglin AFB, and to the best of my knowledge the CIA at the time was responsible for nine of them. I was never involved in any of the other Special Operations, so I do not know what was going on outside of Hurlburt Field. The first several weeks were reserved for those guys who had never been involved in judo training of any sort. The remainder of us had to requalify to the satisfaction of the flight instructors. Nightly drinking parties were to become a common thing for all personnel, and there was no way you could get out of attending them. It reminded me very much of the time I spent in college attending fraternity parties.

The modified T-28-D was a flying machine beyond description and so incredibly exciting to fly. The most significant modification was the addition of the large 1475 horsepowered Pratt & Whitney engine with a three-bladed propeller. The original T-28-A that I first learned to fly in had a 700-horsepower Wright Cyclone type engine with a single propeller blade and wasn't all that fast. With so much additional power it was unbelievable what you could do with this machine. The D-model engine was "redlined" at 420 knots of indicated airspeed, and what fun it was to fly at over 400 mph only a few feet off the ground. We spent the next two and a half months dropping all sorts of bombs, shooting rockets, and trying not to burn the barrels of the .50-caliber machine guns up. For a pilot like me this was indeed Hog Heaven, and to think that I was getting paid to do all of these exciting things.

As we neared the end of the two and a half months, we were told one day to attend a mandatory briefing the next morning. As usual, the briefing was conducted by the local intelligence officer, only this time he had some solid information for all of us. He told us that everything that he was going to tell us was classified Top Secret and that all of us would be leaving shortly for a one-year hazardous duty assignment. He further said that if we survived the one-year hazardous duty assignment, we would have our choice of

Air Force assignments after the year was over. He reminded us that whatever kind of aircraft we chose to fly afterward, the base we requested had to have that type of aircraft. A hazardous duty assignment sheet was passed out to each of us, and we had to certify the sheet with our signatures. The top portion contained a statement indicating that we were volunteering for a classified assignment, and here also was a place for our signature.

The second portion was our individual request for the assignment following this one. I drafted my statement to indicate that I wanted to fly F-105 fighters that were stationed at Kadena Air Base in Okinawa. The reason that I wanted to fly F-105s was because the Thud, as the F-105 was fondly called, was the fastest fighter aircraft in the Air Force at the time and Okinawa was known as the "Country Club" of the Air Force. While we were drafting our responses, the intelligence officer was talking about some of the things that we needed to accomplish, such as drawing up wills and getting our families situated before we left Hurlburt Field. Names that the intelligence officer was using involved the Dirty Dozen, the Jungle Jim Program, and the Farm Gate program. The acronyms didn't really matter, as we considered ourselves commandos and whatever other title someone wanted to use on us was fine. When they asked for volunteers for the First Draft out of our program, I quickly raised my hand along with five other guys. The Intel officer said that we would be departing PCS (permanent change of station) the following month (November).

USS *Barko*, with Marine Squadron VMF-312 on board, somewhere in the Yellow Sea.

The author with one of his Russian Burp Guns, 1950.

Bridge interdiction between Seoul and Kaeson, Korea, September 1950.

While attempting a go-a-round, an F4U snap-rolled and crashed into aircraft parked on the flight line, December 1951.

The author on outer perimeter guard duty at K-6, Korea, January 1952.

The author as a plane captain at K-18, Korea, January 1952.

Building esprit de corps by pilots by VMF-312 Checker-board Squadron prior to combat launch (check out the nifty checkerboard kimonos!).

The author in one of his aircraft, April 1952.

On board the USS Bataan, May 1952, when an F4U crashed on landing.

Getting ready to launch a maximum-effort airstrike from the USS
Bataan.

The author just after his solo flight in a T-34 at
Marana Air Base, Arizona, 1957.

In the cockpit of an A-model T-28 at Moore Air Base, Texas in 1957.

The arrival of the Army's first "Gun Ships" in South Vietnam. The UHE-1Bs are loaded with rocket pods plus two mini-gattling guns.

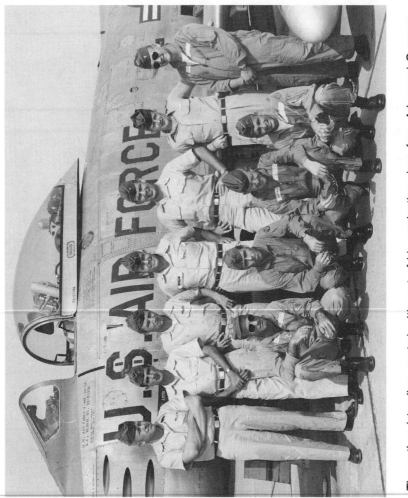

The author (standing, center) with part of his graduating class from Advanced Gunnery School in F-86F jet fighters at Williams AFB, Arizona, 1958.

An F-105 Thunderchief that belonged to the 18th TFW, loaded for a combat mission, December 1964.

A new B-47 bomber being delivered from the Boeing plant in Seattle, Washington.

Greeting a new pilot upon his arrival in Vietnam, December 1963. Author is in center of picture with big smile.

Our strike force at Soc Trang in December 1963. The area between the dirt road and the fence is heavily mined to slow down a VC attack, especially at night.

The author standing by a T-28 loaded with 750-pound canisters of napalm plus two rocket pods.

Flight Commander Floyd Sweet studying a wall map with VC areas circled in black, located just outside Soc Trang, January 1964.

The author and Captain Hal Wagner returning from a combat mission. Note the personal weapons and survival gear.

This is the monkey that bit the Gunny Sergeant at Soc Trang. We tabbed him "the meanest monkey in the world."

This is the Dust-off chopper that flew Captain Anderson and the author down to Captain Shanks' crash site.

500-pound bombs getting ready for loading on nearby T-28s.

This is what was left of the entire U.S. Strike Force in South Vietnam in March 1964.

The author standing by a T-28 with his MA3-1 "grease gun" in 1964.

24

On to Vietnam

I took the only thirty-day Air Force leave in my career, and we left for San Diego, California, in early October. We stayed with Cynthia's parents in La Mesa while we looked for a suitable house for her and the kids. We were fortunate and located and rented a house within walking distance of her parents. While visiting friends from my hometown of Coronado, I ran into one of my classmates who was an instructor pilot in HH-43 helicopters and was stationed at nearby Navy Ream Field. He invited me to fly with him, and for the next two weeks I flew every day and eventually got checked out in the HH-43.

What a blast it was to fly helicopters. In flying any type of Air Force aircraft the one instrument that was the most critical to pilots was the airspeed indicator, especially when getting close to the ground. I almost panicked on my first HH-43 flight as I made an approach for landing and the airspeed indicator went to 0. I was so busy trying to line up for the landing pad that I didn't realize that I was flying backward. Fortunately, I recovered, and seconds later, after the panic factor died down and I realized what was happening, I managed to get the machine on the ground in one piece. I had to buy my IP a beer that afternoon for my carelessness. I never forgot that invaluable flying lesson.

Upon our leaving Hurlburt Field there were six of our names on the same set of secret orders telling us to report to APO-27 with a port of call date at Travis AFB. The six of us talked it over, trying to figure out just where we might be going, but really had no idea except that the assignment was somewhere in the South Pacific Ocean area of operations. The Air Force has two ports of call in the United States. One is Travis AFB, located in Oakland, California, for everyone going somewhere in the South Pacific, while the other port of call is located at McGuire AFB, New Jersey, for people travelling to Europe. The orders did mention our receiving a seven-day secret in-country indoctrination briefing at Clark Air Base, which is located in the Philippine Islands. Since the six of us who had volunteered for the First Draft were all on the same set of orders, I got everyone to readily agree to meet at Travis AFB three days before our departure. The idea was to spend the three days partying in nearby San Francisco. I arrived at Travis AFB in the afternoon on the 18th of October and went straight to the BOQ to obtain a room.

Locating the proper building, I wandered down the hall until I found my assigned room. Upon opening the door I discovered another person lying on the second bed. The guy jumped up off the bed as I entered and introduced hisself. Much to my surprise, he was a member of the U.S. Army's elite and famous Green Berets. He was Lt. Karl Bronson, and there was an instant liking between us. I told Karl that five other Air Force pilot types were meeting me in the officers' club and would he like to come with me for a drink or two. We were quickly on our way.

Within forty-five minutes all seven of us were trying to drink the entire stock of gin in the club. It turned out later that Karl was supposed to catch an aircraft out that evening to Clark Air Base. Somehow the gin caught up with all of us and Karl missed his flight. We told him not to worry, as there was another flight in three days, and that we would take care of everything. We located an airman with a good attitude who understood our problem the next morning in the passenger terminal. He said that there were extra seats on the flight that we were taking and booked a seat for Karl. We were all happy, and Karl accompanied us as we headed out for San Francisco and to the Top of the Mark bar.

We spent a marvelous three days chasing around San Francisco. Mostly we saw the insides of the many local bars. We had so much fun that somehow we missed our designated departure flight back to Travis AFB. When we arrived back at Travis the next morning none of us wanted to go to the passenger terminal, as we were sure that we would get court-martialed for being absent without leave. Having had some experience at traveling around the world onboard military aircraft, I told the guys to stay together as I had an idea. I called and got a taxi to take me to base operations. Going into the flight-planning section of base ops, I located a young captain who was an aircraft commander on a KC-135 tanker-type aircraft. He was in the process of mission planning for a flight to Clark Air Base. I explained our situation and how we overslept in San Francisco and showed him a copy of our orders. He told me that he was departing in three hours and had extra space if we didn't mind canvas seats. He also told me to go get the guys and get back down to base ops ASAP.

After the usual briefing by the flight crew, we got onboard and settled in for the long flight. The captain was right, as there were no passenger-type seats, but there were pull-down canvas racks that worked very well. Approximately two and a half hours out, the copilot came back and informed us that they had lost a generator on their number-two engine and that they were diverting to land at Hickem AFB in Hawaii to get it fixed.

Once on the ground and parked at Hickem AFB, the aircraft commander informed us that we would be on the ground for eight hours. He said that it would only take about two hours to get the generator fixed, but the crew according to Air Force regulations had to go into mandatory crew rest before continuing the flight. We left our gear on the aircraft and went into base ops with the crew. Since we had eight hours to kill, I told the guys that I had an old navigator buddy from my B-47 days who had retired in Hawaii and that I was going to call him. Walt, who had retired two years ago, was delighted to hear from me. I explained to Walt that we were stuck there in Base Ops for the next eight hours. He said, "Not a problem," and that he would be down to pick us up in thirty minutes. About an hour later we found ourselves in the Hickem Officers' Club. For the next six hours or so we told ribald war stories and again tried to deplete the club's supply of Mai Tais. How Walt ever managed to get us back to the tanker I'll never know. Being well fortified, I went to sleep during the long flight, and when I woke up we were in the landing pattern for Clark AB. After deplaning, we thanked the aircraft commander for saving our lives and wished him well.

Somehow, after a lot of confusion we managed to locate the BOQ. Clark was a large base and very spread out. The clerk at the BOQ told us that there was no space available in the main buildings, but that he could put us up in a Quonset hut. We weren't too happy with this, because the nearest Quonset hut was about a mile and a half away from everything, but as the saying goes, "beggars can't be choosers." We were actually so happy just to be where we were supposed to be that no one made too much of staying in a Quonset hut. Since it was late in the day, we quickly unloaded our gear in the Quonset hunt and took off for the officers' club. What a fantastic club it turned out to be, and it was loaded with new schoolteachers and stewardesses. Needless to say, the party was on!

Somehow the next morning we managed to make it to Base Personnel Office. We showed our orders to the desk clerk and asked him where we were supposed to get our secret briefing. The airman told us to wait while he consulted with his NCO. A chief master sergeant came up to the desk and told us that in all of his years in personnel he had never seen a set of orders like ours and had never heard of APO-27. We informed him that the orders were from the CIA and pointed out where they said that we were to receive a classified briefing regarding our destination and mission. The good chief suggested that we get ahold of the 313th Air Division Personnel Office, which was located about a mile away in another building. After looking at Karl's orders the chief told him that there was a passenger aircraft out the next evening for his destination. The chief called for a taxi for us, and we thanked him for his time.

We eventually arrived at the 13th Air Division building and went inside. A colonel met us and listened to our story. He examined our orders and said that he had no idea where APO-27 was, but that wherever the destination was, it was a classified place. He also said that he knew nothing about a classified briefing for us. He further told us that if we would come back the next morning he would be able to tell us where we were going. We thanked him and quickly headed back to the officers' club.

The next morning we tried our best to look sober as we headed for the colonel's office. He seemed to be excited to see us and quickly informed us that we were going to Vietnam. I remember we all looked at one another, and said, "Where is Vietnam?" The colonel's answer was that Vietnam was located in Southeast Asia. Things got humorous at this point as we all looked at one another and laughed. The colonel then told us that a former name for Vietnam was French Indochina. I then asked the colonel if this place was in Burma. The colonel was a little upset that none of us seemed to know anything about geography, and finally he said that at one time the country was known as Siam, if that helped. I quickly told the colonel that it had to be in Burma, because I had only recently seen the movie star Yul Brynner in the motion picture *The King and I,* and he was Siamese and was riding an elephant somewhere in Burma.

The colonel was getting a little exasperated at this point. He said, "Well, do any of you remember a place called Dien Bien Phu?"

I raised my hand and replied, "Isn't that the place where someone kicked the shit out of the French?"

He said, "Yes, it was the Vietminh in the North" and that they were now called Vietcong (VC) in the southern part of the country of Vietnam. I then asked the colonel exactly where APO-27 was located, and he didn't know. He told me that when we arrived in the capitol city of Saigon, someone there would know the location of APO-27. The colonel went on to inform us that there was a C-130 type aircraft going back to Saigon that very evening, departing at 1700 hours. He said that he had already checked and that there were plenty of vacant seats onboard the aircraft. He also mentioned that there was a weekly C-130 flight to Vietnam and that we could either get on the one tonight or wait a week and catch the next flight.

We talked it over among ourselves, and since no one seemed to care, five of the guys decided to stay at Clark and party with the ladies for a week. We were originally supposed to receive a seven-day classified briefing, and since that seemed to fall through the cracks, no one was too worried about his arrival time. I think the main reason was that a Continental airliner was landing that evening and there would be five new stewardesses to chase for four days. Much to everyone's delight, Continental Airlines operated a contract flight out of Clark Air Base every four days. Karl told me that he couldn't stay, as he had to get to his headquarters as soon as possible. Of the six Air Force officers, I was the only fighter pilot and I was getting tired of partying, so I told the guys that I would go on out with Karl that evening. I really wanted to get on with whatever I was going to be doing and was excited about it.

25

Saigon

Karl and I caught the 1700 C-130 flight along with twelve other people. Four hours later we landed at Ton Son Knut International Airport in Saigon, South Vietnam, on November 1, 1963. The final approach and landing at Ton Son Knut was done flying in heavy rain showers, and we were all glad to finally get on the ground. A young Army lieutenant met the aircraft, driving a large Army truck that had no top on it. He was drenched and mad about having to drive out to get us in the rain and therefore wasn't too communicative. He told us to get in the back of the truck and that he would take us downtown. It was close to one in the morning before we got rolling. The lieutenant said that there were no military facilities at Ton Son Knut, so we would have to stay in civilian hotels. He said that he would stop at seven different hotels and that each time he stopped, two of us should jump off. He did tell us to find our way back to the airport the next day and that a liaison officer would take care of us.

His first stop was the Caravel Hotel, and another captain who was sitting on the tailgate of the truck with me jumped off. The hotel had a nice appearance to it, even if we couldn't pronounce the name of the city. It kind of reminded me of a large Holiday Inn type hotel just like the ones back in the United States. It was close to 1:30 A.M. now, and when we approached the registration desk none of the three people could speak English. I tried telling the desk clerk in as many languages as I knew that we needed a room for the night. After a lot of pointless arguing with the clerk, I remembered my pointy-talkie language and pointing to the room keys behind the clerk, I made the sleeping motion with my hands. The captain and I placed a pile of American money on the counter and amid many smiles the clerk took what he wanted and produced a room key. The captain and I both signed something that neither of us could read, and the clerk pointed to the nearby lift. We managed to get ourselves up to the fourth floor, locate our room, and get settled in for the night. It soon was to become a night that no one would ever forget!

Around four o'clock in the morning all hell broke lose. Tanks were rumbling and clanking down the main street outside our hotel window, shooting their heavy guns at something ahead of them. At the same time, we could hear aircraft and they, too, were dropping bombs and strafing the buildings down the street from us. My adrenaline was peaking out well over 500 percent, and the fear factor quickly hit both me and the captain. My initial reaction was that I was back in Korea with the U.S. Marine Corps. I ran from the window to the hallway door and opened it. A Vietnamese man was running down the hallway yelling in his best English, "GIs stay in room!" I stepped back into the room and quickly began digging through my gear for my Colt .38. The captain with me had no weapon, so I loaned him my .38-caliber derringer. While we were sitting on my bed loading the guns, a stray bullet broke the street window to our room, exploding glass all over the place, and scared the hell out of both of us.

I told the captain that I had fought in Korea as an infantryman and that there was no way that I was going to die in a hotel room in a country, especially in a country, that I couldn't even pronounce the name of. He agreed with me, and we decided to go downstairs to see if we could figure out what was going on. Hearing a noise by our hallway door, I jerked the door open and stepped out with my .38 ready to fire. Talk about a shock! Here was one for the books. Standing directly in front of me was an American woman around twenty-five years or so old. She had two six-packs of Budweiser beer in her hands. She looked at me and immediately started laughing. Finally she said, "Are you going to shoot me, or do you want to join me?" I suddenly realized how ridiculous I looked standing there in only my shorts with a cocked pistol pointed directly at her. I lowered the pistol and asked her to give us a minute to get our clothes on. She stood in the doorway while both the captain and I stumbled around trying to look professional while searching for our pants. She told us that her name was Jennie and that she was a reporter for a U.S. newsmagazine. She then invited us to join her up on the roof of the hotel to watch the action that was going on below us. We quickly accompanied her up the stairs to the rooftop of the hotel.

Jennie told us that we were watching the coup d'état of the Vietnamese government. She pointed out the Presidential Palace of Ngo Dinh Diem, which was under a ferocious attack by ground and air forces just two blocks away from us. We got a good lesson in history as Jennie explained that Diem's regime was composed of Ngo Dinh; his wife, Madam Nhu, and his brother Nhu. Only Madam Nhu escaped the bloodbath while both her husband and his brother were killed during this attack. The entire episode reminded me of a giant western-type movie. We watched and threw empty beer cans on the troops below us as they were firing at everything in their way. At the time I was so naïve that I didn't know what a coup d'état stood for and was too embarrassed to ask. The bombs from the attacking fighter planes did not all hit their targets, as some of them landed on the troops that were in the streets below. The concussion from the larger explosions rocked our hotel and broke windows everywhere. Sometime during the excitement Jennie disappeared, and we never saw her again in the hotel. As the sound of gunfire died down outside, we returned to our room, packed our gear, and went downstairs to try to locate some breakfast. Our adrenaline was running so high that the lack of sleep didn't brother either one of us.

We finally located an English-speaking hotel clerk. He told us to be outside the hotel and at 0800 a gray U.S. Navy bus would come by and for us to flag it down. Eventually a gray Navy bus did appear, and we flagged the driver down. He assured us that he would take us to the military section at Ton Son Knut International Airport. Thirty minutes later he stopped in front of a camouflaged eight-man U.S. Army tent that was located somewhere inside the boundaries of the international airport. He informed us that this was our destination. I found a young airman inside the tent who welcomed us to Vietnam. He told me that I was going to Bien Hoa Air Base, while the other captain was assigned to the military advisory group located in downtown Saigon. The airman called Bien Hoa and told me that a jeep was being dispatched to pick me up. He said that it would probably take the driver an hour or so to get here, depending upon whether or not he encountered any VC along the way.

26

Bien Hoa Air Base

Two hours later an American jeep appeared with the meanest-looking guy whom I had ever seen in the driver's seat. His rank indicated that he was a captain, but he was very cocky and reminded me of movie star John Wayne. The captain sat there with a Thompson submachine gun in his right hand as if it were a part of him. He asked my name and only then introduced himself as Capt. Frank Gorski. He wanted to know if I had a gun. I said yes, I had a .38 pistol in my rucksack. He told me to get the gun out, as the ride back to Bien Hoa might be dangerous. He also told me to get the hell out of my Class A uniform as the day's temperature would soon get over 100 degrees. I was hesitant because of his attitude but stepped back into the tent and quickly changed into a more comfortable set of fatigues. Bien Hoa was approximately fifty miles north of Saigon, and the drive was mostly through jungle terrain. I was trying to appear unconcerned to the good Captain Gorski, but inside I was scared as hell. Gorski didn't make it any easier, as he kept his hands on his submachine gun all the time he was driving.

Eventually we arrived at Bien Hoa and Captain Gorski showed me to a tent and to a bunk bed that would become my home for the duration of my stay in Vietnam. The environment of the place that we were staying in was extremely smelly and muddy, and thus all of the tents had wooden floors in them. Between the tents the civil engineers had placed wooden pallets on the ground for everyone to walk on. I quickly discovered that there was no such thing as air-conditioning anywhere. If it got too hot inside the tent, the guys just rolled the outside flaps up to admit any air current. I was told that Bien Hoa was a plush place to stay according to other guys in the tent. These same "other guys" told me that in many of the places where we would be operating at times I most likely would be sleeping under one of the wings of my aircraft. Captain Gorski told me that I was now assigned to the T-28 section of the First Air

Commando Squadron, which was a part of the 34th Tactical Composite Group, commanded by a Col. Ben King.

In my opinion, the inprocessing procedure for the T-28 section was unusual and very unprofessional. I turned in my orders to a very tired-looking personnel clerk and he told me to go down to the PE tent and draw whatever survival equipment I needed. Locating the PE tent was not the easiest thing to do, and there didn't seem to be anyone around to assist me. Eventually I located the proper tent and ran into a very smart-mouthed NCO. He ignored me at first until I got mad and told him that I was assigned to the T-28 section, and he then demanded to see my orders. Once he became satisfied, he asked me if I wanted a .45-caliber automatic or a Colt .38 pistol. Since I had carried a Colt .45 in Korea and was fairly adapt at handling and hitting a target with one, I told him that I preferred a .45.

The sergeant banged a Colt .45 down on the wooden counter along with three boxes of ammunition and stood there smiling at me. I finally looked at him and said, "OK, Sarge, where is the clip?" He smiled back at me and said that they didn't have any clips. I was getting frustrated about this time and asked the sergeant what kind of an air force he thought this was. With the same smile on his face, he informed me that this was not the Air Force. I was really upset with his surly attitude but decided to go along with his private joke. I told him that since there were no clips for the .45 automatic I would go ahead and accept a Colt .38 pistol. The sergeant then slammed a Colt .38 down on the counter and again just stood there giving me that smart aleck smile. Finally, he said that they didn't have any .38-caliber ammunition. I pushed the .38 back to the sergeant and told him to provide me with whatever else I was supposed to get. I left the sergeant's tent madder than hell, wondering just what kind of an outfit I was getting involved in. It seemed that everywhere I turned there was an attitude of complacency facing me, and it wasn't friendly.

It is never fun whenever you are the FNG (fucking new guy) in any outfit, and this was no exception. I discovered that the other pilots in the tent, when they were there, were too busy or too tired to talk to me. It was as if I didn't matter to them at all, and it was some time before I discovered why. They had simply lost too many people and just didn't want to get friendly with me, as I was untested by their standards. I had to wait three days before I got to meet the T-28 section commander, a Major Lengfield. The reason for the wait was that the good major had just returned from a week's TDY assignment and was extremely tired. Major Lengfield was very friendly and told me as much as he could think of about the squadron and what was going on. Major Lengfield went on to tell me that I would get an in-country check ride in the T-28 to see if I was qualified to become a part of the T-28 section. He told me that if I failed my qualification ride I would be reassigned to another section within the 34th Composite Group. Finally, Major Lengfield told me to just hang around the area until there was a free T-28 that was not being used for a combat mission. He said that I would be called to fly the check ride at that time.

Four days later I was told to report to a Colonel Aderholt in another tent who would take me on a combat mission and give me a check ride. I located Colonel Aderholt inside his tent, and during the very short briefing he told me to call him Heini, which was his first name. I thought that was rather unusual, but so was everything else that I had come across. I found Colonel Heini to be a man of very few words. He never asked me anything about my background or qualifications in the T-28. The good colonel did provide me with a combat frequency that we would be operating on. He then told me to locate my aircraft and to check in with him once I got the engine started. At that point Colonel Heini just got up, went outside, got on a bicycle, and headed for the flight line. I had no idea where to go, and one of the guys, a Captain Shank, told me that the flight line was about three blocks away. He said that I best hurry, as Colonel Heini would wait for no one.

There was no flight line taxi service, so I found myself both walking fast and running to the flight line. I eventually located the aircraft that I had been assigned to fly and quickly performed a preflight on the aircraft. I had no checklist for the T-28. While I was fumbling around in the cockpit trying to locate the proper switches to start the engine I noticed the colonel, two aircraft away, with his engine running, waiting for me to call in. The crew chief finally jumped up on the wing and helped me start the engine. As soon as the radio was warmed up I checked in with Colonel Heini. He did not acknowledge my radio call, and as I looked over toward his aircraft he was already taxiing out. I gave the crew chief the signal to remove my wheel chocks and quickly taxied out, trying to catch up with the good colonel's aircraft.

Racing toward the end of the runway, I overheard the tower clearing our flight of two T-28s onto the runway. Colonel Heini wasn't waiting for me, as he turned the corner and continued on down the runway on his takeoff roll. Normally, most pilots spend a few minutes running the engine up, checking the gauges and magnetos before releasing their brakes. I was more than pissed off as Colonel Heini rolled down the runway at full throttle without saying a word. It is proper procedure for all flight leaders to give their wingmen a little power reduction so that they can stay with the leader, but not Colonel Aderholt!

Colonel Heini turned out of traffic immediately after takeoff, and I had one hell of a time just trying to keep him in sight. I think he realized that I was an FNG and very nervous, and he wasn't going to give me an inch. We raced to the target area with him leading me by about two miles. Colonel Heini finally broke radio silence by telling me to orbit over the target area while he made his bomb attacks. He also told me to look out for ground fire. The good colonel made three dive-bomb passes, dropping his bombs somewhat inaccurately on what looked like a civilian house down below.

The colonel finally pulled up and cleared me in to drop my bombs. He again reminded me to watch out for ground fire. I made two hectic bomb runs, dropping two bombs on each pass, never realizing that none of the bombs had exploded. As I pulled off the second pass I heard Colonel Heini, in a somewhat sarcastic voice, say, "Next time, Two, try arming your bombs." Pulling up off that second pass, I searched the sky for Colonel Heini, and it didn't take long for me to realize that he had already left for home, saying nothing to me. I left the throttle at 100 percent and being a combination of both scared and nervous, I selected a heading that I thought might be the correct one to get me back to Bien Hoa. Fortunately, I had selected a correct heading, and the next thing that I heard was Colonel Heini calling for landing instructions from Bien Hoa's control tower.

After landing, I had to do a high-speed taxi job in an attempt to catch up with Colonel Heini before he reached the parking area. By the time that I parked my aircraft and got the engine shut down, Colonel Heini was out of his aircraft and gone on his bicycle. There was no debriefing by the good colonel, and in fact I never saw him again. Later that same evening Major Lengfield informed me that Colonel Aderholt had signed me off and that I had passed my in-country check ride. Major Lengfield told me that I would be posted to the combat schedule sometime during the next few days. It wasn't until several nights later while having a drink in the officers' club that I was to discover what a legend Colonel Aderholt was in the Special Operations branch of the Air Force. I also learned that the good colonel, like many other people, was in the country TDY just long enough to fly one combat mission so that he would receive his combat pay and tax deduction.

It was amazing what I learned during the next few days about combat flying in a hostile and hazardous environment. One of the things that bothered me the most was the absolute lack of naviga-tional aids of any kind. All combat missions were flown by what the Air Force referred to as "dead reckoning." This meant that the pilot had to look at a map, usually always out of date, and try to figure out exactly where to fly and how long it was going to take to get there. Initially flying on someone else's wing for the first few missions was really helpful, as I became more comfortable with the local countryside. The first few times that I flew, I did not have a map with me, and I'm not sure that it would have helped anyway, as the jungle looked the same no matter which way you went.

Several days later I was told to report with a number of other new guys to the group commander's tent at 0800 hours. Here for the first time I was to learn about the various missions of the 34th Tactical Group, and how the T-28 section fit into the big picture. What I really received from Colonel King was a quick history lesson about the country of Vietnam. In so many words the colonel ex-plained that for thousands of years Vietnam had been conquered and controlled by the Chinese. The French eventually conquered the Chinese sometime during the 1800s and controlled the country for almost a hundred years, until 1954. In 1954, the French were defeated by the North Vietnamese forces in a last-ditch battle at a place called Dien Bien Phu.

Prior to the defeat of the French forces, the country was divided roughly into three parts. North Vietnam was referred to as the Land of Tonkin and was controlled by the Communist leader Ho Chi Minh. Tonkin started at the 17th parallel and ran clear up to the

Chinese border. The central portion of the country was known as Annam and ran south from the 17th parallel down to the capital city of Saigon. The southern portion of the country was known as Cochin China, running roughly from Saigon south to the Gulf of Siam and to the South China Sea. South Vietnam is bordered on the east by Cambodia and Laos up to the 17th parallel. From the 17th parallel northward, North Vietnam is boarded by Laos on the east side, with China as a neighbor to their north and with the South China Sea as their west coast.

By the year 1963, the country was divided into two parts, with the border at the 17th parallel. For the purpose of military missions by our forces, South Vietnam was further divided into four equal parts. We referred to the Northern Section as I (eye) Corps, with headquarters at Danang Air Base. At the time, the T-28 section kept four of its aircraft up there on a constant alert status. II (two) Corps was located in the Central Highlands, where we kept three or four T-28s at a place called Pleiku. III (three) Corps area contained the capital city of Saigon and was home to the 34th Tactical Group Composite at Bien Hoa. The final area, IV (four) Corps, was located to the south of Saigon and contained all of the Mekong Delta areas of South Vietnam. The T-28 section kept three or four T-28s at a small U.S. Army helicopter base called Soc Trang.

Colonel King informed us that the group had suffered the most aircraft losses in the IV Corps area. He advised us to be especially on our toes at all times when in that area of operations, and to do nothing that would jeopardize our lives, or the lives of anyone in our flights. Next Major Lengfield took me to his office and explained how the T-28 section's portion of the operation worked. Basically, we would start our TDY tours at Danang for two weeks and then deploy to Pleiku for two weeks. Next we headed south to Soc Trang for two weeks and finally back to Bien Hoa for two weeks. It's always great to have schedules, but I quickly learned that for a variety of reasons in the T-28 section they quite often never held. The most common reason for schedule fluctuation was that pilots got sick or got killed or there wasn't enough aircraft to go around.

Most people back in the States in 1963–64 thought that there was very little actual combat going on in South Vietnam. Most American citizens were of the impression that the small VC forces were only shooting at us with bows and arrows. I can reassure you that this was not the case. The VC in the South were not as well equipped as their brothers in the North were, but they had plenty of single and dual 12mm and 14.5mm Soviet antiaircraft guns. Later in 1964 coming down the Ho Chi Minh Trail there were some Soviet-built 23mm ZPU-23s that were capable of reaching altitudes of 20,000 feet. I was the twenty-fourth T-28 pilot to join the section in November of 1963, and by June of 1964 there were only four of us left in the section.

27

The 34th Tactical Group Composite

The 34th Tactical Group at Bien Hoa mainly hosted the First Air Commando Squadron (Composite) and was composed of a number of sections with different types of aircraft. One section was composed of WW II medium bombers and was known as the B-26 Marauder section. Some people referred to this section as the A-26 section, wherein the A stood for attack-type aircraft. These medium bombers had twelve to fourteen forward-firing machine guns located in the nose of the aircraft and when on strafing missions were really lethal to enemy troops on the ground.

By early 1964, the B-26 section was receiving a few new versions of the B-26 called the On Mark. This new B-26 was named for a company that was rebuilding the aircraft in California. I got to fly several missions in the old B-26s but never got near one of the new birds. However, the pilots who did fly them all raved about them. The pilots said that they were faster and could carry far more armament than the old B-26s. The problem was that their missions were all interdiction (air-to-ground) type missions and the B-26s were not built for the type of stress that pilots were putting on the wings. As a result, many pilots were killed on pullouts, when the overstressed wings frequently came off while in flight. One thing that I do remember about the B-26 was the incredible noise level inside the cockpit. It was absolutely impossible for the pilots to converse while the engines were running.

There was a cargo section, which had both C-47 and C-123 type aircraft. Occasionally from some unknown source some C-130 type aircraft would also appear. We fondly referred to this section as the trash haulers. The C-123 aircraft in addition to carrying cargo were also equipped to be used as defoliation aircraft. I flew many combat sorties in support of their defoliation missions, which I will describe later.

There was also a reconnaissance section that had two types of aircraft. One was the very small Cessna "O-1 Bird Dog" aircraft. The Bird Dog was a quite reliable aircraft but very susceptible to a lot of excitement during the landing phases and prone to ground looping. The problem was that the aircraft, due to its unusual landing gear struts, had a tendency to bounce a lot on landings. These bounces ultimately led to some wild and whirlwind final-type stops for the pilots. The other light aircraft in 1963–64 was a small utility aircraft called the U-10. Pilots of these machines were referred to as the Bullshit Bombers. The reason for this was that on most of their missions they carried powerful loudspeakers that broadcast tape-recorded propaganda messages to the Vietnamese populace on the ground. Because they flew so low and slow they frequently got the dickens shot out of their aircraft. Coming home with twelve to twenty bullet holes was not uncommon for pilots flying the U-10s.

I remember one time making a fifty-dollar bet with a pilot of a U-10 that I lost. The U-10 pilot bet me that he could arrive over the end of the landing runway at 1,000-foot altitude and from that altitude he could touch down in the first 50 feet of the runway. I couldn't believe it, but he did it. The thing that made it possible for this pilot to land on the end of the runway was the very large flaps under the wings. When we came in at 1,000 feet, the pilot put down full flaps and we just came down like a helicopter. At the last second the pilot added just enough engine power to produce a squeak-type landing. I really had to take my hat off to the guys who flew in these two small aircraft. The U-10 is what is considered as a helio-type aircraft. It has a small engine set in an elongated engine housing that just plain looks funny.

As the saying goes, "the pilots of these small aircraft had a large set of balls." The O-1 pilots were frequently referred to as Ravens. They were the unsung heroes as far as I am concerned. Thirty-one of them were killed between 1963 and 1970. Their mission while flying at extremely low altitudes was to first locate the enemy targets and then call for fighters. Once we arrived in the target area, the O-1 pilots who were acting as FACs, would then mark the target, usually with an air-to-ground rocket. The FACs would then direct us to place our bombs exactly where they wanted the bombs to hit.

The final section in the 34th Tactical Group was the T-28 section of which I was a member. In order to set the stage for the reader I need to provide some background on the T-28 aircraft. There were three models that I am aware of, and all were built by the North American Aviation Company. According to historical records, the original T-28 D model was designed as a tandem two-seated, high-altitude, long-range bomber escort fighter. The problem was that WW II ended before the North American Aviation Company could get the T-28 fighters in full production. Therefore, the T-28s never saw a moment of WW II combat. When WW II ended in 1945 all of the U.S. forces underwent large-scale downsizing. With the U.S. economy in trouble and unemployment affecting everyone, especially in the Los Angeles area, President Truman's cabinet informed the Air Force that they would accept 6,000 of the new T-28s.

The Air Force apparently decided that they did not want the T-28s, as there were many other worthy and already-proven fighter-type aircraft around. In the end analysis, the Air Force lost the battle and was forced to accept the T-28s. The Air Force did place restrictions on the North American Aviation Company. The aircraft that the Air Force accepted had to have the gun ports covered over, bomb racks taken off, and the large 1475-horsepower engines removed. The three-bladed propeller, along with the Pratt & Whitney 1475-horsepower engine, was replaced with a Wright-Cyclone 700-horsepower engine with a single-bladed propeller. This model of the T-28 then became the A model and became one of the Air Force's primary flying trainer-type aircraft. The Navy, because of the need to train pilots to land on aircraft carriers, got what was to become known as the B model T-28. This B model was equipped with an 1125-horsepower engine and had stronger landing gear installed.

Prior to 1961 the CIA went to the Air Force's Boneyard located at Davis-Monthan AFB, Arizona, and appropriated a number of the D-model T-28s and gave them to the Special Operations Branch of the Air Force. These D-model T-28s were to be flown by a group of volunteer insurgent pilots during the Cuban Bay of Pigs Operation. Shortly after the Bay of Pigs debacle, these same aircraft were sent to the Vietnam Theater as a part of a covert operation expanding in that country. Most of the aircraft in our section were painted a dull gray and carried no markings of any kind on the fuselage. The original D-Model T-28 had .50-caliber machine guns located inside the wings of the aircraft. The problem here was that the ammunition

201

storage area in the wings could only hold 100 rounds and 100 rounds was of little value in the combat situations that we found ourselves in. Therefore, our ordnance guys modified the aircraft by adding two .50-caliber guns located underneath the wings, each with 1500 rounds of ammunition.

Probably the worst problem that we had with the aircraft was one of too much heat inside the cockpit. Whoever installed the large 1475-horsepower engines did nothing to modify the firewall between the engine compartment and the pilot. As a result, the temperature inside the cockpit after a few minutes of operation became almost unbearable for anyone. For the most part the average daily temperature in Vietnam was over 100 degrees Fahrenheit. Sitting under a Plexiglass canopy for two to three plus hours with the inside temperature exceeding 135 degrees Fahrenheit on an average combat mission had a tendency to greatly dehydrate pilots. In an effort to solve this problem we had our ground crews cut a small hole in the top of the canopies. They then installed a small aluminum air scoop over the hole. This provided a convenient and refreshing source of cool outside air to the cockpit. To further alleviate some of the heat problem we carried canteens with frozen water in them under our seats in the cockpit. The cool water was an absolute lifesaver for most of us.

The North American Aviation Company did not design the T-28 for the type of special operations that we were using it for. As an example, the original aircraft was designed to carry two 100-pound bombs under each wing. We frequently carried two 750-pound bombs or, in some cases, four 500-pounders. Other times we would carry two 750-pound canisters of napalm under each wing with rocket pods on the outboard wing racks. These extremely heavy ordnance loads didn't brother us at most bases. It was only when we operated out of Soc Trang in the Delta area that we always held our breath on takeoffs, as the runway was only 2600 feet in length, with 40-foot-plus trees on the northern end of the runway. It was sort of comical, as there were a lot of propeller swaths cut through the trees on the north end of the runway. We always seemed to have plenty of power for our ordnance loads on takeoffs, but many times we didn't make a drop and had to return and land with those heavy bombs under the wings. Situations like this made for critical short field type landings at Soc Trang. Dropping those birds in on short and unimproved runways with a full ordnance load did nothing for the stress levels on the wings of the T-28s.

We lost Jerry Shank in March of 1964 as a result of the wings coming off his T-28 while on a combat mission. This caused a lot of concern to all the remaining pilots. We knew that the wings were weak, and one look at the aluminum waves on the wings created by G forces during pullouts was enough to scare anyone to death. After discussing this matter one evening, we decided that we would only use a one-half-G pullout on all future combat sorties. Normally we put around four Gs on the aircraft on a normal pullout on either bomb or strafing runs. Limiting ourselves to one-half-G pullouts was not a pleasant thought, as it would expose us to far more enemy ground fire, and that didn't make any of us very happy.

With all of the problems associated with the old T-28s, I absolutely loved to fly them. The aircraft would take an incredible amount of abuse from enemy ground fire and still get the pilots back to their home base. Another significant thing about the T-28 was the fact that you could land it almost anywhere, regardless of the terrain. One thing that I have to admit in combat conditions is that the aircraft was not designed very well for instrument-type flying. Maybe back in the States with radar vectors, et cetera, it was OK, but not so in Vietnam. First of all, we had absolutely zero radar navigational aids of any kind. Oftentimes as you pulled off a bomb run somewhere out in the boondocks it was extremely difficult because of the jungle terrain that looked the same no matter which way you went to figure out which way was home.

One has to remember that we were flying "old" aircraft often at night in terrible weather conditions against sophisticated enemy ground-to-air defenses. Most of the flight instruments in the T-28 worked off a vacuum-type system. Should the instrument that was located in the back cockpit be broken, then the same instrument located in the front cockpit would work in reverse. You can imagine the problems that this created for an already stressed-out pilot.

One of the cover-up operations that I never liked was that of having to train the so-called Vietnamese pilots. The dual cockpit of the T-28 was ideal for this under normal flight conditions. As far as the world was concerned in 1963–64 we were supposed to be training South Vietnamese pilots for combat. Nothing could have been further from the truth—ask our good friend McNamara about this.

Whenever we had a combat flight on alert status at Bien Hoa, we had usually four undesirable Vietnamese soldiers assigned to us. These soldiers were kept locked up in a metal trailer located near the flight line. When we got scrambled, a South Vietnamese technical sergeant armed with a submachine gun would bring these young Vietnamese soldiers to our individual aircraft. He would then provide the soldiers with parachutes, a helmet and force them into the backseats of our T-28s. As he strapped them in the backseats he always told them in Vietnamese that if they touched anything in the cockpit during the flight we would kill them. The main idea was that should we get shot down and killed, there would be a Vietnamese body onboard the aircraft. This then would provide the cover-up for our secret operations from the media.

What frequently happened was that these undisciplined Vietnamese soldiers would get bored after several hours in the backseat. Because they were usually short people, they would then place their feet up on the instrument panel to stabilize themselves as we rolled the aircraft over into a split-S type maneuver for a bomb run. By doing this they many times broke the glass covering the instruments in the rear cockpit, and we usually wouldn't know it until we flew into IFR flight conditions. As a result of these instruments working backwards we spent a lot of hectic time when we were forced to fly through a cloud formation.

Another problem that plagued us was oftentimes whenever we went into a vertical dive these undisciplined soldiers would kick the stick or try to help the pilot pull the aircraft out of the dive. This really had a tendency to piss off our pilots, especially as they were concentrating on a target during a bomb run. Usually what the pilots would do to prevent this from happening again was during their pulloff from the target roll the aircraft inverted and blow the rear canopy open. At the same time, the pilots would jockey the stick back and forth while in inverted flight. Normally this would get the rear occupant's attention, and he would very rarely ever touch the stick again. I must say that on a few occasions the soldiers would fall out of the aircraft, and to my knowledge nothing was ever said about the loss. None of the pilots in our section liked the idea of having inexperienced and untrained pilots in the backseat, but that was the way it was.

This was the second "political war" that I had fought in, and sometimes it was difficult to believe in what we were doing. I just kept the thought in front of me that if I should survive this hazardous duty assignment, then I would have my choice of aircraft and bases. Secretary McNamara's Rules of Engagement that we had to operate under often placed us in a very hazardous situation. For example, we couldn't fire upon an enemy unless he shot at us first. What a stupid rule that was! All it accomplished was to force us as American fighting men to expose ourselves more than we should have. I can assure you that after being scrambled and arriving over a hot target area we would do anything to get the VC to fire at us.

This procedure of getting the VC to fire at us brought about a number of amusing incidents in the air. First of all, we could not engage the VC on the ground even though we could plainly see them, unless a FAC told us that the VC were shooting at us. In this case the FAC usually then cleared us into the target. We always hoped for American FACs, but many times there were South Vietnamese FACs in the O-1s. After a scramble from home base, the flight of T-28s would proceed out a specific heading and fly for a certain amount of time. Normally the flight would set up an orbit at 2,000 feet while our flight leader would make every effort to contact whatever FAC we were supposed to be working with for that mission.

If the FAC was an American, he was always on frequency and waiting for us. If the FAC was a South Vietnamese pilot, he usually would not answer our radio calls. When this occurred, the T-28s would circle the target area until someone finally spotted the FAC. Once we found the FAC, the pilot who located him would have the honor of zooming down below him at a great airspeed and pulling up right in front of him. This maneuver usually resulted in the FAC's immediate loss of control of his aircraft, occasionally causing him to go into a spin. Whenever this occurred, the FAC upon recovery would rapidly come up on the proper frequency and provide us with all sorts of target information. Usually within minutes he would mark the target with an air-to-ground rocket and clear us in.

For the new pilot like me, it was difficult enough to find my way around flying during the day and at night it was almost impossible. One of the most interesting things about night missions was finding the actual location of the target. Most often our flight would arrive over the target area and the FAC would say to us, "Watch for the fire arrow" on the ground. Fire arrows were very primitive devices, oftentimes just a large piece of wood shaped like an arrow with burning pots depicting the head of the arrow. The idea was for the friendly ground forces to show us which way the VC were coming in from.

If we were fortunate enough to have communications relayed from the ground forces through the airborne FAC, they would many times request us to drop our ordnance as close as twenty meters off the point of the arrow. This was not always easy to accomplish. Once a pilot rolled his aircraft over and started downward he was frequently distracted by the large amount of enemy tracer bullets flying up at the aircraft. Target acquisition not only was difficult, but trying to drop a 500-pound bomb twenty meters from the end of a flaming arrow was not the easiest thing to do. If the pilot gave it any thought, he would quickly realize that a 500-pound bomb would completely destroy anything within fifty meters of ground zero. My heart really went out to those guys on the ground, and just trying to respond to their many urgent requests often placed us in very hazardous situations. I often flew missions where the defenders, when getting overrun by the VC, requested ordnance drops at ground zero. This was never a pleasant task to accomplish, as we invariably lost communications with the defenders. When this occurred, we could only zero in on the antiaircraft gun emplacements that were firing at us.

There were so many things that we as pilots did with the T-28s that were "not in the book." This next incident will provide the reader with a good idea of how we as pilots did things using good old American common sense. When I arrived in Vietnam in 1963, I was of the impression that I was a member of the most professional air force in the world. My positive thinking was put to the test during the next several months in so many small ways that it was hard to believe. The use and delivery of napalm bombs was a thing that none of the T-28 pilots had ever experienced before. One day while we were at Bien Hoa, a large shipment of napalm arrived and we all wondered what the stuff was. Napalm in its generic state looks exactly like Blue Cheer soap. We had received many calls by friendly forces for us to use napalm, especially when their positions were under direct attack by the VC. At the time, we had no way of dispensing napalm.

Our section ops officer, however, was quick to figure out a way that we could possibly make use of the napalm. He returned one day from Saigon with a truckload of WW II 750-gallon aviation drop tanks that he had located in an old warehouse outside of the city. These drop tanks were made available to the French Air Force shortly after the close of WW II. It seems that the U.S. Navy was directed by Congress to provide the French Air Force with two complete wings (approximately 150 aircraft) of the latest Navy fighter, the F-8. The drop tanks were part of the U.S. Lend-Lease Package and were designed to extend the combat range of the F-8. The F-8 was a small yet heavy and unusual fighter and difficult to fly under any circumstances by anyone. The primary problem was that the aircraft was way overpowered. In addition, the landing gear was too close to the fuselage, thus causing stability problems especially on landings on unimproved runways. If you used full engine power on takeoff, the aircraft would snap roll, just about the time that the plane broke ground, and would usually spoil your whole day. The problem was that there wasn't enough vertical rudder to control the yaw caused by the tremendous torque of the engine. It turned out that the French had a lot of problems flying the F-8s, especially while flying them off unimproved jungle airstrips. By late 1954 most of the original F-8s that had been given to the French were lost and scattered throughout the Vietnamese countryside.

Luckily for us, these F-8 drop tanks required very little modification and would fit snuggly into the wing bomb racks of the T-28. We did, however, encounter a number of other small problems, the least of which was how to set the bombs off once they were dropped. One of our ground crew members solved the problem for us. He was able to get hold of some thermite hand grenades, and with a little modification these grenades were installed into the napalm bomb in place of the fuel caps.

The neat thing about the thermite grenades was that they had a little propeller on top of them and it only had to make one revolution to arm itself. By running an arming wire from the bomb rack through the grenade propeller the system was made safe until released. Our next problem was that no one knew exactly how much Blue Cheer to pour into the 750-gallon tanks. Remembering from my combat experience in Korea, I mentioned that one had to mix the napalm with aviation gasoline and then let it set up overnight very much like Jell-O. Everyone thought this was a good idea, and that afternoon we installed four F-8 belly-tank napalm bombs under the wings of two T-28s. Capt. Jim Tally and I would fly out the next morning and see what kind of success our operation was. I was curious that night as to how these very old WW II belly tanks would hold up.

From my days as a plane captain on F4-U Corsairs while in the Marine Corps I remember the excitement when we had napalm missions scheduled the next morning. The plane captains had to arrive at the flight line early and warm the Corsairs' engines up. The napalm, having been mixed and poured the night before, would coagulate in the tanks. By morning this blue mixture would ooze out around the igniter tank caps, hanging in large gobblets over the sides of the napalm tanks. Corsairs all had what was known as down-type draft carburetors installed in them. When the engine was primed with raw fuel for the first morning start, the raw gas from the carburetors ran down into the exhaust stacks and always caught on fire. The napalm bombs were always snuggled up tight against the underside of the Corsair's wings between the landing gears and right below the exhaust stacks. As the burning gas exited the exhaust stacks it usually fell right on top of the napalm bombs. The sticky residue of napalm that was coagulated around the igniter caps on top of the napalm bombs always caught fire and literally scared the heck out of the plane captains as they sat in the cockpits of the Corsairs. There was many a morning that I held my breath while watching the napalm burn off the sides of the napalm tanks.

Our first several napalm missions out of Bien Hoa were total failures. As the bombs were released they tumbled through the air, eventually striking the ground. Quite often upon impact the thermite grenades would be ejected into the sky and we got zero fireballs. When this happened, the pilots had to return low-level and strafe the jellied mess in order to get it to burn. This very low-level type flying was not conducive to long life for pilots engaged in combat situations. Also, the napalm when finally ignited by our tracer bullets just didn't burn effectively, as there was no fireball, just a large kerosene fire. The T-28 section at the time was really chagrined with the results of these test flights.

After our trial napalm drop missions Captain Tally and I did agree on one thing: no matter what the situation, a pilot dropping napalm should always drop both tanks at once. We discovered that with a 750-gallon weapon hanging under just one wing there wasn't enough aileron and rudder left on the T-28 to hold both wings level. When a pilot delivers the napalm around thirty to fifty feet off the ground, if one bomb hangs up then there also isn't enough altitude to recover the aircraft safely.

We had a stand-down one night for our section due to inclement weather, and all of the T-28 pilots who were at Bien Hoa at the time congregated in the officers' club. We were doing the usual thing that all fighter pilots do when inactive, i.e., drinking, discussing missions, arguing combat tactics, and deciding who was the greatest jock. No one was feeling any pain when someone came up with the idea of a contest to enhance the poor performance we were having with the use of napalm. We eventually arrived at a consensus that each of us would put five dollars in a pot, with the winner of the contest taking all. Someone located a case of medium-sized Mason jars, and we were off and running. Into these jars we inserted a live fragmentation hand grenade with the pin pulled. We numbered all jars on the tops of the lids. Next we placed three tablespoons of Blue Cheer into each jar. Each pilot was given a numbered jar and told to embellish the contents of the jar with whatever secret mixture he wanted to include. He was then told to return the jar within one hour, wherein all jars would be locked up in the section safe for the night.

None of us were chemistry majors in college, so there were a lot of laughs about the contents of many jars. I personally put a tube of Colgate toothpaste, a dash of bourbon, and the powder out of a .45-caliber bullet into my jar. An hour later, when all jars were returned to the club, we filled each jar up to the brim with aviation gasoline and screwed the lids back on. Next morning all pilots assembled on the flight line with pencils and paper. This was going to be a democratic contest, with everyone in attendance judging the results. One of the base pilots volunteered to fly his Cessna O-1 aircraft with a volunteer in the backseat. Prior to takeoff the volunteer in the backseat was given a cardboard box with twenty-four Mason jars that had live hand grenades in them. The O-1 was to make twenty-four low-level passes down the taxiway, and on each pass the backseater would call off the number of the Mason jar and drop it as they flew by. As each Mason jar hit the ground and exploded we all rated the size of the fireball, using a simple scale of 1 to 10, with 10 being the best score.

The winner of our very professional contest was Capt. Brooks Morris. His fireball was definitely the largest and best, and we dubbed it the Madam Nhu Cocktail. Captain Brooks's secret contents turned out to be three tablespoons of Tide soap plus three charcoal briquettes. The next evening, to each 750-gallon tank we added a large economy-size box of Tide soap plus a large bag of charcoal briquettes. The results were fantastic, as we got giant fireballs out of each tank dropped. Very rarely from that day forward did we ever have to return and strafe a napalm bomb to get the contents to burn.

28
Ranch Hand Missions

With the buildup of UN forces in South Vietnam, large amounts of international marine ships were coming into and departing Saigon on a daily basis. New problems for the South Vietnamese government arose as a result of this increased shipping. Since the lowlands surrounding the Saigon area were predominantly located in a jungle environment, the VC would frequently shoot at the ships as they passed by. This had a tendency to make ship captains very nervous, and they complained on a daily basis to their respective embassies. As a result the South Vietnamese government requested assistance from our Military Advisory Group (MAGV), and the Ranch Hand Program was initiated.

Our "Trash Hauler" section quickly converted a number of their twin-engine C-123 cargo aircraft into crop dusters. They equipped the 123s with special spray nozzles under the trailing edges of their wings to dispense the herbicide chemicals that they would be using. Whenever a ship, whether coming into or departing Saigon, was fired upon by the VC, a defoliation mission was quickly scheduled for that particular canal or river.

Nothing ever works like it's supposed to, especially when a bureaucracy is involved in the process. This is true even in a combat zone. Even though it was a political-type war, I often wondered who was responsible for making some of the stupidest mistakes imaginable. The way in which the "Frag Order" worked was as follows: A request would come into MAGV requesting a defoliation mission. MAGV would then via Ops-Orders dispatch a U-10 psychological warfare aircraft out of Bien Hoa. This U-10 would then fly down both sides of the canal/river one week before the defoliation mission was going to take place, announcing the fact that at 0600 next Thursday the C-123s would be flying in to spray chemicals over this area. These U-10 utility aircraft also carried powerful loudspeakers that broadcast tape-recorded propaganda messages and dropped leaflets to the VC who lived along the waterways. We often called these guys the Bullshit Bombers, but they probably received more enemy ground fire than anyone else did. Exactly twenty-four hours prior to the defoliation mission the same U-10 pilot would again fly over the area and using his powerful speakers, tell the people to get out of harm's way the next morning. What really irritated us was that the real message to the VC was that "Hey, VC, get your guns oiled up, as tomorrow morning at 0600 there will be a turkey shoot for you." And nine out of ten times there was!

The ground fire from the VC guns got so bad that the C-123s would often abort their missions unless they had T-28 fighters to escort and protect them. Having flown sixty-six of these Ranch Hand escort missions, I fully understand how the guys inside the C-123s felt. If the 123s went in without our protection, they would frequently lose an aircraft and crew, plus the remaining members of their flight would get the dickens shot out of their aircraft.

When we first started escorting the C-123s, they were defoliating with a herbicide called Agent Purple. It was followed sometime in late 1963 with a new herbicide called Agent Orange. No one knew at the time what the herbicide actually was; it just came in fifty-gallon drums with an orange or purple stripe on the outside of the container. Hence the name Agent Orange/Purple stuck with everybody. We quickly discovered that this undiluted herbicide when used at 100 percent was absolutely lethal to any kind of plant it touched. Right after a defoliation mission you could actually watch the leaves fall off the trees and other plants. I know that the U-10s were telling the VC that this chemical wouldn't hurt their children and animals, but I never believed it for a minute.

When an MAGV Ops-Order came down to escort a Ranch Hand mission, we usually sent a three-ship fighter escort for every two C-123s involved in the mission. The way the mission worked was that the lead fighter would have iron bombs and guns available and once joined up would lead the gaggle (five airplanes in trail) by flying down the defoliation track about twenty feet off the ground. The lead C-123 would be right behind the lead T-28 at about fifty foot altitude dispensing his herbicide. The number two T-28, armed with two 750-pound cans of napalm plus guns, would fly directly behind the lead C-123 at about two-hundred-foot altitude. The idea was that if any VC machine gun opened up on the lead C-123, the number-two T-28 would roll in instantly and napalm the machine gun. The second C-123 would be right behind the number-two T-28, and as long as there was no ground fire he would drop down to fifty feet or so and commence his defoliation run. The third T-28 would be armed with iron bombs, guns, and rockets. He would follow the second C-123, only he would remain at 1000-foot altitude. Should anything out of the ordinary occur, the third T-28 was in position to bomb and strafe any target in the area. The stacking of our fighters much like the steps of a staircase proved to be very sound and quite effective. In most circumstances the VC would not fire on the C-123s if they had fighter escort, and this made the C-123 crews extremely happy.

On April 1, 1964, I was assigned to a Ranch Hand mission, #91126. I was flying the number-two T-28 in a flight of three-T-28s, and therefore, I would be carrying the napalm on this particular mission. The target area was located along the Song Long Tao River about 110 miles south of Bien Hoa. It was the first napalm mission that I had flown in some time, and for some reason my thinking cap was not on for this mission. We proceeded south after takeoff and quickly rendezvoused with two C-123s that were climbing on-course to the target area. We spent several minutes arranging our flight and then proceeded to the target area, descending all the while.

Receiving our clearance from the Command Post, the lead T-28 descended and began his sweep of the target area. The lead T-28 was followed immediately by the lead C-123, which began to spray his Agent Orange chemicals. As I looked down, I saw a dual-mounted antiaircraft gun open up on the lead C-123. I called the lead T-28 and told him that I was in hot on a VC antiaircraft gun. Here is where things got real crazy. The VC gun emplacement was located at the apex of a canal that split into a Y. Instead of using the jungle foliage to cover my approach, I came straight down the stem of the Y about five feet off the canal water. My aircraft was so low that I was picking up water with my propeller during my approach. Looking at the target area, I became mesmerized by the tracer bullets arching toward me in what appeared like counterrevolutionary circles. The VC bullets seemed to be floating in the air, forming a large tunnel that I was flying through. I was so distracted that I failed to fire my own machine guns at the gun emplacement, and I couldn't figure out why none of the enemy bullets were striking my aircraft.

This was all happening very rapidly, yet it seemed like things were happening in slow motion. The strange part was that the VC bullets were indeed striking my aircraft and I just didn't realize it, as I was concentrating so hard on the target. The next dumb thing that I did was violate the very same combat tactics that I had helped to develop in delivering napalm on a target. While in my opinion flying a perfect approach, I only armed and subsequently dropped the right napalm tank beneath my aircraft. What happened next is difficult to describe, and I am not quite sure why I am here today to explain what happened. As the 750-gallon napalm bomb dropped off my right wing the aircraft lurched, and suddenly I didn't have enough rudder and aileron to get the left wing up and level. I was only approximately twenty feet in the air and things were happening in microseconds. I had applied full throttle and was straining to both pull the nose of the aircraft up using full right rudder and right aileron. With both hands on the stick I couldn't release the back pressure and reach the salvo switch located on the front instrument panel.

To this day I do not fully understand how I recovered from this stupid mistake and lived to tell about it. I did somehow manage to hit the salvo button, but at the same time my left wing was striking bushes on the ground and for sure I thought I was going to crash. My belief in "guardian angels" improved considerably after this flight. After returning and landing at Bien Hoa, the ground crew counted twenty-three bullet holes in my aircraft. I caught hell from the T-28 section commander and from the other pilots who were flying with me for failure to follow my own combat delivery techniques. That evening I bought a round at the bar for everyone. Sometimes I really think that someone was looking out for me. Strange things happen in combat, and there often is no reasonable way to defend or describe the actions that you took. In this case I was just flat lucky to be alive.

All Ranch Hand missions were considered dangerous by all personnel involved in flying them mainly because of the constant exposure to intense enemy ground fire. The extreme low-level type flying that we had to do in order to provide fire support to the C-123s also compounded the exposure problem. I always had the feeling that all T-28s were built by the John Deere Tractor Company, simply because of the large amount of battle damage that they could sustain and yet still bring the pilot home.

An incident occurred during one of our Ranch Hand missions on April 24, 1964, that I would like to describe. On that date while operating in the IV Corps area of South Vietnam we launched four T-28s out of Soc Trang Air Base at 0520 to provide escort for the four C-123 Ranch Hand aircraft. Of the four T-28s, I was flying in the number-two position and was carrying two 500-gallon canisters of napalm, plus two rocket pods under each wing. All of our F-8 belly tank napalm bombs came in only the 750-gallon size. Since we had experienced major flight control problems trying to release a single 750-gallon canister, we decided to reduce the contents of the napalm inside the F-8 belly tanks to 500 gallons. Should anything go wrong and a napalm tank fail to release, pilots still had enough rudder and aileron left to be able to control the aircraft without crashing.

We rendezvoused with the C-123s over the town of Vinh Loi and proceeded south to the tip of the Ca Mau Peninsula, where the C-123s were to defoliate an area that contained a large number of VC insurgents. The weather from the rendezvous point to and including the target area was inclement, with thunderstorms, heavy rain, and ceilings that varied from 300 feet up to 2,000 feet.

Upon our reaching the target area, the weather was so bad that we had to revise our approach into the target area. As the C-123s were maneuvering into position, they flew over the northern boundary of the target area. Figuring that the C-123s were coming in at this point, the VC gunners had set up a trap, and they opened fire on the C-123s using three well-emplaced heavy machine guns. Watching the incoming tracer bullets, I called the C-123 flight leader and told him to break left immediately. I informed my flight leader that I was going in hot on one of the enemy gun emplacements in an effort to draw the attention away from the other two heavily loaded and slow-flying C-123s. With both of my machine guns blazing, I headed straight for one of the gun emplacements at approximately twenty feet of altitude and delivered one of my 500-gallon napalm bombs. I don't know how many hits I took from the VC guns, but my engine was still running smoothly when I pulled off. Without hesitation, at approximately fifty feet of altitude I yanked the old T-28 around and went straight for the second enemy gun emplacement. Luck was riding with me, as I dropped the second canister of napalm directly on the second VC gun emplacement.

All of this action was happening very fast, and at the completion of my second napalm drop I pulled up to allow the number-four T-28 to take my place in the formation, as he still had two canisters of napalm. The defoliation mission went ahead as planned from the now burned-out entry point until the C-123s reached the last 500 yards of their combat flight plan. It was at this point that the unexpected happened. The VC had set up gun emplacements at both the original entry point and exit points. The lead C-123, as he pulled off his defoliation run at approximately fifty feet of altitude, came under intense enemy ground fire. Realizing what was about to happen, I called for the lead C-123 to break right immediately in order to get away from the hostile ground fire. The problem was that the C-123 wasn't moving fast enough to get away from the hostile enemy ground fire. The C-123 already had smoke coming from his starboard engine as I made my move.

There wasn't time to strafe the gun emplacements, so with full throttle I dived down somewhere between twenty and thirty feet of altitude and placed my aircraft beneath the crippled C-123, allowing him more time to get away. I knew that I was absorbing the brunt of the enemy gunfire, but there were more people onboard the C-123 than there were in my T-28. While pulling away, my aircraft received repeated hits in the left wing area, but I managed to maintain control as I headed away from the target area. The crippled C-123 sustained major battle damage and made an emergency landing at nearby Ca Mau. Rejoining my own flight, I was able to make it back to Soc Trang. It was discovered after landing that my T-28 had suffered severe damage to the left wing, requiring a complete wing change before the aircraft was flyable again. The maintenance ground crew figured that I had received somewhere over fifty enemy bullet hits in my aircraft on this mission. Once again my faith and confidence in the old T-28 was renewed, and I silently thanked the North American Aviation Company for this great airplane.

29

Nha Trang and the Green Berets

We could never figure out how they did it, but the VC had pictures of all the T-28 pilots who had been assigned to units in South Vietnam. These pictures were distributed throughout South Vietnam and much like the "wanted posters" of the old West, their posters advertised 44,000 U.S. dollars for the head of any pilot. This figure equated to around $144,000 on the South Vietnamese black market. Early in December two of our pilots were shot down, and before we could get a helicopter in to pick them up the VC had captured them. One of the problems that we experienced, should any of us survive a crash, was that all we had to defend ourselves from the VC was either a .38- or .45-caliber pistol and it just wasn't enough to keep the VC away. In both instances the VC cut the heads off the American pilots and paraded the heads throughout the nearby local villages.

We were discussing this problem one evening in our club when I informed my section commander that I possibly had a solution to our problem. I told him that I was certain that I could get enough submachine guns so that everyone in the section could have one. The idea was that should one of us get shot down, he could at least have enough firepower with him to keep the VC at bay until we could effect a rescue. I informed Major Lengfield that I had a good friend who was a Snake-eater and that he was stationed at the Green Beret headquarters in Nha Trang. I figured the price for the submachine guns would be several cases of good gin. A frag order came out the next day and one of my good friends, Bob Schoen, was to accompany me up to Nha Trang on the following day.

We took off that next morning with four cases of Beefeater's gin strapped into our backseats. Nha Trang, our destination, was a coastal city and located about four hundred miles northeast of Bien Hoa. When Karl (my Army buddy from Travis AFB) and I departed last October, he told me that he would be going to the headquarters for the Green Berets, which was located in Nha Trang. He also told me that if I should ever need any help with guns or anything, to look him up. Later that same morning, arriving over Nha Trang, we discovered that there was no airfield at that time in the immediate area. We did see helicopters on the ground but no landing strip for a fixed-wing aircraft.

As we were looking around, I saw an American jeep coming down a dusty road toward town. I told Bob to stay at altitude while I let down to make sure that the jeep was driven by an American. On my first pass I crossed so low in front of the jeep that the driver while skidding to a halt almost turned his vehicle over. As I swung back around, the driver was shaking his fist at me. I wagged my wings at him and placed my landing gear and flaps into the down position. The field alongside the road didn't look too bad, and I informed Bob that I was going to land as close to the jeep as I could. I also told Bob to cover me with guns until I established contact with the jeep driver.

After landing I taxied over as close as I could get to the road and motioned for the driver of the jeep to come over to my aircraft. I was happy to note that the driver of the jeep was a technical sergeant and very definitely a Green Beret. The good sergeant climbed up on my wing and over the noise of the aircraft engine he told me that the headquarters for the Green Berets was indeed just down the road. I radioed Bob telling him to land and to taxi over and pull in behind me so that we had guns pointing both ways should we need them.

Once Bob was safely on the ground and in place, we cut our engines and told the sergeant that we needed to borrow his jeep. We informed him that we wouldn't be gone too long and that we would give him a forty-ounce bottle of gin to guard our aircraft until we returned. He was really nice and quickly agreed to our request. The sergeant said that it wasn't every day that two Air Force fighter planes dropped out of the sky and landed next to him. I'm sure that he was a little surprised, especially when we proceeded to load four cases of gin into his jeep, but he didn't say anything. Once we had the jeep loaded we took off for town, and once we were in town locating the Green Beret headquarters area was not difficult.

We asked the first person we came to, if he knew Lieutenant Bronson, and the soldier told us to follow him. Karl came out of a tent with a wild yell upon seeing us. We bear-hugged and slapped each other for several minutes with both of us trying to talk at the same time. While this was going on Bob walked back to the jeep and, borrowing a steel helmet from one of the soldiers standing around, poured the helmet full of gin. We passed the helmet around until it was empty. I told Karl why we were there and what we needed. We then presented him with what was left of the four cases of gin. I also told him that we had left one of his sergeants guarding our aircraft. Karl said that he would get a detail out immediately with more firepower to relieve the sergeant, and for us to not worry about our aircraft.

Karl insisted that we stay the night and gave us a choice of an Army cot or a room in a nearby French hotel. We both opted for the hotel, and Karl, after getting the gin stashed away, drove us the short distance to the hotel and got us registered. The hotel, which was run by French-speaking Vietnamese people, was actually what I would call a motel, as it was a single-storied affair with room for parking cars in front of the individual units. The rooms were small, with two single beds, but certainly adequate for our needs. We threw what little gear we had on the beds and returned with Karl to visit the Green Beret compound. We met Karl's commanding officer, explaining what we needed and why, and he was most helpful, telling Karl to fix us up with as many weapons as we needed. All of the Green Berets in the compound wanted to go out and look at our aircraft, as none of them had ever seen these fighters up close. Bob told the commander that he would accompany as many men as wanted to look at the T-28s, and everyone was excited about that.

Karl told us that he was taking us to dinner that evening and that it would be a dinner that we would never forget, and he was absolutely right! We tried our best to remain sober that afternoon, but I'm not sure who won, i.e., the bottle or us. We departed the Green Beret compound in a jeep just before sunset, and Karl drove for about forty-five minutes south along the coastline. Arriving at the restaurant, we were met at the door by the restaurant owner, according to Karl, who requested that we check our weapons prior to entering the restaurant. Karl then told us that there would most likely be some VC officers eating in the same restaurant that night. Karl said that an agreement had been worked out by the restaurant owner so that everyone was safe once inside the restaurant. It reminded me of the old days of the West wherein local sheriffs made everyone check their guns when they came to town.

Although I was a little uncomfortable with the VC officers in the same room, the meal itself was outstanding. With Karl ordering in the native language we had lobster tails the likes of which I have never seen. Each individual lobster tail must have weighed between three and five pounds. The house wine was also excellent, and we most certainly drank our share of it. Collecting our hardware upon leaving the restaurant, we drove out to where our aircraft were parked, and sure enough, Green Berets were guarding both T-28s. I have no idea how much liquor I drank that afternoon and evening, but it was plenty. Returning to Karl's tent, we opened another bottle of gin and shared the contents with a number of his buddies. After several rounds of drink, Karl wanted us to go downtown and see a local French sex show. Bob said that he was too tired and would Karl drop him off at our motel. Neither one of us could remember the room number, but we knew approximately where it was located. I told Bob to leave the door slightly ajar several inches and that I would be back in an hour or so.

What happened next is still funny to me even this many years later. A couple of hours later Karl brought me back to the motel and dropped me off. Even today I do admit to being slightly inebriated. I staggered down the side of the courtyard where our room was located until I found a door that was slightly ajar and entered the room. There was a body in one of the beds, and I didn't pay any attention to it; I just assumed that it was Bob. It was a typical Vietnamese motel room as there was only a small night-light burning and the room smelled awful. Besides the two small beds there was a half-wall separating the bedroom from the bathroom. As in most Vietnamese bathrooms, the men urinated on the wall and there was a small collection tray located at the base of the wall. For women there was a small slit trench that emptied into the same collection tray. They did provide a bucket of water to rinse the place out with, but you can imagine the smell.

I was standing in the latrine portion of the room getting rid of some of the beer when I looked up and noticed a pair of women's panties, plus a brassiere on top of the half-wall. My initial reaction was, *That son of a gun Bob.* I stepped around the corner and ripped the sheet off what I thought was Bob. What a shock I was in, for there lay a naked American woman. It turned out to be Jennie from Saigon, for the second time in my life! After she put her pistol down I explained what had happened, and we both then had a good laugh. She was not aware that her door had been ajar. She told me that she was in Nha Trang trying to do a story on the Green Berets' activities, but that she wasn't having much luck getting inside their compound. I told her that I could take care of that the next day.

The next morning when Karl came over to pick us up, I introduced Jennie to Karl. I was certain that Karl would give her all the information that she wanted to know about their activities. In any event, we spent most of the day on the local beach, planning our takeoff for late that afternoon. Karl told us that I had all of the submachine guns in my aircraft, while Bob was carrying all of the ammunition in his backseat. Arriving late that same evening at Bien Hoa, we unloaded our aircraft and discovered that we had thirty-nine submachine guns of every make and possible description. Bob and I had our pick of the lot; then we let the other guys fight over who wanted what. I decided on a WW II Tanker's M3A1 .45-caliber submachine gun because the clip held thirty rounds. I taped two separate clips upside down to the first clip, giving me a total of ninety rounds of ammunition. For a fun weapon I kept a Thompson submachine gun because it looked macho and I remember John Wayne carrying one in most of his WW II combat movies. With everyone having a submachine gun, the section morale improved considerably. During the next several months, we had guys get shot down, but we never lost another pilot to the VC, thanks again to the Green Berets.

30

Back to Bien Hoa

There was only one South Vietnamese Army in South Vietnam, and it was stationed at Bien Hoa. Bien Hoa in 1963–64 was the largest base for military operations in the country. To our delight there was a 13,000-foot concrete runway. The 1st Air Commando Squadron (Composite) was located on the southwest side of the Vietnamese base, as far away as we could get from the Vietnamese ground troops. We lived in a tent city, with wooden pallets forming the walkways between tents. We combined several large tents together to form both a small mess hall and an adequate officers' club. Since we were involved in covert-type operations, military regulations were very lax and we found that we could wear anything that we wanted for flying purposes. Due to the excessive heat and high humidity conditions I quickly modified my flying suits by cutting the legs and sleeves off them. At first I carried all sorts of things in my survival vest such as clean socks, an extra T-shirt, a fishing kit, cigarettes, candy, a first-aid kit, a whistle, plus many other dumb things that I considered important. After several combat flights I wound up carrying nothing but spare ammunition in the survival vest.

The 1st Air Commando Squadron adopted Australian bush hats as our daily headgear, with a 1st ACS patch located on the turned-up portion of the side of the hat. Most guys had cobra-skin bands around the tops of their hats. The way it worked, a pilot had to get a bullet hole in his aircraft before he could wear the cobra-skin band. It took me seventy combat missions before I earned my cobra-skin band. This snake band may seem but a small thing to most people, but in those days it was a mark of distinction and everyone yearned for one. Most all T-28 pilots had cobra-skin bands except me. I would often fly missions where one aircraft might get shot down by enemy ground fire and everyone else would get hit at least one or more times, but not me. It got so bad that while I was back at Bien Hoa guys started calling me the Preacher. If I was walking down one of the wooden pallet walkways and someone was coming toward me, he would step off in the mud and just stare at me as I passed by. I told one of my bunkmates whom I flew many combat missions with that on the next mission (number 70) I was going to land for a few minutes on one of the many dirt roads leading to Saigon while on the way home. My idea was to take my submachine gun and spray the tail section of my aircraft just so I could be "one of the guys." Fate solved the problem for me the next day, as I picked up my first VC bullet hole on mission number 70 and subsequently became "one of the guys." I will explain this mission later.

Living anywhere in South Vietnam in 1963–64 as an American was always stressful. Since there was a $144,000 price on all fighter pilots' heads, all of the South Vietnamese felt obliged to shoot at us. As a result of both friendly and enemy gunfire, we lost four aircraft shot down in the traffic pattern at Bien Hoa. Too many times as a pilot pitched out while in the traffic pattern over the confines of the base there at Bien Hoa he could see South Vietnamese troops shooting at him. It gave one a very uncomfortable feeling, especially when we were supporting the South Vietnamese government in their fight for democracy. After we lost the fourth aircraft, we decided to do something about it regardless of whom we attacked.

Mostly the South Vietnamese troops would fire at the slower-moving support-type aircraft, unless they could catch a T-28 on final approach. One morning we launched a DC-3 on what looked like a normal mission. About thirty minutes after the DC-3 took off, we launched an O-1 FAC aircraft, then fifteen minutes later scrambled two T-28s, both armed with napalm canisters. To anyone watching, this would appear to be part of a normal day's combat operation. On a normal mission we would then fly out several miles from the base and establish contact with the DC-3. We would then tell the DC-3 pilot to make a normal approach for landing at Bien Hoa. Usually what happened next was that either the VC or the outer South Vietnamese base guards who were hidden in the tree line that ran parallel to the runway would open fire on the unsuspecting DC-3. The second that this happened we would leave our low orbit descending at maximum speed and drop all four 750-pound napalm canisters along the tree line. This was a very effective combat technique, and usually no one got shot at for three or more weeks in or around Bien Hoa. I was always surprised that the South Vietnamese base commander never said a word to our commander about this procedure. It was as if he knew about it and just didn't want to say anything.

We, for the most part, always took off from Bien Hoa with a heavy load of ordnance on our aircraft. Probably the most terrifying experience of all my combat flying occurred during these early-morning takeoffs from Bien Hoa. Strong VC forces continually operated just to the north of our base. Oftentimes during the night the VC would set up a .50-caliber machine gun just north of the runway. It was during these early-morning flights that the VC would wait until the T-28s just broke ground and were in the most critical phase of flight. Suddenly just in front of the aircraft would appear incoming tracer bullets. Fortunately, the VC were poor marksmen, but the floating tracer bullets would most certainly get the pilot's attention. As quick as we could get our gear and flaps up, we would turn away from the gun positions until we got enough altitude and airspeed. We would normally be too low to drop iron bombs, so we would turn directly back into the machine-gun positions and rake the entire area with our own guns. This maneuver, although dangerous due to our heavy loads, usually stopped the VC gunners.

31

Soc Trang

Soc Trang was located in the IV Corps area of South Vietnam, about 120 nautical miles southeast of Bien Hoa. The major river of Vietnam, the Mekong, separated itself into four major branches after exiting Cambodia. Soc Trang itself was about twelve miles south of the southernmost branch of the four branches of the Mekong River. The U.S. Army's 121st helicopter squadron owned the base. They called themselves The Soc Trang Tigers, and the Army aviators all wore a patch on their left sleeve depicting a tiger flying a helicopter. The aircraft that they flew were Shawnee H-21s. The H-21 looked like a flying banana with twin rotors, and the only weapons they carried were door gunners.

I quickly learned that these Army aviators were indeed among the unsung heroes of the Vietnam War. It was incredible what those guys could do with one of those flying bananas. I have escorted the H-21s on many combat assault missions and could not begin to explain how courageous or heroic those Army aviators were. In order to perform our escort over the H-21s, we had to slow our T-28s down to seventy knots in order to stay with them. This meant that the pilot had to fly the T-28 with the canopy open plus having both the gear and flaps down as he slowly wove the fighter back and forth over the assault helicopters. While circling overhead many times while looking down I watched in horror, as you could see the enemy bullets fly right through the sides of the H-21s.

Like all good military units, the army guys slept in tents just like ours. However, with what limited resources they had they built an officers' club right next to their flight line. Much like the Air Force personnel at Bien Hoa, the Army guys combined several large tents together; however, the Army guys built wooden sides all around their club, which added just the right touch to make it a special place. Outside this club their mascot, a 241-pound Bengal tiger, was tied to a stake during the daytime. During the evenings while most of us were eating our supper the tiger was allowed loose inside the club. The Army guys kept a large bowl of gin on the floor near one end of the bar for the tiger. Never having been around a large cat of this size, although he was docile, according to the Army guys, I did my best to keep my distance from him. As a morale thing each of the Army aviators had his picture taken with this tiger and all of their pictures lined the walls of their club.

Food was something else while we were TDY from Bien Hoa. When in the field we only had a choice of which C ration we were going to eat, and none of them were very good. One of the pleasures of being at Soc Trang was the wonderful resourcefulness of the Army aviators. They had somehow secured an old flat-surfaced wood stove and placed it in one corner of their club. Every few days the Army would dispatch a helicopter to Saigon and the crew would return with a load of steak, ham, or turkey. The Army guys hired a Vietnamese cook from the local village to come in every night and prepare meals for the officers. What a marvelous thing this was for us.

Solving the furniture problem for the Army club was an easy one. Since there were lots of trees in the nearby forests, we borrowed a chain saw from the civil engineers at Bien Hoa and cut a number of trees down. From these downed trees we made small tables with accompanying stump chairs to fit, and placed them throughout the club. One of the situations that we never solved was the hunger problem of the tiger. The tiger always seemed to be walking around somewhere in the club whenever we wanted to eat. All we had for dishes were the top halves of military mess kits. This proved to be somewhat awkward, especially when trying to cut a steak while trying to balance the mess kit on your knees. To this day I feel that the Hoover Vacuum Company got their secret patent from a Bengal tiger. I would swear that this crazy tiger could turn his head from three feet away and suck the steak off your plate faster than you could imagine. And there was absolutely nothing that a person could do about it, short of getting mauled.

Because the Air Force fighter pilots had saved so many of the Army aviators' lives during their assault missions, we could not buy a drink while in their club. We didn't worry too much about this, as the cost of a drink was only five cents. The thought was there, for those Army aviators, and we truly appreciated it. By February of

1964 we were down to about fourteen T-28 pilots left in the country. Since we were so few in number, we gave up trying to maintain fighters at Danang in the I Corps and later at Pleikeu in the II Corps. During this time period most of the rough ground fighting had shifted to the III and IV Corps areas. We still responded and flew missions into the I and II Corps areas upon request, but it was difficult to remain over a target area for any length of time due to our fuel consumption and the distance to recovery bases. In addition, it was extremely difficult to navigate when flying over the mountains located in the I and II Corps areas. About this same time, the 34th Group commander decided to consolidate what few fighters he had left between the III and IV Corps areas of operations. This new consolidation between the Third and Four Corps for T-28 pilots provided far more familiarity with the surrounding countryside and made it much easier to navigate for everyone concerned. At the time of this consolidation I just happened to be at Soc Trang, so that is where I flew most of my remaining combat missions.

Due to inclement weather one night, we stood down and partied hard with the Army aviators in the club. The Army guys kept bugging us to have our pictures taken so they could be placed in positions of honor right above their main bar. We decided that we first had to have a commando mascot of our own, as none of us wanted to hold on to the tiger for a picture. The next day we sent our intelligence officer who could speak the Vietnamese language into the local villages to try to locate something special for us in the way of an animal. He certainly did not fail in his mission, as two days later he returned with the largest snake that I have ever seen. We were not sure whether the snake was a boa constrictor or a python, but he was between nineteen to twenty feet in length, depending on how he was stretched out. We also discovered that the snake was very docile and didn't seem to mind being around humans. We named the snake Charlie and estimated his weight to be somewhere between four and five hundred pounds. It was impossible for even two guys to pick up and hold Charlie.

Having never been around a snake of that size, I found him fascinating. The girth of Charlie was between two and three feet around, depending on where you grabbed him. Anyone could grab Charlie and hold on as tightly as he could and then could feel Charlie moving inside his skin—it was a weird feeling. We quickly built a very large chicken coop type cage and placed Charlie inside. He didn't seem to mind at all, and every evening around five o'clock the Intelligence officer would pick up Charlie behind his head and lead him out of his cage. Charlie would then follow the intelligence officer over to the nearby rice paddy, where Charlie was allowed to swim. The first few times that the Intel office did this we all held our breath as the rice paddies were all mined. However, Charlie never seemed to strike one of the mines while swimming. In the interim the Army was really pleased, as we all had our pictures taken with Charlie draped somewhere over or around our bodies. These pictures were carefully placed above the main bar in their club.

Because Charlie was so docile, his evening swim in the rice paddy became commonplace and no one thought anything about it. This was a grave mistake that almost cost the life of our intelligence officer. No one had given a thought to Charlie ever getting hungry. One evening when the intelligence officer came over to the cage to let Charlie out for his evening swim, Charlie grabbed the intelligence officer. Before anyone heard the screams, Charlie had gotten two coils around the intelligence officer. It took six guys to get Charlie unwound and off the intelligence officer, and Charlie was not pleased. We forced him back into his cage, and he was not a happy camper. His hissing was incredibly loud and really scary, and we worried that he would break out of his cage and attack someone else that night.

We had to have the Army's Dust-Off medical helicopter fly the intelligence officer to the hospital in Saigon that evening, as his rib cage was crushed and he was having difficulty breathing. We all decided that was one hell of a way to get a Purple Heart medal.

The next morning we talked several of the South Vietnamese soldiers into going to the nearby village to try to find some food for Charlie. Charlie in the meantime had settled down, but he had that hungry look about him and no one wanted to enter the cage that morning. A couple of hours later the South Vietnamese soldiers returned with four crates of ducks. There were sixteen ducks in all, and the soldiers said that supposedly this was what large snakes liked to eat. We therefore threw all sixteen ducks into Charlie's cage. For the next thirty minutes absolutely nothing happened and eventually we all got bored watching nothing happen.

Two days went by and still Charlie refused to admit that there were sixteen ducks in his lap. Finally we placed a chart on one of the walls of the club, and for a dollar a square you could guess when Charlie was going to eat these ducks. I can't remember exactly which day it was, but someone yelled and soon there was a large crowd surrounding Charlie's cage. Charlie had consumed all sixteen ducks and appeared to be sleeping with a smile on his face. One of the army aviators won the $350 Charlie Eating Pot.

Charlie quickly became famous throughout South Vietnam, and every visiting general and congressman from the States managed to finagle a trip to Soc Trang in order to have his picture taken with Charlie. One thing that we did not do was allow Charlie into the Army's club at night, what with the loose tiger. There was constant bickering about which animal would win should they be allowed to get together.

By March we were down from four to three operational aircraft at Soc Trang. We always had one more pilot than we had planes should someone get sick and could not fly. Since by this time American airpower in South Vietnam was hurting, we often found ourselves flying three to five combat missions a day, and everyone was getting tired. We rotated the flying schedule, allowing those who had the day off to sleep as much as possible. One of the problems that confronted all of us was excessive drinking. After flying two or three rough combat missions on a daily basis it was awful easy to drown your emotions in cocktails. I cannot remember a time in my life when I drank more alcohol than I did while in Vietnam. This is nothing to brag about; it was just a way of life for those of us who survived, and it did seem to calm the nerves. However, like many other things in life, it did eventually catch up with me.

Before I discuss this next mission let me describe Soc Trang in more detail. I mentioned earlier that the runway was somewhere between 2,600 and 3,200 feet long, but I failed to mention what happened to braking conditions when it rained on the compact dirt. It was like being out of control on snow skis. The Army kept their H-21 helicopters lined up the best they could up and down each side of the runway—this barely under normal landing conditions allowed enough room to slip between the large rotor blades

229

of the H-21s. We kept our T-28s on the northeast end of the base in sandbagged revetments. A dense jungle forest was located north of the base. On the east perimeter and farther out on the west side there were mined rice paddies that extended beyond the base for about a thousand yards.

There was a small wooden control tower, but there was no one to man it, which caused some hair-raising and very close near misses during takeoffs and landings between our aircraft and the Army's H-21s. To prevent mishaps we told the Army aviators that we would always buzz the base prior to our landings, and this seemed to work fairly well. Whenever we received a scramble order we taxied out and down the runway, regardless of which way the wind was blowing. This procedure let the Army know to clear the runway, that we were going to be taking off shortly. This procedure seemed to work out satisfactorily for everyone.

Flying at night in the Delta Area always presented major problems for us. First of all, and foremost, was just trying to locate the base whenever we returned, as there were no base lights at all. If we had three T-28s on alert at Soc Trang, we always had four pilots available. The fourth pilot had several important duties to perform. As soon as we launched in the evening he would drive up and down the flight line in an old pickup truck and place one-gallon cans of sand soaked with kerosene in strategic places. Upon our return the flight leader would make a low pass over the field and the fourth pilot would then race down the runway lighting the cans of kerosene. When he completed his lighting task, he would park the pickup truck on the end of the runway with the headlights on. It was difficult enough landing at Soc Trang during daylight conditions; however, when darkness and occasional incoming enemy tracer bullets were added to the equation every night landing had to be perfect.

Should the weather be marginal at Soc Trang, then we would have to recover back at Bien Hoa. This could make for a long and dangerous flight, and frequently when we did this our engines would be running on fumes by the time we located Bien Hoa. If we knew ahead of time that we couldn't get back into Soc Trang, then we would just head north after our combat mission until one of us spotted the city lights of Saigon.

By military regulations all military aircraft have anticollision lights installed on them. These are rotating red beacons located on the bottom and near the center of the aircraft fuselage. They are designed so that other aircraft can see you at night and to visually prevent midair collisions between aircraft. In South Vietnam these anticollision lights also provided a neat beacon for VC antiaircraft gunners, so unless absolutely necessary we did not use them. This made formation flight join-ups at night extremely difficult and called upon all the professionalism and skill of our guys. Often it became impossible for the number-three fighter after takeoff at night to locate the lead aircraft. He would then ask the lead to turn on his anticollision lights for a few minutes. Usually within seconds there would be a stream of incoming enemy antiaircraft tracers following the lead aircraft. That was one of the many reasons that none of us liked to be the lead aircraft, especially on night missions.

Generally, we flew all of our combat missions between 1500- and 1800-foot altitude. This was just enough altitude to keep out of antiaircraft-gun range. Occasionally we would run into heavier enemy gun emplacements and have to fly higher. Whenever this occurred the entire flight would be zigzagging around the sky in order to get away from the flying shrapnel. I don't recall ever losing a T-28 to enemy antiaircraft flak, but we did pick up occasional shrapnel holes in our flying machines when flying near flak.

At Soc Trang we had a small South Vietnamese artillery detachment that manned a large 105mm cannon, which was located about ten feet east of our parked T-28s. The Vietnamese gun crews would often fire this artillery piece at all hours of the night, using starburst flare shells to try to locate incoming VC insurgents. Frequently they would also fire the 105 during daylight hours. These conditions always created havoc with the pilots' sleep time, but it served the purpose of preventing night attacks by the VC.

Eventually the Air Force airlifted a large three-bedroom trailer to Soc Trang, and did we ever love it. Since it was air-conditioned, we spent most of our waking time inside it. I remember relaxing one day after a mission inside the trailer with one of my fellow pilots. Hal was from Texas and was proud of it, and he spoke in the usual slow Texas drawl. As we were sitting there sipping Cokes, the 105mm cannon located about forty yards from the trailer went off. Within seconds it went off again and again. I remember clearly Hal saying,

"Gosh, those guys are getting good with that cannon." About that same instant the shrapnel hit the side of our trailer with a loud crash. Seconds later we were both on the floor looking at each other and laughing. This was a daylight VC mortar attack on the base. We quickly grabbed our gear and raced for our aircraft, hoping that the ground crew had gotten some gasoline into the tanks. We both pulled our landing gear chocks and climbed into the cockpits. Cranking the engines, as there wasn't time for an engine warm-up, we both opened the throttle and headed for the active runway. It was scary as hell accelerating down the runway, because there were Army aviators running across the runway in order to reach their helicopters at the same time. To add to this excitement there were VC mortar shells going off all over the place.

Hal called smoke from beyond the east perimeter of the base and we both headed for it. In my excitement to get airborne I forgot to pull the ground safety landing gear locking pins. Consequently, I could not retract my landing gear and had to keep my airspeed below the gear-down structural limitation. Hal had his gear up and locked and made a perfect bombing run on the VC positions. I followed his bombs with two 750-pound canisters of napalm. We watched to see that no helicopters were taking off and came back in for a landing. After landing we decided that this was the shortest combat mission either one of us had ever flown.

While flying out of Bien Hoa, we mostly got shot at from north of the base. However, there were VC all around the base at Soc Trang, and many times they were in too close to the base at night. No one got killed, but often aircraft got hit with small-arms fire during the landing phase.

Our section commander came up with a great idea that really put the fun back into flying while at Soc Trang. I think he got his idea from the Army helicopters, as they never came in from the same direction whenever they were landing at Soc Trang. We decided to apply Baron Von Richtofen's flying tactics to our landing patterns. By this I mean that from that day forward we never flew a normal traffic pattern and never landed the same way twice. As an example we would approach the field from ninety degrees to the runway while flying about fifteen feet off the ground. As we hit the edge of the runway we would pull straight up into a loop, reversing the direction ninety degrees at the top of the loop, and basically land out of the loop. This maneuver is quite like an Immelmann loop except for the reverse at the top of the loop. There is no doubt that we showed off to a great extent for the Army troops, but they always seemed to enjoy our air shows. Even though combat losses were excessively high in the IV Corps area, everyone was beginning to enjoy flying out of Soc Trang.

There occurs in everyone's life a time that one knows will be the last few seconds on the face of the earth for you, and I am no exception to this rule. This nerve-ending event happened to me twice while flying combat missions during 1963–64. The first time that it occurred was in December of 1963. I found myself on my first rotation visit to Soc Trang and I was scheduled to fly a mission with an old buddy from the Air Force's ROTC Program at San Diego State College. Tom O'Brian (Oby) was two years ahead of me while in school and was currently TDY out of Hurlbert Field, Florida, to finish up some missions.

Oby briefed me that we were going to escort a Gooney Bird (DC-3) that was going to be dropping supplies to an Army A Team located somewhere in the Seven Mountains area of the Delta. At the time, this area due to its closeness to the Cambodian border was considered to be a rather "hot" area, as there were numerous large antiaircraft guns in the vicinity. After takeoff Oby and I rendez-voused with a Gooney Bird near the town of Can Tho and proceeded to the Seven Mountains area of the Delta. Completing the escort duties, Oby then contacted an FAC who was operating in the same area. The FAC told us that the area was full of VC insurgents and wanted to know what type of ordnance we were carrying. Oby in-formed the FAC that we were carrying four 250-pound fragmenta-tion bombs on each of our aircraft. The O-1 aircraft was being flown by an American FAC, and he was delighted to see us. The FAC told us that there were some heavy antiaircraft guns in the area and for us to be careful, but he had several excellent targets for us. Joining up with the FAC, we armed our weapons and under his guidance proceeded to the target area. The FAC after marking each target with a white phosphorous rocket was really impressed with our bombing results and told us so. Oby and I made several strafing passes at his request before leaving the target area.

Oby was an old head-type fighter pilot and had flown many combat missions in South Vietnam. After joining up and climbing out from the target area, Oby, who was a man of few words, told me that we would be going home on the deck. As we started a descent, Oby wagged his rudder, which was the signal for me to move out about one thousand yards into a tactical formation position. We then came home in what is called a hedge-hopping flight maneuver. This means we were flying anywhere between five and fifteen feet off the ground with our airspeed in excess of 400 mph. It was an incredibly exciting way of flying, and I was enjoying it to the limit. As we were approaching Soc Trang somewhere to the northwest, Oby asked me if I had ever flown a tactical overhead flight pattern. I knew what a tactical overheard pattern was but had never flown one, so I lied to Oby and told him I had.

Normally when flying a tactical overhead landing pattern the aircraft, when on final approach, descends down to within fifty feet of the runway going as fast as it will go. As the aircraft reaches the far end of the runway, the pilot rolls to the left or right and begins a climbing turn to the downwind leg of the traffic pattern. Upon reaching the downwind leg with wings level, the pilot then flies a normal descending turn from base to the final landing heading. This sharp pullup maneuver while speeding down the runway is called a chandelle. I figured that if Oby could do it, then so could I. What a mistake that assumption was!

Nearing the base Oby told me to go "in-trail," which means that he wanted me right underneath him and just to the rear of his aircraft. I gradually moved over the 1,000 yards, and as I closed on his aircraft I thought to myself, *He is so low, how am I going to get underneath him?* For professional and macho reasons I didn't want to say, "Hey, Lead, give me some room." Moving carefully into position, I wasn't sure exactly how low he was, and I couldn't take my eyes off his aircraft to even glance at the altimeter. When you are moving over the ground at over 400 mph things happen fast and an inch is a lot of room. I kept moving in behind and below Oby's aircraft, as I wanted us to look good in formation should anyone be looking. (How stupid of me.) Even though I could feel the ground below my aircraft, I wasn't sure just how close to his aircraft I should get. I knew the propeller of a T-28 was approximately five feet long from the hub, and I couldn't see the tip. So I kept moving in until I started getting oil from his engine exhaust stacks on my windshield.

We flew for what seemed like an eternity, and I was really working hard to stay in position. Suddenly without warning Oby pulled straight up. I naturally attempted to stay in position with him but blacked out from putting too many G forces on my aircraft. While in that microsecond limbo of time I heard Oby call, "Gear down!" I relaxed my pull on the controls for just a second, allowing blood to flow back into my eyes and brain. Looking out of the cockpit, I was shocked to find myself upside down over the runway at the top of a loop. Pulling the power off, I quickly opened the canopy and put both gear and flap handles in the down position, as the nose of the aircraft started down through the horizon. I found myself momentarily hanging from my seat belt as the negative G forces hit me. I was well below normal traffic pattern altitude, and as I looked down at the runway coming up at me in that instant I knew exactly what the last two words were going to be before I hit the ground—"oh shit." I was certain that I was going to make a big hole in the runway right before everyone's eyes.

I give all the credit to that good old T-28 and its large flaps. As the flaps were coming down I remember the aircraft slowly rotating around the flaps, and the next thing I knew I was on the runway. To this day I do not know how I survived that landing. I do know that as I was taxiing in I was so scared that I could not talk even after shutting the engine down. In the parking area Oby, looking over from his aircraft, smiled and gave me a thumbs-up. For several years afterward I experienced numerous nightmares over this harrowing landing. Three weeks after this flight Oby was shot down and killed while participating in another combat mission. Everyone who knew Oby felt the loss of a gallant and true fighter pilot.

One of the most hazardous combat missions that I ever flew occurred one night while at Soc Trang. It was my scheduled night off, and I wasted no time in warming up a seat at the bar. I was on my seventh or eighth martini when Jim Tally came running into the bar and told me that there was a night scramble and that I had to fly. Jim said that one of the alert pilots was too sick to fly and that they needed all of our aircraft on target. It was a three-shipper flight, and I was to fly in the number-three position.

I experienced very little trouble taking off and joining the flight. The flight (call sign "Lion") headed northwest toward a small town called Phu Vinh. The weather was absolutely terrible above 1800-foot altitude, and we were inundated by heavy rainsqualls as we proceeded to the target area. We could see the target area at a distance, because 200,000-candlepower flares that were being dropped from a flare ship flying above our altitude were lighting up the clouds.

Arriving over the target area we were given a quick briefing by the airborne FAC. The FAC indicated that the A Team hamlet located below us contained both American Special Forces and South Vietnamese troops and was being attacked by a strong force of VC insurgents from four sides. Orbiting the area at 1500-foot altitude there were large amounts of enemy antiaircraft tracer bullets floating up in the sky. The FAC cleared us in hot in any direction that we wanted to attack. The flare ship orbiting directly above us was dropping flares from 6,000 feet on a continual basis. As the flares burnt out, the empty flare cases continued to come down in their parachutes. The problem was that the flare canister when empty weighed thirty-seven pounds and could no longer be seen. Prior to rolling in, I caught one of the empty canisters' parachutes on my right wing, and the noise of the empty canister banging on my wing scared the pee out of me. Immediately I pulled out of the dive, and my first thought was that I had been hit by some of the heavy antiaircraft ground fire. Inside my cockpit I was screaming so loud that I'm sure the enemy could have heard me on the ground. Lion Lead brought his ship over close to mine and flew around me looking for battle damage. I was sweating profusely when I heard him laugh. Lead told me that I had struck one of the empty flare canisters and that it was hung up under my right wing on my outboard machine gun.

Before this mission was over, Lion Two struck a flare canister with his propeller, scaring the hell out of him, and it made me feel a lot better. The parachute cords holding the flare canister to my machine gun finally broke loose, and the noise level inside the cockpit became bearable again. This hung canister problem was minor compared to what was about to happen. Up until it was my turn to roll in on the target, I had been watching the lead and number-two ships in our flight. As I rolled over into a split-S type maneuver and

236

pulled my nose down to the vertical position I got a sudden bad case of vertigo. The magnitude and light intensity of the many 200,000-candlepower flares were reflecting off my canopy and the water in the rice paddies below me. Quite suddenly it became extremely difficult to determine which way was up and which way was down.

Aborting my first bomb run, I was fighting for my life just to get the aircraft under control, with not a lot of airspace to work with. Poor instrumentation and lack of good instrument lighting additionally hampered my recovery problems. It was like being momentarily blinded. The light of the flares one second contracted your eye pupils, while during the next second you were looking into total blackness. I think that the only thing that saved my life was the enemy's tracer bullets being fired at me.

Once I determined that the tracer bullets were coming from the ground, I pulled the power off my engine and rolled violently into a climbing left-hand turn. I was breathing and sweating so hard that I'm sure my heart rate was over 200. Lion Lead was watching my erratic flight, and he was certain that I was going to crash, as I barely missed hitting the ground. Before that mission was over I really felt that God was with me that night. I remember telling Him that I would never drink and fly a mission hereafter and thanking Him for his forgiveness. The weather was too inclement to return to Soc Trang and land. I felt a lot more sober as we headed north and recovered at Bien Hoa. After landing and taxiing in to our parking spots, I felt like kissing the ground once out of the aircraft. I scared myself so bad that night that I, in fact, swore off drinking for the next month or so.

Several days after this mission a captain from the Army's famous Green Berets flew down to Soc Trang in a helicopter. He presented the three of us who flew this combat mission with authentic Green Beret caps to wear. He told us that our precision bombing and subsequent strafing of the VC positions had very definitely saved their asses and that his troops would forever be indebted to us. That Green Beret cap hangs in my den today.

I find that most all Americans love animals of some kind, and military men particularly do so. There were all sorts of pet animals around Soc Trang beside the Army's tiger and our snake, Charlie.

A particular animal event stands out in my mind that I would like to share with you.

It seems that one of the airmen assigned to our maintenance section had adopted a small dark brown monkey. Each evening, the airman would ride around the perimeter of the base on a bicycle with the monkey sitting on the back fender of the bike. During the day the airman kept the monkey chained to a stake that he had put into the ground near our area. The problem was that the chain was just long enough that a person had difficulty getting by the monkey on his way to or from the flight line. All of us found this particular monkey hostile to everyone except for the airman who owned him. Should someone happen to get near the monkey, he would shriek, bare his fangs, and lunge, as if he were going to attack. A person had to be very fast to stay out of the monkey's way.

One day I was returning from a mission and had so much on my mind that I forgot all about the monkey. As I was walking near where the monkey was staked out, I felt something grab at my leg. Before I realized it, the monkey had grabbed my sunglasses out of my lower flight suit pocket. I knew that the monkey did not like me, and the feeling was mutual. I was mad as hell at the monkey, because we were going to launch again just as soon as our aircraft were refueled. I made an attempt to be nice to the monkey, but that proved to be useless. Because of my need to get back to the flight line, I pulled out my .38 and got one shot off before the monkey's owner came running over to where I was. The young airman pleaded with me to not shoot his monkey. I told him that his monkey was a damn nuisance and that I needed my sunglasses in a hurry. The airman quickly grabbed the monkey's chain and pulled the monkey to him retrieving my sunglasses from the monkey's grasp. I put my .38 away but told the airman that if it ever happened again my next shot wouldn't miss. The airman told me that he would work on the monkey's disposition.

Several days later our mutual problem was resolved in a most unusual manner. A DC-3 Gooney Bird landed with some replacement people onboard. This was always a major event at Soc Trang, because it meant that someone was getting to go home, plus there were new people to welcome into the fold. We all gathered around as the new people started climbing down the DC-3's detachable ladder. The first person down the ladder was what I would call an old gunny sergeant. The name gunny sergeant was given to Marines during WW II when they made the rank of technical sergeant. As the gunny's feet hit the ground, he shouldered his duffel bag and asked directions to our area.

We were all kind of shocked standing there, as none of us had seen a gunny sergeant like this before. The gunny's face was dark-tanned and looked like an old piece of leather. He commanded respect just by the number of hashmark strips going down his sleeves. We all fell in at a respectable distance behind as the gunny made his way toward our containment area. We watched as the gunny approached the place where the airman's monkey was staked out. I think that we were all sort of stunned as the gunny stopped and placed his duffel bag on the ground near the monkey. The gunny then began talking to the monkey as if he had known the monkey.

As the gunny continued to coo and talk, he approached the monkey with his right hand held out in what I would call a friend-ship greeting. The monkey seemed rather docile until the gunny got about a foot from him. Suddenly the monkey leaped at the gunny, sinking his fangs into the meaty area between the gunny's thumb and first finger. The gunny never uttered a word. He calmly reached down and pulled the stake out of the ground with his other hand and started walking toward the nearest rice paddy. Meanwhile the monkey was furiously ripping up the gunny's right hand and blood was flying all over the place.

The scene was very dramatic, to say the least, and we all watched in fascination. The gunny stopped at the edge of the rice paddy and quite calmly worked the monkey's fangs out of his very bloody right hand. The monkey, chattering for all he was worth, was trying to get away. Reaching the end of his chain, the monkey was violently jerked off his feet. The gunny was holding the other end of the chain and began swinging the monkey in large circles around his head. All of a sudden the gunny released the chain and both monkey and chain flew about twenty feet out into the water.

Everyone watched with fascination as the monkey, dragging the chain, eventually made it back to the shoreline. The gunny walked over and reached down to pick the monkey up. However, the monkey again bared his fangs and hissed at the gunny. Once again the gunny jerked the monkey up by the chain and began swinging him around in large circles above his head. Again the monkey, stake, and chain all landed about twenty feet out into the rice paddy. This time the monkey was struggling just to keep his head above the water. As the monkey disappeared for the third time, the gunny jumped into the rice paddy and locating the chain, pulled the monkey up to him. We were all screaming to the gunny that the rice paddy was mined, but it didn't seem to faze him. Ignoring us, the gunny, although dripping wet, cuddled the monkey in his arms and carried the monkey back to his original place. The gunny then placed the stake in the ground and stomped on it with his foot, driving it securely into the ground, and carefully put the monkey down, all the while patting him on the head and talking to him. Finally the gunny stood up and asked the nearest person where the medic's tent was, and with that walked off as calmly as possible.

Later we learned that the gunny had been a Marine during the invasion of Iwo Jima during the Pacific campaign of WW II. He told us one night that what he did to our monkey was exactly how the Marines made so many pets out of the monkeys they found on the many Japanese-held islands. The gunny said that the Marines would attach about four to five feet of chain to a monkey's neck and that they would then throw the monkeys out into the surf. The gunny said that it would usually take no more than two or three times before the monkeys would become tame. I personally never tried to pick the monkey up even after the gunny's treatment, but many other guys did and said that the monkey's attitude had really changed.

32

Bear Flight

Another of my "go to hell and back" missions occurred on February 26, 1964. I would like to share it with you. I called this combat mission Bear Flight simply because that was the permanent radio call sign that was assigned to me whenever I was the flight leader. We originally had three T-28s at Soc Trang, but one of the machines came down with a major maintenance problem that day and was flown back to Bien Hoa for repairs. Capt. Jim Tally and I were on alert duty that February day, and by four o'clock that afternoon we had already flown two lengthy combat missions. Jim and I always traded off being the lead aircraft, and he had just led the second of our day's combat sorties. While sitting in the club that evening talking about our combat missions for the day we received a radio alert message from the command center at Bien Hoa.

The message told us to take off at 1900 hours and to contact the Command Post once we were airborne. It was my turn to lead the flight, and with the current weather the way it was I was not very happy about being the leader or even taking off. The South Vietnamese weather can be bad enough when flying during the daylight hours but absolutely horrible when flying a T-28 at night. Taking off that evening, neither Jim nor I gave much thought to the local weather, since we were both "test pilots" for the T-28 section and disciplined combat pilots. Our erroneous assumption was that flight conditions had to get better. How many times have I been wrong about weather forecasts in my military flying career and been stupid enough to fly anyway?

There was so much water on the runway that I wasn't sure that I would even be able to break ground during my takeoff roll. It was still light enough that you could see, but not well. It was raining so hard that I remained at 1,000-foot altitude and told Bear Two that I would leave my anticollision light on so that he could find me. After Jim joined up on my wing I turned my anticollision light off, and turning to a westerly heading we began our climb. Bear Two was really tucked in close as we were flying in heavy clouds. I told Bear Two that we would climb up to eight or nine thousand feet and if we were not then in the clear we would abort the mission and head for Bien Hoa. It would have been impossible for us to return to Soc Trang while flying under IFR flight conditions. The turbulence that we were flying through was unbelievable, and to this day I don't know how Bear Two managed to remain on my wing. We finally broke out of the clouds at 8,000-foot altitude. This was an unusually high altitude for our T-28s, since our aircraft were not equipped with antiicing devices nor did we have oxygen onboard the aircraft.

We hadn't been able to run a proper after-takeoff check on our aircraft as we had both been too busy with just getting our aircraft in the air. Once we broke out in the clear I told Bear Two to move out and to check his cockpit and to be sure that he had plenty of carburetor heat on. We flew a time and distance type flight, since we could not see the ground. In the distance we did see flares being dropped by a Gooney Bird and headed for the lit-up sky. Setting up a lower orbit upon arrival near the Gooney Bird, we established radio contact and received a briefing on what our target was going to be. The aircraft commander of the DC-3 told us that a large force of VC insurgents was attacking an American Special Forces compound below us and that they were desperate for help. We were unable to communicate with the Special Forces because they only had an FM band radio frequency while we were operating on a UHF radio frequency. The Gooney Bird, however, had both types of radios in his aircraft, and he was relaying messages between us and the Special Forces commander.

The Special Forces commander said that the VC were within forty feet of their compound and requested that we drop our bombs that close to their position. Both Jim and I were carrying four 250-pound iron bombs, and we were reluctant to drop that amount of killing power so close to friendly forces. While we were thinking about this predicament I asked the Special Forces commander what the weather was like around their compound and could he estimate the height of the cloud base above his position. His response was that he thought that the bottoms of the clouds were at least 100 feet above his head. I informed him that we couldn't drop our bombs from 100 feet without blowing ourselves out of the sky, but that we could support him with our machine guns. Making a quick decision, I told Bear Two to remain at 8,000 feet while I let down through the clouds. I wanted to be sure that we could safely use our machine guns to assist the guys on the ground.

Presetting my altimeter to 29.92 inches of mercury, I entered the clouds and began a very slow circling descent, which believe me required the utmost of concentration and flying skills. What made flying conditions so difficult was that I was surrounded by total blackness punctuated with 200,000-candlepower flares. Adding to this equation was the addition of terrible weather conditions plus fluctuating instrument cockpit lights, all combining to make flying all the more difficult. Eventually I reached an altitude of 100 feet and leveling off began a variation of flying patterns over what I hoped was the target area. Calling the flare ship, I asked them to contact the ground forces and see if they could hear my aircraft engine as I passed over or near their position.

The message came back that no, they could not hear my aircraft engine. Based on where the flares were floating down, I informed the ground forces commander that I would widen my flight path over his area in the hope that they could hear me. Flying a crisscross flight pattern, I remained at 100-foot altitude for approximately fifteen minutes. During this time the ground force commander began begging me to drop my ordnance at ground zero. I told the Gooney Bird pilot that I just could not do that, especially since I could not locate their position. I was also fearful of getting any lower, thinking that I might strike the ground or a tree at any time. These flying conditions were compounded by the fact that I was also flying in and out of heavy rainsqualls while using an unknown altimeter setting for this area. I remained at this altitude for another ten minutes with no success.

It was a feeling of total exasperation. While I was flying around in unstable weather conditions trying to keep my aircraft in the air I could overhear the communications from the ground forces commander to the Gooney Bird pilot. Things were apparently going from bad to worse for the guys on the ground. Finally all radio contact was lost between the Gooney Bird and the ground forces. Applying power, I began to slowly climb in large circles back up through the weather to 8,000 feet. I do know that I was hyperventilating and sweating profusely by the time I approached 8,000 feet.

Breaking out of the clouds, I probably came the closest to a midair crash that I had ever experienced. I found myself directly under Bear Two. I couldn't have missed him by more that a few inches. Instantly I pushed the nose of my aircraft down hard and proceeded to lose control of my aircraft. I can only guess that this was a case where constant training proved to be the only thing that saved my life. Dropping back into the cloudy murk, the aircraft began to spin to the right. While locking my eyes on the instrument panel I pulled the engine power off and stepped on the left rudder until the spin stopped. During the process of trying to recover on instruments I lost close to 3,000 feet of altitude. Once I leveled off I called Bear Two and told him that I was climbing back to 8,000 feet and requested him to increase the size of his orbiting circle.

The second time that I broke out above the clouds I found that I couldn't talk for a few minutes. Turning on my anticollision lights, I requested Bear Two to join up with me, which he accomplished in seconds. Going off radio frequency, I called the pilot of the Gooney Bird, explaining how terrible that we felt about the results of being unable to assist the guys on the ground. After a few minutes of conversation, I informed him that we were terminating the mission and requested a heading from him that would get us to Bien Hoa. Bear Two moved out into a tactical position and we proceeded toward Bien Hoa at 8,000 feet.

Flying for some thirty minutes, we were unable to see the city lights of Saigon. I told Bear Two to move back into a tight weather formation and that we would begin a descent on our current heading down to 1500 feet. Again, how Bear Two managed to remain in position was beyond me as the severity of the up- and downdrafts while flying through thunderstorms was just awesome. Bear Two proved beyond a doubt how incredibly good he was as a professional pilot.

Still in IFR flight conditions at 1500 feet we continued our descent and finally broke out of the clouds at 1100 feet. At this point I told Bear Two to move out into a tactical flight position so that we could both look around for familiar land objects on the ground. Twice Bear two lost me and requested that I turn on my anticollision lights. Both times, enemy tracer bullets began floating close to my aircraft before Bear Two finally located me. The ceilings of the clouds kept getting lower and lower as we went in and out of the rain showers. At one point after getting separated I had to request Bear Two to turn on his anticollision lights before we were able to locate each other. Eventually we did locate the lights of Saigon. We made several circles over what we thought was approximately the center of the city, selecting a northern heading to fly that should get us safely to Bien Hoa.

It was around this time that Bear Two informed me that his engine was running on fumes, and so was mine. I told Jim to join up again and that we would fly an International Triangle flight pattern until we ran out of gas, with the hope that someone would see us bail out. It was during the second leg of the triangle that I suddenly spotted the runway lights at Bien Hoa and vectored Bear Two in for an immediate landing.

Contacting the tower at Bien Hoa, I explained that Bear Two and I were both running on emergency fuel and that Bear Two was on final approach for a full stop landing. I began a level 360-degree turn to the right at 1000-foot altitude in order to give myself enough spacing behind Bear Two. Rolling out on the downwind leg of the traffic pattern, I ran into a solid wall of water. It was like being hit by a tidal wave! Once again I found myself flying on instruments, as flight visibility dropped to zero. Completing my turn from the downwind leg, I rolled out on the runway heading and continued my descent.

This again was one of those times that all of your life experiences suddenly passed before your eyes as you knew without a doubt that you were going to crash. My only thought at the time was that I hoped that I crashed close enough to the base so that crash personnel could find me. At some point while all of these hyper thoughts were going through my head, my engine quit running. I wasn't even aware that it had quit, for suddenly I broke out of the wall of water and was approximately ten to twenty feet in the air off the right side of the main runway. This was going to be three out of four times in my military flying career that I would dead-stick an aircraft! Coasting down the right side of the runway I saw Bear Two for a second or two before losing him in the rain showers. Bear Two's engine had also run out of gas. While still rolling down the runway I switched over to the ground control frequency and listened as Bear-Two was calling for a fuel truck and ground assistance.

Some time later a fuel truck arrived and gave us both enough gas to be able to start our engines and taxi to the T-28 parking ramp. By the time we finished our debriefing with the intelligence guys, it was past three o'clock in the morning. The intelligence guy was unaware that we had not had any sleep, so told us that we had to be airborne at 0500 that same morning for another emergency mission. There were not enough T-28 pilots left to argue over who should fly the next mission, so Jim and I didn't waste any time heading for the sack. We both concluded that this flight had been one of the most harrowing combat missions in our tour. Reflecting back, I knew that I should have never survived this mission, yet what was it that seemed to be protecting me?

As my thoughts went back and forward that morning, I recalled another exciting flight, mission number 70, where technically I shouldn't have survived. I remember explaining earlier about how important that cobra-skin band was on our hats. At the time it was really a very much needed morale and bonding issue among all of the combat-qualified pilots in our section. My cobra-skin qualification mission occurred in early January of 1964. I was flying the number-three aircraft in a flight called Tiger Flight. Our target area was in the extreme southern portion of the IV Corps area (WQ280/910). The VC had attacked and taken over a small hamlet located near a small river and had set up numerous antiaircraft guns in the immediate area. Tiger Lead and Tiger Two were both carrying four 500-pound iron bombs, while I was carrying two large rocket pods plus two 250-pound fragmentation bombs.

Reaching the target area, the flight was cleared "in hot" by the FAC. Pulling off my first rocket pass on the target, I happened to be looking out to my right when I saw a bullet tear through my right wing. Being very unprofessional at the moment, I screamed and yelled as I continued my pull-up. I was so excited that I completely forget about flight integrity and my second pass. Tiger Lead caught up with me as I was careening through the sky babbling about a bullet hole. Both Tiger Lead and Tiger Two thought because of the unusual commotion by me that I had personally been bodily hit.

Tiger Lead finally got my attention, telling me to pull my power back, as I still had the throttle wide open. Flying around me, he inspected my aircraft and suggested that since the bullet had gone through the wing spar I'd best fly very carefully, or the right wing might come off. That thought sobered me immediately since several wings had already come off T-28s. Tiger Lead aborted the sortie, and began escorting me back toward Soc Trang. Slowing the aircraft down, I watched the right wing with an intensity that you can't imagine. I knew that should the wing decide to separate from the aircraft there was no way I was going to be able to get out alive.

Tiger Lead and Tiger Two joined up on either side of my aircraft. They both later had to laugh simply because my radio calls from that point on were almost down to a whisper. Arriving near Soc Trang, Tiger Lead suggested that I make a long, slow, and gentle straight-in approach for landing and not worry about the VC guns surrounding the base. After I landed and parked, the maintenance guys told me that the battle damage was so extensive to the wing that the aircraft had to be grounded until a new wing spar could be flown in. That evening we partied hard at the club while I wore my new snakeskin hatband, and finally I lost the title of Preacher. From that day forward I could hardly fly a mission without getting hit, and sometimes many hits.

I hope you can understand why I was often possessed with the feeling, *Why me?* I knew that other pilots had been killed when they received lesser battle damage than I had. I am still unable to completely answer that question other than thinking that my time was just not up yet! For a long time I considered that it was possibly because of my Christian upbringing plus my training as an Eagle Scout. Later, reflecting back over two wars, I realized that there are no rules in warfare. Sometimes you survive, and sometimes you do not.

33

Captain Bernie Lukasic

I couldn't complete this book without the mention of Captain Bernie Lukasic. Bernie was one of our senior T-28 pilots and was considered to be a perfectionist as a fighter pilot. He was great to fly with, because he always seemed so knowledgeable about almost everything. He took great pains in developing good wingmen and always took care of whoever was flying with him. Bernie was continually looking for new methods of ordnance delivery and ways to improve flying safety in combat conditions. Sometimes Bernie was extremely difficult to fly with, simply because he would take his wingmen by surprise by performing a sudden new maneuver. Only afterward, once the flight was back together, would he try to describe why the maneuver was important to everyone.

Captain Lukasic was the first person in our outfit to receive the Air Force Cross, our nation's second-highest award for heroism. This occurred in late March of 1964. Bernie was flying cover for a South Vietnamese pilot who had been shot down. The VC had advanced to within thirty yards of the downed Vietnamese pilot's position. Bernie and his wingman had made strafing pass after strafing pass trying to keep the VC away from the downed pilot. Bernie's accuracy with air-to-ground machine-gun fire was second to none in our outfit. Eventually Bernie ran out of ammunition, but the VC didn't know that, as he continued to make extremely low-level passes on their positions while he waited for the incoming helicopter to pick up the downed pilot. When Captain Lukasic finally returned to Bien Hoa his aircraft had eighteen bullet holes in it from the VC ground fire.

The following day I flew on a combat mission with Bernie. We ran into a situation where a fairly large force of VC insurgents was in the process of trying to overrun a South Vietnamese combat position. Using our machine guns, we chased a portion of the VC insurgents down into a streamed that had high banks they were able to hide behind. By this time in his combat tour Bernie had become notorious for inventing a maneuver that we subsequently called the Lukasic Maneuver. It was a maneuver that very few of his fellow pilots ever attempted to duplicate due to the dangerous recovery, especially at such low altitudes.

In performing this maneuver Bernie would frequently come off a target while performing a low-angle strafing pass. While outbound as best as I can describe it, Bernie would cross-control his flight controls, chop his power, and, as the aircraft started to skid while flying an arc, carefully advance the power, all the while centering the flight controls. As the nose of the aircraft reversed 180 degrees, Bernie would again gently apply full throttle and suddenly be coming straight right back at the target. This maneuver, although difficult to perform, was quite effective when used against enemy ground forces, as it did not give the ground forces enough time to retrain their guns back on you.

This indeed was a wild maneuver, but Bernie could fly it to perfection. He was performing this maneuver on the day that he was killed. The only thing that we could figure out was that Bernie must have taken a direct hit to his body as he bore back toward the target. There was no communication as Bernie flew his aircraft straight into the side of a river embankment where the VC were hiding. Watching something like this happen absolutely shocks you and then saddens you, as you realize that the U.S. Air Force has just lost one of their finest fighter pilots.

During the final weeks of March 1964 we received the word that General LeMay, who was then the chief of staff of the U.S. Air Force had removed the covert name restrictions on our program. Suddenly the world's media arrived in Vietnam en masse. Originally the Air Force used the secret name of "Farm Gate pilots" to describe the covert operations that we were flying in South Vietnam. The declassification of our program title in no way affected our future combat missions. We would still be flying classified missions as a part of the 34th Tactical Group's Composite Strike Force.

Many of the reporters who arrived in our area wanted to know about Captain Lukasics's death, since he was the first American pilot to receive the Air Force Cross in the Vietnam Theater. To my knowledge, not one pilot would speak to the media about the circumstances. On March 16, 1964, much to our surprise, Jim Lucas, a

Pulitzer Prize–winning war correspondent, was given permission to fly on a combat mission with our section. Most combat missions are scrambles and you never know where you are going until you get in the air, and this one was no exception. I found it difficult to believe that Mr. Lucas had been authorized to fly with us, especially when this combat mission was flown into such a dangerous area of the Mekong Delta. In the area where we were targeted absolutely no civilian should have been onboard a fighter-type aircraft.

After the mission Mr. Lucas telephoned his story about the mission to the *Washington Daily News*. The story was titled "It Takes a While for a Town to Die." In this article Mr. Lucas described how I placed a 100-pound white phosphorous bomb directly through the window of a house that a contingent of VC was hiding in. According to him, that bomb set the entire village on fire. Jim Lucas later turned out to be a really concerned war correspondent. Several years later he published a book titled *Dateline Vietnam*, in which he identified a number of our pilots by name and described many of their combat missions. However, he never got the facts on Bernie Lukasic's last mission.

34

Change of Command

In true military tradition, Change of Command ceremonies are very formal affairs accompanied by a military band with all of the commands' troops parading and passing in review. I cannot remember the exact date, but one day those of us who were left in the T-28 section were told to stand down from our various TDY locations and return to Bien Hoa. After parking their aircraft on the flight line, pilots were told to report to the briefing room ASAP. Of the some twelve to fourteen pilots in attendance, all were dressed in various parts of the flying uniform and everyone was armed to the teeth. Our section commander came in and told us to all get up and to stand in the back of the briefing room.

We were in the process of getting into some order along the back wall when suddenly someone called the entire room to attention. Into the room walked three U.S. Navy admirals and one U.S. Air Force brigadier general, followed by several civilian congressmen. As our motley group of guys tried their best to come to attention, many of the submachine guns that guys were carrying fell to the floor; fortunately, none went off. I watched the eyes of the congressmen as they tried to get settled in, and I'm sure that we scared the hell out of them. All of us were armed with submachine guns of all sizes and descriptions, plus most of us had one or two pistols in belts, with large knives attached to the belts. Most of us were wearing our Australian bush hats complete with cobra-skin bands, and none of us had bothered to shave for several days. I personally had an unauthorized eight-inch highly waxed handlebar mustache, and I was really proud of it.

Our current 34th Group commander, Colonel Preston, walked in and introduced another Air Force colonel, Bill Bethea. Colonel Preston said that Colonel Bethea was the new 34th Group commander. It was the first time that I almost lost my military discipline and laughed. Colonel Bethea looked exactly like the famous Frito

Bandito right out of Hollywood. Colonel Bethea stood about five feet five inches in height and had a very large mustache that hung down well below his chin on both sides of his head. He had a huge belly and like us was wearing an Australian bush hat. Below his large belly on his very narrow hips were strapped two pistol belts, both with polished bullets. Each belt contained a pearl-handled .45-caliber six-gun that seemed larger than he was. He accepted the command from Colonel Preston and quickly began a very formal briefing for the benefit of the civilian congressmen and generals and admirals, whom he introduced as a part of the congressional committee from Washington, D.C.

Completing his typical commander's "dog and pony" show, he asked if there were any questions from the congressional committee. I recall this one admiral looking at us distastefully and asking Colonel Bethea if he thought that we, "his pilots," were in good-enough physical shape to be flying combat missions. It was at this point that the new colonel, Bethea, scared the living hell out of all of us. Looking the admiral in the eye, Colonel Bethea removed his bush hat and threw it so hard at the floor that everyone in the room jumped. You could really hear a pin drop at this point. Colonel Bethea next dropped to the floor and quickly completed twenty-five-one-arm pushups. Jumping up, and in a very normal voice, he told the admiral that he wouldn't ask any of his men to do anything that he could not do. There was a deathly silence in the room for the next ten to twenty seconds as Colonel Bethea stared at the admiral. There being no further questions, Colonel Bethea quietly dismissed us from the room. This was the first that any of us had seen Colonel Bethea, but he was instantly liked by all of us.

Several weeks later I returned to Bien Hoa with a mechanical problem on one of our aircraft that couldn't be fixed out in the field. After getting settled in that evening, I decided to go over to the club and see who was there. It was almost dark as I entered the tent area by the club. About twenty feet from the door of the club I heard this wild scream, and a body came flying right through the screen door of the club ripping the door right off the hinges. This body did about six to ten back flips down the boardwalk, and only when it stopped upright did I realize that it was Colonel Bethea. He turned out to be one hell of a commando and consistently built our morale to new heights. I later discovered that Colonel Bethea was always trying to sucker some guy into seeing how many one-arm pushups he could do for a dollar per pushup. I'm sure that the colonel won a considerable amount of money in the bar during combat tour.

35

Combat Fatigue

There is a saying that "it always happens to the other guy, but never to you." Our squadron flight surgeon constantly harped on the subject of combat fatigue at every mission brief, and mostly pilots never listened to him. Combat fatigue is always in the back of a pilot's mind, but fighter pilots always think that it just cannot happen to them, right? Well, wrong in my case. Normally we would only fly two or three combat missions in a day, but occasionally, due to circumstances beyond our control, we would find ourselves flying four or five missions in a day. Whenever this happened, pilots got very little sleep if any at all, especially should they be tasked for a five-mission day. As the days passed, I began to observe other guys being afflicted with the combat fatigue phenomenon and eventually killing themselves. But I somehow felt that it could never happen to me. How wrong I was!

Late one afternoon four of us were returning to Bien Hoa after having flown our fourth combat mission that day. The runway was wide enough at Bien Hoa that it was customary for two T-28s to land together in formation. On that particular day I was flying in the number-two aircraft with the lead aircraft just to my left. We had made a normal approach to the traffic pattern and had been cleared for landing by the control tower. Probably the one thing that saved my life that day was the fact that there was an American sergeant on duty in the control tower instead of the usual Vietnamese controllers.

Approaching touchdown I heard this voice screaming at me, "Two, take it around!" My aircraft was lined up perfectly with the right side of the runway, and I thought everything appeared to be going smoothly. My natural reaction as the voice continued to scream at me was to say, "Fuck you. I'm flying this aircraft and my position is perfect, and I know what I am doing." As I was approaching touchdown, two bright red flares flew up in front of me.

This is an international sign for any pilot that there is an emergency and to get out of the way immediately.

I was tired and there was so much noise in the cockpit, what with the sergeant's continual screaming, that I decided to make a go-around. With much haste I threw the power in and automatically reached to bring the gear handle up. Much to my surprise, it was already in the up position! Anytime while flying an aircraft that you drop below a certain airspeed and the gear handle is not in the down and locked position a number of things happen. First of all, a red light inside the gear handle flashes continually, plus a very loud gear-not-down warning horn also blares in your ears. As the realization of my situation hit me I broke out into a very cold sweat and couldn't even think for several seconds. I was so tired that I simply didn't comprehend what the control tower operator was saying to me. In addition, there was the distraction of the gear-not-down warning horn blaring so loudly in my ears.

Continuing my go-around maneuver, I called the tower requesting to reenter the traffic pattern for a full stop landing, and it was granted. Once on the ground after parking my aircraft I immediately went to the officers' club and purchased a case of beer. U.S. Air Force tradition says that should a pilot screw up during the landing phase of the traffic pattern he shall purchase a case of beer for the tower operators. It was the first time that I realized that there were ninety-four steps from the bottom to the top of the control tower and no elevator. I gratefully carried the case of beer up those ninety-four steps. It wasn't necessary to say "thanks"; this was just one of those never-to-be-forgotten moments in my flying career. As the stress wore off and my stomach returned to normal, I realized that I, too, was human and had made a grave error in judgment that could have easily cost me my life. It was really a wake-up call for me, because I had already watched on two separate occasions as pilots flew their aircraft into the ground. Thereafter, I found myself always listening whenever the squadron flight surgeon was passing out free advice and doing my best to get as much rest as possible.

255

36

The John Wayne Story

When I was a young kid growing up during the times of WW II, my personal hero was none other than Hollywood movie star John Wayne. The "Duke", as he was known to everyone, was just an incredible example of what an American male should be like. His parts in the movies during the late 1940s and early '50s emulated what I thought America was all about—what it stood for and what it ought to be! Not only was the Duke proficient in almost any kind of flying machine, but he could also ride the hell out of the meanest horse on the range. While riding he was able to employ deadly accuracy with his six-guns. The Duke was a real college football hero at the University of Southern California and was a fellow Sigma Chi fraternity brother. Also on the list of his many talents was the ability to drive the largest bulldozers, trains of any kind, and military tanks. He was also adept at steering Navy destroyers and large aircraft carriers. In addition, and most important, the Duke was a common man, a foot soldier of the highest character, and represented the cream of the crop of our country's best fighter pilots. Mr. Wayne put "honor" back into the role of every young American and made you feel especially proud to be an American.

The Duke made so many movies that I couldn't begin to remember all of them. There is one, however, that had a significant impact upon my life as a future fighter pilot. It seems that the Duke was a squadron commander of a Marine Corps F4-U Corsair squadron in the movie *Back to Bataan*. I probably saw the movie a half-dozen times, and came to believe everything the Duke not only said but also did. The movie was all about a supposedly invincible Japanese heavy cruiser that was causing havoc with Marine ground forces in and around the Marianas Islands. American cryptographers had broken the Japanese code, and the approximate location of the heavy cruiser was determined. The Duke's squadron took off in hot pursuit of the Japanese cruiser. As the movie went along, deadly air-to-air battles were the order of the day, and planes from both countries fell as burning wrecks from the skies.

The Duke's squadron after locating the Japanese cruiser expended all of their bombs in dive-bomb run after run trying to sink this invincible ship. After exhausting their entire bomb loads to no avail, the Marines were not about to give up. In desperation attacks those Corsairs that were left began strafing the cruiser from stem to stern. Meanwhile the music in the movie's background was increasing in tempo as each Corsair dived toward the cruiser, and almost everyone watching the movie was sitting on the edge of their seats. Looking haggard and with smudges on his face, the Duke decided to make one final desperation-type strafing pass. He dove his F4-U right down on the deck and was headed for the cruiser using full throttle. He was so low that he was picking up seawater with his propeller blades.

Around what looked like about one to two hundred yards out, the Duke began walking his remaining bullets into the waterline directly into the center of the cruiser. One of his last rounds apparently struck the ships' armory, and the cruiser suddenly disintegrated before his eyes in a spectacularly large explosion. The next thing that everyone saw was the Duke joining up with his wingman on the other side of the explosion. The music score had now changed to a light and flowery consistency! The Duke casually opened his canopy and wiped the smudges from his face. He managed to locate a cigar and quickly lit it up. Moments later the movie ended, and everyone went home happy.

It wasn't until fourteen years later before I realized that something was not right about this movie and my hero. On April 18, 1964, while on alert status at Bien Hoa three of us were scrambled on a combat mission, call sign "Camel Flight" into the Delta area to coordinates WS696/556. Arriving over our target area, the FAC who had been circling the combat zone marked the location of the enemy soldiers with rocket fire, and our flight delivered ordnance according to the FAC's wishes. The VC insurgents who were attacking an Army Special Forces A Team broke their attack off after losing too many men to our bombs.

Completing our air-to-ground mission, we joined up into a loose-spread formation and headed back toward Bien Hoa. On the way home we had to fly over the Mekong River. The Mekong River of South Vietnam is much like our own Mississippi River; i.e., it is long and quite wide in many places. Looking down, Camel Two spotted a large two-masted schooner on the Mekong River in a location where it shouldn't have been. Camel Lead told us to remain at altitude and that he would go down and make an identification pass over the schooner to determine if it was friend or foe. We already suspected that it might be a foe, since it was operating in an area that had been determined to be a "free zone." The next thing we heard was Camel Lead screaming for assistance as antiaircraft guns from the ship were firing at him. Both Camel Two and I dived to his assistance, and we were amazed to discover that there were four antiaircraft gun emplacements on the ship.

In those early days our command section told us to make only one hot gun pass on any enemy target, as the probability of getting shot down was too great to make more. I will be the first to admit that no one paid much attention to this order, because a pilot just could not get the job done with only one pass. We swiftly silenced all four antiaircraft guns using only two passes. The next thing that came to our minds was, *How do you kill a ship of that size with only machine guns?* We did our best but couldn't seem to do anything to stop the ship. It was at this point that my mind flew back fourteen years and I remembered what the Duke did in order to sink that Japanese cruiser.

Like the Duke I was on my 10th and last strafing pass, with most of my ammunition already gone. I brought my aircraft down to where I was almost in the water and, very much like the Duke's, my propeller was picking up water from the river as I pressed in toward the ship. I, too, was walking my bullets into the center of the ship when just what happened to the Duke happened to me. The enemy ship disintegrated in a gigantic explosion right before my eyes, and I was headed right into the fireball with no way to escape. I knew instantly that someone had lied! How I survived the flight through the fireball and came out alive is beyond description.

My T-28 was violently thrown out the other side of the fireball, but somehow I managed to regain control and stabilize the aircraft. There was no light and flowery music, and I had no cigar! There was a piece of lumber stuck through my right wing and some sort of cable embedded in my fuselage. I made it back to Bien Hoa, but wow, was the ops officer ever mad at me. He told me that he was going to court-martial me, but somehow he never did, because I did manage to sink the ship. I still idolize the Duke for his patriotism and courage but have decided that his combat tactics were strictly Hollywood stuff.

37

Significant Emotional Events

From what I've learned, almost everyone I know has had one or two significant emotional events occur in their lives that truly changed their lives, and I am no exception. One of those significant emotional events occurred to me on May 18, 1964. Although I have always owned and used guns both in recreational shooting and in wars, I just flat do not like shooting at animals. Over the years while a youth I shot lots of rattlesnakes, ground squirrels, and birds, plus one deer. I remember shooting a deer while up in Northern California and after shooting the animal I made the mistake of looking into its eyes as it was dying. I couldn't even clean it and drove fifty miles back to the city and gave the deer to my Uncle Hack. I don't mind shooting at people during wartime simply because they, too, can shoot at me; however, animals do not have that same privilege.

In any event, three of us were scrambled during the morning of May 18, 1964 to provide aid to a U.S. Army A Team that was located in the Delta area of South Vietnam at coordinates WS424/842. With the help of a Vietnamese FAC who identified the positions of the VC, our flight was able to destroy the majority of the enemy attacking forces. Once the mission was completed, we rejoined up in a loose formation and picked up a heading back to Soc Trang. While flying along, our flight leader, Andy, spotted a large herd of water buffalo below us. The animals were located in what we called an enemy-free zone. A free zone is an area on a map that is completely under the control of VC insurgents, and anything in that designated area is free game for our forces to engage. Camel Lead quickly called our Command Post and reported the finding. We were then instructed to descend and destroy as many of the animals that we could. The reason was that the VC were using the water buffalo to transport guns, ammunition, and other supplies into their various war zones.

Since the FAC didn't require us to make strafing runs during our mission, we all had plenty of machine-gun ammunition onboard our aircraft. Camel Lead told us that he would make the first pass and would try to split the herd. He said for Camel Two to take the animals on the left flank, while Camel Three was to hit the animals on the right flank. Since there were no antiaircraft guns in the immediate area we choose to use very low-angle strafing passes on our targets. At the time I did not question the orders, as these targets were located in a war zone and a lot of unusual things happened in war zones. Pressing the targets, I watched animals being blown apart as the ground below the water buffalo turned a bright crimson. There were several VC located in the center of what was left of the herd who were trying desperately to shoot our aircraft down with automatic weapons. Both Camel Lead and Camel Two each made a strafing pass on the VC but failed to suppress their fire. I was very pleased with my air-to-ground gunnery, as I nailed the VC on my next pass, and received yells of congratulations from the other two members of our flight.

Each T-28 pilot expended all of his ammunition sometime during the next fifteen minutes while chasing water buffalo. Camel Lead finally told us to rejoin the formation, as it was time to head for home. Pulling in close to Camel Lead's ship, I noticed that the entire bottom of his aircraft was covered with blood and small chunks of animal flesh. I looked over and observed Camel Two opening up his canopy and throwing up. That was when it hit me like a bolt of lightning. I didn't throw up, but I was sick to my stomach beyond words. Here I was a professional fighter pilot shooting and killing innocent animals that in no way could harm me, and I was overcome with emotion.

I have always said after the experience of having fought in two wars that I didn't mind killing human beings, because they in turn could just as easily have killed me. But to kill an innocent animal was just too much for me. From that day, which was definitely a significant emotional event day, to my present time in life I have never been able to hunt deer or ducks as I once did.

Another very emotional event for me occurred later that same month. One evening three other pilots and I were sitting around inside a tent just relaxing and shooting the bull and solving world problems. As a part of our covert operations, whenever we flew no pilots could carry identification on them that would distinguish them as Americans. In addition, our aircraft had no markings on them that would identify them as belonging to the USA. Also, we as American forces could not even fly an American flag on what we considered our portion of any base in South Vietnam. It is difficult to make folks back home understand just how important the American flag is, especially to combat veterans in overseas assignments. Someone had earlier pinned a small American flag on one of the walls on the inside of the tent where we currently talking, and it made all of us feel a whole lot better just to look at it.

The topic of discussion that evening had eventually drifted into life, liberty, and the pursuit of happiness. I do not remember exactly how or when it happened, but somehow the subject of Boy Scouts came up. What was astounding was the fact that three out of the four T-28 pilots who were left in the section at the time were Eagle Scouts. We all stopped our thinking process for a few seconds and just looked at one other.

It was too difficult to explain in words what that bonding did for us, but somehow it got into each of our hearts. I thought to myself as I quickly reflected back over my career as a member of the Boy Scouts of America, *What a marvelous program, and look what the program did for leadership.* More important was to think that three out of the four survivors of the T-28 section were Eagle Scouts. Many people over the years have asked me how come I survived both wars and came home alive when the odds against coming home were so terrible. My answer was always, "On my honor I will do my best—to do my duty to God and country." And to that statement I would always quietly add from my days as a member of the Marine Corps, "Semper Fidelis."

It's not often that you get the opportunity to personally meet the president of your own nation or, for that matter, the president of a foreign nation. I couldn't conclude this chapter without describing how I met South Vietnam's president Nguyen Cao Ky. When I first met Ky in 1963, he was a lieutenant colonel and commander of a Vietnamese Air Force (VNAF) squadron stationed at Bien Hoa. At that time in history the VNAF had mostly T-28 fighters, with some of their units just starting to transition into A1-E fighter aircraft. All of their aircraft were aluminum silver in color, with South Vietnamese markings on their fuselage and wings, except for the one aircraft that Ky himself flew. Then lieutenant colonel Ky, as a squadron commander, was one of the first South Vietnamese pilots to check out in the A1-E. He had his personal A1-E aircraft painted solid black.

During 1963–64 most American pilots had very little respect for the VNAF pilots, and for good reasons. As combat pilots we were often directed into the same target areas, and if there were any indication of VC ground fire the VNAF pilots would not attack. They would often leave the target area with bombs under their wings, and later when they returned to Bien Hoa the ordnance would be gone. We strongly suspected that the VNAF pilots were landing somewhere and selling their bombs, rockets, and gun ammunition to the VC, but we couldn't prove it. Also, Vietnamese pilots would never respond to emergencies at night even in support of their own countrymen, no matter how critical the situation was. Should one of their pilots get shot down, they would flee the area if there was the slightest possibility of being hit by enemy ground fire.

I am painting a very poor picture of South Vietnamese pilots primarily because of their inability to accept responsibility in combat situations. However, I will admit that there were some distinguished VNAF pilots, especially their helicopter pilots who were always very courageous. However, I have personally watched VNAF pilots drop their bombs while remaining in level flight in the vicinity of the target area instead of using dive-bombing tactics. Quite often both the VNAF and we would be targeted for the same area. Upon arrival should the FAC explain that there was enemy ground fire in the area, the Vietnamese pilots would suddenly experience some sort of engine problem and have to return home.

On the other side of the coin, one of our pilots and I were returning from a combat mission northwest of Bien Hoa one day when we spotted two VNAF A1-Es below us headed the same way as us. My flight leader looked over at me and pointed down toward the VNAF aircraft. Since we were up higher and behind them with the sun to our back, the idea was to zoom down and bounce them for effect. It was at this point that I was about to learn an invaluable lesson in aerial combat maneuvers. The lesson was one that I would never forget: never underestimate your adversary! Neither one of us realized that one of the A1-Es was painted black until it was too late. To this day I do not know how Ky managed to spot us, but spot us he did. He waited just like a bird of prey until we were both committed and ready to yell, "Gotcha!" The next thing I knew was that we were in for one hell of a dogfight, with Ky and his wingman coming out the winner.

After ten or twelve minutes of heavy dogfighting Ky eventually waggled his wings, and we all joined up for the remainder of the flight back home to Bien Hoa. Just before Ky pitched out for his landing, he told us to report to his office as soon as we had landed and secured our aircraft. My flight leader and I were a little concerned, because we knew that we were not supposed to get involved, especially in dogfights, with the VNAF pilots. Neither of us had ever been in the VNAF area of the base, but we reported as requested to Ky's office.

It was the first and only time that I ever met Lieutenant Colonel Ky. He was dressed in an all-black flight suit and was all smiles as the four of us sat down. Since it was after a flight, we enjoyed several bottles of Vietnamese beer with Colonel Ky while everyone reflew the dogfight. Ky's English was excellent, and in my opinion he had proven beyond a doubt that his flying skills were outstanding. He was "one hell of a fighter pilot!" Ky later rapidly advanced in rank in the South Vietnamese Air Force and eventually became premier of his country.

38

My Favorite Meal

This has always been one of my favorite combat stories from my days in South Vietnam. It actually began back in a BOQ room at Travis AFB, California, when I first met Karl Bronson. We were both headed for somewhere in the South Pacific area of operations. Karl was what we called a Snake Eater, i.e., a Green Beret. By the time that Karl and I had finally reached Vietnam some ten days later we had become close friends. Karl told me prior to our departure from Clark Air Base in the Philippine Islands that if I ever needed help of any kind to try to contact him at the Special Forces headquarters. The Green Beret headquarters was located near the seaside village of Nha Trang in South Vietnam. As you well know from a previous story, Karl was responsible for furnishing the submachine guns for all of the pilots in the T-28 Section, and we were all most grateful to Karl for that.

Approximately two and a half months after Karl and I said our good-byes to each other in Nha Trang, I found myself on a two-week TDY tour at Soc Trang. In those early days of the war we were oftentimes still flying two-ship combat formation flights, and this story is about one of them. I was scheduled to fly with an old Air Force ROTC buddy from San Diego State College days. His name was Tom O'Brian, and he had gone by the nickname of Oby ever since I had known him. This particular morning Oby was Tiger Lead while I was flying in the Tiger Two position. We had been scrambled southeast to coordinates VS897/568, which was located near the Cambodian Border in the Seven Mountains area of the Mekong Delta. This was a very dangerous area, and we both knew that it was heavily infested with various types of antiaircraft weapons.

Arriving over the Seven Mountains, we rendezvoused with an Air Force Gooney Bird whose mission was to make some low-altitude resupply drops to an Army Special Forces A Team that was located on the side of Phnom Kto Mountain. The Gooney Bird crew was really counting on us being there, because when they tried to make resupply drops in this area without fighter protection they usually got the dickens shot out of their aircraft.

Upon completion of our escort, Oby contacted a South Vietnamese FAC who was flying in the same area. The FAC was very happy to get our call because there were numerous enemy targets in the area for us to work over. Once we located the FAC, he rolled his aircraft in and marked a target using a white phosphorus rocket. The FAC then cleared us in hot on the target. For the next fifteen or twenty minutes we hit a number of enemy targets with our various bomb loads.

Pulling up after our final bomb run, Oby asked me if I had ever seen big-time ack-ack, and I responded, "No." Oby then told me to get into the trail flight position about five hundred yards behind and below him. Descending to 1000-foot altitude, we crossed into Cambodia. Suddenly, without saying anything, Oby dived for the ground, and wow, did the action ever begin. What he did was buzz the Cambodian antiaircraft gun crews located along their border. Their gun crews responded immediately with both 37mm and heavy 57mm antiaircraft gunfire. Large puffy clouds of black smoke abruptly surrounded my aircraft, and the smooth air suddenly became very bumpy.

I remember screaming at Oby and called him everything that I could think of before I realized what terrible gunners the Cambodians were. They were obviously tracking us using manual targeting methods, and they were almost as bad as their VC buddies across the border were. Pulling off my fifth or sixth pass, I heard Oby tell me to rejoin with him. I had just about made it into position when Oby told me that he had a problem and was running out of gas. He started an immediate descent toward a country road below us. He asked me to climb up to 8000-foot altitude and attempt to contact our Command Post. Leveling off at 8000 feet, I made every effort to establish contact with the Command Post, even using the International Guard channel, but radio contact was impossible, as we were too far away.

My aircraft wasn't out of gas, but the fuel tank was getting mighty close to empty. Since I was still relatively new to the combat theater in the Delta, I decided that the best thing to do was follow Oby down and land on the highway behind him. Because I was flying as Tiger Two, I had not looked at a map prior to departure and had no idea where we were. I broke out my map and, looking around, guessed that we were landing on the Kinh Mac Duhn road that was heading toward the town of Can Thonh. After landing, I taxied up to Oby's aircraft and, getting as close as I could, completed a 180-degree turn so that we would have guns going both ways down the road. After shutting the engine down, Oby jumped up on my wing and said that we needed to get the aircraft closer together. Unlocking my brakes, I got out of the cockpit and jumped down to the ground. We physically pushed my aircraft back toward his so that the tails of our aircraft were approximately three feet apart.

Oby said that we were probably safe so long as it was light, but when darkness arrived the VC would own the entire area. Thinking to myself, I remembered stories of what had happened to other pilots who had been caught by the VC, and I wanted no part of being captured. While we were discussing our fate, many Vietnamese buses and trucks began arriving, and the drivers were very angry with us because they were unable to get their vehicles around us. About six or seven of the drivers got together and began shouting and waving their fists at us. Minutes later they got a little bolder and started toward us. Oby raised his submachine gun and fired a short burst over the drivers' heads. This had a tendency to quiet them down, and they subsequently kept their distance from us. After several hours of this cat-and-mouse game Oby suddenly called me and said, "We had grave problems approaching us." Looking to the north across a large field, we could see what looked like an entire company of VC insurgents approaching our position. They were wearing the typical VC conical straw hats and black pajama-type pants and appeared to be armed to the teeth.

I told Oby that I would not allow the VC to capture me alive and he felt the same way, so we both crouched down behind the landing gear of my aircraft and prepared to go down fighting. Suddenly we heard this voice shouting in English, "Are you Americans?"

We got up and climbed up on the wing and shouted back that yes, we were. The next thing that I noticed was what looked like a very large Vietnamese man in the center of their formation coming toward us, and he appeared to be in charge. Getting closer, he shouted, "Are you American commandos?"

We both responded with an immediate, "Yes."

By the time this person got close enough for us to physically recognize him, we realized that he, too, was an American. Not only was he an American, but it was none other than Lieutenant Bronson. What a relief and reunion we had. Karl explained that his troops were Montagnard soldiers from a village approximately five clicks (kilometers) to the north of where we currently were. We explained what our problem was, and Karl turned and began speaking to the Montagnards in their own language. Instantly the Montagnard soldiers began running toward the parked buses and trucks. Everyone in the buses and trucks got out and ran for their lives. Karl explained that all of the Vietnamese people in the area were scared to death of the Montagnard tribesmen.

Karl told us that there were approximately thirty-nine separate tribes of Montagnards located in the hills and jungles of South Vietnam. He also said that the VC left the Montagnards completely alone, as they were too fierce and unpredictable to fight. Karl told us that he had given his men orders to gather up anything that would hold gas. He then told his soldiers to punch holes in the gas tanks of the buses and trucks nearby and pour the gas into the main tanks on our aircraft. It was an incredible thing to watch this operation. As the tanks of the buses and trucks were almost empty, the Montagnards would then drive the vehicles off the road so that we would later have enough space to take off in. Oby and I were not exactly sure that our aircraft would burn a mixture of automotive fuel, but we were in no position to say anything.

Meantime, Karl told us that he had parachuted at night into this Montagnard village several months before. He hoped that the Montagnards would not kill him before he could establish himself and make friends with them. The only thing that he had to protect himself with was a radio. It seems that the Montagnards hated the VC so much that they would gladly accept help from any source, provided it helped kill VC. Once Karl had been accepted by the tribe, he had guns, medical supplies, and other things dropped into the village. His mission was to organize and train the men of the village into a guerilla-type fighting outfit. Karl's troops had been out on a training exercise today when they saw the two T-28s descending down toward the ground. I was so relieved to see Karl that I couldn't thank him enough for saving our skins.

The refueling operation took several hours, and during this time while visiting with Karl I asked him all about his experiences in the tribe. I was also curious about what he and the tribesmen ate, and how did he keep from getting sick? He laughed and showed me a small bottle of yellow-green pills that he said that he took religiously. Karl also mentioned that he had several Montagnard wives back in the village who took good care of him. Karl said that while they were out on training exercises the tribesmen cooked whatever they could find to eat. Karl went on to say that we were to be the guests of honor this day for his soldiers. He further said that very soon his soldiers would be preparing a meal in honor of this occasion. Karl was also quick to tell us both that no matter what the tribe members offered us to eat, we should just smile and eat it regardless of what it was. Karl reminded us that these people were a primitive people and should we fail to accept something that they offered they would be offended. Karl went on to say that should one of Montagnards become offended, he couldn't predict what they might do, and that it could be dangerous for us.

Now it is extremely important to understand just what these tribesmen looked like up close. The majority of them were fierce- and ferocious-looking, with hair that looked just like a primitive caveman's hair might look. Some had black pajamas on, while others simply wore a loincloth around their lower body. Most had teeth missing, and their individual breath would knock you over if they got close to you. The Montagnards were shorter than the average South Vietnamese people yet had much broader chests. These tribesmen actually reminded me of pictures that I had seen of the Australian Aborigine Bushman people. All of the Montagnards in addition to new automatic submachine guns carried large machete-style knives. Some of the soldiers even had bows and arrows with them.

While we were talking and watching the refueling operation, Karl had some of his troops dig a fairly large fire pit off to one side of the road. I was fascinated as I observed one of the tribesmen actually starting the fire in the pit with a bow and a stick. Several hours later we heard a lot of commotion from the tribesmen and watched as a member of the tribe approached us with a rather large net over his shoulder. At first we couldn't tell what was in the net, until he got close enough for us to hear the chattering and squealing of the animals in the net. It was definitely a bunch of brown monkeys inside the net.

Karl again reminded us to be very careful, as the Montagnards according to him were extremely superstitious people and wouldn't hesitate to kill us if we should dishonor them. He smiled and said that we would be offered what they considered to be the choicest piece of meat from the monkeys. He had my curiosity aroused as the tribesmen began to extract monkeys from the net. One of the tribesmen grabbed what looked like a medium-sized live monkey by the back of its head. The tribesman stepped up in front of me and, taking his machete, hit the monkey first on the right side of the head and again on the left side of the monkey's head. Next he quickly changed his grip and hit the same monkey in the back of its head. The monkey all this time was squealing loudly, and blood was running all over the tribesman's hands.

While all of this was going on, several of the Montagnards began circling around me. All of them at the minute seemed to have bloody machetes raised and pointing right at me. The tribesman directly in front of me then pulled the top of the monkey's head off, thus exposing the brain. He had this incredible smile on his face as he offered the monkey to me. I was gasping as Karl through clinched teeth said, "Eat the brains." I do remember saying, "What?" and Karl replied, "The brains."

Well, needless to say, with this Montagnard tribesman standing right in front of me with his bloody machete raised, I didn't hesitate to place as much of the monkey's brain as I could in my mouth.

At the same time, another Montagnard tribesman was offering the same delicacy to Oby, and he, too, like me, accepted the offering. Karl by this time was doubled over laughing and couldn't speak for several minutes. In fact, all of the nearby tribesmen were laughing either at us or with us. To this day I am not sure which it was. However, both Oby and I had a bloody monkey in our hands and were doing our level best to consume what was left of the monkeys' brains.

Once Oby and I had started eating, the rest of the tribesmen began killing the remaining monkeys in the net as fast as they could. The tribesmen were all dancing around enjoying this wonderful delicacy with us. When Karl finally managed to stop laughing, he told us that the entire thing had been a setup for their entertainment, but that we both had come through with flying colors. The tribesmen actually considered monkey brains to be a delicacy, according to Karl. He went on to say that they would not have killed us even though they appeared to want to do so. Karl had instructed the Montagnards without our knowledge, and everyone was having a great laugh over the whole situation. The tribesmen additionally roasted a large lizard that had been placed on a spit over the fire pit. The meat of the lizard was indeed tasty. About this time Oby informed Karl that he felt that we had enough fuel in our tanks. Oby told Karl that we needed to get back to Soc Trang before it got too dark as there were no runway lights on the base. We asked Karl to thank the Montagnards for their outstanding efforts in fighting the VC and for their very gracious meal that they had prepared for us.

Saying good-bye for the last time, I again thanked Karl for what he had done and hoped that in the near future Oby and I could return the favor that we both owed to him. We cranked our aircraft engines, and after warming up they seemed to be running fine. The Montagnards had cleared all of the vehicles off the road to the east of us, and we took off in that direction. I suggested to Oby that we make a high-speed pass with a victory roll for the Montagnards, and he said, "Absolutely." We came back in about twenty feet off the ground around 400 mph and performed several aileron rolls over their position. Pulling up sharply, we could see Karl and all of his troops waving at us, and we in turn wagged our wings back to them. Unfortunately, I never saw Karl after that incident. I only hoped that in the number of missions that lay ahead of us someway somehow we could provide some support for him. And yes, that was definitely one of my most unusual meals, and one that I shall never forget.

Later that evening we arrived safely back at Soc Trang. Everyone thought that we had both crashed or had been shot down since we had been gone for so long. Oby explained that on our way back we had experienced some engine problems. He also said that we were too far away for radio contact, so we had landed while en route at the Army's Can Tho Air Base. We were in the hopes that the Army mechanics there could help us. No one ever questioned Oby's remarks as far as I know. Oby was subsequently killed several weeks later while on another combat mission. We shared some precious time together, and I shall never forget what an outstanding pilot and leader he was.

39

Saigon and the Arrival of the A1-Es

Because of the unusual classified environment that we found ourselves in we were not privileged to receive normal Air Force benefits. We still could have thirty days of annual leave on the books, but we could not leave the theater for more than two weeks, the theater being the South Pacific. If we chose, we could go anywhere military flights went in the South Pacific, such as the Philippine Islands, Japan, Okinawa, or Hong Kong. We, however, could not come back to the States, including Hawaii. We were told that the reason for this was that several guys had gone home and when the time came to return were unable to get transportation back to Vietnam.

Oftentimes due to aircraft shortages or sick pilots we had to deadhead home from Soc Trang to Bien Hoa. What this amounted to was catching a ride on the daily Army helicopter that went up to Saigon for food. Upon arriving in Saigon we normally had to stay overnight in what was known as the "Safe House." We tried to be as discreet as possible when in Saigon, especially about carrying firearms, because it seemed to upset the REMs (rear echelon motherfuckers) who were assigned to the many soft administrative duties of the headquarters staff. One thing for sure: we learned the hard way that you never caught a taxicab at night without being fully armed. Since all of us had such a high price on our heads, we were never safe no matter where we were. Two of our people were killed in the backseats of civilian taxicabs in downtown Saigon, and later all that was ever found were their beheaded bodies.

One evening I was en route from the Safe House to Ton Son Knut Airfield in a civilian taxi, the driver suddenly swerved into a dark alley. Being alert, I quickly placed my .38-caliber derringer next to the driver's ear and cocked it. I didn't have to say anything, as the driver quickly put on his brakes and backed out of the alley faster than he went in. I then kept the gun next to his head all the way to the airfield. There was a South Vietnamese guard at the entrance to the airfield so I stopped the taxi and requested an interpreter all the while keeping the taxi driver covered.

Once the interpreter arrived, I explained what had happened. The interpreter said something to the South Vietnamese guard, who in turned pulled the Vietnamese driver out of the taxi and hit him several times with the butt of his rifle as he questioned him. The interpreter searched the taxi and found an automatic pistol under the front seat along with some VC propaganda materials. I felt lucky to have survived that very close shave, and I never went to town again without my submachine gun in hand.

While waiting for a ride out to Bien Hoa one day, I ran into a young second lieutenant who turned out to be the commander of the Seventh Aerial Port Squadron. While talking, the lieutenant explained that his squadron's mission was to escort and transport all of the top-secret materials from U.S. military forces from Vietnam to PACAF headquarters in Hawaii. He further told me he had a large backlog of materials and that he didn't have enough personnel with top-secret clearances to do the escorting. I told him that I might be able to help him out so long as he helped me, since I still had a top-secret clearance.

I had some time off coming, and I figured out that if I could guarantee my way to and from Hawaii, my section commander just might consent to let me go. I had the lieutenant type up a special set of orders that I took back to Bien Hoa with me. I also asked him to call my section commander. Arriving back at Bien Hoa, I took the special orders and presented them to Major Lengfield. He looked at the orders and finally said for me to put in for two weeks of leave. I called the lieutenant and we confirmed a departure date of June 26, 1964, with a return flight on the eighth of July. It worked out perfectly with my TDY schedule, as I would be back at Bien Hoa for three weeks during that time period.

Using the military's Autovon Telephone System, I contacted the U.S. Army's Fort Derussy in Hawaii and got confirmed reservations for eight days beginning June 30th. I told them that I would be arriving from Vietnam on the twenty-seventh, and they were most helpful in arranging reservations at one of the local hotels in downtown Honolulu for three nights. I next coordinated all of this information with Cynthia, and she was as delighted as I was with the good news. She as usual accomplished all of the necessary arrangements (no easy task for her) from her end, i.e., airline tickets, transportation to the airport, baby-sitters for the kids and dogs, et cetera.

By the middle of June 1964 there were only four T-28 pilots left in the commando squadron in South Vietnam. Under Secretary of State McNamara's orders, the first contingent of the Air Force's Al-Es had arrived in late May at Bien Hoa. Secretary McNamara's programs called for an escalation of the in-country war by U.S. forces, yet at the same time he also wanted to end the war as soon as possible. He was responsible for the arrival of the Air Force's Al-E squadron in Vietnam. When the Al-E squadron arrived, their pilots were really a cocky bunch of smart-asses who didn't want to listen to or believe the information that we were trying to tell them about Vietnam and the VC.

The four remaining T-28 pilots were given the opportunity to check out in the Al-Es depending on how much time they had left in the country. I flew four or five missions in the aircraft, but after experiencing the maneuverability of the T-28 I didn't care much for the Al-E. My instructor pilot was none other than a former SAC pilot from the 384th Bomb Wing at Little Rock AFB: Bill Dugan. Like me, Bill had always wanted to be a fighter pilot, and now was his chance. Much to my chagrin, Bill was killed a few months later while flying a combat mission against a heavy force of VC insurgents.

On the good side, the Al-E could carry a significantly larger ordnance load than the T-28. To me, the best thing was the addition of four 20mm cannons in the wings instead of the smaller .50-caliber machine guns that we had in the T-28s. The big problem with the Al-E was that it had a dual side-by-side cockpit with only one set of flight controls located on the left side. This caused many pilots to want to consistently pull off a target to their left, which made them very susceptible to enemy ground fire. Worse, should you be a second pilot on board, there were no flight controls for the right-hand seat, which usually made most pilots very uncomfortable. I felt sorry for the instructor pilots who were giving us checkout rides, because the aircraft was really touchy when you threw the power to it, but somehow we all four qualified. Because the Al-E pilots were not certified for in-country missions for the first thirty days, the remaining T-28 pilots led all of their combat formations. I got used to thinking that the Al-E had only one airspeed for everything and that was 131 knots. You broke ground at 131, climbed at 131, and cruised at 131!

On June 7, 1964, we received a frag order from Washington, D.C., ordering us to fly an all-out maximum-effort combat mission that according to Secretary of State McNamara would end the war in Vietnam. All twenty-four A1-Es were loaded with three 2,000-pound bombs between their landing gear plus twelve 500-pound bombs on each wing rack. My job was to fly a T-28 and lead this gaggle of A1-Es to coordinates XT370/550, which was located about fifty miles northwest of Bien Hoa. The target area was supposed to house the headquarters for the 9th VC Training Battalion, which was the mother unit located in South Vietnam. At the time the A1-E pilots were not combat-ready and thus were not allowed to dive-bomb. Leading this gaggle I set a course to the northeast and flew straight and level into the target area at 1800-foot altitude. I had the A1-Es move into the tightest formation that they could fly, and on my command they armed their bombs. When we were over the primary target, my command was: drop now, and the entire gaggle of A1-Es salvoed their bomb loads. I had to laugh, because when the A1s dropped their ordnance loads all twenty-four of them were suddenly so light that they popped straight up approximately two hundred feet above me. Watching them try to recover without hitting one another would have caused anyone to laugh. This mission in no way impacted the outcome of the war, but it certainly served notice to the VC that American airpower was becoming more formidable.

During the in-country combat indoctrination program we got into some really hot arguments with these cocky A1-E pilots. All of their combat missions during the checkout phase had been located in the III Corps area in and around Bien Hoa. The T-28 pilots considered combat missions flown in this area to be ''milk-run'' type missions when compared with the other three corps areas. The reason was that there were very few VC antiaircraft guns located in the III Corps area. What these missions did for the A1-E pilots was present them with a false sense of security regarding the VC antiaircraft guns. It seemed like every time we led a flight of A1s into a target area, the A1-E pilots all insisted on pulling off their bomb runs to the left. No amount of arguing by the T-28 pilots seemed to correct this error.

During postflight briefings we told the A1-E jocks that once they started flying missions into the IV Corps area things would become very different for them. They again refused to believe us. For some reason beyond our comprehension, the A1-E pilots thought that the VC were extremely primitive and backward in their use of combat weapons. The A1 jocks would laugh and joke each night in the officers' club as they talked about how invincible they were to the VC bows and arrows. This was certainly not the first time that our own military forces refused to believe us in terms of what was really happening in South Vietnam.

Somewhere around the 18th of June the A1-Es flew their first night solo combat mission into the IV Corps area. On that particular four-ship mission three of the four A1-Es were shot down and the pilots were killed. The following day, Colonel Bethea called a mandatory meeting for the A1-E pilots. The atmosphere in the briefing room was very subdued as Colonel Bethea insisted that the A1-E pilots reconsider what the T-28 pilots had been telling them. For the first time the A1-E pilots listened to us, as we helped plan their next mission.

40

June 25, 1964

I haven't kept track of all June 25ths in my life, but enough things have happened to me on this particular date so as to get my attention. On June 25, 1950, the Korean War started. On June 25, 1951, I was supposedly killed while onboard the USS *Baroko*. On June 25, 1961, I landed a B-47 that had run out of gas on a runway covered with close to a foot and a half of snow at Goose Bay Air Base in Newfoundland, Canada. On June 25th, 1962, I recovered from a night-inverted spin in a B-47 out over the Atlantic Ocean. On June 25, 1963, I crash-landed a B-47 bomber at Little Rock AFB, Arkansas. Finally, on June 25, 1964, I got shot down by VC antiaircraft guns in South Vietnam.

This following story is about my getting shot down in South Vietnam, and it is a day in my life that will always remain vivid in my memory. By the middle of June 1964, as mentioned earlier, there were only four pilots left in the T-28 section, and we were all located at Bien Hoa. Our daily schedules kept us busy, what with getting checked out in the A1-E, plus leading all combat training flights for the A1-E pilots in our T-28s. Since the A1-E pilots were not combat-ready yet, the four T-28 pilots were still responsible for all in-country combat missions. On the morning of June 25, we had only three T-28 pilots available for duty.

We were awakened at 0430 that morning and told that we had to scramble three aircraft ASAP. The weather there at Bien Hoa that morning was miserable for takeoffs, with low clouds and heavy rain showers. What was new? The combat situation was so critical that Colonel Bethea decided that he would send only the experienced T-28 pilots on this mission. Apparently around 0200 hours that morning a large force of VC insurgents had surrounded and attacked a Special Forces camp located on the west side of Tay Ninh Mountain. The target area was located about seventy-five miles due west of Bien Hoa and was in the same general vicinity where we had recently conducted the maximum-effort mission with the A1-Es.

The Special Forces commander who was under attack was requesting immediate drops of ammunition, water, and medical supplies. The Special Forces compound was located at the far upper end of a very narrow valley. The terrain and flight conditions were so bad that pilots coming in for low airdrops would try to make an immediate left turn after their drop. Because of the low clouds, turning right in most cases caused the C-123s to go into IFR flight conditions, and with the existing mountainous terrain so close no one really wanted to do that. But for obvious reasons it was the safest way to turn. The main problem was that the VC had set up a dual mounted antiaircraft machine gun above the Special Forces camp on the left side of the valley. Before our arrival the VC had shot down three American aircraft that had turned left, and everyone was running scared. The C-123s had refused to make further airdrops without fighter escort after the loss of the third aircraft. Hence the call for our emergency scramble that day.

Our job was to provide escort and air cover for the C-123s that were trying to drop the supplies to the besieged Special Forces. Much like our combat tactics for the Ranch Hand missions, we elected to place a T-28 with iron bombs about one hundred feet off the deck, followed immediately by a C-123. Five hundred feet above the C-123 was the second T-28, loaded with two cans of napalm. The third T-28, loaded with iron bombs, was flying in and out of the rain showers around fifteen hundred feet watching and waiting for the VC gun to fire.

Once we arrived on the scene and began our escort duties there were no more aircraft losses to the VC antiaircraft guns. On each mission we rotated in and out of the C-123s flying in circles for approximately two hours while over the target area. When the last C-123 on each mission completed its drop and departed for Saigon, a FAC who was flying in the immediate area contacted us and said that he had many targets for us. We joined up and under the FAC's direction made multiple bomb drops on the VC forces below us. The FAC kept cheering and was ecstatic with the accuracy of each of our bomb drops.

I flew in the number-two position on the first mission, led the second mission, and flew as number three during the third mission that day. Each mission that day was roughly two plus hours in length, and none of us escaped getting hit by the heavy VC ground fire. By the time we took off for the third mission, it was late in the day and the weather had gone from bad to considerably worse. All day long we had been on the lookout and searched diligently for the VC antiaircraft gun that had shot down the three cargo planes earlier that day. The frustration of not being able to locate the gun was getting to all of us.

In talking it over, the three of us figured that this was not the average VC antiaircraft gunner. An average VC gunner would have fired at every aircraft that got within distance of his guns. This particular gunner fired only short bursts at passing aircraft from his concealed position, thus making it extremely difficult to track the tracer bullets back to his location. In addition, the side of the hill where the gun was located was covered by jungle terrain, thus making it all the harder to see anything. By the time we had finished the third mission that day all three of us had over nine hours in the air with a combined twenty-plus bullet holes in our three aircraft.

It was around 1700 hours during the third mission, that a C-123 showed up and for some unknown reason we were unable to talk with him using our UHF radios. The C-123 pilot had been properly briefed as to how we would escort him, but apparently no one told him about which way to turn after his drop and he turned left. I was flying at around 1600-foot altitude when I saw the VC gunner cut loose at the C-123 as he was banking left. Calling Lead, I told him that I had the gun located and was going in hot. I pulled the aircraft up vertically on instruments and climbed into the clouds to 1800 feet. Arriving at 1800 feet without leveling off, I rolled my aircraft over performing a split-S maneuver while still flying on instruments.

During the vertical descent toward the side of the mountain I began to really get scared. For some reason it was taking too long and I was not breaking out of the clouds as soon as I thought I should be. Suddenly warning horns in my head were going off and I was sweating profusely. During the next few seconds my life began passing before my eyes. When I finally did break out, several factors instantly confronted me. Up to this time we all had used vertical dives on our bomb runs, and pilots got used to the ground coming up straight at them. However, in this case the ground was coming up rapidly toward me from a sixty-degree slant angle, which both scared and confused the heck out of me. To this day I am embarrassed about the accuracy of my bomb drop during that dive. By this time in my combat career my bombing accuracy was such that I could normally place a bomb through a particular window of a Vietnamese hooch (house) if necessary.

In the microseconds that were left during that dive I guessed the location of the enemy gun and instantly salvoed my entire bomb load. Pulling the stick back as hard as I could, I knew full well that I was going to get hit from the shrapnel of my own bombs as I bottomed out of the bomb run. Coming off the target, I not only felt bullets hitting my aircraft, but also observed tracer bullets going by my cockpit. At this moment in time I was mad as hell and all I could think of was Bernie Lukasic. For the third time in my combat career I quickly performed a Lukasic arc-type maneuver and found myself headed straight back into the VC guns.

My machine guns were making so much noise and I was pressing the target so hard that I do not remember exactly when my engine quit. I was firing constantly and the only thing that I can think is that I must have gotten the VC gunner while he was nailing me. I was extremely low on altitude as I started my pull-off. It was only then when I applied power with the throttle that nothing seemed to be happening—my engine had definitely quit. Gliding down the hill, I did everything wrong from the standpoint of preparing for a crash landing. Foremost on my mind was the thought that Cynthia was going to be in Hawaii in a few days and I wouldn't be there to meet or see her.

Looking down the side of the hill, I noticed a dirt road heading west back toward Saigon. I immediately headed the aircraft toward that dirt road. The ground was coming up faster than I anticipated while I was making every attempt to slow the aircraft down to less than forty knots. I quickly placed both the gear and flaps into the full down and locked position and opened the canopy. Hitting the road the first time, I bounced back into the air and very quickly came right back down in a cloud of dust. The second time the aircraft hit the ground, it stayed glued to the ground, and the noise of breaking brush alongside of the road with my wings was awesome as the aircraft finally came to a stop amid a huge cloud of dust and debris. My main goal during that crash landing was aircraft control, which I devoted my undivided attention to.

I couldn't have sat there for more than a minute when a bullet came through the left front side of the forward canopy. This bullet clipped off the left earphone of my headset and killed the VNAF who was in the backseat of the T-28. My first reaction was that I needed to get out of there. First, I got out of the aircraft to see what was wrong with my engine. What a stupid thought that was, as it almost cost me my life. As I was stepping out of the cockpit onto the wing, a bullet struck the side of the aircraft and passed through the pant leg of my flying suit. This really pissed me off and I quickly jumped back inside the cockpit. While attempting to restart the engine I happened to look out and saw about 150 yards away several VC infantrymen coming toward me. This is where my fellow pilots really saved my life. Each pilot strafed both sides of the road and out in front of my aircraft, trying to keep the VC away from me.

During my third attempt using the starter switch, and much to my amazement, the engine coughed several times and quickly came to life. I quickly flipped my ground override switch for my machine guns on and turned the nose of the aircraft back and forth, spraying the area immediately in front of me with .50-caliber bullets. Even though the engine was running very rough, I didn't hesitate to make a quick decision. Looking down the road, even though it wasn't straight I pushed the throttle fully forward, and somewhere between forty and sixty knots I yanked the T-28 into the air

Getting the gear and flaps up as quickly as possible, I selected a heading that I hoped was toward Bien Hoa. Within minutes every engine instrument on the panel was operating close to the red zone. I dared not touch the throttle, for I knew that I had a terrible oil leak and was afraid that the engine would seize at any moment. My goal was to get as far away from the VC forces as I could before the engine quit again. The fear thing, for pilots, is always with you, especially when under extreme stress. I didn't recognize any of the terrain, but I knew that there was a paved road to the south of me that went from Tay Ninh to Saigon, and that's where I headed. Once I was airborne, neither of my fellow pilots could catch up with me, as I left the throttle in the full open position. Both pilots later said that all they could see was a small dot with a large smoke screen behind it heading toward home. Finally locating the correct road back toward Saigon, I roared down the road, flying about one hundred feet over the tops of the trees. I figured that if the engine seized I could put the aircraft down on the road and take my chances with the VC from there.

One of my problems was that during the crash landing on the side of Tay Ninh Mountain I lost my headset and could not communicate with anyone. Due to the extreme rainy and inclement weather, both of my wingmen finally lost sight of me. Between them, after they contacted Bien Hoa's tower they decided that I must have gone in somewhere, as they could not raise me on the radio. To this day I cannot remember being as scared as I was during that eventful flight back toward Saigon. I flew for some distance before I realized that I had not closed my canopy. While closing the canopy, with my high state of anxiety, I also realized that I had lost my radio headset and in addition was not strapped into my cockpit seat.

It was getting really dark and my greatest fear at the time was not being able to figure out exactly where I was. Seeing a village to my left, I swerved off the road that I was following and circled the village, hoping to see something that I could recognize. I was sure that it was Xom Dan Han, which would place me approximately fifteen miles from Bien Hoa as the crow flies. I could see the lights of Saigon to the south of me through the rainstorms, but since I had no way to communicate with the tower, I elected to head for where I thought Bien Hoa was located. This, of course, was another stupid mistake on my part. I was running out of flying time, especially with all of my engine instruments now redlined. Keeping that old T-28 in the air was my most immediate problem.

To this day I do not know what kept that old T-28 going, but at approximately six miles out I saw the runway lights of Bien Hoa. This is the point where a "guardian angel" or whatever you want to call it had a hand in the outcome of my life once again. The second that I recognized the runway lights at Bien Hoa, I pulled the power off, as I was going too fast. The minute I pulled the throttle back the engine seized and the propeller stopped. Suddenly it got extremely quiet in the cockpit. My concern was now to try to stretch my glide—trading altitude for airspeed in an attempt to get across the Song Dong Nai River, which was the eastern border of Bien Hoa Air Base. Somehow with God's help I managed to accomplish this feat.

There were so many problems facing me at that particular time in space that it was impossible to recognize them all. Besides having no engine, having lost my helmet and not being strapped in while crossing the river at no more than fifty feet above the water definitely held my attention. I held my flaps in the up position, trying to stretch my glide until I saw land below me. At the absolute last second I placed the gear handle down and held my breath. I actually touched down on the runway's overrun, heading slightly to the right, and finally came to a stop in the dirt along the right side of the main runway, sitting there for how long I do not know, as it was dark. Finally I removed my .38-caliber derringer from my boot and fired two flare shots into the air toward the control tower. Within minutes a security truck with red lights on came highballing down the runway and located me.

Since I was still in the cockpit, the security guys called an ambulance. When the ambulance arrived, I climbed out of the cockpit and rode on into the base with the medics, who dropped me off at the T-28 section. I reported the loss of another T-28 to Colonel Bethea. He wasn't too concerned about the loss, as there was just too much going on to be bothered with the loss of an old T-28 that was on its last leg anyway. Three months later, as a member of the 18th Tactical Fighter Wing, in Okinawa I was awarded the Silver Star for these three missions. U.S. Army Special Forces intelligence reports indicated that not only did I silence the gun position, but also over 400 VC had been killed in this single action that day. That night the squadron flight surgeon there at Bien Hoa insisted that I report to the Air Force hospital the next day in Saigon for a complete medical checkup. For the first time in my military history I disobeyed orders. I was not going to let anything come between me and that C-124 flight that was leaving the following morning for Hawaii.

I stayed up most of the night and was actually waiting beside the C-124 when the crew arrived. Once airborne, I never realized just how long it took for a C-124 to fly from Saigon to Hawaii. The first leg of the trip was to Wake Island, and it took twenty-one hours. Touching down on Wake Island's runway, the aircraft commander of the C-124 told me that the crew had to get twenty-four hours of crew rest before going on to Hawaii. I was frantic with this news. Looking out the cockpit window, I saw another C-124 on the ramp with its engines running. I told the aircraft commander that I had an appointment with General Harris the following morning and pleaded with him to call the other C-124 to see if they would help me. It was a wild shot, as General Harris was the Supreme Allied Commander of all forces in the Pacific Ocean, but it worked. By the time the two C-124 pilots were through talking, the second pilot agreed to take me on with them to Honolulu. With the assistance of the two crew chiefs and a truck we moved 750 pounds of top-secret material so fast you wouldn't believe it. The total flying time combined for both C-124s to Hawaii was thirty-one hours. The combat fatigue plus the effects of yesterday's incredible combat mission were rapidly catching up with me as we approached Honolulu.

Unbeknownst to me, the aircraft commander of the second C-124 believed what the aircraft commander of the first C-124 had told him. Upon landing, the AC contacted the Command Post at Hickim AFB and had them notify General Harris's office that I was onboard his aircraft. While the C-124 was parking, General Harris's staff car rolled up beside the entry hatch. General Harris's aide met me and told me that I was to go with him immediately to meet with General Harris. I informed the aide that I had 750 pounds of top-secret material onboard the C-124, and he told me to not worry about it. The aide said that he would have the intelligence section come to the C-124 and pick the stuff up.

I got in the staff car and we drove straight to the general's office. Never in my military career did I feel so conspicuous. I hadn't slept much during the past thirty-one hours, hadn't shaved, and sure as hell wasn't in any kind of uniform to be reporting to a general officer. I was wearing a very worn-out and cut-off flying suit, and my only headdress was the Australian bush hat with the cobra-skin band around it. I worried a little about my armament, but the aid told me to not worry about it. I was carrying my submachine gun, two .38-caliber pistols, and a .38-caliber double-barreled derringer in my left boot, plus I had a bolo machete in a leather case down my back.

As I entered the outer administrative office, General Harris came out to meet me. He was a short man in stature and was wearing his Air Force blue cloth cap. There I was, totally intimidated, staring at twelve silver stars. I had seen pictures of four-star generals but had never spoken to one, and the initial impact was one I shall never forget. I apologized and told General Harris that I was not prepared to meet with him simply because I had no Air Force uniform with me. I also told him how I had used his name in order to get onboard the second C-124. General Harris shook my hand, went over and closed his office door, and asked me to sit down. The general laughed while pouring coffee for both of us and said that sounded like what one of his fighter pilots would do and to not worry about it. The general said that I was the first T-28 combat pilot he knew of who had returned from the combat zone and he wanted to know firsthand what was going on in the field. Once I relaxed and got over my fear of just plain talking to a general, we enjoyed several more cups of coffee and talked for almost two hours.

The general finally asked me how I had managed to get to Hawaii, since he knew that combat pilots flying in-country missions were not supposed to be able to do that. I told him about my top-secret clearance and how I had met the Aerial Port squadron commander by accident and that the lieutenant had worked it out with my section commander to use me as a top-secret courier. The general then asked me why I had wanted to come to Hawaii, and I told him that my wife was waiting for me in one of the downtown hotels. General Harris literally jumped up, shouting for his aide, all of which scared the heck out of me. The general then turned and thanked me for the information that I had given him and told his aide to take me downtown immediately. General Harris also gave me his telephone number and said that when I was ready to return I should call his office for transportation.

Leaving the base, the aide asked me where I wanted to go. I looked at the aide and suddenly panicked. For some reason, probably because so much had happened to me in the last forty-eight hours, I simply could not remember where I had told Cynthia to meet me. Also, I was in such a hurry to get out of Bien Hoa and get to Saigon and to that C-124 that I forgot to bring my last correspondence from Cynthia with me. I asked the aide to give me the names of some of the better downtown hotels, and the only one that sounded familiar was the Mapes. Because I couldn't think of anything else, I suggested that he take me there. The captain pulled up in front of the Mapes Hotel and let me out.

This was still 1964, and most Americans had absolutely no idea what was going on with the war in Southeast Asia. Stepping out of the staff car, I grabbed my B-4 bag and headed for the main desk. Immediately people stopped and started staring at me. I guess I must have looked like something out of a Hollywood war movie. I think the thing that got these people's attention first was my Australian bush hat, and then all of the guns that I was carrying. I'm sure that my eight-inch handlebar mustache got some laughs, because it most certainly was not in alignment with current U.S. Air Force regulations.

Stepping up to the main counter inside the hotel, I asked the desk clerk what room Mrs. Hunter was in. He stared at me and finally said, "Room Four-oh-six." Turning around, I had started toward the elevator when the desk clerk said in a very loud voice, "Excuse me, sir, but is that a real gun?"

I had completely forgotten about my submachine gun. I said, "yes," and turning back, I set the submachine gun up on top of the counter.

At this point the head clerk intervened, asking me if the gun was loaded.

I replied, "Yes," and quickly ejected the large clip from the gun, again laying it on the counter. By now a large crowd had gathered behind me, but no one said anything to me. I said to the head desk clerk, "You probably want my thirty-eight pistols, too." Extracting the shells from both .38s, I put the bullets onto the top of the counter, placing them in a nice neat pile. The looks on all of the clerks were ones of absolute disbelief. I said, "You probably want this, too," as I pulled the large bolo machete from behind my back and placed it, too, on the counter. Turning to leave, I remembered the .38 derringer in my boot and quickly unloaded it and placed it also on the counter. I asked the clerk for a receipt for my weapons and suggested that he place them in the hotel safe. I told the head desk clerk that if there were a problem to call General Harris's office and that his office would clarify the situation. I also told the clerk that I would be checking out several days later and that I would need all of my weapons back. I don't think any of these folks had seen anything like this since WW II had ended.

Several gentlemen behind me in the crowd of people wanted to know where I was from, and I replied, "Vietnam." No one said anything; they just all stared at me as I picked up my B-4 bag and headed for the elevator.

Of course Cynthia was extremely happy to see me. She insisted that I had lost a lot of weight, which was probably true. Sometime during the next several hours she asked me if I had received the message that she had left with the main desk from the other hotel. I remember giving her a stupid look but didn't say anything. She went on to say that she just didn't like the accommodations in the other hotel and decided to move over here to the Mapes. This was one of those occasions where it was best to just not say anything, so I didn't.

There was just no way that I could tell her that I had been shot down three days ago and that I had avoided checking into the hospital in Saigon. My mental state at the time was one of complete fear, and I just couldn't tell her the truth. After what I had been through during the past three months and with only four T-28 pilots left alive in South Vietnam, I had the feeling that I would never see her again. I was chagrined at myself for even thinking like this. I remembered what had happened to some of my other buddies for feeling the same way, but I couldn't help it. Cynthia and I decided that we would just live "high on the hog" for the next nine days and not worry about what the future held. We enjoyed one of the finest posthoneymoon experiences there in Hawaii that anyone could ever imagine.

By the time that I returned to Vietnam, I was really spooked. I was almost afraid to fly another combat mission. I did, however, fly several more combat missions, but my heart just wasn't in them like it had been before. It's difficult thing to put your finger on, but whatever it was, I had a bad case of it, and I didn't want to tell anyone else about my feelings. One of my closest friends, Bill Dugan, recognizing my problems, did his best to keep my spirits up, but it was a hard thing even for him to do. I flew my last mission in a T-28 on July 18, 1964, delivering one of the last of our two flyable T-28s to the CIA operations base at Nha Xom Phaxom in Thailand. From the eighteenth of July until I left in September, I flew my remaining combat missions in the A1-E.

In early September an emergency request came into the 34th Group asking for anyone with a career specialty of 1435 to go to Okinawa immediately. I quickly checked with personnel and discovered that I had a secondary Air Force Specialty Code (AFSC) as an air operations specialist, or a 1435 in Air Force language. I told Personnel that I still had two months to complete my duty requirement. They in turn said that they were desperate enough for a 1435 in Okinawa that they would give me complete credit for the year if I would volunteer. At the time I really felt like I had worn out my welcome mat in Vietnam and readily volunteered for Okinawa.

41

Okinawa

After I left Saigon as a passenger on an Air Force C-54 cargo-type aircraft, it took almost eight hours to reach Kadena Air Base in Okinawa. A really unusual situation occurred as the C-54 came to a full stop in front of base operations. Since I was the only passenger getting off, the aircraft commander of the C-54 shut down only the two engines on the passenger-door side of the aircraft. The transit alert crew pushed one of those large ladder-type ramps up against the passenger door of the C-54, and I prepared to get off. Much to my surprise climbing up the ladder came the commander of the 18th Tactical Fighter Wing.

In my short eight years in the Air Force I had never heard of a wing commander meeting a lowly incoming captain, and I was really shocked. As Colonel Cardenas arrived at the top of the ladder he held out his hand to me. I was astounded to see a large Sigma Chi emblem on the ring of his right hand. Immediately I slipped him the Sigma Chi social grip, and the bond of truth materialized between us. He later told me that I was the first combat-qualified pilot in the wing and that was why he wanted to meet me upon arrival.

Colonel Cardenas told me that I would be working in the wing's Command Post and that I could check out in any aircraft on base except the F-105. The colonel told me that after flying 166 combat missions I needed a rest. He did say that after I got my feet on the ground I could check out in the Thunderchief if I wanted to. I thanked him for meeting me and headed for base operations, where I could catch a taxi to the BOQ housing area.

Two other pilots, Dick Fleitz and Wes Shireman, both captains like myself, were checking in at the same time, and the BOQ clerk gave us adjoining rooms. Since it was the middle of the day, all three of us walked the short block over to the officers' club for lunch. While we were in the process of eating our lunch, suddenly without warning klaxons and sirens started going off all over the place. Over the base loudspeaker system a voice was repeating, "Typhoon Condition One." Since we were all new to Okinawa, we asked the waiter what was going on. He said if we were smart we would go next door to the Class Six liquor store and stock up on as much booze as we could carry back to the BOQ. We quickly followed his advice and then headed back across the street to our BOQ.

That same day, unknown to us, 425 schoolteachers had arrived at Kadena and they also had checked into the same BOQ. The teachers were headed for assignments into the American school systems in Korea, Okinawa, and Japan. We discovered that during a Typhoon Condition One, everyone on base was restricted to his or her quarters. An incredible weather phenomenon subsequently occurred. This typhoon, which was very real, circled around the island of Okinawa for the next seven days. Wow, what a way to get initiated into a new assignment, with only three guys and 425 women. We really partied hard while the typhoon went around and around the island, and we became very good friends over the time period. Both Wes and Dick were F-105 pilots new to the 18th TFW wing. Dick was assigned to the 44th Tactical Fighter Squadron (TFS), while Wes went to the 67th TFS. Dick later gave me my first checkout rides in the F-105. Wes was later shot down over Hanoi, North Vietnam, and spent six years in the Hanoi Hilton prison camp. Three weeks later all of our families arrived, and we all found Okinawan-style houses in the same neighborhood off-base.

I was told when I first got commissioned that somewhere down the road I would experience a bad assignment during my Air Force career, and believe me this was about to be it. I had never been around a Command Post, and all I can think to say is that it was like being hired as a cheap telephone operator. The Command Post commander, since I was the "new guy," put me on the swing shift duty rooster, which meant that I worked a twelve-hour shift starting at eight o'clock each evening. I quickly learned to hate those night shifts. The worst part was that after eleven long hours of trying to stay awake, the night duty officer had to conduct the morning 0800 stand-up briefing for the wing.

The briefing room was about thirty feet long by eight feet wide. The briefing officer had a two-foot-wide runway and had to face all the wing colonels in attendance. Directly behind the briefing officer was a floor-to-ceiling plastic aircraft status chart with every aircraft assigned to the wing, with the condition of each aircraft on it. What made these briefings so difficult was when some colonel would want to know exactly where the part was for a particular aircraft. With 111 aircraft on the board, it was extremely difficult to not only locate the aircraft in question but then also give the nice colonel a good guess as to when the missing part would arrive. I sweated out many morning briefings trying to explain why some part was not where it was supposed to be.

The night Command Post shift consisted of myself plus a staff sergeant. Thank God for intelligent staff sergeants, as this one kept me out of so much trouble, you couldn't imagine it. I worked directly for a senior captain who had to have the worst attitude case of any officer I had ever met. The commander of the Command Post was an alcoholic major, and he, too, was very difficult to get along with. Working nights and being off days was not conducive to a good social life, either. The only highlight was that frequently Colonel Cardenas would come into the Command Post late at night and we would share war stories for several hours. I remember one night that Cynthia called and told me that there were two inches of water on the floors inside our base house, and what was I going to do about it? We both laugh about it now, but at the time and especially during typhoons it was "do your best to solve the problem yourself" and don't worry about the outcome.

After four months in the Command Post, an interesting event occurred. One of my high school classmates, Rusty Rumney, came through Okinawa on his way to Vietnam and wanted to meet me for lunch. It was my day off and I had flown a training mission earlier that same morning and had not changed out of my orange flying suit when Rusty called. I drove over to the club, not giving it much thought, as we walked into the formal dining room for lunch. I didn't particularly feel out of place in the formal dinning room, because there were other pilots in the same room also wearing their orange flying suits. That evening as I reported for my night shift, the day shift advisor told me that he was going to write up a disciplinary action in the form of an Article 15 on me for wearing my orange flying suit in the officers' club. I was absolutely furious with this senior captain for being such a jerk. However, I didn't want an

Article 15 on my Air Force promotion record jacket. That night I broke out my thesaurus and spent about four hours writing a rebuttal letter, telling the good captain exactly what I thought of him. The next morning I left the letter on his desk and promptly forgot about the incident.

Three days later Cynthia woke me up early in the day and said that I was to report to the wing commander's office in a Class A uniform immediately. Arriving in the command section of the wing early, I told the commander's secretary that I was reporting as requested. The fear of waiting outside the wing commander's officer is enough to scare anyone to death, and I was no exception. Fifteen to twenty minutes later the secretary finally told me to report in to the wing commander, Colonel Cardenas.

Marching in, I stopped three paces in front of Colonel Cardenas's desk, saluted, and informed him that Captain Hunter was reporting as requested. In my peripheral vision I could see three other full colonels sitting quietly in their chairs which scared me all the more. I knew something was wrong but was unable to figure out exactly what it was. Colonel Cardenas kept me standing there for what seemed like a full five minutes. However long I remained standing there, it was it was enough for sweat to form on my forehead. Finally, Colonel Cardenas looked me right in the eye and said, "Captain Hunter, did you write this letter?"

Still standing at attention I glanced down to his desk and saw the letter that I had written to the day shift advisor in the Command Post. There were red marks up and down the margins of the letter, and I just knew that my career in the Air Force was over at that moment. Replying, I said, "Yes, sir, I wrote that letter."

He finally smiled after what seemed like an eternity, and I could hear the other three colonels snickering in the background. Colonel Cardenas then said, "Captain Hunter, I want you to go down the hallway to the Director of Personnel's office and take everything out of Lieutenant Colonel Upchurch's desk and place all of his items in a box." Colonel Cardenas then said that anyone who could write a letter like that one deserved to be in a better position. "You are now officially the new director of personnel and wing executive officer for the Eighteenth TFW."

All three of the colonels who had been seated stood, cheered, and congratulated me on my new position. What a shock and surprise it was for me. I was so excited that I wouldn't have to work night shifts any longer and could hardly wait to go home and tell Cynthia the good news.

The following morning as I was getting settled into my new desk, a civilian gentleman approached my desk and asked who the TSCO (Top-Secret Control Officer) for the wing was. I looked at my brand-new chief master sergeant, who himself had just reported in that morning, and asked him who and what was a TSCO? The chief looked at me very strangely and replied, "Sir, you are the TSCO." Standing up, I quickly introduced myself to the civilian and told him that this was my first day in this position. I further told him that if he would explain what a TSCO was, I would be most happy to help him. By this time everyone in the office was laughing—most of them at me.

The civilian turned out to be a Mr. Hadley from Fifth Air Force headquarters in Japan. He produced a copy of his orders and told me that he was here to conduct an inspection of our Command Post. Mr. Hadley said that he was particularly interested in how we were handling top-secret messages. I told him that I had been in the Command Post from December until just yesterday and that yes, there were a lot of top-secret messages in the Command Post. I told Mr. Hadley, from what I knew, the Command Post had received only one top-secret message in the previous five years. Since December the CP had received well over 380 top-secret messages. Mr. Hadley informed me that the Air Force had very strict procedures for the handling of top-secret messages and that was why he was here to ensure that we were following U.S. Air Force directives.

Verifying Mr. Hadley's credentials and clearances, I informed Colonel Cardenas as to who was onboard and then took Mr. Hadley over to the Command Post. Upon arrival at the Command Post, Mr. Hadley asked to use the rest room before we proceeded with the inspection. Several minutes later he returned and was flaming mad. Since there weren't enough filing cabinets in the Command Post, top-secret messages were piled in stacks on the floor all along one wall. What had happened when Mr. Hadley entered the latrine was that an Okinawan cleaning lady had taped a top-secret message to the glass part of the door indicating that she was in the process of cleaning the latrine. When Mr. Hadley finally caught his breath he told me that what had just happened was beyond belief. He said that our wing commander could be fired over this incident. Mr.

Hadley then asked me how I had gotten assigned to my current position, and I told him. During the course of our conversation Mr. Hadley discovered that I had only recently been raised to a Master Mason in the local Masonic Blue Lodge. Mr. Hadley then calmed down and suggested that we return to see Colonel Cardenas. Mr. Hadley sat and talked with Colonel Cardenas for fifteen minutes and finally told him that this would not be a 5th Air Force inspection. Mr. Hadley said that in light of the current wartime situation he would just evaluate Command Post operational procedures.

The handling of nuclear weapons and the Air Force procedures that apply to using or dropping them are extremely stringent. For a fighter pilot to drop a nuclear weapon, the pilot must have a validated "Go-Code card." These cards are normally passed out and signed for by each pilot as he comes on alert duty. When the pilot accepts and cocks his alert aircraft, the Go-Code cards are placed in a small holder located inside the cockpit of the fighter. The alert aircraft are located inside a fenced-in area with multiple armed guards circulating among the aircraft and around the area. When an alert changeover occurs, the pilots going off alert bring in their old Go-Code cards and return them to the wing intelligence officer. Local procedures for the handling of these highly classified top-secret Go-Code cards were a little complacent in the 18th TFW in 1964–65. Pilots who were in a hurry to get off alert frequently would just throw the Go-Code cards on the table and walk off, leaving the intelligence officer to sort them out by number.

It was an alert changeover morning, so Mr. Hadley decided to inventory the wing's Go-Code cards. I watched him as he stood there aghast at what he was seeing. Pilots involved in the changeover would just throw their Go-Code cards on the table and walk off. The new pilots coming on alert would amble over and pick any Go-Code card and proceed out to their assigned aircraft. According to regulations, anytime a Go-Code card was handled by anyone, all Go-Code cards had to be then verified and accounted for. Approximately every three months or sooner all Go-Code cards had to be destroyed, and new cards would be issued out of the JCS office in Washington, D.C. The accountability of handling these cards was extremely sensitive, as we were dealing with the authority to start a nuclear war.

On this particular morning as Mr. Hadley was observing the alert changeover, one of the Go-Code cards came up missing. This is the kind of incident that gets wing Commanders fired really quick by higher headquarters. Mr. Hadley insisted on opening an immediate investigation by recalling all of the pilots who had gone off alert that morning. He requested that I order all pilots back to the Command Post instantly. By the time we got everything sorted out, it was apparent that the card that was missing had been assigned to a good friend of mine, Captain Laws.

During the interrogation of Captain Laws, it seems that the Go-Code card he had might have accidentally fallen down inside the cockpit of the F-105. We quickly pulled the F-105 off the alert line and proceeded to have maintenance personnel tear the cockpit apart looking for the card. I then informed Colonel Cardenas what was going on and told him that I would remain with Mr. Hadley until this problem was resolved. It took over five hours to remove the cockpit from the F-105, and we found nothing. We sent the pilots home after three hours, and sometime during the fifth hour Captain Laws called back telling me that he had located the Go-Code card.

When Captain Laws had gone home, his Okinawan maid had gathered up all the dirty clothes in their hamper and had taken them down to a local stream to wash. The glitch was that the Go-Code card was in the lower pocket of Captain Law's flight suit. His maid had proceeded to lay each piece of clothing on a flat rock and beat it with another rock when she noticed this funny card in the pocket of his flying suit. The maid brought the flight suit with the card still in the pocket back to Captain Laws's house, and he in turn called me. Because the card was dented we had to recall all Go-Code cards and inform the JCS in Washington, D.C. We explained to the JCS office that the card had fallen inside the cockpit of the F-105 and was damaged during the removal of the cockpit. Fortunately, the JCS's office bought our excuse, even though it necessitated changing all Go-Code cards throughout the entire U.S. Air Force. Mr. Hadley was really very understanding about this mishap and said that he, too, would keep our secret quiet so long as we cleaned up our act. Thank God he had decided to turn this experience into a training session and not into a real inspection.

My life was never the same after the first few weeks in this new position. I had no idea what a director of personnel and wing executive officer's duties were, but I worked night and day trying to learn them. One day Colonel Cardenas called me into his office and explained that the situation in Vietnam was getting more serious and he was afraid that we might be tasked to send one or two of our fighter squadrons down there. Colonel Cardenas asked me if I would mind going down to the three fighter squadrons and talk to the young pilots about my experiences in flying combat. I told him that I would be delighted to do this. The first squadron that I visited was the 67th TFS commanded by Lt. Col. Robbie Risner. You would have to fully understand what makes fighter pilots tick to imagine the reception that I got. Much like the A1-E pilots, the F-105 jocks literally laughed me out of their briefing room. Those pilots insisted that I was not a true fighter pilot because the VC had only been shooting arrows and throwing spears at me for the past year. I couldn't believe how foolish and naïve these young pilots were. What little they knew about Vietnam and combat techniques at the time you could place on the point of a pin.

After my reception in the 67th TFS I decided to not even brother with the other two Thud squadrons. I informed Colonel Cardenas of my decision and why, and he concurred. About a month after this disastrous experience, the 67th TFS was the first all jet fighter unit to become involved in the Vietnam War. The 67th TFS deployed to Danang Air Base in South Vietnam in December of 1964. During the first thirty days of combat operations the squadron lost eighteen out of their twenty-four assigned aircraft. When the six pilots returned to Kadena, we had to really shuffle pilots from other squadrons to try to get the 67th TFS back up to tactical readiness status. We relied heavily upon accelerated replacement pilots from the States to bring all of our fighter squadrons back up to twenty-four pilots per squadron level.

As soon as Lt. Colonel Risner returned to Kadena, he contacted the commanders of the other two squadrons, and all three commanders asked Colonel Cardenas if I would speak to the entire wing about combat tactics. This time you could hear a pin drop in the auditorium during any part of my presentation. Shortly after this presentation Colonel Cardenas cleared me to check out in the F-105. I flew two familiarization flights and was subsequently cleared for a solo flight. Because I was still considered a "wing wienie" and not assigned to a fighter squadron in particular, I could only fly four hours a month in the F-105. Colonel Cardenas would not allow me to deploy with any of the squadrons, as he felt that I had more than filled my square of combat missions. I didn't like his decision but learned to live with it. Worst of all while getting my four hours of flying time I was restricted to the local flying area only. After two months, I elected to give up flying the F-105, because I could only fly in the local training area.

One of my main reasons for coming to Okinawa and Kadena Air Base was to fly the F-105. My first flight in the F-105 was one I shall never forget. I was in the backseat of an F model, with the pilot in the front seat being a very good buddy of mine. Lou as a typical Thud jock, considered himself, like most fighter pilots, to be the "greatest fighter pilot" in the U.S. Air Force. Lou was incredulously humorous in his approach to life. We took off and climbed to 23,000 feet in just a few seconds and headed northwest for the Ie Shima bombing and gunnery range. Our mission was to drop a rack of iron bombs and then strafe some gunnery targets. Arriving over the bombing range, we received permission for our first run. Having flown over 166 combat missions in South Vietnam, I was very familiar with what was about to happen—the only difference was the initial roll-in altitude.

During my combat missions in South Vietnam, we usually rolled in on a target between 1800 and 2000 feet above the ground. Rolling in on a target was usually a very coordinated and comfortable maneuver in the T-28. The pilot just flipped the aircraft over upside down, smoothly pulling the nose down to the vertical position. Lou was talking to the range officer, telling him that we were coming in hot. Lou then rolled the F-105 over, snapping the nose down, and lit the afterburner. Even without the use of the afterburner, it is difficult to communicate between the two cockpits of the F-105. When in afterburner, it is absolutely impossible to communicate. I was used to seeing the ground come up at me, but not at this speed. It was like being in an elevator that had broken loose from the eighty-fifth floor and was speeding straight down at a supersonic speed with nothing to stop it. I remember screaming at Lou to "Pull out! Pull out!," as I was certain that we were going to plant ourselves in the ground. Just microseconds before Lou began the actual pull-out, I had finally located the ejection handles and was within seconds of ejecting from the runaway aircraft.

Later, during the debriefing, I learned that it was a standard operating procedure to light the afterburner during a dive whenever the pilot had a full load of bombs on the aircraft. The reason, as Lou explained to me, was that should the bombs fail to release, the pilot could pull the stick back and the aircraft would actually rotate on its own axis. However, without the afterburner to provide the additional thrust, the aircraft, due to its heavy weight, would continue on down, eventually striking the ground in a horizontal position. I never fully trusted Lou after that flight and was quick to tell him so, but he was one hell of a good fighter pilot. We remained good friends even though he continually harassed me about being a wing wienie pilot.

Many people have asked me what it was like to fly an F-105 Thunderchief. The aircraft was the largest and noisiest jet fighter in our Air Force inventory. When parked next to another fighter-type aircraft, you just couldn't believe the enormous size of the Thud. It was powered by a J-57 turbo jet engine with an afterburner. It was the last of what was considered a "hard burner" type afterburner in a fighter aircraft. Probably the most exciting thing about flying the Thud was when you actually used the afterburner. No matter what airspeed a pilot flew, at the noise level inside the cockpit of a Thud was indescribably loud. The minute the throttle was moved from full military power outside and forward into afterburner, the noise level inside the cockpit would drop to almost 0 for a few microseconds, followed by the largest and loudest explosion imaginable. The pilot would be first thrown forward in the seat as the plane went into afterburner. Then suddenly the pilot would be pinned into the back of the ejection seat as the plane accelerated through the Mach. Every time I lit the burner, the explosion was so loud that I couldn't help but look in the three small mirrors located on the top of the canopy to see if I still had a tail section on the aircraft.

Factory representatives from the Republic Aviation Company were always present on a base where their products were being flown, and Kadena was no exception. They were especially attentive to new pilots who were checking out in the F-105. The company reps would always explain to each pilot that the Thud in 1964 was still the fastest fighter in the world. The F-105 had held the international speed record for the past ten years. Here is how the factory reps described the speed. According to them, you first needed to take two F-105s, a D model with a single-seat cockpit and an F model with a two-place tandem-seated cockpit. Place the aircraft side by side at any altitude and airspeed. If the pilot in the backseat of the F model were to hypothetically roll his side window down and fire a 30-06 rifle outside the cockpit while at the same instant the pilot of the D model lit his afterburner, the D-model aircraft would outaccelerate the 30-06 bullet. This then put the tremendous speed potential of the F-105 into perspective where a nonflier can hopefully understand it. I have to admit that any time that I rolled the F-105 over and pointed the nose at the ground and lit the afterburner I always got the thrill of my life as the ground came up to meet me.

After Cynthia and the kids arrived in Okinawa, life was never the same. Our first house was rather substandard even by Air Force standards, but we were together and nothing else mattered. As a family, we shared some incredible experiences while stationed on Okinawa. The first that comes to my mind was the arrival of our household goods from the States. At the time, captains were allowed to send 1,500 pounds of household goods overseas.

When our shipment arrived at Kadena, my first thought was that Cynthia had lost her marbles. I was expecting dishes, furniture, and things like that. The Okinawans from the transportation organization first unloaded a large children's swing set. Next came the 1,000-pound player piano, a king-sized bed and a deep freezer. It was at this point that I really thought that she had lost it. But her thinking was way ahead of mine. The deep freezer was a lifesaver for not only us but also our immediate neighbors, as every food product had to be imported into Okinawa. We entertained many a party with that old player piano accompanied by a "gut bucket" (a washtub with a G string attached to a broom handle), and everyone loved the music. Because Okinawa was considered a remote military assignment, we as a family were able to take advantage of the many free flights and fly all over the South Pacific on military aircraft. The aircrews who flew these passenger carriers loved having the children onboard and always let them come up to the cockpit to help fly the aircraft. The kids especially loved every minute of their time at the controls of the C-130 type aircraft.

My first form of transportation on Okinawa was a cheap motor-scooter. Although it was hard to start, I managed to get along fine until the rainy season started. Once the family arrived, I managed to purchase a 1950 Ford Sedan for $1.25 from a departing pilot. His only stipulation was that when I rotated I was to sell it again for $1.25 to another pilot. The body of the vehicle was completely rusted out, which provided plenty of outside air, and you could actually see the ground below your feet as you drove along. That Ford had a three-speed manual transmission; however, the clutch had long since gone out on it. In order to move, what you would do was carefully listen to the engine rpm and, as the rpm started falling off, quickly jam the gearshift lever into the next gear and take off. This made for some rather unusual starts, but the old Ford never failed me. I drove that car "maintenance-free" for almost four years before finally selling it to another pilot for $1.25.

Sometime during our second year at Kadena, Cynthia was elected to the position of vice president of the Officers' Wives Club. With her in that position, we both learned a lot about international politics. The wives' club had a profit from sale of items from their store. They were not allowed to donate any money to the American Dependent School System and therefore bought air-conditioning units and television sets for the local Okinawan School District. Wasn't it a shame that our children were roasting in the classrooms and we could only spend the money on the Okinawan schools?

The second incident had to do with our own foreign aid policy. It seems that the U.S. government had been providing annually $25 million to the Okinawan government since the end of WW II. What made this so interesting was the fact that these annual monies had gone into the hands of only five Okinawan families for all this time. Another political thing that galled all of us was the fact that the U.S. Army had at the end of WW II left two large generator ships in the harbor at Buckner Bay. During the war these two ships provided the entire island with electrical power. We discovered that after the war ended the same five Okinawan families had taken over the operation of these generator ships and were now selling power to everyone on the island. Woe to those American families who lived off-base and had to pay the Okinawans for electrical power. One

301

time I pulled the electrical circuit breaker on our house and the lights went out in five nearby Okinawan houses. We lived for four months on the local economy while waiting for government housing. Our electrical bills averaged between $200 and $250 per month, while the Okinawan families who lived right next door to us paid what amounted to $1.00 in U.S. currency. We spent many an evening trying to figure out how to jimmy the electrical meters attached to our houses. We never succeeded, as the Okinawans always won. Our only salvation was to move into base housing as soon as possible.

Once I got the F-105 out of my system and returned to base ops type flying, I got to check out in every type of aircraft that we had on the base. I especially enjoyed flying the executive twin jet engine T-39. The aircraft was normally used to haul generals or other high-ranking personnel around the South Pacific. However, since there weren't too many generals around, we found lots of other uses for this aircraft. Fresh vegetables and fruits were always a problem, as only one shipment arrived monthly for the U.S. military forces stationed on Okinawa. Unless we were able to get to the commissary on the day that the vegetables and fruits arrived, we usually got extremely wilted lettuce and spoiled fruit. To reduce this problem we would lay on a T-39 mission to either Taiwan or the Philippine Islands. During these very important missions we would come home loaded with all sorts of fresh fruits and vegetables. In addition, when going to Taiwan we would bring back incredibly good rolled pork roasts and lots of bananas, which Cynthia made into banana bread, keeping it in our freezer.

By 1966, I was one of two T-39 pilots on the base who were qualified and selected to fly the high commissioner of Okinawa to wherever he wanted to go. The high commissioner was the equivalent of the president of the country and he never seemed to keep normal hours. One night his aide called our Command Post around 2300 hours and said that the commissioner and his wife wanted to travel to Tokyo immediately. Arriving at base ops, the copilot and I were briefed that the weather en route to Tokyo was bad, as well as the destination weather. We decided to climb up to 44,000 feet in the hope of flying over the tops of most of the clouds and thunderstorms.

Arriving over Tokyo, we were informed that the only navigational aid available to us for penetration was an old-fashioned twenty-four-year-old automatic directional finding (ADF) beacon that still had an instrument landing and approach system (ILAS) that was working. The center had lied to us, as it was not an ADF approach but was, in fact, an aural-knoll type approach. I had not flown an aural-knoll type approach since pilot-training days. On this type of approach, if and when the pilot intercepted the proper heading, should he get a half-degree off to the left side, he would hear in Morse code the letter *A*. However, should the pilot wander a half-degree off to the right side of the beacon, he would then hear the letter *N*. This might sound easy and it probably was easier when pilots were flying slower propeller-driven aircraft during these types of approaches. However, in a jet aircraft things happen much faster due to the higher airspeeds and there is far less room for error. The problem was additionally compounded by the fact that the directional beacon's heading needle was affected by thunderstorm activity in the immediate area.

Tokyo Center had cleared us to descend from 44,000 feet down to 20,000, which placed our aircraft inside clouds, and it became very hazardous and bumpy-type flying. I truly felt sorry for the commissioner and his wife, but orders are orders! When we arrived at 20,000-foot altitude, Tokyo Center suddenly called and cleared us for an immediate penetration. Initially I was disoriented and scared stiff, because I knew that there were plenty of mountains in the area surrounding Tokyo, plus my comfort with a night aural-knoll type penetration and approach was not good. Going in and out of thunderstorms we descended to 1,000 feet in heavy rain showers, never quite sure exactly where we were.

Just about the time that we were ready to abort the landing approach, the horizontal and vertical needles on the ILAS instrument started to center, indicating that we had reached the glide slope, so we decided to continue the approach. I was sweating profusely trying to keep all of the needles centered while flying a smooth platform. Using the ILAS instrument requires a pilot to keep the two needles centered inside the instrument until eventually arriving over the end of the landing runway. This works in all American airports while using the ILAS system. Pilots just need to keep the two needles centered and the plane will arrive exactly over the approach end of the active runway.

This was not the case at Tokyo International Airport! Approximately a mile out, I could see the runway lights and started feeling much better about getting this machine down safely. I was still concentrating on flying the instrument approach when out of my peripheral vision I kept seeing runway lights go by the aircraft and we were not on the ground yet. To further disturb my already-shocked sense of security, I quickly realized that the Japanese ILAS system was not adjusted to the end of the approach runway. I dived the T-39 onto the runway just as the copilot yelled that there were only 3,000 feet left to try to stop the aircraft in. Needless to say, I should have for safety's sake made an immediate go-around, but I made one of those quick decisions and we were committed to land. I had to get on and off the brakes rapidly to keep the aircraft from hydroplaning due to the large accumulation of water on the runway.

Arriving at the end of the active runway, we continued on to the overrun portion and eventually ran into fairly deep mud before finally getting the machine stopped. For a few minutes I felt that we had blown all three tires, but that wasn't the case—thank God. Pushing one of the throttles up to 100 percent I managed to get the aircraft turned around and, by jockeying both throttles, eventually got the aircraft back upon the runway. We immediately contacted Tokyo Ground Control on the radio and were vectored back toward the parking area for Very Important Persons (VIPs). The rain was coming down so hard that it washed most of the mud off the aircraft by the time we reached our parking space. The copilot opened the outer door once the engines were shut down, and we both assisted in getting our passengers' luggage off the aircraft. We bade them both a happy good night and thought to ourselves, *If they only knew what really happened during this flight.*

After the commissioner and his wife left, we quickly inspected the aircraft for damage. Finding nothing wrong, we called for a fuel truck. I told the copilot that we were going to refuel and take off as soon as possible, heading back to Okinawa, regardless of the takeoff time. At the time that we received our clearance, I informed Tokyo Center that the navigational approach they had given us was an aural-knoll and not an ADF. I'm not sure that they ever understood what I was trying to tell them. On the way home the copilot confessed to me that he had never seen or flown an aural-knoll type penetration and approach. I just smiled and said nothing! (If only he had known?) As far as I was concerned, this was just one of those "Hail Mary" type flights that you were pleased to have survived and that it was all behind you. After landing at Kadena, I told the copilot on the way to our cars to not say anything to anybody about this unusual flight and to just chalk it off to good luck!

Surviving typhoons was to become a common experience while living on Okinawa. Whenever a typhoon got within a hundred miles of Okinawa, Kadena would go into Typhoon Condition Four. At seventy-five miles we upgraded to Typhoon Condition Three and at fifty miles into Condition Two. In Condition Two all base military personnel except for the pilots are sent home in order to get their homes prepared for the typhoon. During Typhoon Condition Two, all base aircraft would normally be evacuated to either Korea, Japan, or the Philippine Islands, depending upon where the weather was the best. As the typhoon reached the twenty-five-mile limit, the base would go into Typhoon Condition One, and absolutely no one was allowed outside his or her individual homes.

One of my jobs as the wing executive officer during a Typhoon Condition Two was to ensure that all nuclear weapons and aircraft that were carrying them were secured inside typhoon-proof hangars. I was in the process of completing this job one time when I received an emergency telephone message from base operations. The base had just upgraded into Typhoon Condition One and they needed a pilot to evacuate a T-33 that was still on the flight line. By the time I responded and reached base operations, it was raining so hard that I could hardly see twenty feet in front of me. The surface winds were up to eighty-five miles per hour and the rain was coming in horizontal instead of vertical. I asked the base operations officer where he wanted me to take the T-33, and he replied, "To nearby Naha Air Base."

I couldn't believe that he was serious, as Naha Air Base is on Okinawa and is only eight miles south from Kadena Air Base as the crow flies. For clarification purposes, there are two American air bases located on the southern tip of Okinawa. Kadena Air Base is operated by Tactical Air Command, while Naha Air Base, located twenty-five ground miles away, is on the extreme southern tip of the island and is controlled by the Air Defense Command.

First of all, to even take a T-33 off the ground with winds in excess of eighty-five knots is extremely dangerous. To compound this problem, the T-33 had a full load of fuel on board, which meant that I would have to burn all of the fuel out of the wing tanks before I could bring the aircraft in for a safe landing. It had been so long since I had been in the front seat of a T-33 that I had to request the crew chief to get up on the wing and help me start the engine. Once I had the engine going, I asked the crew chief if he would like to accompany me to Naha, and he couldn't get away from me fast enough. The takeoff was not an easy one, as I had quartering headwinds of eighty-five knots or more and visibility was almost zero. Since there were no other aircraft in the area, I climbed straight ahead, going out to sea and into the approaching typhoon. My goal was to drive out about ten miles while staying above the waves and make a large circling turn back toward Naha. Leveling off at 200-foot altitude I left the flaps and gear in the down position to help create drag and burn more fuel off as soon as possible. Even at that low altitude I wasn't sure whether I was getting saltwater spray or rain on my windscreen.

Flying conditions were some of the worst that I have ever experienced, and several times I almost lost control of the aircraft, as the high winds would suddenly lift one wing up almost to the vertical position. Flying along, I realized what a "no win situation" I found myself in. I decided to put the speed brakes out with the idea of creating even more drag on the aircraft. Doing this I found myself needing 100 percent of the throttle just to keep the T-33 airborne. At the ten-mile limit I used every bit of experience that I possessed just trying to make a simple turn back toward the island.

The buffeting and turbulence inside the cockpit were so bad that I cracked my helmet open on the side of the canopy. For those who have never flown a T-33 jet, the cockpit is extremely narrow and small, especially for a big guy. Apparently mine was the only aircraft still flying in the vicinity of Okinawa, and suddenly both towers, using the emergency Guard Channel on the radio, were screaming for me to land immediately. My first thought was that why in the hell had Kadena Tower asked me to take off in the first place? I tuned in Naha Tower and told them that I was flying circles

306

five miles out from their field trying to burn off enough fuel to effect a safe landing. Throughout all of my flying maneuvers, I found myself using full military power on the engine. I informed Naha Tower that I would call them when I was on final approach. Their comment to me was that the typhoon had suddenly sped up and was rapidly approaching landfall.

The only approach to Naha was over the water, and finally deciding that I needed to get this aircraft on the ground or go in the water, I lined up on the initial approach heading and began a slow descent. The high winds were whipping the onshore waves into a frenzy to the point where you couldn't tell where the surface was. The strong winds were also so bad that I found myself crabbing the aircraft almost thirty degrees from the landing heading just to stay lined up with the runway while on final approach. My largest concern while attempting to land was to handle the unpredictable wind gusts while actually trying to get the T-33 on the runway. There were approximately two to four inches of moving water on the runway as I touched down, and the aircraft immediately began to hydroplane. At one point I was almost ninety degrees to the runway heading, sliding and scared shitless. I was afraid that the extremely strong wind gusts would actually flip me over, but eventually I gained control and was able, with the tower's assistance, to taxi to an open hangar door. Man, was I ever glad to get inside that hangar. Ground crews quickly closed the doors behind me. Several hours later I was able to get a bus ride back to Kadena. The typhoon swept over the island for three days. Calling Naha Command Post on the fourth day, I told them that I would be there at twelve noon and requested that they put a light fuel load on the aircraft. Landing at Kadena some thirty minutes later, I decided that I never wanted to get involved in another typhoon evacuation debacle like this again.

Okinawa is actually a very small island, with all of the people living on what would be considered the southern one-third of the island. The actual island is seventy-five miles long, with the width varying between eighteen miles at the widest point to less than two miles at the thinnest part. The many small Okinawan villages always seemed to have some sort of celebration going on. The center attraction of their many festivals was always a mongoose–*habu* (snake) fight. Neither animal is native to Okinawa, but the natives seemed to love them. The average mongoose looked to be the size of an average American gopher while the *habu* snakes varied in length from four feet to seven feet and, like a rattlesnake, were extremely poisonous. Usually the villagers would place the *habu* in an elevated cage approximately three feet square about three feet off the ground. Next they would harass the *habu* with sticks while an incredible amount of betting was going on. Once the snake was really pissed off, they would drop the mongoose into the cage.

Most of the time the fights were very quick, with the mongoose winning most of the events, but occasionally the *habu* would win and then lots of money would change hands. Oftentimes one mongoose would live long enough to kill five or six *habus*. I learned to respect the quickness of the mongoose! It seems that the *habu* snakes were brought to Okinawa by the Germans sometime during the eighteenth century to supplement their food chain while they occupied Okinawa. I was told that most of the current mongoose population were imported from nearby Thailand.

There is a large form of tropical grass that thrives on Okinawa, and it is called *habu* grass primarily because that is where most of the *habu* snakes live. The grass grows to about three feet tall and normally blooms twice a year. The blooms look like large white puffy yucca plant flowers and are very willowy in nature. Whenever they bloomed I took as many TDY trips as I could in order to get off the island, as I was extremely allergic to the pollen.

42

A Small World

Earlier I mentioned having met one of my high school classmates
(Rusty Rumney) for lunch while I was still in the Command Post at
Kadena. Rusty had always been my closest friend while growing up
in Coronado, California. We were "buds" from the third grade on
through graduation. We were not only members of Boy Scout Troop
#75 but also in the same Flaming Arrow Patrol. I do not remember
exactly how far Rusty got in scout rank, but I finally made it to Eagle
Scout. We both played trumpet from about the eighth grade on and
constantly vied with each other for the solo chair. All the way
through high school we both worked part-time for Rusty's father,
who owned Perkins Flower Shop in Coronado. Since I played football while Rusty ran cross-country, this arrangement worked out
incredibly well for both of us. During football season Rusty would
work part-time after school and we would both work on Saturdays,
while the reverse was true during track season. What the work schedule did was provide enough money for both of us for weekend dates,
et cetera. We both worked during all of the holiday seasons, and
like brothers, we were inseparable throughout our high school days.

Rusty's dad was Coronado High School's cross-country coach,
and as a result Rusty became good enough over four years to win a
full-ride scholarship to the University of Arizona. Our careers parted
shortly after graduation from high school, as I was called to active
duty as an enlisted man with the U.S. Marine Corps in July of 1950
while Rusty went on to college. While he was at the University of
Arizona, Rusty joined the U.S. Army's ROTC Program and subsequently was always ahead of me rankwise throughout both of our
military careers.

Back at Kadena sometime during the month of May 1965, I
arranged a cross-country flight down to Saigon with the sole purpose
of looking up Rusty. I knew that he was assigned to the Army's
headquarters staff, and what an experience that was trying to work

my way through the Army's bureaucracy to locate him. Rusty was always a workaholic, and nothing had changed. Normal people usually work an eight-hour shift, but never Rusty, as he always managed to somehow turn an eight-hour workday into a ten-hour one at the minimum. He was just an incredibly outstanding and competent officer while in the Army. As a major he had already received the Legion of Merit medal, which is the highest award you can receive for meritorious service in any branch of the U.S. military services.

After finally locating Rusty's work area, I had to wait around for another two or three hours before he felt that he could leave. We finally settled into seats on the outside veranda of a French-Vietnamese restaurant looking over the main street of downtown Saigon. About halfway through our second Bomie Bom (Vietnamese beer) we were getting pretty well caught up on the years that we had been apart. We were laughing and going over some of the humorous experiences at our school when suddenly Rusty jabbed me and pointed down the street. Here walking along the sidewalk was one of our classmates (Larry Jordan) from Coronado. We held our breath and waited until Larry came abreast of our position and simultaneously both pitched beer bottles at Larry. Watching Larry jump for his life was worth every second of our joking around. Rusty and I both decided that it was definitely the highest that we had ever seen Larry jump! The three of us tried drinking the restaurant's bar dry that evening. Larry was an Air Force B-66 pilot and had only been in-country several hours when we assaulted him with beer bottles. Before we departed, I suggested to both of them that they should work it out with their respective commands so that they could come to Okinawa for Christmas. They couldn't go many places and I knew it, but Okinawa was on the good-place list and they both agreed to come and share Christmas with my family.

Somewhere around December 20 Larry made it to Okinawa, and the following day Rusty showed up. Rusty had used the excuse of being an official escort officer delivering some Army prisoners to the federal facility on Okinawa. We started out having a great time, as both Russ and Larry were good family men and they really enjoyed Cynthia and the kids. Here is where the story really gets interesting as far as this being a small world is concerned. Two days after both guys arrived, I had to fly a night refueling mission for proficiency training in the F-105. I was to hit a KC-135 tanker that was TDY from somewhere in the States. Once a quarter we had to hook up to an airborne tanker using what the Air Force calls a probe-and-drogue (Funnel) maneuver in order to get an off-load of fuel. Unlike the flying refueling boom that we normally used with our probes, this god-awful procedure required that we hit this airborne drogue that was attached by a rubber hose to the end of the flying boom. This was never an easy way to get fuel, even in good flying weather, and this night was no exception for me.

The refueling probe on the F-105 extends outside the left forward side of the cockpit area, and as the pilot closes in on the drogue he has to actually drive the probe into the center of the drogue in order to obtain a hookup. For me this was a difficult maneuver even in broad daylight. I was experiencing difficulties and getting really frustrated with my inability to obtain a hook-up. The boom operator on the tanker said something caustic about fighter pilots, and I quickly told him to go fuck himself. He advised me that he was going to formally report me to his AC, a Major Bullock, and I told him to do so immediately. Something then caused me to ask the boomer exactly who his AC was. He came back with a "Major Earl E. Bullock."

I asked the boomer to put his AC on the command radio frequency so that I could talk to him. I backed my aircraft away from the tanker and waited for the good major to come up to my frequency. When he finally did come up to my frequency and wanted to know why I wanted to speak with him, I said, "E.B., fuck you and your fuel very much."

He shouted, "Who is this?"

I told him it was an old buddy from the Flaming Arrow Patrol.

He then shouted, "Hunter."

We talked for a few minutes, and since he was headed back to Kadena, too, I told him that I would meet him at base ops after landing. Earl and his crew were assigned to Kadena for an SAC fifty-nine-day TDY tour of duty. We had not seen each other since graduation, and here we met 13,000 miles away in the middle of the South Pacific sky at night. Before leaving, I asked Earl to come over for dinner two nights later without telling him that Rusty and Larry were already there, staying with us. Earl was unable to make it to dinner that night due to a priority flight schedule.

Several weeks later I was sitting in base operations waiting while Maintenance repaired a part on the T-33 that I was scheduled to fly. While sitting there, I overheard a conversation between two pilots from nearby Naha Air Base and the base ops officer. Out of curiosity I eavesdropped on their conversation, and lo and behold, one of the pilots was Capt. Kenneth Lamberton. Ken was also a classmate from Coronado High School. I couldn't believe my eyes. I immediately interrupted the conversation and grabbed Kenny. He was an F-102 pilot and had been stationed at Naha Air Base for two months. I asked him over for dinner that night, telling him that he had just missed Rusty and Larry. Since Kenny was unable to make it that night, I asked him over for dinner the next night; however, Earl had to fly that night. As far as I know, Kenny and Earl were able to get together on another occasion before Earl left Kadena for the States.

The irony of this situation is that all of us were in the same graduating class of 1950 that had only thirty-two boys in it, and now here we were as men 13,000 miles from our hometown, Coronado. You must understand that Coronado Island was only a mile in diameter when we grew up. It seemed really strange that fate would have us meet fifteen years later together on another small island in the South Pacific. Four of us, Rusty, Larry, Earl, and I have remained in contact every year since that occasion. Kenny Lamberton was later killed in the crash of an F-105 that he was checking out in back in Kansas.

I couldn't complete the story of Okinawa without including the story about a great American fighter pilot and very close friend. While I was the 18th TFW executive officer, Capt. Marvin (Monty) Montgomery was the chief of plans and intelligence, and we both worked together on a daily basis. Monty died while flying an F-105 in a most unusual set of circumstances. I personally wrote the narrative up regarding the flight, and the wing commander, who thought the world of Captain Montgomery, then turned the story over to war correspondent Bob Considine, who published the story in the *New York Journal* on March 30, 1965. Monty's loss was truly felt by every pilot and administrator in the 18th TFW. As a senior captain he was in charge of the Operations and Plans Section of the 18th TFW. To place his professional skills and incredible intelligence into perspective, he as a captain was filling a slot that called for a person at the rank of lieutenant colonel.

Captain Montgomery was probably the most knowledgeable officer I ever met during my entire career in the Air Force. Monty was personally responsible for drafting, writing, and developing all of the 18th TFWs' plans for both conventional and nuclear contingencies in the South Pacific. This responsibility included mission planning, strike timing, conflict resolution and source data submission on all F-105 sorties assigned to the 18th TFW by the JCS. His security clearance was so high that he was restricted from flying combat missions in routes 4 through 6 over North Vietnam. As a result, most of his combat-accredited missions were in the delivery of F-105s to advanced combat units in Thailand.

On March 20, 1965, Captain Montgomery and Capt. William Burkett were tasked to deliver two F-105 Thunderchiefs from the 18th TFW at Kadena, Okinawa, to the PACAF Maintenance Repair Facility at Taipei, Taiwan. On the way to Taiwan the rare drama of courage and professional flying skill of Captain Burkett averted what could have easily become an extremely dangerous international nuclear incident, since both of these fighters were capable of carrying nuclear bombs. As far as the military forces on the Chinese mainland were concerned, all of our F-105 fighters carried nuclear weapons all of the time. This made the Chinese forces very uneasy, especially when these same two F-105s penetrated Chinese airspace over Shanghai. The Chinese Air Force immediately launched interceptor fighters to shoot the F-105 fighters down.

The entire incident took place at an altitude of 26,000 feet as the two Thunderchiefs were proceeding toward their first airborne checkpoint. Captain Montgomery was flying the lead aircraft, with Captain Burkett as his wingman. After Captain Montgomery failed to make a left turn to their new heading and upon reaching their second required en route position reporting point, Captain Burkett became alarmed as he had not heard Captain Montgomery return any calls to Okinawa Center regarding their flight's position. At the time, Captain Burkett was flying approximately 150 feet off the right wing of Captain Montgomery's aircraft in a loose formation. Because Captain Burkett received no radio response when he called

Captain Montgomery, Captain Burkett moved his aircraft in close to see if Captain Montgomery had experienced a radio failure.

Closing in on Captain Montgomery's aircraft, Captain Burkett discovered that Captain Montgomery appeared to be unconscious and slumped over in the cockpit. Monty's head was drawn up, left and back between the headrest and canopy. Captain Burkett tried everything that he knew to try to get Captain Montgomery to respond to his radio calls. It was at this point that Burkett noticed that Monty's body was now slumped forward toward the instrument panel and that he was totally incapacitated. Captain Montgomery's aircraft at the time was on autopilot and both aircraft were traveling somewhere around 650 mph and slowly accelerating. Captain Burkett moved back out into a loose formation position and consulted his aerial maps and quickly realized that they were about to penetrate Chinese airspace.

Captain Burkett, using his radio, informed both ATC and the Kadena Command Post to explain the situation. The CP quickly diverted two KC-135 jet tankers to try to intercept the stricken F-105 fighters. While all of this was taking place, Captain Burkett decided to try to move in and change the heading of the aircraft that Captain Montgomery was in. As Captain Burkett was attempting to move in and place his wing under the wing of Captain Montgomery's aircraft, the weather was going from bad to worse. Burkett's idea was one based on the aerodynamic principle of disturbed airflow.

While traveling at 650 mph in weather and early night flying conditions, Captain Burkett moved in and placed his left wing under the right wing of the disabled aircraft. The idea was to raise the right wing of Captain Montgomery's aircraft enough so that Burkett could begin to change the heading of Monty's aircraft. Burkett was successful in making small jerky turns, but frequently the autopilot on Captain Montgomery's aircraft would react and slam Burkett's left wing down, very definitely placing Burkett in harm's way. While all of this was going on, Burkett was informed by ATC that there were Chinese fighters inbound to his position. Refusing to give up after numerous tries, Burkett finally managed to get Captain Montgomery's aircraft turned enough so that they were now on a northeasterly heading and back out to sea.

It was shortly after the completion of the turn that Captain Montgomery's tip tanks went dry and his aircraft flamed out while still on autopilot and altitude hold. Once Captain Montgomery's aircraft engine flamed out, his fighter slowed to a stall and subsequently entered a violent spin down into the Yellow Sea. As Captain Montgomery's aircraft spun down, according to ATC there were over thirty-nine hostile Chinese intercepts on it. Captain Burkett wasted no time getting out of the hostile area and established a rendezvous with the airborne tankers as soon as he could. When he returned to Kadena, Captain Burkett's eyes were red and moist and his face drawn with fatigue. He informed Colonel Cardenas that he would have gotten out of his aircraft and walked across the wings to help Captain Montgomery if he could have done so.

The estimated impact area based upon Captain Montgomery's flamed-out aircraft position turned up no evidence of the twenty-ton supersonic fighter or its pilot. Without Captain Burkett's remarkable intervention, Captain Montgomery's aircraft would have crashed in hostile territory, with imponderable international consequences. Sometimes in the flying profession the loss of a fellow pilot really impacts other pilots, and this was one of those times for all of us in the 18th TFW. It was as if it could never happen to such an invaluable person. Captain Burkett later was awarded the Distinguished Flying Cross for his courageous and heroic attempt to save his longtime friend.

The last part of this chapter before departing Okinawa concerns itself with the ugly receipt of my next military assignment. I had already worked out a deal with one of my good fighter pilot buddies who not only owed me a favor but also controlled assignments for all U.S. Air Force fighter pilots. This person owed me a favor, and I called in my marker, as I wanted to fly one of the new A-7 fighters that were stationed at Luke AFB in Arizona. About a month before my rotation date, I called Randolph AFB in Texas and was informed that everything was taken care of. I therefore forgot about reassignments for the time being.

Several days after this telephone call, PACAF headquarters informed me that twenty full colonels from Air University would be arriving at Kadena AB. Their mission, according to the message, was the mandatory interviews of all senior captains on the base who were about to rotate back to the States. One of my good friends, who was also a wing administrative officer, and I both decided not to attend the mandatory interviews.

About a week later the shock wave hit as we were both notified that we had been selected for assignments as Air Force ROTC instructors. During the next ten days I had two Air Force Generals try their best to get my assignment changed. Both generals informed me that they had to deal with a major air command, i.e., Air University, and that Air University would not budge for anyone. Air University was kind enough to consider my choice of areas in the United States, and I elected to go to the Pacific Northwest. Needless to say, there were heel marks all the way back across the Pacific as we rotated out of Kadena.

I was headed for the University of Puget Sound (UPS), which was located in Tacoma, Washington. I was also assigned to the 318th Fighter Interceptor Squadron (FIS) located at nearby McChord AFB to maintain my flying proficiency. I sent a message to the 318th FIS ops officer telling him what I was currently checked out in and asking him how I could help him. The ops officer responded by telling me to get checked out in a T-33 single-engine jet. I was quickly running out of time there at Kadena, so I asked my neighbor who was in charge of the base flight aircraft if he could get me a formal check ride in the T-33 ASAP, and he agreed to do it. Several nights later I was scheduled to fly on a night local area check ride mission with me in the backseat and the base ops officer as pilot in the front seat. Even though I had flown the T-33 before, I never got to touch the flight controls during the two hours that we were airborne, and upon landing, my neighbor signed me off as being checked out as pilot in command in the T-33. This quick good favor would later haunt me when I arrived at McChord AFB.

43

Tacoma

We as a family rotated back to the States during July of 1967, and our first stop was San Diego, where we visited with all grandparents. Although I was assigned to UPS, the U.S. Air Force amended my orders to include a six-week stay at the Air Force's Academic Instructor School located at Maxwell AFB in Montgomery, Alabama. After a week in San Diego I headed for Maxwell AFB, where Air University managed to pour four years of academic instruction into our class in just six weeks. Never before had I stood in front of a bunch of people and tried to entertain anyone for any reason, and I found it very difficult. What happened in the end was that I received a quick education in the latest and proper educational techniques before completing that six-week course.

Arriving back in San Diego and before leaving for Tacoma, Washington, I purchased a brand-new four-wheel-drive two-door Jeep Commando vehicle. I bought the Jeep because of the thought of how bad the winters must be that far north in the United States. This particular sports model was the first of its kind for the Jeep Company, and it was fully loaded, including a newly designed V-six engine made by the GMC. Leaving the family in San Diego, I took off for Tacoma and made it as far as Mount Shasta before my problems began. It seemed that each time I shifted gears with the manual gearshift lever, the clutch pedal got harder and harder to push in. By the time I reached Ashland, Oregon, the cable running from the clutch pedal to the gearbox broke. I pulled off the main road into a gas station where the manager told me that the nearest Jeep dealer was located twenty-one miles north in Medford, Oregon. The gas station attendant helped me pull the broken cable up through the floorboards, and using a pair of pliers I managed to get the vehicle into second gear. I drove the twenty-one miles in second gear and finally arrived at the Jeep agency. The people there were really nice, but the vehicle was so new that they had never seen one

317

like it and had no parts for it. I explained my problem, telling them that I had to report to McChord AFB in two days and really needed their help. One of their mechanics said that he could fix the Jeep good enough for me to make it to Tacoma. He drilled a hole directly through the floorboard and ran the cable up through the new hole. He then welded the cable to a piece of metal and told me that each time I needed to shift gears all I had to do was to pull up on the cable. The system worked and they never charged me for the quick fix. I was able using this primitive system to make it on into Tacoma the next day.

Several days after getting settled into a motel in Tacoma, I drove down to Winthrop Motors, the local Jeep dealer for Tacoma. The service manager was extremely nasty to me and told me that they would not touch the vehicle. He called the owner of Winthrop Motors over, and we got into a shouting match. Finally, in exasperation, I told both of them what I thought of their dealership and informed them that I was going to write a letter to the president of the Jeep Company. They laughed in my face and told me to get my vehicle out of their service department. What a way to get welcomed into a new town! I went home and did write a letter to the president of the American Jeep Company but never received an answer.

A month later I was taking three ROTC cadets out to McChord AFB to give them an orientation ride in the T-33 jet. I didn't know all of the cadets by name yet, and one of them asked me how I liked my new Jeep. I told him the sad story just as I have described it. He said that he would take care of the matter for me, and at the time I was unable to make the connection of what he was talking about. His name was Kim Kaiser, and his dad was the owner of Kaiser Aluminum, which, in turn, owned the American Jeep franchise. Two days later I received a call from Detroit, Michigan. A nice gentlemen informed me that he would be in Tacoma in two days and that he wanted to pick up my Jeep, and I told him OK. I still had not made the connection between Cadet Kaiser and the Kaiser Aluminum Company.

Two days later, true to his word, one of the senior vice presidents from the Kaiser Aluminum Company arrived at UPS. I was called over to Dr. Thompson's office, where he made the introductions. The man from Kaiser Aluminum told me that he was only going to be in Tacoma for a short stay, and could he possibly see

318

my Jeep? I quickly explained what had happened, and the Kaiser gentleman asked if he could have my Jeep for a week or so. The man explained that he would have my Jeep fixed and in the meantime he offered me a new Chrysler rental car for my use. He told me that the owner of Winthrop Motors would call me once my vehicle was fixed and that I could turn the Chrysler in to him when my car was ready. By the end of our conversation I had finally made the connection between Cadet Kaiser and his father.

This was one of those rare and significant times in your life that you just love, will never forget, and will talk about for years. Approximately a week later I received a call from the owner of Winthrop Motors explaining to me that my Jeep was ready for pickup. Arriving at Winthrop Motors, I delivered the keys to the Chrysler to the owner's secretary and went downstairs to pick up my Jeep. I couldn't believe my eyes when I saw the changes in my Jeep. There were new chrome strips down each side and matching mud flaps for each wheel. The vehicle was completely detailed in every respect. Not only was the shifting cable fixed, but also the interior now had been changed from rubber floors to a matching ruglike material on the floor and included matching rubber floor mats for each side. As I was driving toward the exit, the service manager and the owner were standing there to see me off. As I stopped and rolled down my window, I remarked to both of them, "Wasn't it amazing what a simple letter could do?" To me they both looked like they were in a state of shock! I continued to have my Jeep serviced at Winthrop Motors for two more years and always received service that must have been reserved for CEOs.

I had Cynthia fly up to Tacoma, since this was to be our first major purchase of a new home and I couldn't make up my mind between the three or four that I liked. We both agreed on a three-bedroom house located about four blocks from the university. Since this was our first home, we were both extremely proud of it. On my first working day I dressed up in my Class A uniform and reported to my new boss, Col. Bob Denomy, who was the ROTC commander of Detachment 900. After welcoming me onboard, Colonel Denomy told me that I had a 0900 interview with the university president, Dr. Thompson. Dr. Thompson was known as "Doc T.," and he always insisted on interviewing all new employees in his office on their first day of employment. The new varsity basketball coach, Don Zeck, and I were both ushered into Doc T.'s office at the same time.

Upon completion of our interview by Doc T., Don and I both started walking back across campus toward our new offices located in the fieldhouse. On the south end of the campus there was a street that separated the football field from the fieldhouse. As we approached the street we noticed a large bonfire in the middle of the street, where the university chaplain was in the process of burning a large American flag. He had a student beside him holding a staff with a large replica of a VC flag flying from it. The show was all for my benefit and we both knew it. Students tried to spit on me as we walked around the bonfire, and they were all shouting terrible antimilitary slogans as Coach Zeck and I climbed the steps up into the fieldhouse. I had been out of the country for the past five years and was not fully aware of the hatred that had built up toward our military forces as a result of the Vietnamese war. In addition to the bonfire, students were holding up copies of the student newspaper that had a full-length picture of me on the front sheet with two-inch letters saying, "Professional Killer Arrives." I have never forgiven the university chaplain for this incident.

Life at UPS was delightful compared to where I had just come from; however, there were some hectic moments. The faculty for the most part wanted nothing to do with the ROTC Department and, given a chance, made life as difficult as they could for the ROTC Department staff. On the high side, our individual offices were located on one side of the fieldhouse, while the UPS coaching staff was located on the other side. A highlight for our children during the UPS basketball games was for Anne, our youngest daughter, to go into my office and draw on the chalkboards. I got involved immediately and volunteered to assist the varsity football coach in any way that I could. Coach Ryan asked me to stay close to Coach Paul Wallrof, who was the defensive coach for the team. In the short months ahead, Coach Wallrof taught me more than I could ever imagine about the game of football. By the end of the first year, the athletic director (AD), Doug McArthur, asked me to accept the position of varsity ski coach for the university, and I quickly did.

What an incredible experience this turned out to be for the ski team. The first year I had only seven students turn out, with a budget of just $300. What a laugh that was, as the ski team spent all of the $300 on the first meet. We were later invited to the International Intercollegiate Championship Meet in Banff, Canada. Mr. McArthur put another $300 in our account since we qualified for the International Championship meet, and we started preparing for the event. The problem was that we had to have a Nordic Ski Team as well as an Alpine Team in order to participate in the upcoming meet. I drove cross-town to Pacific Lutheran University (PLU), and borrowed two pairs of cross-country skis from their coach. Dr. Christopherson, the PLU coach, had made his cross-country training skis out of old wooden military surplus skis, and they were extremely heavy. I wasn't choosy at this point, as I knew absolutely nothing about Nordic skiing. I told my team captain, Grant Middlestat, and another student that they would both have to run in the cross-country event in order for us to qualify for the meet. Both students agreed to the torturous event.

The team packed up and we drove to Vancouver, British Columbia, and caught the overnight train to Banff. Since we didn't have enough money for sleepers, I spent most of the night in the train's Skylight bar. Having never been involved in a ski meet at this level, I was totally unprepared for the events as they unfolded. Prior to this meet I had never skied on anything but wooden skis. The first metal skis had only recently appeared in the commercial stores, and I had purchased a new pair just for this meet.

On the first morning after the coaches' meeting I took the Alpine Team up on top of the mountain to make some practice runs on the slalom course. The ride up to the top of the hill was in small two-person chairs, and the weather was terrible, with intermittent snow, fog, rain, and hail. I had a forty-pound radio pack inside my backpack, which didn't make things any easier for me. As the chair lift neared the discharge area, there was only a small trail approximately ten inches wide next to a small picket fence about ten feet long for both of us to maneuver in. I quickly pushed forward with all my strength to give Grant more room.

Approaching the end of the picket fence I tried to make a 360-degree turn, and this is where the trouble commenced. The area around the end of the fence was solid ice; and I was totally unprepared especially with my new skis. I slipped, and the last thing I remember hearing was, "There goes the UPS coach on the course."

I slid for more than a hundred yards before I was finally able to turn over and try to get myself under control. When I eventually stopped I could see no one. After getting up, I experienced one heck of a time just getting down the very steep hill on those new metal skis. Since I was used to wooden skis, I continually found myself overturning on all of, what should have been simple, turns. My students got a great kick out of my ride down the hill, and it served to lessen the stress level for everyone.

The slalom course was very steep and had two runs, with seventy-five gates on each of them. A skier had to successfully navigate and complete the first course in order to qualify for the second run. This was no easy task for anyone, and only one UPS skier, Grant Middlestat, successfully made it through the first seventy-five gates. Grant crashed about halfway through the second course, and I had to get down to him in a hurry, as we only had fifteen minutes to get Grant over to the start of the Nordic cross-country race. Grant was just one of those persons described in Elbert Hubbard's "A Message to Garcia" type individuals. He never whimpered or said anything about having to run nine miles on cross-country skis even though he had never had a pair of cross-country skis on in his life.

Arriving in the vicinity of the starting gate, I started getting Grant's skis ready. Grant had borrowed a secondhand pair of Nordic shoes, which he was trying desperately to get adjusted to his feet while I was attempting to locate some Nordic wax. At that point I knew absolutely nothing about Nordic ski wax. Locating the varsity coach from the University of Washington, I explained my problem, and he agreed to help me. Both he and his team laughed when they saw the skis that Grant was going to use, as their Nordic skis were of the latest technology.

At that time most cross-country skiers used a gooey hot pine mixture on the bottom of their skis. The better college teams all used a Klister paste-type wax, which came in small colored tubes, that they rubbed onto the bottom of their skis. As the UW coach began to wax Grant's skies I realized the secret of their success. They had somehow managed to change the wax inside the Klister canisters to another color so that other teams would not be able to copy or know which wax they were using. I had no idea just how much secrecy was involved in winning these events!

Grant ran the entire sixteen kilometers and eventually crossed the finish line a very tired yet courageous person. Of the seven skiers on that first team, six of them were from the Sigma Chi fraternity.

The following year, due to our success and press coverage, we had fifty-eight students turn out for the ski team. My team captain for the second year was Sara Eaton, and she turned out to be one of the best ski team captains I was ever associated with. Sara was simply a natural student leader. Every school day she was in early and got the team's daily training practices organized. I was really perplexed that second year, as I could only seed three skiers in each event and many of the students wanted to race in all Alpine events. I also knew that my budget could not handle fifty-eight racers and I wasn't sure what I was going to do to eliminate some of them. I took my problem to the school AD, Doug McArthur. Doug felt that the best way to eliminate most of the students was to have them run a mile in a specific time. He felt that the boys should be able to run the mile in six minutes, thirty seconds, while the girls should qualify in seven minutes, thirty seconds. This seemed like good advice at the time and I complied with it, but was I ever in for a future shock.

One of the young UPS skiers had failed to qualify in the run, and he came into my office the next day. This young man had a speech impediment, and it was very difficult to understand him at times, especially when he was excited. Vince was just one of those persons who could not run fifty feet without stumbling or falling. He explained his desire to be a member of the ski team, particularly because he came from a ski family and his younger sister was currently a member of the U.S. National Ski Team. I explained how sorry I was that he did not qualify for the team, but that I did have an alternative in mind for him. I told Vince that I felt sure that I could get him a job as a ski instructor at Crystal Mountain, and he reluctantly agreed to accept my offer.

About a month later we were involved in a very large ski meet at Crystal Mountain. It was what became the annual UPS Invitational Meet, and we had 351 skiers from twenty-two different universities competing. At the time I was the vice director of the newly formed Northwest Intercollegiate Ski Conference (NCSC). Since UPS was sponsoring this meet, I found myself so unbelievably busy that I barely had time to coach my athletes. One of my downhill racers, against my advice, had loaned his downhill skis to another racer the evening before the actual downhill race so that he could make a practice run. The racer who borrowed the skis had changed the binding settings and had forgotten to mention this to Dan when he returned the skis. Dan's home was in Seattle, and he thought that he knew everything there was to know about skiing. Another problem that I had with him was his insistence that he use long thong straps on his ski bindings. This was the era before ski brakes were invented, and the idea was that should the skier fall and the ski come off, it would remain attached to the skier's boot by a six-or-seven-foot strap. Thus a skier could fall and quickly get his or her skis back on and hopefully continue on with the race. I had reminded all of my racers that I was adamantly against anyone using long thong straps because I felt that they were a danger to the skier.

What ultimately happened was that Dan started the race and on the first turn of the downhill he stepped right out of the binding on his right ski. In the process of the ensuing fall the right ski left his body until it reached the end of the long thong. At this point, we all watched with fascination as if the accident were in slow motion. The ski extended out and upon reaching the limit of the thong whipped back around Dan's body and subsequently broke one of his legs. He was quickly bundled up and strapped into the rescue toboggan and taken to the first-aid station at the bottom of the hill by the ski patrol. This was the only mishap that I experienced in my years of coaching at UPS.

While I was waiting outside the emergency room, Vince approached me and asked if he could replace Dan in the afternoons slalom race. I told Vince that I had a coaches' meeting in an hour and would bring the subject up and coordinate it with all of the other ski coaches. During that coaches' meeting, I explained to the other coaches that I had cut Vince from the team simply because he could not qualify in a preliminary mile run. I also told the coaches that even though he had been cut from the team, he had continued to voluntarily work out every day with the team. The coaches all agreed that Vince could race; however, the stipulation was that he had to start dead last in the race. This meant that Vince would be the 84th racer on the slalom course.

By the time that Vince stepped into the starting gates at the top of the hill, the ruts in the course were so bad that we almost stopped the race. I was the course referee and was located at the finish line when Vince started the race. Dr. Christopherson from PLU was the starting referee, and shortly after Vince left the starting gate, Dr. Christopherson called me and wanted to know if this racer was one of my kids. Dr. Christopherson was a man of few words, and rarely did he ever say anything on the radio unless there was something wrong. From the bottom of the hill you could not see the start of the race at the top, as the hill bowed in the middle.

My first reaction was, *Oh, darn, another accident.* About that time I looked up and saw Vince and couldn't' believe my eyes. At this level in collegiate racing, the top ten racers would usually always finish within one-hundredth of a second of one another. Vince not only won the Gold Medal for the race, but his time was four seconds faster than that of his closest competitor. I took a lot of heckling from the other coaches, who all wanted to know if they could have my future rejections. The most significant thing that I learned was that I would never cut a future skier simply because he or she could not run the mile in a specific time period. I immediately placed Vince back on the team, and the following year we were considered the "powerhouse" of the NCSC thanks to Vince.

Another interesting problem occurred toward the end of that second year. I was informed by the school's AD that I could not give varsity letters to female athletes. This really upset me, as I had such an outstanding women's team. The Title Nine legislation had just come into being, but not too many people were paying it much attention in 1968. The AD told me that my real problem was coming from the Men's Lettermen Club, and without their OK there was no way that I could give varsity letters to my female athletes. The following week I attended the next meeting of the Men's Letterman Club. I challenged them to send two of their varsity athletes to attend one of my daily woman's ski team workouts. Several days later two young men showed up for our ski team practice. Sara led the practice and the two men finally gave up after trying to run the stairs of the football stadium with the girls' team. The next week I was invited back to the Men's Letterman Club. The club gave me a complete endorsement to give varsity letters to the girls on the ski team. Thanks to Sara and to all of those wonderful ladies who worked so hard to make that a successful season.

Crystal Mountain personnel were incredibly good to our ski team in those early years as we ran all of our weekly practices on their slopes. Ed Link, the hill manager, was instrumental in the development of the hill for intercollegiate ski racing. In the late 1960s the downhill course at Crystal Mountain was considered one of the best in the nation. In addition Ed helped us construct and build a thirty-meter ski jump, which was now required for NCAA-sanctioned ski meets. The jump was located just to the right side of the T-Bar hill. Needless to say, being so involved in skiing was great for the family. On Thursday nights I used to take both Jane and David up on the hill and they would help me set poles on the giant slalom and slalom racecourses. They both went on to become expert skiers. At the time, Anne was too small to carry the race poles, but she, too, became an excellent skier.

I think that the reason Ed Link and I got along so well was because he was a retired lieutenant colonel from the U.S. Army. During the school weeks I used to fly the AFROTC cadets on training flights in a T-33 jet out of McChord AFB. My standard flight with a cadet onboard was to take off and head straight for Mount Rainier. I would then circle around the mountain with the T-33 climbing all the while. Eventually reaching the top at around 14,400 feet, we would mush over the peak and wave at the mountain climbers who were there. From there we would race down the back side of the mountain and into Cayuse Pass until reaching my cutoff mark for Crystal Mountain.

Coming up over the top of the C-4 hill I would roll the fighter inverted and start down about thirty feet over the top of the chair lift. Reaching the bottom of the C-4 ski run and now being right side up, we would turn left and climb out of the canyon doing aileron rolls over the main chair lift until passing less than a hundred feet over the restaurant at the top of the hill. Ed knew that it was me all the time, but he never complained, as everyone seemed to enjoy the air show and the cadets loved the flying thrills. Only once in three years of flying this route did a cadet ever get sick while in the aircraft.

What made my AFROTC assignment so exciting while there at UPS was my additional duty assignment of flying T-33 single-engine jet trainers with the 318th FIS at McChord AFB. In July of 1967 there were sixteen T-33s assigned to base operations at McChord AFB, which was an unusually large amount of trainer-type aircraft. Base ops didn't want to lose any T-33s, so they assigned one of the aircraft to me to use as my personal aircraft while I was assigned to UPS. Whenever I was not required to fly a mission for the 318th, I could fly the T-33 for any reason I choose to and could fly anywhere inside the continental limits of the United States.

Each year our ROTC summer camps were held across the state at Fairchild AFB in Spokane, Washington. The encampment was six weeks long for instructors, and each year I would make the seven-hour drive a day early based upon the SAC courier schedule. Upon arrival at Fairchild AFB, I would go immediately to base ops and book myself a seat on the SAC courier airplane for the next day to McChord AFB. I was really lucky, because most SAC couriers only went to SAC bases. However, a lot of SAC aircrews departed out of McChord AFB for TDY assignments around the world, and there was usually one seat empty to McChord AFB. In any event, I would pick up my T-33 at McChord and head back to Fairchild, arriving in less than one hour's flying time. The camp commanders at Fairchild were always pleased to see me with the T-33. By bringing the T-33 to Fairchild I managed to get out of most all extra daily details that other TAC officers had to be concerned with. My extra duty detail was to fly as many of the cadets on orientation flights as I could get into the air each day. What a deal this was for both the cadets and me, and a great way to spend six weeks of my summer.

The first two years at UPS, I was considered as an assistant professor of aerospace studies, and I taught Astronautics and Space for one semester and the History of Flight the second semester. The final year I became the professor of the Aerospace Studies Department for the last six months of my tour at UPS. One of our most difficult tasks each year was to hold the annual Awards and Decorations parade on the university's football field. The actual parade was an excellent opportunity for the cadets to pass in review before a visiting general from different commands within the Air Force. With the detachment being so close to McChord AFB, we were fortunate to have the use of the McChord AFB Air Force Band to support our parades. The problem that we encountered each year was the large amount of student protestors against the war in Vietnam. Each succeeding year their activities seemed to get worse. These students were sponsored each year by the Students for Democratic Society (SDS) of America foundation from both UW and UPS.

The SDS students would set up ten-foot-tall speakers on all four corners of the football field and play acid rock music as loud as they could get the speakers to go. The idea was to disrupt the military music, and they managed to do a fairly good job of it. In addition, they would hurl rotten eggs and fruit at the cadets. As the war in Vietnam continually got worse, so did the insults and hatred for America's military services on campuses across our great nation. The Army and Air Force ROTC detachments at UW held their annual parade one month before ours in 1969. The UW protestors became extremely violent as the SDS students attempted to burn the Army ROTC facilities down during their parade.

Doc T. called me over to his office shortly after the news broke about the violent conditions that were experienced on the Washington campus. He told me that he had received word that the UW chapter of the SDS was going to send delegates down to UPS to show the UPS chapter how to conduct a really violent protest. Doc T. wanted me to conduct business as usual and not worry too much about the SDS student threat. He said that he had already contacted the FBI and that they, plus undercover policemen from Tacoma, would be on hand to assist us.

As the parade day approached, I became more and more nervous. What bothered me most was the arrival of two Air Force generals instead of one and all of the protocol necessary to take care of them in proper military fashion.

Doc T. came over two hours before the parade to inspect conditions around the field and on campus. Sure enough, the ten-foot speakers were in place but at the time were silent. He assured me that he felt everything was under control.

The two Air Force generals showed up right on time, and I invited them upstairs in the fieldhouse for coffee prior to the parade. Later as we were descending the steps in front of the fieldhouse it appeared as though a normal class period had ended and students were in the process of changing rooms. One of the students in passing, who was an All-American tackle for the football team, yelled at me not to worry about a thing. I wasn't quite certain what he was referring to so I just smiled and thanked him. As the generals and I approached the stadium entrance there were two young ladies in white dresses passing out antimilitary literature. This was to be the only form of protest that we were to experience that day. The parade went off like clockwork while the McChord Air Force Band, without the harassing music from the ten-foot speakers outdid itself with military music.

After the generals departed in their staff cars I was walking back across the street when once again there was a large exodus of students coming down the steps of the fieldhouse. The same All-American tackle said, "Hey, Coach, I told you so."

I stopped and said, "What are you talking about, Bob?"

He placed his arms around me and said to follow him and that one look would be worth a thousand words to me. Athletes from all of the male sports had organized themselves into several teams located in the men's football locker room. These students had set up two barber chairs in the adjourning shower room. This organization of students caught four of the SDS students from UW, as well as two student leaders from UPS. These SDS students were escorted to the locker room, where they were stripped of their clothing. Each one of the SDS students, according to the UPS football players, had his long hair cut off and was given a lye soap shower, then physically thrown outside the fieldhouse. Word apparently quickly got around campus, and subsequently the planned protest became a complete failure.

After all of the flak that I had taken as a Vietnam veteran from various students on campus, this turned out to be one of those significant emotional events that occurred in my life. I was so overwhelmed with the display of red-blooded American patriotism, especially from the football players and varsity skiers, that I decided then and there to dedicate my future career to teaching and coaching. I immediately started working on a master's degree in Education and received it from Ball State University in June of 1974. Today, after twenty-four years in education, my association continues with a number of those guys who renewed my faith in the youth of America. Three of the kids off that UPS football team later became very successful high school head football coaches, while one of them still today is the head football coach at a nearby PAC-10 school.

I couldn't conclude this chapter without this story, as it pertains to one of the four times in my Air Force flying career that I had to dead-stick an aircraft after running out of fuel. When I first arrived at UPS I was also on orders to report to the 318th FIS located at nearby McChord AFB. I checked into personal equipment at the 318th, and later met with the squadron commander. Since I had recently flown F-105s, he gave me my choice of flying the Air Defense Command's F-106 or the T-33 jet trainer.

I initially wanted to fly the F-106 simply because it looked like such a neat aircraft. It had the look of exceeding the speed of sound just sitting on the ground, and I chose it to fly. Shortly after I passed my checkout ride in the F-106, the squadron commander informed me that I would have to go on the weekend alert schedule with the rest of the squadron. That was not what I wanted to do at all, as I had pulled enough time on alert during my time in SAC flying B-47s.

I told the squadron commander that I would just as soon fly the T-33, and he quickly agreed with me, as he did not have enough T-33 pilots. I was told to turn in my Form 5 (flight records) to base ops and to inform them that I was assigned to the 318th and not to base ops for flying. I drove down to base ops and gave a copy of my orders to the clerk on duty. The clerk informed me that they were extremely short of qualified T-33 pilots and welcomed me onboard. The clerk also told me that base ops had sixteen T-33s assigned to McChord AFB and that I was the fourth T-33 qualified pilot to check in.

Approximately one week later I received a call from the 318th operations officer informing me that I was on the schedule for a three-day mission starting the next day. The ops officer told me to report in three hours early, as I had to wear a "poopy suit" and it would take a minimum of 45 minutes to get into it. I had no idea what a poopy suit was, so I told him that I would be on time. It turned out that all Air Defense Command (ADC) pilots who were scheduled to fly over water or cold landmasses had to wear a poopy suit for survival purposes.

A poopy suit looks like what today's astronauts wear when they prepare for space flights. It is made out of heavy rubber, and like a woman's girdle, it was extremely difficult to get into. There were two special equipment airmen assigned to assist each pilot in getting the poopy suit on. The pilot's entire body had to be dusted with a liberal amount of powder first before attempting to get into the suit. By the time the pilots finally got the poopy suit arranged and zipped up it was time to strap on your Mae West water survival vest, plus another cold-weather survival vest, and you could hardly move.

Having never flown for the ADC, I found their flight-planning procedures quit different from those of other flying commands. After reporting in at the 318th, I was handed a computerized flight plan indicating that I was one of three T-33s that would be going to Namao Air Base in Canada. Normally Air Force pilots report to base operations, where they draw lines on maps, figure fuel times and distances, and coordinate the total flight plan with the base weather officer. Using this procedure, you could always look at a map and get a pretty good idea of where you were going and what the terrain was like. You could also locate where the nearest alternate bases were located for in-flight emergencies along your flight path. I felt really uneasy about this flight, but since I was flying in the number-two position of a three-ship formation I figured I would just follow the other two aircraft and say nothing, as my professional pride was on the line. How stupid this decision was became real apparent a few hours later.

It was about four-thirty in the afternoon and, very typical of Tacoma, raining hard, and the weather was going from bad to worse. The squadron bus delivered us to our aircraft one at a time. I gave my parachute to the crew chief, who proceeded to place it in the open cockpit while I began my outside walk around the T-33. Trying to look very professional, I kicked the right forward landing gear and shook the right wing as I walked around it, eventually looking up into the tailpipe as if I were to find something unusual located there. Finally I arrived back at the ladder and began my climb up to the cockpit in a hurry to get out of the rain. This is where my real problems began! In order to get inside the cockpit I had to stand up on the pilot's ejection seat and twist my body fully to the left in order to get into the cockpit.

Because the front cockpit was unfamiliar to me at the time, I was using my checklist, but having trouble locating all of the proper switches. Having not started this aircraft in many years, I called the crew chief up to the cockpit using hand signals. He jumped up on the wing thinking something was wrong. I informed him that nothing was wrong other than I didn't remember how to start the engine and asked him if he would show me how. I remember the crew chief giving me a real funny look as he said, "Are you sure that you want to fly this machine, Major?"

I replied, "Yes," and he began to start the engine for me. He was talking to me all the time, but I couldn't hear him very well, as there was so much noise with the engine turning over. He finally leaned over and gang-loaded all of my fuel switches and gave me a thumbs-up. I wasn't sure as to why he did this but said nothing. The real reason, I learned later, was that there were seven separate fuel systems in the T-33 and unless you knew exactly how to use them you could find yourself in deep kimchee real quick.

By the time I got things settled down and checked in on the ground frequency with the lead T-33, both the number-one and number-three aircraft were starting to taxi out to the active runway. Once I got with the other two T-33s, we taxied out as a very professional-looking three-ship formation and proceeded to the end of the active runway. The lead aircraft and I received instructions from the tower to taxi into the takeoff position on the end of the active runway and to hold for Air Traffic Control (ATC) release. We were taking off on runway 160 to the south. ATC informed us that we would be taking off with a twenty-second separation between aircraft. Upon receiving takeoff clearance the lead T-33 pushed his power up to 100 percent and started to roll. Just about the time I was about to release my brakes, the pilot in the lead T-33 shouted that he was aborting his takeoff. The tower told me to hold my position until the lead T-33 had cleared the active runway, and I acknowledged. This meant that I suddenly was to become the leader of the now two-ship formation, and I wasn't really prepared for that responsibility. However, due to professional pride I said nothing.

About the time that the tower cleared me for takeoff, it was raining so hard that I could barely make out the yellow centerline of the active runway. Accelerating down the runway as I reached takeoff speed I lifted the T-33 off the ground and began to clean the aircraft up. I was cleared by departure control for an immediate right-hand turn to a heading of 360 degrees. By the time my gear came up and locked into position I was already in the clouds and had to instantly resort to instrument flying conditions. It was about this time that I heard the number-three, now number-two, T-33 aborting his takeoff.

I quickly found myself in very deep kimchee again, as I had never flown an ADC mission before and all that I knew was that my destination was somewhere up into Canada. I was very carefully following the clearance that I had received from Seattle Center when I broke out for the first time between layers of clouds as I was climbing through 8,000 feet. Going back into the clouds almost immediately, I again broke out and for some reason looked out toward my left side and discovered that my left wing was almost up to the vertical position. I quickly slammed the stick over to the left to level my wings and the aircraft stalled and immediately went into a spin. This was the second time in my flying career that I had to recover from a spin while flying on instruments, only this time I wasn't quite as familiar with the aircraft's flight characteristics. I lost 4,000 feet before finally getting the aircraft under control and straightaway turned to my original heading and began climbing again.

Seattle Center was quick to ask me if I was experiencing flight control problems. I lied, telling them that I had encountered severe turbulence at 8,000 feet and had gone into a tailspin, but that now everything was under control and that I was climbing back out on my departure heading. Up to this point I had only flown a few times north of Seattle, and I knew that there were mountains in almost every direction and I wasn't sure exactly how high they were. It's like your life is quickly passing before your eyes, but you are unable to do anything about it. I continued to climb out on the original heading that I had received and just hoped for the best.

While passing through 8,000 feet the second time I was prepared to break out into the clear, and sure enough, I did. As I looked left, my wing was still up into the vertical position, and I quickly cross-checked my instruments. I realized instantly that I had a case of vertigo and tried to ignore the position of my wings. Believe me, this is not an easy thing to do especially, since I had never experienced the conditions of vertigo before. I did know that a lot of pilots had been killed while experiencing this flight phenomenon. Going back into the clouds, I returned to instrument flying conditions as my heart was going sixty miles per hour beyond where it was supposed to be.

I glued my eyes on the attitude gyro indicator, trying desperately to keep my wings level, and continued to climb. I just couldn't believe that my eyes had deceived me. I broke out again around seventeen thousand feet between layers of clouds and asked Seattle Center if I could level off for a while. I explained that I had a severe case of vertigo and needed a few minutes of VFR flying to reorient myself, and they cleared me to remain VFR until I was ready to climb again. I glanced left and sure enough the left wing was almost in the vertical position. After glancing at the attitude indicator, which indicated that my wings were straight and level, I quickly closed my eyes for about ten seconds—and the results were the same, i.e., my left wing was still in the almost vertical position. I just couldn't believe this phenomenon, so next I tried holding my breath with my eyes closed, and this still didn't help matters. Last, I placed my left arm on the cockpit railing, locking my chin into position with my hand and eyes closed, and again this didn't help. I finally called Seattle Center and told them that I experiencing a severe case of vertigo and requested to continue to climb on my original course until I broke out on top of the clouds. The center told me that the tops of the clouds were about thirty thousand feet, and they were correct.

By the time that I broke out on top of the clouds, my vertigo had gone away and I felt much better. I continued flying on the last heading that Seattle Center had given me and eventually leveled off at 34,000-foot altitude. As I looked down at the ground, everything was white, as it was still wintertime in Canada. Flying on for a ways I eventually became concerned, as I hadn't heard from Seattle Center in a while. I made several attempts to contact Seattle Center but received no response. Glancing back at my flight log, I couldn't make heads nor tails out of it, and my anxiety level was definitely on the upswing again. It is always embarrassing for an Air Force pilot to use the International Guard radio frequency, but I had reached the point of no return by this time. I was definitely lost and had no idea where I was. I was definitely embarrassed to declare an emergency, so I pushed the control button down and asked if any aircraft could hear me. A Canadian mutilengine aircraft answered me immediately, and I told them that I was a single-engine Air Force fighter at 34,000 feet and needed a radio frequency for Edmonton Center. They were especially nice and quickly gave me a UHF radio frequency for Edmonton Center, and I thanked them.

Placing the new radio frequency into my radio, I called Edmonton Center as quickly as I could, and they responded immediately, wanting to know how they might assist me. I informed them that I was inbound to Namao Air Base, and could they provide me with flight following? They requested me to change the numbers in my aircraft's transponder and to make a ninety-degree turn to the left followed by a return to my original heading. Within seconds they informed me that they had a positive identification on my aircraft. Wow, was I ever relieved, but the feelings of euphoria were to quickly disappear. By not paying attention to my surroundings I failed to realize that clouds had been forming below me and began to cover the entire landscape. Suddenly I received the radio call that all pilots fear when Edmonton center called and said, "The weather at Namao is currently below minimums." In the next breath Edmonton Center wanted to know what my intentions were.

Quickly looking over my computerized flight plan, I could find no suitable alternates, and I had no in-flight map to assist me. It took me a while to collect my thoughts and return the center's call. It has always been my experience when flying that whenever things like this begin to happen they snowball, and this time was no exception. The thing that caught my eye the quickest was the blinking yellow light on my fuel panel. This meant that I was experiencing a low level of fuel and that I should get the machine on the ground ASAP. Responding to Edmonton Center, I told them that I did not have a map, and could they tell me where the nearest alternate military landing site was? Their speedy response was that the only military base that was in the clear was Moose Jaw.

By the time I got through laughing at the strange name and got myself under control I asked them exactly where Moose Jaw was. The center answered that it was directly on my tail and 600 miles from my current position. My mind was racing and I thought to myself that I could never make 600 miles in my current state of not having much fuel to burn. I informed Edmonton Center that Moose Jaw was out of the question, as I just plain did not have enough fuel to make it there. The center responded in a rather hostile manner by reminding me that Namao Air Base was now closed due to accumulations of snow on the runway and also for being below safe landing minimums. They again asked me what my intentions were.

I had no alternative at this point but to declare an in-flight emergency, as I now had all seven low-level fuel lights up on my master fuel panel. I requested an immediate descent from the center with flight following to Namao. The center reluctantly complied with my request and cleared me to start my descent from 140 miles out and gave me a radio frequency for Namao Approach Control. Flying an airplane is very much like being the captain of a naval ship, as the pilot in command always has the final decision. Quickly establishing communications with Approach Control, I found myself passing through 10,000-foot altitude. At the same moment, I entered the clouds and immediately was back flying under instrument flight conditions. Like Edmonton Center, Approach Control again reminded me that the runways at Namao were closed with an accumulation of close to two feet of snow on them. Since this was an official emergency Approach Control did turn me over to their Ground Control Agency (GCA) unit. I was at less than 2,000-foot altitude when the GCA unit called me. I acknowledged their radio call and informed them that I now had red lights "blinking on" on my master fuel panel.

From former flying experiences I knew that my anxiety level was about as high as it could go at the present moment. When the GCA unit responded to my call I asked them if they had a master controller on duty, and they said that he would be right with me. Seconds later the most comforting voice that I had ever heard came up on frequency requesting that I continue my descent and turn left one half-degree. Now, only a master controller can accomplish something like this, as most controllers would have turned me three or four degrees one way or the other instead of one half-degree. The master controller requested my fuel state, and I responded by telling him that my engine was currently running rough and that I would shortly most likely "flameout."

The master controller continued talking to me in a steady voice, as if there were nothing wrong, telling me to place my gear handle in the down and locked position just as if it were another normal landing. He continued talking me down and told me that in exactly five seconds my wheels would hit the snow. This master controller was absolutely correct, as I felt the gear strike first the snow and then the ground. While all of this was going on, the noise of impacting the snow was terrifying as it flew up and over the aircraft's canopy. The master controller was still with me as he quietly told me to hold my current heading as best as I could until I could gain control of the aircraft. Things had happened so fast that I never did know exactly when my engine "flamed out."

After the aircraft finally came to a complete stop and I could once again talk, I thanked the master controller and requested a Ground Control radio frequency from him. I made numerous attempts to contact the tower's Ground Control, but all to no avail. My feelings were that they must have gone home when the runway was closed. My aircraft batteries were going fast due to the extremely cold conditions. Returning back to the GCA radio frequency, I informed the controller that I was unable to establish contact with the tower. The controller advised me that he had already contacted a tractor tug and that they would be out looking for me as fast as they could. He also said for me to stay inside the aircraft and not open the canopy. It took close to forty-five minutes before the tug crew found my aircraft. The tug crew manually cranked open the canopy so they could communicate with me.

I had not been that cold since my combat experience during the Korean War, and I was really thankful for the poopy suit. Once the aircraft was hooked up to the tug it seemed like it took forever for the tug to get from the runway into the aircraft parking area. By this time the tug stopped, I was really shivering; my fingers were hurting the most, since I only had on summer flying gloves. Before I left the aircraft the tug crew told me they would close the canopy later once they got a power unit attached to the aircraft. I placed the ejection seat safety pins in the ejection seat and got out of the aircraft as quickly as I could. With all macho fighter pilots, it is traditional to place your helmet on the top of the forward canopy railing, and was I ever going to pay the price for this mistake later on.

A crew truck picked me up and took me to base operations. I got on the military autovon telephone as fast as possible and called the 318th FIS. I explained what had happened to me and that the aircraft was OK. I told the ops officer that it might be several days before I could get out of Namao due to the snow on the runway. The ops officer told me to take my time, that he was just happy that nothing more serious had occurred. He said that he would cancel the ADC intercept mission and that I should return home whenever

337

conditions were safe enough to fly. He also said that he would inform my wife and for me to enjoy the Canadian hospitality in the meantime.

As it turned out I was to enjoy a complete week of that wonderful Canadian hospitality. Unlike the situation at most American military bases, the Canadians were still addicted to their officers' club in the evenings. With the weather finally clearing, I spent approximately three hours in base ops planning my own flight back to McChord AFB.

When I went out to my aircraft I found the canopy open and my helmet sitting on the front of the cockpit just like I had left it. The helmet liners were frozen solid inside the helmet, and since I am baldheaded, wow, did I ever hate putting that helmet on. This time the return flight was a piece of cake, and was I ever happy to get back to McChord in one piece. I spent the next few weeks studying ADC flight plans, telling myself that I never wanted to get caught up in a fiasco like that again.

Those three years while assigned to the 318th FIS for flying were most enjoyable. There was a lot of rapport among the pilots assigned to the 318th FIS, and competition among sections was always high. The T-33s were the target ships for all of the ADC scrambles of F-106 fighter-interceptors. We had two military corridors in Washington State that we used for training exercises. The eastern training range was located between Lake Roosevelt (north) and Walla Walla to the south, while the western range was located over the Olympic Mountains. There were mainly two types of air intercepts, high and low, plus front or rear approaches. The high-altitude frontal intercepts were always the scariest for a number of common reasons. We in the T-33s were never sure whether the F-106 was being hand-flown by the pilot or on autopilot with the controller flying the aircraft while sitting behind a computer screen in the NORAD Center.

The T-33s on a high-altitude intercept would be flying normally around twenty thousand feet, and the aircraft were armed with two chaff tanks. The idea of using chaff was to deploy it in small bursts after the F-106 had a lock-on with the idea of breaking the F-106's lock on the T-33. We also had Electric Counter Measure (ECM) pods on the T-33 to further assist us in jamming the F-106's radar.

In addition the T-33s could descend or climb 500 feet and turn no more than thirty degrees off the flight planned heading during the actual intercept. According to ADC both aircraft were supposed to always have a minimum 500-foot clearance between each other. The T-33s would be traveling around 500 mph while the F-106s would be accelerating through the Mach while bearing down on you. This would equate to a 1260-mph closer rate, and believe me, things happen fast when you are involved in this type of closure with another aircraft. The F-106 pilots always had to make a forty-mile mandatory radio call as they approached you. On a high-altitude head-on intercept the T-33 pilots usually could not see the F-106, but you could see the smoke from the 106's afterburner as the aircraft accelerated toward you. Should you be 500 feet high in the T-33 and the F-106 500 feet low, the actual pass could really get your attention, especially when you went by each other.

The F-106 pilots enjoyed the tail chase passes the most, especially if they knew who the pilot of the T-33 was. The 106 pilots would always try to get close enough to dust the T-33s off as they passed by in supersonic flight. Many times the impact of two aircraft passing so close to each other would cause one of the aircraft to lose control, and guess which one it was? The F-106 jocks got their jollies during these intercepts, but when it came time for the low-level intercepts, we in the T-33 had the most advantage. The T-33 pilots could fly low enough so that the F-106 pilots could not see the T-33 in their radarscopes due to the ground clutter on the 106's radarscope.

During these low-level missions most T-33 pilots would not drop chaff or use our ECM jammers, because these devices would just highlight the T-33 on the F-106's scope. Once we got down to less than fifty feet from the ground it was next to impossible for the F-106s to locate us. As the F-106 pilots sped by there would be lots of joking chatter on the radio frequency, as the 106s only had the opportunity for one pass before they had to head for home, due to low fuel conditions. The F-106s would beat the T-33s home by an hour, but once we finally arrived there would always be an extra can of iced beer for the T-33 drivers during the debriefings.

My second flameout in a T-33 came during one of the many national ADC exercises where we, the T-33 target aircraft, were deployed twenty-four hours ahead of time to a secret ADC base. Once on the ground at the secret base the T-33 pilots would stay on alert until the ADC launch message came down. The T-33s would then deploy on a classified flight plan, while ADC facilities along the T-33's flight path would try to make airborne radar intercepts on us all the way home. Our secret launch site for this particular mission was Nellis AFB in Arizona, and our flight path to Las Vegas took us down the central corridor of California. Normally on any ADC mission the T-33s were armed with two external chaff tanks that resembled large 2,000-pound napalm bombs. Under normal flight conditions these tanks caused a lot of drag on the aircraft and reduced the fuel consumption considerably while airborne.

By this time I had flown enough ADC missions so that I was very comfortable with the computer-type flight plans. Flying the missions had by then become second nature. The one thing that happened on this particular mission, which I did not pay enough attention to, was the maintenance crew had inadvertently uploaded an additional chaff tank on the centerline position of my aircraft without telling me ahead of time. I didn't think too much about it until after I got airborne. However, once I was airborne, it was like carrying three 2,000-pound bombs between the wheel wells of the T-33. The extra drag created by the third chaff tank began to tell on the fuel gauge by the time I leveled off at 24,000 feet. The second of the other two T-33s had taken off fifteen minutes before my departure time, so I was all alone in the sky.

By the time I crossed over the southern boundary of Oregon State I began to worry about my fuel state. There was no way that I was going to make it all the way to Nellis AFB in Nevada, and I started thinking about where I could land. I called Oakland Center and told them that I needed to make a fuel stop very soon and they suggested that I try the Sacramento area. Since I was currently south of Redding, California, and there were no military air bases in the immediate area, I told them that the Sacramento area would probably be OK.

I tried very hard not to watch my fuel gauges, but the tension was beginning to build and I was getting worried, especially since several of my fuel tank low-level lights were blinking on. As I was passing Yuba City VOR facility, all seven low-level lights came on and I called Oakland Center and declared an immediate emergency. I told them that I had Beal AFB in sight off to my left and that I was going to land there. I knew that Beal AFB had runways that were at a minimum of 13,000 feet long and I was sure that I could land somewhere on one of their runways. Oakland Center cleared me instantly to depart 24,000 feet and turned me over to Beal AFB Approach Control. Placing the speed brakes out to get more drag on the aircraft, I dropped like a rock. Somewhere between six and five-thousand-foot altitude the yellow low-level lights turned to red, indicating that my engine was about to flame out, and they were correct.

While I was passing through 5000 feet, Beal AFB Approach Control called me and told me that I could not land my aircraft at Beal AFB. I immediately canceled my IFR flight clearance with Approach Control and went to Beal's tower radio frequency. The tower had been monitoring my conversation with Approach Control, and the minute I established radio contact the tower informed me that the field was closed and that I could not land there. By this time I was passing through 1500 feet on a straight-in approach for the runway. The tower was screaming at me that I could not land, yet I could see nothing on their runway and besides, I had already committed myself. As low as I was at the time, I was completely focused on the empty runway ahead of me. Nothing was going to deviate me from the approach and landing at that moment. I quickly reminded the tower that I had already declared an in-flight emergency and that I was now flamed out and would be on the ground in less than two minutes.

Placing the gear down as close to the runway as possible, I continued my descent until touchdown. All the time I was rolling down the runway the tower was screaming at me, so I changed my radio frequency to channel three, the standard Air Force ground control, and informed them of my location and requested assistance. By the time I came to a complete stop there were security vehicles on every side of my aircraft with guys out pointing guns at me.

I couldn't believe what was happening and thought to myself, *Are they really pointing guns at me?* After opening the canopy, I was in the process of removing my helmet when two security policemen jumped up on both sides of the cockpit. While one of the policemen kept me covered with his weapon, the other policeman reached in and placed a black bag over my head. The two policemen told me to very carefully get out of the cockpit. Once outside the cockpit I sat down and carefully slid off the wing onto the ground.

I was placed inside a military van and taken to base operations. Once I was inside the building the black bag was removed from my head and I found myself confronted by several enraged colonels. I couldn't understand why they were so mad, and I told them so. They asked me if I didn't understand that Beal AFB was classified as a secret base and accepted no aircraft outside of SAC flights. I told them that I thought that Beal AFB was still a U.S. Air Force base. I further informed the colonels that I had declared an official in-flight emergency with Oakland Center. By that time I had no choice as to where I was going to land. I gave the colonels a copy of my ADC Secret Orders from McChord AFB and suggested that they call the 318th FIS and get this straightened out between the major air commands.

The colonels finally left me alone. Eventually one of the colonels came back later and apologized to me. The colonel told me that Beal AFB was an operational base for the supersecret SR-71 Blackbirds. The colonel then took me into the pilots' briefing room and made every effort to help me in the refiling of a flight plan that would get me to Nellis AFB. The colonel told me that my aircraft was currently being towed and that it would be parked in front of base ops. The colonel then asked me how much of a fuel load I wanted put onboard, and I responded, "A totally full load in every tank."

I knew at the time what SR-71s were, but I didn't know very much about their capabilities or missions. I also knew that everything about them was classified. What I did know came from my association with one of the original project officers who was now flying with the 318th FIS. This pilot had flown both the SR-71 and the YF-12.

By the time that I got ready to depart Beal AFB, everyone had become really friendly with me and I was offered all kinds of assistance. One of the SR-71 pilots in the briefing room showed me a picture on the briefing room wall that had been taken by the cameras of an SR-71. The picture according to this pilot was taken from around one hundred thousand feet, and the picture was of a golf ball sitting on a tee. The picture was so clear that you could read the "Wilson" label on the golf ball. I just couldn't believe what I was seeing and have never forgotten that picture.

After filing my flight plan I was escorted to my aircraft by one of the colonels who by now was extremely friendly. I cranked up the engine in the T-33, and while I was awaiting my flight clearance an SR-71 came taxiing by right in front of me. The rare beauty of this aircraft astounded me as it passed by me. What really got my attention was the amount of raw fuel that was dripping out of the aircraft onto the ground as it taxied along. There were two fire trucks on both sides of the SR-71 and two fire trucks directly behind the taxiing aircraft. What I learned from the folks in base ops was that while the SR-71 was on the ground if left alone all of the fuel would eventually leak out of the unsealed fuel tanks.

As a part of standard SAC procedures, a tanker aircraft always took off three minutes ahead of any SR-71. Once the SR-71 was airborne, the SR-71 had to hit the tanker immediately or abort the mission. When the SR-71 received a full fuel load from the tanker, the SR-71 would immediately climb to 40,000 feet for another refueling from another tanker. After the second refueling, the same SR-71 would then climb to its maximum altitude. While the SR-71 was accelerating, the fuselage of the SR-71 would expand due to the immense heat and the fuel tanks would then seal up. What fun it must have been for the aircrews to fly that machine, and how I envied them!

The remainder of the ADC mission was what we called ops normal, although I had difficulty explaining to my comrades why and how I had managed to flame out. They couldn't believe the problems that I experienced by landing at Beal AFB. We all agreed that it would be better to land somewhere else in the future.

The summer of 1970 was time to press on with my Air Force career. In the Air Force, like every type of bureaucracy, a person needed friends in the right places. I had a few "marks" to call in, and it was now time to do that. About a month before my rotation date from Tacoma, I called the Military Personnel Center (MPC) at Randolph AFB in Texas and spoke with Captain Matthews, a good friend who owed me a mark. Matt at the time was in charge of fighter assignments for the entire U.S. Air Force. Matt asked me what I wanted, and I told him that I wanted to fly F-7 fighters at

Luke AFB in Phoenix, Arizona. Matt said, "No problem," and I thanked him and comfortably awaited my next set of orders.

Several weeks passed and I had received no orders and had heard nothing from Matt, so I called MPC and asked to speak with him. I didn't get Matt, but some other captain told me that Matt had gone TDY to Vietnam to finish out his 100 missions. I explained who I was and told him that Matt had assured me that I would get an F-7 assignment. Well, the captain was not a friendly type, and I received zero help from him. Two weeks later I received a call from MPC wanting to know whether I wanted SAC and B-52s or C-141s in MAC. Once I was able to control my emotions and speak, I told the caller that I would take C-141s at McChord AFB. He said to send MPC a night letter requesting the same, and I did.

A week later and now for the second time in my Air Force career, I got screwed back into SAC with a B-52 assignment to Ellsworth AFB in South Dakota. Realizing that things were now out of my control, I called Ellsworth and asked to get on the base housing list. I was told that they had only a few houses left and that if I wanted one I would have to report in and sign up on their housing list. *Welcome back to SAC* was my only thought! The very next day I flew to Ellsworth AFB via the SAC courier service and signed their stupid housing list. Cynthia and I placed our house in Tacoma on the market and, fortunately, sold it the first day that it was advertised.

I subsequently left a few days later for a three months' B-52 training class at Merced AFB in California. Ellsworth AFB Housing Unit called me the same day and said that there was a house available if I wanted it. I explained that I did and, Cynthia and the kids having already gone to San Diego, left the next day from San Diego pulling a trailer behind our 1969 Ford station wagon. I couldn't believe how responsible my son, David, had become to the family. David was in the fifth grade when I showed him how to change a tire. Never did I realize how important this training session was as David changed a flat tire for his mother while en route to South Dakota. How absolutely proud I was of David.

44
B-52s

Arriving late one evening at Merced AFB, California, I checked into the Base Housing Office (BOQ). Since I was a senior major at the time and the BOQ was currently out of single rooms the BOQ clerk said that I could have VIP quarters if I wanted them. The VIP quarters turned out to be a small house complete with two bedrooms with everything included. It was getting late and I hadn't stopped for food that day, so I unpacked rapidly and headed over to the officers' club for dinner. Approaching the club I heard this incredible commotion coming from the stag bar and immediately headed in that direction. Pushing through the swinging doors, I spied a guy standing on top of one of the tables shouting at the entire audience of pilots. I immediately recognized the guy (Ed Mitchy) as a former fighter pilot from the 18th TFW in Kadena. Ed was slightly intoxicated and was prepared to take on the entire SAC crew in a fistfight.

For the record, all fighter pilots disliked multiengine pilots and especially SAC pilots. I quickly climbed up on the table and things suddenly got a lot quieter in the room. Ed's antagonists decided that they didn't want to take on two fighter pilots and left grumbling to themselves. Ed, like me, had recently been screwed into SAC and to a B-52 assignment and wasn't real happy about it. Ed had arrived at Merced about an hour before I did. We talked for a few minutes and I discovered that Ed had not checked into the BOQ office. After dinner we stopped back by the BOQ office and the clerks were very happy to put Ed in the same unit with me. We were delighted to learn in the next few days that we would be flying together as an upgrading AC team with the same IP.

Entering the flight briefing room the following day, we were introduced to our new instructor, a Major Philpot. Our first mission in the BUFF (Big Ugly Fat Fucker) created a real uproar in the training school. Word had already reached the instructors about our little fracas in the officers' club and about our attitude toward

SAC. The instructors, however, were a little leery of Ed and me since we both had recently returned from combat tours in Vietnam and we didn't hesitate to display our dislike of multiengine pilots.

Our first mission had us taking off at 0600 hours on a beautiful California morning with me in the left seat and the instructor in the right seat. We flew for several hours in the traffic pattern with both Ed and me alternating in the left seat making numerous "crash and goes" until the instructor, Major Philpot, decided that we were both safe to land and take off the BUFF. We then proceeded to an area where we were scheduled to practice air-to-air refueling with a KC-135 tanker. By this time we had become very comfortable with Major Philpot as an instructor. Major Philpot had remarked that we both were exceptional pilots and that he was completely satisfied with our flying skills. By the time that we neared the tanker's flying track, the three of us were all laughing and telling jokes to one another.

Again, as we entered the in-flight refueling phase, I was in the left seat. Major Philpot, flying from the right seat, contacted the tanker and began to move the B-52 in for the first hookup. Major Philpot stopped the B-52 about fifteen feet short of the refueling boom and then proceeded to tell us how to obtain a successful off-load of fuel from the tanker. Major Philpot then made the initial hookup with the tanker's flying boom and after receiving a fifteen-minute token off-load of fuel told us that he was going to demonstrate the limits of the flying boom to us.

The flying boom on a KC-135 aircraft is a tubelike straw that extends between two aircraft. It is approximately twenty-eight feet in length, with a small set of wings called ruddervators attached to the flying end of the boom. These ruddervators assist the boom operator, who is lying on his stomach in the very back of the tanker, to move (fly) the boom toward the receiver aircraft's refueling receptacle. The refueling portion of the boom, which is inside the actual boom, extends on outward about twenty feet from the end of the boom itself. At the exact center of the extended refueling tube there is a green luminous area that the receiver pilot tries to keep his aircraft in as his aircraft moves up and down.

Above and below the green luminous area is a yellow luminous area, which means to the receiver pilot that he is out of position and needs to make a correction up or down immediately. The yellow luminous area is followed by a red luminous area indicating that the receiver pilot has reached the full extension (approximately fifteen feet) of the boom and that there is imminent danger to both aircraft if no corrections are made. When this red limit is reached, either the boomer or the receiver pilot must instantly disconnect the refueling operation and break away. In addition to the up limits of twelve degrees and fifty-degree down limits, there are also thirty-degree lateral limits on each side of the centerline of the boom. These limits are designed for the protection and safety of both aircraft.

Flying at about 300 mph, the good major moved the BUFF into position and got a perfect hookup. Major Philpot then began to demonstrate the up-and-down limits of the flying boom as well as the side-to-side limits so that we would have an idea of how much area we had to work in. Major Philpot remained connected to the boom for approximately ten minutes, then disconnected and moved the BUFF back into the approach position below the tanker.

I have never been a real lover of multiengine aircraft, and especially one of this size, but I had to admit to Major Philpot that the BUFF D model was really sweet and easy on the controls. With its eight J-57 jet engines the BUFF had enough power to make a pilot appreciate the aircraft even though it weighed up to 450,000 pounds at takeoff. Sitting there in the left seat, I played with the flight controls and throttles for a few minutes, waiting for clearance to move into the refueling position. As the boomer talked me in toward his aircraft, this was one of those times that I felt very confident about my flying skills. After hooking up to the tanker's boom I managed to keep the BUFF hooked up for thirty-five minutes.

I told Major Philpot that I felt comfortable enough to demonstrate the limits of the boom to him. Major Philpot gave me the green light, and I went through the exact demonstration that he had performed for Ed and me. I then said to the major, "Watch this." Without out explaining what I was going to do, I quickly cross-controlled the flight controls using full left rudder and full right aileron and again demonstrated the full limits of the boom. At a point between between the outer limits I quickly swapped over to full right rudder and full left aileron and again demonstrated the limits to the good major. Major Philpot was completely aghast. He said in all of his flying days he had never seen anyone do anything like that. I got my full forty-five minutes on the boom during that flight, which was one of the requirements in order to pass the AC upgrading course.

Pulling the throttles back, I slowed the BUFF down and backed off from the tanker, and Ed quickly replaced me in the left seat. Ed proceeded to do the exact same thing that I had done, and we were all laughing by the time Ed finished up his forty-five minutes on the boom. We told Major Philpot that after both of us flying combat missions in fighter aircraft in Southeast Asia this formation flying was a piece of cake. I didn't mention my 1500 hours flying the B-47, which included numerous airborne air refuelings. During the postflight debriefing, Major Philpot told us that he was going to do something that he had never done before. He signed both of us off on the AC upgrading class for the B-52 program.

The only thing that Ed and I had left to do to satisfy SAC requirements was complete the low-level training portion of the program. I had a very difficult time with this part of the program. The problem was learning to trust the little "black boxes" that actually flew the aircraft once you leveled off at one- or two-hundred-foot elevation above the ground. The worst part was having to close the cockpit curtains during the descent to the entry point of the low-level route and hence basically fly blind. Two things made me feel very uncomfortable: the accuracy of the radar altimeter and the wing span of the aircraft.

Technically, a rectangular box appeared in front of the aircraft with the lower limits of the box at 100-foot altitude and the horizontal limits just a little over the span of the B-52's wings. While the BUFF is flying along the low-level route, should the top of a tree in front of the aircraft be 115 feet high, the second that the top of the tree penetrated your magic radar box in front of the aircraft, the aircraft would violently pitch up the fifteen feet needed to clear the obstacle. Once by the obstacle, then just as suddenly the aircraft would pitch back down after clearing the object. Even though there were three modes that you could set into the black box, i.e., light, moderate, and heavy, no matter which mode you selected, the ensuing constant up-and-down motion of the aircraft was violent enough to make almost all crew members sick.

If this wasn't bad enough, in this same black box a pilot could watch the terrain ahead of him on a very small light green televisionlike screen. What really got the pilot's attention happened when the horizontal limits of the pass he was flying through began to encroach on the aircraft's wing tips. Sometime the aircraft only missed the edge of a cliff by a few feet. Looking back, I think that the absolute worst problem beside the mistrust of the black box was the constant buffeting motion of the aircraft while at low altitude. I was never really sure if the wings would handle all the violent motion. Taking an aircraft that large, that low to the ground, with airspeeds in excess of 400 mph even when the ground in front could be seen really put the pilot to the test. Every time I was scheduled to fly one of these low-level missions I always told the IP that I was not going to close the cockpit curtains. I further informed him that he could fail me if he so desired. They never failed me, so I figured that they felt the same way that I did about black boxes and that portion of the flight. Other than the low-level phase, I really learned to enjoy flying the BUFF.

Time flew by rapidly there at Merced AFB, and prior to departing I had one rather unpleasant experience. During my annual flight physical the flight surgeon discovered a nodule on my thyroid and told me that it would have to be cut out. At the time I wasn't even sure what a thyroid was, but it didn't take long to find out, as I was directed over to the internal medical department of the hospital. The doctors there told me that I would have to have a radioisotope scan and that the nearest place to get one was at Travis AFB in Oakland. Two days later I reported to the internal medicine section at Travis AFB Hospital. The results of the scan very definitely showed a large, round nodule on my thyroid. The doctors were aware that I had been exposed to Agent Orange while in Vietnam, and they were worried about the nodule being cancerous. They informed me that the nodule would have to come out immediately.

Arriving back at Merced I explained to the doctors that my health otherwise was outstanding, that I had been running six miles a day, plus playing two to three hours of raquet ball each day. What I wanted the doctors to do was allow me to complete the BUFF upgrade training program and then, when I arrived at my next duty assignment, I could have the nodule removed. After much consultation the doctors finally agreed with my request, only if I had the nodule removed immediately upon my arrival at my next duty station. I quickly agreed with their request.

There wasn't much flying for Ed and me toward the end of the program, so we spent many a day up in the hills around Sonora, California, panning for gold. We didn't have a lot of luck, but it sure was fun. I called Cynthia one night to tell her that I would be home the following week. She informed me that she had seen a large sign outside of Rapid City advertising that the NCAA National Ski Races were going to be held at nearby Terry Peak. I told her that I couldn't believe it, as to my knowledge the Black Hills just were not high enough to allow for all of the events in the national combined ski races.

45

Ellsworth AFB

Since I was still certified as a NCAA college ski coach, I could hardly wait to get to South Dakota and Ellsworth AFB. Sure enough, Cynthia had all of her information right, and we drove up to nearby Terry Peak the weekend after I arrived home. In addition to getting accepted by the NCAA to work for them during the races, we discovered that a land development company from Taos, New Mexico, was selling lots on Terry Peak, and we quickly purchased a large lot. The lot that we purchased was located approximately in the center of the area being developed. Once the paperwork was completed we drove back to the area where our new lot was to further inspect our purchase.

While we were walking over the lot trying to decide exactly where we wanted to build our house, Jane (our oldest daughter) suddenly called us and said that there was a large hole in the ground. We dropped rocks down the hole and it was so deep that we could not hear the rocks hit the bottom. It scared the daylights out of Cynthia and me. We got the children out of there and returned to the development office to discuss our problem. The development company later determined that the hole was an airshaft belonging to one of the many mines of the Homestake Mining Company. By the time we got through threatening them with a lawsuit the development company said that they would work out an exchange of lots, if we would agree.

It turned out that they offered us the second lot that had been sold for an investment. The lot was located on a high bluff with a ninety-five-mile unrestricted view of Wyoming forests. We were thrilled with the exchange and began to immediately work out plans to build an A-frame type ski lodge on the new property. Winter was coming on fast, so we hired two local carpenters to lay out the foundation and frame the structure up. We had to blast a waterline through solid rock for over 200 feet to get the waterline low enough so that the water would not freeze during the wintertime. I located an old stonemason in the nearby town of Lead, and he agreed to build a stone fireplace that would cover one complete wall of the living room. We hauled the stone up from the bluff located just in front of the A-frame. The stone itself was variegated in color and made a beautiful fireplace and wall. It didn't take me long to realize that being a carpenter was not one of my better vocations.

Skiing at Terry Peak in the mean time was a new experience for all of us. The daily winter temperature was usually somewhere between fourteen and twenty below zero and necessitated wearing of heavy ski clothes, including a ski mask. The snow was absolutely the best powder snow that I have ever skied in. As you charged down a hill, a large plume of snowy white particles followed your every move. It gave one the sensation of flying through cirrus clouds. The kids and I would ski all Saturday morning on the ski slopes, and then we were able to ski home about a half-mile to our ski lodge. Cynthia would always have great lunches for us and there would be a large fire in the fireplace to warm us up. During those winter months, I got involved in a lot of local ski races and thoroughly enjoyed the competition.

When I checked into the bomb wing at Ellsworth AFB, a personnel clerk informed me that I was one of the most senior majors in the wing. The clerk also told me that there were special orders authorizing me to now wear command pilots' wings, and I was delighted. I wasn't quite as happy when I had to turn my medical records into the base hospital, as they immediately grounded me. I was informed that I could not return to flying status until they knew what was going on with my thyroid. I met the flight surgeon who was going to perform the operation, and after examining me he felt that it would be an easy operation. The surgeon told me that he would just cut the nodule out and that was all there would be to the operation.

It was during the postsurgery that I discovered that he had taken over two-thirds of my thyroid out along with the nodule. I wasn't happy with this news, but there wasn't much that I could do about it at this point. Ellsworth Hospital did not have a pathologist on their staff, so they sent the thyroid specimen to nearby Minot AFB. The pathologist at Minot was a close friend of the surgeon who had performed my operation and in a telephone conversation informed my doctor that he would conduct the diagnosis of the specimen.

Four or five days later, while I was still in the recovery ward, four senior officers walked into my room and closed the door. In attendance were the base commander, the wing commander, the surgeon general, and the base chaplain. In my days in Okinawa as the wing executive officer on numerous occasions I accompanied the wing commander and base chaplain into the base housing area whenever we lost a fighter pilot over North Vietnam, and I knew that something unusual was up here. Each of the colonels hemmed and hawed around, and finally I said, "All right, what the hell's the matter?" The base chaplain was the first to speak, informing me that my thyroid specimen had come back positive and that I had a cancer in my throat.

Their report indicated that I most likely had four to six months to live. I thanked the chaplain for a difficult analysis and requested that they leave my room. As soon as they were out of sight I got out of bed quickly, got dressed, and sneaked out of the hospital. I was feeling OK at the time, but for some unknown reason I just wanted to be near my family. It was almost two hours later that the base MPs located me at home. The security police returned me to the hospital, where I remained for another week before being discharged. Nothing was ever said about my disappearance on the night that the colonels visited me.

Since I was now a grounded flyer, the base personnel officer offered me four different jobs. Ellsworth, being an SAC base, had a B-52 wing with a squadron of KC-135 refueling tankers, a strategic missile wing, plus an air division that supervised both wings. The job that I selected was to be an air operations specialist for the 313th Air Division. The 313th Air Division's officer staff consisted of a brigadier general, one colonel, and two senior majors. I had the responsibility for all flying activities on the base, while the other major oversaw the missile wing's problems. This meant that we both were exposed to a lot of senior brass. It turned out to be the worst job that I ever held while in the Air Force, because there was no job description and basically nothing for me to do. I created many staff studies in the time that I was there, but my heart just wasn't in politics at that level.

One day another significant emotional event occurred that very definitely affected my future. The commander of the local helicopter squadron came bursting into my office shouting at anyone and everyone he saw. By the time I got the captain settled down, his complaint was that the missile wing operations officer was again dictating weather conditions to his helicopter pilots. The U.S. Air Force has standard weather operating conditions for all Air Force bases. If the weatherman says that the cloud ceilings are less than 100 feet above the ground, then all flights for that base are canceled until the cloud ceiling rises. What the colonel was doing was telling the helicopter pilots that the cloud ceilings were at 200 feet and that they needed to fly. Weather personnel throughout the Air Force are responsible for local weather conditions, but the pilot flying the aircraft has the final authority as to whether he will fly. The base helicopter squadron's mission was to deliver on a daily basis all of the security personnel to the 425 missile sites located around the state of South Dakota, and the weather was frequently below safe minimums for flying. I told the captain that I would take care of his complaint and quickly informed Colonel Norton, my boss, of the situation. Colonel Norton directed me to go down to the missile wing and inform the operations officer to immediately stop dictating weather conditions to the helicopter pilots.

The missile wing headquarters was located inside a huge aircraft hangar that must have been used to maintain large B-36 bombers right after WW II. I struggled through the many mazes inside the hangar finally locating the ops officer's office. One of the NCOS informed me before I went into Colonel Burnett's office that he had a nasty disposition. Wow, was that ever an understatement! As I entered his office, Colonel Burnett jumped up and wanted to know what the hell I was disturbing him for. I told him who I was and where I was from and that I had a complaint about him dictating weather conditions to the helicopter pilots. He became so mad that he rushed around his desk and physically shoved me back a few feet, telling me to get the hell out of his office and never come back.

I returned to the air division and quickly told Colonel Norton what had happened. Colonel Norton in turn went straight into General Adams with the problem. Colonel Norton told me to stand by, and seven minutes later a flustered missile wing colonel reported into General Adams's office. General Adams called both Colonel

Norton and me into his office, telling us to stand at ease. What happened next is almost beyond description. Since my days in the Marine Corps I had never heard as good an ass chewing as General Adams gave to the missile wing colonel. General Adams kept the colonel at attention the whole time he was shouting at him. As the general finished, the last thing he ordered the colonel, who was by this time sweating profusely, to do was formally apologize to me, and the colonel reluctantly did so. This incident would later come back and haunt me.

Meanwhile, about eight months passed by. My health was excellent and on a daily basis I was playing raquetball two to three hours a day. Finally one day my boss, Colonel Norton, called me into his office and said that it appeared that there was really nothing wrong with me medically, and I agreed with him. He told me that one of his classmates was the surgeon general of the Air Force, and with my permission he would call him and ask to have my medical condition reviewed. I immediately concurred with his suggestion.

Two weeks later a message arrived on base from the U.S. Air Force's surgeon general's office. The contents of the message indicated that I be returned to full flying status immediately, that a mistake had been made by the reviewing pathologist's office. What had actually happened was that the pathologist at Minot AFB, who was a friend of the flight surgeon there at Ellsworth AFB, who had performed my operation, had gone on leave before my specimen had arrived. When the specimen arrived at Minot AFB, it was sent to a local civilian pathologist in downtown Minot for review. Apparently somehow my specimen had gotten mixed up with another person's specimen, and the wrong report had been forwarded back to Ellsworth AFB. The thing that saved my flying career was that all military specimens of any kind are kept on record in the National Pathological Institute of Research in Washington, D.C.

The commander of the 313th Bomb Wing (BW), Colonel Lawson, contacted me and welcomed me back on flying status and into the B-52 program. After three training flights in the D model of the B-52 I was upgraded again to the status of AC. The 313th BW had both D and G models of the B-52. The wing was in the process of changing over completely to the new G models but still had fifteen D models on station. Since I had never flown the G model, the wing commander asked me to continue flying the D model. The reason was that the wing had to deliver all of their D models to the Bone-yard in Tucson, Arizona, as soon as they were phased out of the wing's combat role. I had no problem with this request because I did not have a specific crew yet.

One day I was called to fly an upgrade mission for one of the wing navigators. Upon reporting to the flight line, I discovered that my copilot for the mission was a lieutenant colonel and former squadron maintenance officer from one of the BW's three bomb squadrons. To this day I cannot remember the lieutenant colonel's name, but I do remember that his colonel's insignias were so tarnished that they appeared to be black in color instead of silver. During the mandatory walk-around and preflight, the colonel said nothing to me and gave the appearance of being mad as hell about something. I figured that he was mad because he outranked me and possibly felt that he should have been designated as the AC for the flight.

Together we finally got all eight of our engines running and taxied out to the end of the active runway. A KC-135 tanker had taken off three minutes ahead of us, and we were supposed to establish a hookup with him at 23,000 feet and get a night heavyweight off-load of fuel. Approaching the refueling altitude, I was slightly high on both airspeed and altitude. While pushing the nose of the aircraft down slightly I also reached over and grabbed the handles on the eight jet engine throttles in order to reduce some of the power. SAC has a procedure whereby the pilot who is not flying the aircraft can communicate with the pilot in command by briefly tapping his hand on the other pilot's hand if something is wrong. In this case the colonel without saying a word slapped my right hand so hard that he broke my wristwatch band. Maybe it was the fighter pilot aggressiveness in my blood: I came around with my left hand doubled up in a fist and hit the colonel so hard that I knocked his oxygen mask off and bloodied his mouth. For the next eight and a half hours neither one of us spoke to the other.

Some eight hours later as we arrived back into the local flying area for Ellsworth AFB, I called the Command Post and told them that I wanted to see the wing commander immediately upon landing. Once on the ground and after completing the postflight briefing, I went directly to Colonel Larson's office and requested permission to speak to him. I told him exactly what had happened from the first contact with this lieutenant colonel who was the designated copilot all the way through the mission. I further told Colonel Lawson that I no longer wanted any part of flying B-52s. Colonel Lawson did his very best to try to talk me out of my decision and even offered me probably the best job that I could have asked for in the wing, i.e., the 313th wing operations officer's position.

Refusing to change my mind, several days later I was assigned to the base flight section of the wing and started my checkout in the T-29 transport aircraft. The T-29 was similar to the civilian Convair 440 aircraft, and was a delight to fly. I found myself flying the SAC courier routes between South Dakota, Nebraska, Kansas, Colorado, Wyoming, Montana, and North Dakota. The T-29 carried sixty passengers and, although a good aircraft in my opinion, was very definitely not equipped to fly in the horrible weather conditions that we frequently encountered, especially while flying in Wyoming and Colorado.

I remember one afternoon we had to make an emergency landing at Bismarck, North Dakota. It seemed like the entire town turned out to see our aircraft and to watch us land on one engine. While we were waiting to get the engine fixed, the mayor of Bismarck took the entire crew out for dinner. It was great to witness such incredible and true American spirit in this small western town.

Several months after I began flying the T-29, SAC headquarters decided to start downsizing their SAC commands around the country. The 313th Air Division was one of the first units to be disbanded. General Adams called me into his office one day and said that he felt that I was ready for a command. The general went on to explain that he was assigning me as the squadron commander of the 821st Transportation Squadron there on base if I wanted the job. I was so surprised at first that I couldn't find the words to thank him. In order to accept the position I had to go down to the base personnel office and volunteer for the Air Force's rated supplement program, which meant that I now would join the combat support side of the Air Force. Orders were immediately cut sending me down to Wichita Falls, Texas, to attend the Staff Transportation Officer's School.

Because the timing was critical, we put Duke, our Labrador, in a local kennel in Rapid City. Since the kids were out of school for the summer, we packed up and headed out for Wichita Falls, Texas. We were unable to find a house to rent for two months, so we stayed in a local motel. The kids were really excited, as the motel had a large swimming pool. Our stay was made even more enjoyable as one of the other students in the class, Brad Hallock, and his wife, Carol, were staying in a motel close by ours and we played bridge almost every night.

We left Wichita Falls in the middle of a giant storm as big as they can get in Texas. The same storm had struck Rapid City several days before, and the ensuing floods in Rapid City made national headlines. Seven inches of rain in three hours, and the local dam broke above Rapid City. What we didn't know until our arrival back in South Dakota was that our dog, Duke, had become a national hero. It seems that as the floodwaters enveloped Rapid City, Duke, who weighed close to 110 pounds, had saved the life of the lady who ran the dog kennels where we had placed him. Duke swam to the railroad tracks with the lady and forced her to stay on higher ground. For this feat Duke received his picture in the local papers and was considered a canine hero. Duke always was an incredible dog, and we loved him dearly in spite of the fact that he chewed the tops off all the fences that we put around our yards. Duke had been a birthday present to me from Cynthia when we first moved to Tacoma, Washington, in 1967. Duke's father had been a national champion for the state of Washington. Before we left Tacoma, Duke had graduated twice from a hunting school located in Roy, Washington. Upon his second graduation, Duke graduated magna cum laude! Duke loved to hunt, and worked on either voice, whistle, or by hand signals that he had learned while in the hunting school.

The 824th Transportation Squadron, which I was now assigned to, was the largest transportation squadron in 15th Air Force. There were in excess of 322 personnel assigned to the squadron when I first took command. One of the many requirements for squadron commanders was to conduct a squadron commander's call once a month. I'll never forget my first commander's call. The most people I had ever spoken to at one time was my B-47 crew of two, and here before me in a very large room were 322 strange faces—all looking hostilely to me! *Scared stiff* wouldn't even begin to describe my feelings at the time. The first mistake that I made was to memorize my speech, and boy, did I ever blow that one before all those hostile faces. I'm sure that the squadron enlisted personnel thought, *Boy, here is a rated pilot for our commander and look at him sweat.* Before we left Ellsworth, I finally learned to relax and became very adept at giving highly motivated speeches to my troops.

All squadron commanders have occasional nightmares, and I was no exception. It seems that on one quiet Sunday with only a small standby crew on duty, two of my young airmen decided to see just how fast a loaded fuel truck would go. They were racing each other down the flight line when one of the drivers lost control of his vehicle and rolled it over right next to a parked fully loaded KC-135 refueling tanker. Arriving on the scene, I discovered volatile aviation fuel was leaking all over the flight ramp and the situation was rapidly becoming critical. Within minutes, there must have been fifteen full colonels out there on the flight line, and each one of them felt that he was in control of the situation. I had to contend with all of them yelling at me at once. It was a very stressful situation.

My first problem was to somehow get the refueling truck that had turned over back on its feet. I finally got the vice wing commander from the BW to get everyone away from the accident scene. With the help of one of my staff sergeants, using a large crane, we eventually got the refueling truck back upright. This was no easy, task as under no circumstances could we cause a spark of any kind during the righting of the refueling truck. For my actions I quickly developed a reputation for being able to get the job done and subsequently received a Letter of Commendation from the commanding general of 15th Air Force.

The thing that I didn't realize was that when I volunteered for the U.S. Air Force's Rated Supplement I suddenly became "number one" on the Air Force's list of qualified people for an overseas assignment as a nonrated transportation squadron commander. It didn't take the Air Force personnel shop long to locate and reassign me to an overseas air base. During the next month I received orders to three separate air bases in Germany, i.e., Bittburg Air Base, Hann Air Base, and finally Frankfurt Air Base. With the knowledge that we were going to Germany, Cynthia located some German-language records in the base library. We then, as a family, tried to learn from the records enough of the German language so that we would be able to communicate once we arrived in Germany.

46

Change of Orders and the 401st Transportration Squadron

Just prior to leaving the Transportation School in Texas, I was informed that my orders had been changed once again from Frankfurt, Germany, to Torrejon, Spain. The new set of orders would send me to Madrid, Spain, instead of Frankfurt, Germany. I called Cynthia, who had returned earlier to South Dakota, and she was delighted with the change of assignments. Getting all of our household goods packed, we departed Ellsworth AFB in September. As we deplaned at the terminal in Frankfurt, a Colonel Peoples met us and identified himself as the deputy commander for transportation for Europe. Colonel Peoples told me that the commander of 15th Air Force had forwarded a recommendation to General Jones, the Supreme Allied Commander for U.S. Military Forces in Europe, about me. The recommendation indicated that I was a person whom he could count on to get the job done. Colonel Peoples said that General Jones had then requested that I be diverted to Torrejon. Colonel Peoples informed us that our new assignment was to the 401st Transportation Squadron, located on Torrejon Air Base in Madrid, Spain. Cynthia was wild with excitement and could hardly wait to get back on the aircraft, while I tried to understand what was going on. We were both excited about Spain due to the fact that the weather was similar to that in Southern California, whereas the weather in Germany is horrible most of the year.

Colonel Peoples informed me that I didn't have to accept this change in orders if I chose not too. What could I say to the recommendation of a four star general? Colonel Peoples went on to say that the U.S. Air Forces in Europe (USAFE) Command needed a strong commander to take charge of the 401st Transportation. He further said that the 401st Transportation Squadron had had eleven commanders in the past fourteen months, none of who could, apparently, handle the squadron. The current squadron was in a complete state of disaster. He went on to say that General Jones had what was referred to as his famous "Christmas tree charts" on one of his office walls, where he compared the success of all units stationed in Europe. Colonel Peoples used the example to explain the general's charts to me by saying that at any time General Jones could tell exactly how many vehicles a squadron had in commission or how many were down and for what reasons. Also listed on the charts was all the legal information, such as violations of military discipline problems by members of each command. Colonel Peoples went on to say, that the information was so bad from the 401st Transportation Squadron that it didn't even meet the minimum standard required by General Jones. Peoples further informed me that I would encounter some of the worst racial problems associated with any of the U.S. squadrons stationed in Europe.

I thought about the information that Colonel Peoples had provided me and told him that I would accept the command so long as USAFE headquarters would back me should I encounter problems beyond my control. He was extremely pleased with my decision and told me to get back on the airplane and to go on down to Torrejon. He asked me to look the squadron over for a week before giving him my final answer.

We arrived in Madrid that same evening and eventually got settled into the base BOQ. The next morning I put on a Class A type uniform, and not telling the dispatcher who I was, called the transportation squadron for a taxi. Twenty minutes later a taxi finally arrived, and I informed the driver that I wanted to go down to the transportation squadron. I discovered that Torrejon Air Base was laid out like a giant rectangle, with the transportation squadron located on one of the short base legs. The driver pulled up before what looked like several pole barns from the midwestern part of America and told me that this was the transportation squadron. I was immediately repulsed by what I was seeing. There were dirty vehicles parked all over the place with no semblance of organization, and military discipline appeared to be nonexistent. Getting out of the taxi, I asked one young airman where the commander's office was, and he didn't know. He asked several airmen who were standing around and one of them finally responded that he thought that the commander's office was located somewhere on the other end of the base in a barracks.

I walked over to what appeared to be the vehicle dispatch section, located in one of the pole barns, and told the young airman behind the counter that I needed transportation up to the commander's office. Without looking up he responded, "We haven't got any." I looked directly at him again and repeated my request, knowing that there were at least five vehicles parked outside. I mentioned to him that I knew for a fact that there were at least five vehicles parked outside, and again he responded in a belligerent manner, "We don't have any."

At that moment, a Chief Master Sergeant Lazotte stepped forward and identified himself as the new noncommissioned officer in charge (NCOIC) of the 401st Vehicle Operations section. He quickly informed me that he had just arrived himself and had not yet had time to complete processing in on the base. He said to me that he was sorry and that what the airman meant to say to me was that he did "not have any taxies available, sir." Chief Lazotte went on to say that he would personally locate a taxi for me, and I thanked him.

Once again, I asked the driver to take me up to the barracks where the transportation squadron personnel where billeted. Arriving outside a somewhat ugly-looking barracks, this time I told the driver to wait for me. Upon entering the barracks and looking down the hallway I noticed a sign that said: COMMANDER. As I entered the office there was a secretary's desk but no secretary. I stepped on through the open door and discovered a young staff sergeant sitting behind the commander's desk reading a magazine. I asked the sergeant where the commander was, and without looking up the sergeant informed me that he didn't know. I then asked the sergeant if he were sitting in for the commander, and again never looking up, the sergeant replied in a rather hostile voice that he didn't want to be bothered. I then asked if I might use the telephone. Finally looking up from the magazine he was reading, the sergeant looked me over glancing at my pilot's wings, and probably thought here was another lost pilot. The sergeant then pointed to the telephone and said nothing further.

Fishing around in one of the desk drawers, I located a base telephone directory, and called the base personnel office. While I was waiting for the director of personnel to come on the line I asked the sergeant for his identification card. With another very hostile stare the sergeant very reluctantly gave me his ID card. A few minutes later a Lt. Col. Jerry Lawrence came on the line, identifying himself as the base personnel officer, and wanted to know what he could do for me?

I introduced myself as the newly assigned transportation squadron commander, and told Colonel Lawrence that I had a little problem that I was sure that he could help me with. Informing him of where I was, I gave him the name of the staff sergeant who was sitting at my desk. I further told Colonel Lawrence that I was sending the sergeant over to his office and that I wanted the sergeant off the base in twenty-four hours. There was a long pause, and finally the good colonel said that he couldn't do that. I then informed him again that I wanted this particular sergeant off the base in twenty-four hours or that he could answer to USAFE. Colonel Lawrence hesitated for a few minutes and finally told me to send the sergeant over to him. The sergeant was off the base that very same afternoon and I never heard of him again.

There are three operating sections to all Air Force transportation squadrons. There is the Vehicle Operations Section, which handles all moving vehicles on base, the Vehicle Maintenance Section, which repairs and keeps all base assigned vehicles operational, and finally the Traffic Management Operations (TMO) section. TMO handles the movement of all personnel entering or departing the base plus the forwarding of their individual baggage and household goods.

For my second day onboard I visited each section and introduced myself to as many of the squadron personnel as possible. It didn't take me long to realize that the current vehicle maintenance commander was having an affair with the wife of one of his enlisted men. I fired the captain and had him off the base in twenty-four hours. I was unable to locate the assistant commander of the vehicle maintenance section as he was away playing on the base football team. Checking into this captain's absence, I soon discovered that he had been gone for over three weeks and no one knew exactly when he might return. What a way to get started into a new organization!

By now the fall season was upon us at Torrejon, and the rainy weather had begun in earnest. As I was touring the vehicle maintenance section that second day late in the afternoon, I was appalled at what I found myself seeing. I found a sergeant working under a pickup truck lying on one of those floor scooters that all mechanics use while working underneath vehicles. The problem was that the water level inside the maintenance building was higher than the floor scooter that the sergeant was using. I kicked the sergeant's booted foot and asked him what he was doing.

The sergeant rolled himself out from under the pickup truck, and the force of the cascading water from his scooter covered my shoes. The sergeant told me that he was attempting to repair a broken shock absorber on the pickup truck. About that time, the NCOIC of the vehicle maintenance section, having seen me, came running over. His name was Senior Master Sergeant Hollyfield and he appeared to really be flustered. It seems that my reputation had gotten around the squadron, especially after having the one sergeant deported from the commander's office the day I arrived.

I told the sergeant who was working under the pickup to get out of there and to go get into some dry clothes immediately. Master Sergeant Hollyfield asked me if I would accompany him over to his cubbyhole of an office, where he proceeded to in brief me on the many problems associated with the vehicle maintenance section. He apologized for the water on the floor, then told me that there were fifty-four holes in the roof over the vehicle maintenance section. Master Sergeant Hollyfield then showed me a stack of three years' worth of squadron requests to the Civil Engineering (CE) squadron to fix the roof that had all been disapproved by the CE squadron. Master Sergeant Hollyfield also told me that the commander of the CE squadron, a Lt. Col. Joe Devlon, was a Citadel graduate and had a reputation for being one of the meanest commanders on base. I told Master Sergeant Hollyfield to give me the stack of requests and that I would get his roof fixed. He quickly reminded me that several of the previous transportation squadron commanders had tried to get the CE squadron to fix the leaks, but all had failed. I smiled at him and told him to watch my dust.

This wasn't the first time that I had run into someone who thought he or she held all of the marbles, and I wasn't going to be intimidated by him. The next morning after calling for an appointment with the CE commander, Lt. Col. Joe Devlon, I jumped into my staff car and drove over to the CE area of the base. I took the stack of three years' worth of requests to fix our roof with me. Locating the command section, I introduced myself to Lieutenant Colonel Devlon's secretary, and before I knew it a loud booming voice came out of the next office. It was Lieutenant Colonel Devlon and he wanted to know why I was wasting his time. Stepping into his office, I stuck out my hand and introduced myself. Lieutenant Colonel Devlon refused to accept my handshake and wanted to know what the hell I wanted. I explained exactly what I wanted and he threw a fit, telling me to get the hell out of his office, as he was too busy to worry about my problems. Returning to my area, I went over to the vehicle operation section and visited with Chief Master Sergeant Lazotte.

CMS Lazotte had reported into the squadron the same day that I did and he was the one responsible for getting a taxi for me. Chief Lazotte said that he knew a very good way of getting Lieutenant Colonel Devon's attention but told me that I had to be prepared for a fight. The chief went on to explain that the CE squadron had thirty-four dump trucks and, according to our squadron records none of the dump trucks had ever gone through a mandatory safety inspection. Chief Lazotte said that he could legally recall all thirty-four of them, but that I might pay a price, as the dump trucks were currently involved in a critical priority "1" base runway renovation project. I then gave CMS Lazotte a direct order telling him that I wanted all thirty-four of the CE dump trucks recalled immediately for a safety compliance check. The chief smiled and walked away.

Returning to my office, I sat and waited for the telephone call that I knew was sure to come in short order. Sure enough, within twenty minutes I was informed to report to the 401st base commander's office immediately. I was ushered into Colonel Winger's office, and there sitting at the far end of Colonel Winger's desk with a smug look on his face was Lieutenant Colonel Devlon. Colonel Winger took a few minutes to work up a good "mad-on" and started out by wanting to know exactly who the hell did I think I was? He told me to release Lieutenant Colonel Devlon's dump trucks immediately. I responded by asking Colonel Winger if I could use his telephone for a minute. I'm quite certain that he thought that I was calling my vehicle ops section, but I had actually used a military Autovon telephone number and had called Colonel Peoples in USAFE headquarters. When Colonel Peoples came on the line I quickly explained what had happened and why. He asked to speak with Colonel Winger, and all we heard for the next few minutes was: *Yes, sir; yes, sir; we will comply immediately.* Hanging up, Colonel Winger thanked me for coming in and said that I could return to my squadron.

The next morning Lieutenant Colonel Devlon arrived at the transportation squadron with all twelve of his CE officers. The good colonel was all hearts and flowers, as his team inspected my facilities. Lieutenant Colonel Devlon wanted to know what else his engineers could do while they were there. Thanking him, I explained that I wanted a commander's office located between the vehicle ops and vehicle maintenance sections, and Lieutenant Colonel Devlon said that would be no problem. I also told him that I wanted offices for both my vehicle ops officers and vehicle maintenance officers built inside the current structures.

In addition, I mentioned that I would like the outside of the squadron buildings painted after all repairs were completed. Lieutenant Colonel Devlon wanted to know what color I wanted, and I responded by telling him that I wanted a light blue color on the Vehicle Maintenance building while I wanted the vehicle ops building painted a light yellow. Lieutenant Colonel Devlon quickly reminded me that those were not standard Air Force colors, and I told him that I was not a standard person. I received everything that I asked for from the CE squadron, and more. We released the CE dump trucks that very same day. From then on and until I left the base Lt. Col Joe Devlon and I became very good friends.

While the civil engineers were repairing the roofs, I had them jackhammer the edges of our floors and install internal gutters that would handle the overflow of any future water that ever got inside the building. We had them also paint and seal all of the floors inside the building. I decided that while making drastic changes I might as well pay a visit to the base supply officer. During my little fireside chat with the supply commander, I told him that I wanted white coveralls for all of my maintenance troops, the reason being that their current military uniforms were all eaten out with acid and grease. The supply commander balked at first but then remembered what had happened with the CE dump trucks and quickly decided that he would comply with my request. The mechanics assigned to the 401st Transportation couldn't believe it when they saw the white coveralls. I told my mechanics that from now on I didn't want to see any dirty coveralls in the squadron area, as they could now exchange coveralls daily from that day forward.

Sometime during my second week as the commander I overhead a discussion between two young airmen in the vehicle ops section. They were discussing the inequalities of disciplinary actions among black and white airmen in the squadron. It seemed to them that mostly it was only the black guys in the squadron who were receiving disciplinary punishment in the form of Article 15s and court-martials. I interrupted their conversation and asked the most vocal airman to accompany me into my new office. This young airman's name was Aerial Jackson and he had no stripes on his uniform, although it appeared that there had been stripes on his sleeves before. I couldn't get over how personal and caring Airman Jackson was.

I called the squadron first sergeant and asked that he bring Airman Jackson's personnel file into my office. During the course of our conversation I discovered that Aerial Jackson was originally from the Canary Islands. Airmen Jackson told me that he had been a professional baseball player prior to enlisting in the U.S. Air Force and that all he wanted to do was ensure that the black guys assigned to our squadron got a fair shake. I noted from his records that he had indeed been a staff sergeant only last year. I asked Airman Jackson about that, and he told me that he had received two Article 15s mainly because no one would listen to his side of the story. I then asked Airman Jackson if he would explain his side of the story on both of the Article 15s. Before dismissing Airman Jackson, I asked him if he would like to become involved in a human relations program for the squadron, and he replied, "Most definitely yes."

The next morning I went to the base legal offices and reviewed Airman Jackson's article 15s. Much to my delight, I was informed that I could withdraw both Article 15s any time that I wanted to. Later that same morning I called Airman Jackson back into my office. Once he was seated, I asked him if he had seen the new office that was being completed just down the hallway, and he replied, "Yes, sir." First I pulled out his legal folder and extracted both Article 15 and handed them to him. Second, with the first sergeant present, we presented Airman Jackson with his staff sergeant's stripes. I told him that he was now reassigned as the 401st Squadron's human relations officer and that he now reported only to me. Further, I informed the new Sergeant Jackson that his human relations office was just down the hall and he was to coordinate with the first sergeant for the internal furnishings.

Sergeant Jackson and I discussed human relations in great detail, and from the day that I left the 401st Transportation Squadron, the squadron never experienced another Article 15 or court-martial on anyone. I know for a fact that Sergeant Jackson took several of our so-called hotheads out behind the squadron area and beat the heck out of both of them. No one ever complained to me, and more important, no one in the squadron ever got into trouble again. Later Sergeant Jackson came up with a rough draft on a Human Relations (HR) manual for the squadron. Sergeant Jackson and I worked together finalizing the document, and we finally published the manual for the squadron. The HR program became so successful that USAFE headquarters requested a copy of our manual and later reprinted the manual for the entire European command. Sergeant Jackson is one person whom I shall never forget.

When Captain Buck, our squadron maintenance officer, finally returned from his football sojourn, he couldn't believe the changes in the squadron that he saw. Captain Buck was an All-American football player from San Jose State University and was just one of the nicest guys that you could ever hope to meet. During our in-brief, Captain Buck told me that he just couldn't tolerate the previous commanders and that was why he went to play for the base's football team. Capt. John Buck turned out to become my "right hand" in the squadron. In my absences I always left the command and control of the squadron in Captain Buck's hands, and he never let me down. Later when I was promoted to the deputy base commander's job I saw to it that Captain Buck, even though he was only a captain, got the 401st transportation commander position.

And now for the incident that became the lowest part of my Air Force career. While all of this was going on, the new lieutenant colonels list came out and I received my only "pass-over" for my entire U.S. Air Force career. It was the first time in my professional career that I had failed at anything. I tried desperately to not let it affect me, but I know that it did. The base personnel officer was the one person instrumental for keeping me on track. I was really considering getting out of the Air Force and looking for employment with the airline industry.

Many times through out my life I have been possessed with the feeling that someone upstairs must be looking out for me, and here is why. Two months after I had been passed over for Lieutenant Colonel General Jones's, the Supreme Allied Commander for all Military Forces in Europe, aircraft was forced to land at Torrejon because the weather in Germany was below minimums. General Jones was supposed to be on the ground there in Spain for a two-hour weather hold. I was happily sitting in my new office when I received a telephone call from the 401st wing commander. The 401st wing commander informed me of the situation and said that he was bringing General Jones down to inspect my squadron area. I couldn't imagine a four-star general taking time out of his busy schedule to come and visit a transportation squadron.

I called the first sergeant and told him to inform everyone what was coming down immediately and for all personnel to be on their best behavior. I was a little bit worried, as I knew that the wing commander was a little taken aback because I had violated Air Force Regulations and painted my buildings pastel colors instead of the usual Air Force gray. Much to my astonishment, when General Jones arrived at the transportation squadron he was accompanied by a staff of nine other general officers, each of whom had a writing pad in his hands.

General Jones had told Colonel Collins, the 401st wing commander, that he especially wanted to meet me. The general's reasons were that the 401st Transportation had gone from last place as far as transportation statistics were concerned, to first place for all of the transportation squadrons in Europe, and he wanted to know how we did it. For answers, a lot of the credit had to go to Sergeant Jackson and his human relations program, as we reported zero disciplinary actions for the squadron. In addition, we had more vehicles in commission than any other squadron in Europe, and General Jones also wanted to know how we had accomplished that in such a short time period.

As General Jones got out of his vehicle and looked at the squadron buildings, his first comment was, "Wow." General Jones quickly turned and asked me if I would give him a tour of the facilities. I was never so proud of my men as they went about their assigned tasks during the general's tour of the squadron. All squadron facilities were absolutely spotless. General Jones was especially pleased to see the floor mechanics all in white coveralls. One of the things that the 401st Civil Engineers had done for us was build a large wash rack outside our facilities. Every vehicle that came to us no matter how small the reason, was first washed and the engine steam-cleaned before any of our personnel would touch them. The vehicles were then lined up with squadron codes on their windshields waiting their turn into our maintenance shop. General Jones couldn't get over how spotless the inside of the maintenance shop was. He was impressed with the white lines that had been painted on the floor for each vehicle stall and with the fact that all of the floors were sealed with a heavy plastic solution that added even more light for the mechanics working underneath vehicles.

As the general got to the center of the vehicle maintenance shop he was astonished to see Captain Buck and Sergeant Hollyfield working on the finishing touches to our new Vehicle Maintenance Command Center (VMCC). The command center was about 90 percent completed when General Jones arrived. The VMCC was octagonal in design, looking very much like a large lighthouse. We had placed lighted plastic panels on the upper half of the octagonal walls with every vehicle on the base annotated as to its status. General Jones insisted on going inside the VMCC, where one of our sergeants was updating the side panels. It turned out that this sergeant was from the same small hometown in Missouri that General Jones was from.

Before entering the command center General Jones asked if we had any hot coffee in the squadron. Captain Buck returned in a few minutes with a pot of coffee, and General Jones asked for all of us to wait outside the VMCC. General Jones spent the next forty-five minutes inside the VMCC talking with the NCO. It was sort of humorous watching the remainder of General Jones's staff walking around the VMCC with their notepads in hand waiting for the general to come out. Colonel Collins, who had disappeared earlier, came rushing back with important information for General Jones. Colonel Collins had received a message that the weather was now good enough for the general to continue his flight home to Germany. As General Jones was leaving the squadron, he turned to Colonel Collins and said that he knew that I had recently been passed over for lieutenant colonel and that he wanted to see an Officer's Effectiveness Report (OER) in his office within the next two weeks.

General Jones then came over and asked me if I knew why I had been passed over. I told him about the incident that had happened at Ellsworth AFB, and he shook his head and said that he would see what he could do. Later I discovered that he had called the Military Personnel Center (MPC) located at Randolph AFB, Texas. The next thing that I knew, I had orders to return to Randolph AFB to attend a hearing and to immediately protest my last OER. Colonel Barnett, from Ellsworth, had also been summoned to Randolph AFB. During the next few days there at the MPC in Texas, the situation was completely cleared up and the downgraded OER was taken out of my personnel file. Two months later, on Special Orders from the MPC, I was promoted to lieutenant colonel. What a thrill for me!

Shortly after putting on my lieutenant colonel's leaves I was asked by the base commander if I would consent to take over the 401st Base Special Services Squadron until they could get a new qualified commander in. What an incredible task that turned out to be. The previous special services squadron commander had been fired, and I couldn't even spell *special services*. I quickly discovered that the special services squadron was responsible for all the entertainment activities on the base, i.e., movie theaters, golf courses, bowling alleys, and flying clubs, just to name a few. I was in the process of taking an inspection tour of the facilities, accompanied by the senior NCO of special services, when we came upon a warehouse that had its doors padlocked and chained. I asked the NCO to open the locks and to undo the chains and he said that he didn't have a key. Having my portable radio with me, I called Chief Lazotte, telling him where I was and asked him to bring a large bolt cutter with him.

Before Chief Lazotte arrived on the scene the Special Services NCO suddenly found his keys. When we opened up the warehouse doors we discovered a surplus of over 70,000 dozen boxes of golf balls stacked inside. I immediately contacted both the 401st base and wing commanders, and very rapidly the stuff hit the fan. The Special Services senior NCO was also fired and sent back to the States. I had only uncovered the tip of the iceberg, as I got further into Special Service activities. Later I discovered that one of our Air Force Aero Club aircraft had been on a personal loan to a private citizen, and the problems continued to mount.

I held the position of 401st special services commander for approximately four months before I was asked to move up and take over the deputy base commander's job. About the same time, General Jones had called Colonel Collins and requested that I come to Ramstein Air Base in Germany for an interview to select future base commanders. I was told that the interview consisted of being interviewed by ten general officers, the final interview being with General Jones himself, and that was all. I was scared to death by the thought of the interviews but pressed on.

Several days after my interviews I was informed that I had been accepted on General Jones's list for NATO base commanders. I was given my choice of NATO bases and quickly selected my choice of countries that I would like to serve in. In looking over the choices I selected Greece first and Turkey second. I was then informed that I would receive orders for that assignment at the end of my four-year tour in Spain in 1976. Less than a month after I arrived back from my interviews in USAFE I was personally called one evening by General Jones himself. General Jones wanted me to be in place at a base in Turkey within twenty-four hours. I naturally said yes, and General Jones said that he would send his personal aircraft down to Torrejon to pick me up the following day. General Jones informed me that he wanted to personally brief me the following day prior to my going to Turkey. I couldn't believe how fast things were happening in my life.

47

Turkey

The next morning after I feverishly packed, General Jones's T-39 picked me up at 0600 hours and I was off to Ramstein AB in Germany. Several hours later, after I reported in to General Jones, he explained why he needed me immediately in Turkey. It seems that the former U.S. Air Force base commander at Murted Air Base had been bodily kicked out of Turkey by the Turkish military and the base was without an American commander. In more detail General Jones explained that the Turks were apparently conducting an Operational Readiness Inspection (ORI) at Murted and the American commander from inside his Command Post was counting the number of trucks and iron bombs that the Turks were sending onto the base. All of this was happening while Turkey was still totally involved in the Cyprus War with Greece, so emotions were running high on the part of the Turks.

It seems that the young American commander had sent a top-secret message to General Jones explaining his concerns about the Turks. The Turkish base commander, General Tuncman, was so mad that he sent his executive officer over to the American Command Post, and asked the American base commander to come to his office immediately. The Turkish executive officer insisted that both officers ride in the general's car because with the car's radios and staff flags the driver could go across the active runways and not have to drive the long way around. As they approached the runway, the general's driver turned down the active runway and the Turkish executive officer stuck a pistol into the face of the American commander. The Turkish driver stopped the general's car near the end of the runway where a Turkish O-11, the equivalent of an American C-45 twin-engine transport type aircraft, was waiting with engines running. The American commander was told to get onboard the O-11, and he was subsequently flown to Istanbul. From Istanbul the

American commander was taken to the Communist border of Bulgaria and bodily thrown across the border into Bulgaria. According to what we heard, it later took the American Consulate in Bulgaria approximately three months to get the displaced American commander safely back into American hands.

General Jones then told me during our interview that if I ever experienced any trouble or needed special help I should call him directly and not send messages other than routine types. General Jones went on to tell me that if I could somehow change the relations between the Turks and the Americans at Murted he would back me on any reasonable request. With all of this in mind, several hours later I departed for Incerlik Air Base in Turkey, again on General Jones's personal T-39 jet aircraft.

Due to my rather rapid departure from Spain, the 401st wing commander had the base personnel officer at Torrejon out-process me. Torrejon's base commander called me several days later and told me that Cynthia and the kids would now have to move out of base housing. Cynthia had two choices, i.e., to go back home to the States or to move out onto the Spanish economy until the end of my new remote tour. Cynthia quickly chose to live in Madrid, as she was currently teaching school at the nearby military dependents' high school, while I was assigned to Turkey. Somehow Cynthia located an apartment in downtown Madrid and with Captain Buck's assistance the 401st Transportation Squadron moved her and the kids into her new apartment. What an invaluable educational experience this was to prove for our three children. They had to learn the Spanish language in order to get by. Cynthia continued working full-time as a teacher in the U.S. Department of American Schools and really loved her job. She wasn't about to return to the United States while I was still located somewhere else in Europe.

Since Turkey is such a unique and incredibly exciting country historically, I would like to spend a paragraph or two providing the reader with a quick overview of that nation. Personally, I found Turkey to be one of the most fascinating places in the world that I have visited. According to Turkish historical documents, Turkey was the geographical and cultural bridge that separated the East from the West. Turkey has over 7000 years of recorded history. I literally found the country to be like a museum without walls. Three seas surround Turkey as a nation, on the western end: the Black Sea, Mediterranean Sea, and Aegean Sea.

On the central plain lies the capital city of Ankara. Its name comes from the former Hittite city of Ankura, which flourished around 1900 B.C. Around 900 B.C. the Citadel of Saint Augustus was built in what is now known as Ankara. Alexander the Great traveled extensively throughout Turkey and wintered near Ankara in 334 B.C. There is a small fascinating city located about thirty kilometers south of Ankara called Gordium, which was built around 1200 B.C. In the town of Gordium is a gazebo where Turkish history says that King Midas had a laborer tie a hemp knot that was one meter in diameter.

According to one of King Midas' oracles, whoever could untie this hemp knot would become a king and would conquer the world, as it was known to the Hellenistic age. It seems that Alexander the Great arrived in Gordian sometime during 334 B.C. and spent three days trying to untie the then-famous Gordian knot. Alexander became so frustrated on the third day that he whipped out his sword and successfully cut the knot in half. According to legend, Alexander went on to conquer the known world. Interestingly enough, the sequel to this story occurred in another land at about the same time involving the great sword Excaliber. Anglo-Saxon history indicates that whoever could pull the sword Excaliber out of the stone would go on and conquer the Anglo-Saxon world, as it was known at that time.

Upon my arrival, my in-country briefing was conducted at Incerlik Air Base in southern Turkey. Here the intelligence officers gave just enough information to absolutely scare the hell out of a person. The second day at Incerlik, we were taken on a field trip to a local Turkish prison. The condition of the prison and the prisoners was unbelievably horrible. Much to my surprise, there were members of the American Air Force locked inside this stockade. The intelligence officer who conducted the briefing told us the following story about one of the inmates.

It seems that an American sergeant after arriving in Incerlik, had gone into a local town for an evening of entertainment. As the sergeant was paying his bill in one of the local pubs, a quick wind came up and blew some of his new Turkish lira away. The sergeant quickly stomped on several of the Turkish lira to prevent them from blowing away. The sergeant was subsequently arrested by Turkish police and thrown into this local prison. At the time that I was there, this same sergeant had been in this Turkish prison for over two years and the American authorities were still unable to effect his release. The sergeant's crime was stomping in public on a picture of the Turkish president Atatürk. In Turkey, Atatürk's picture is printed on all denominations of Turkish lira. We were also told to never stare at a Turkish citizen, especially women, as this was also an offense that could land you in jail.

The next day after in-processing my paperwork, I was able to obtain a ticket on a Turkish civilian airliner to Ankara. Arriving late that night, I stayed in a hotel in downtown Ankara. It was a night that I shall never forget. Since we were not fed during the flight from Incerlik, I was really hungry by the time that I finally got squared away in my hotel room. By the time that I got downstairs and located the dining room it was closed. I attempted to speak with one of the Turkish waiters about where I might locate something to eat, but the waiter couldn't speak English and I could not speak Turkish. I left the dining room totally frustrated and went into the bar.

Again I ran into the same problem; however, this time I was rescued by a young Turkish fighter pilot who could speak English. During the course of getting acquainted, I offered to buy the Turkish lieutenant a drink, and he told me that American Scotch was his favorite drink. I told him that I in turn would drink whatever the national drink of Turkey was. What I received was a tall glass of what the lieutenant called Raki, which looked very much like straight American gin. The taste wasn't too bad, but the kick on an empty stomach was awesome! After three or four of these drinks I do not know when I left the bar or how I got back into my hotel room. By the time an American staff car picked me up the next morning, I was suffering from a tremendous hangover and starved to death. I quickly learned from that experience to never drink Raki straight again.

Thinking about my situation to date in Turkey, I was a little embarrassed by how little of the Spanish language I actually knew after two years in Spain. In those two years I had mastered mostly *Si* and *No* which was pretty pathetic. I vowed that when I got settled into my new job I would make every effort to learn as much of the Turkish language as I could.

The Turkish driver told me that we were first going to Bulgat Air Base, which was the main American support base for the Turkish fighter base that I was being assigned to. I went through the usual administrative in-processing at Bulgat and eventually was ushered in to meet my new boss, a Major General Elliot. It was instant liking from the get-go. General Elliot informed me again about what had happened to the previous American base commander at Murted and cautioned me to be very careful and delicate in my communications with my Turkish counterparts, as they were currently really ticked off with the Americans. I assured him that I would give the job my best shot. He said that General Jones had informed him that I was coming in highly recommended and that he would back me as far as possible.

That afternoon the same driver took me out to Murted. It turned out to be an eighty-five-mile drive from the outskirts of Ankara. While I was checking into my command section, the first shock that I received was to learn that General Tuncman had assigned a personal interpreter to me. The interpreter introduced himself as Mehmet, and he turned out to be an absolutely invaluable asset to me while I was assigned there at Murted. Mehmet was a retired sergeant from the Turkish Army and was thus familiar with all of the protocol of the Turkish military. Mehmet informed me that he had already made an appointment for me to meet General Tuncman the next morning. I knew that Turkish military traditions were definitely different from those of the U.S. military, and I didn't want to make any mistakes, especially when meeting a Turkish general. I informed Mehmet that I wanted to spend the next several hours learning the proper way that a Turkish officer would report to a Turkish general.

The following morning Mehmet took me over to the Turkish command section for my appointment with General Tuncman. Instead of knocking on the door to enter the general's office, the visitor was required to stand before the open door with head bowed where the general could see him and "pop" his heels together three times. If the general acknowledged you, you then took three steps forward and repeated the same head-bowing and heel-popping process. Again, and only if you received an acknowledgment, you were to take two steps forward, repeating the same process, only coming to attention after the last heel pop. After my final heel-popping performance, General Tuncman with a smile on his face jumped up, came around his desk, and gave me the traditional Turkish hug and kissed both of my cheeks. General Tuncman told me in his best English that I had done my homework well and welcomed me to Murted Air Base.

We shared several cups of Turkish *chi* (tea) together, and I told General Tuncman that whatever he required of me I would be most happy to assist him with. The general then told me to go down the hall and introduce myself to his deputy, Colonel Aykut, whom I would be working with on a daily basis. Before leaving, I called Mehmet in and he presented General Tuncman with two cartons of American cigarettes plus six bottles of Scotch.

This introduction to Colonel Aykut was to become one of the most interesting introductions of my life. Before going down the hall, I asked Mehmet to return to my office and get two more cartons of cigarettes plus another six bottles of Scotch so that I could present them to the general's deputy. Stopping in front of Colonel Aykut's office door, I popped my heels together the accustomed three times and waited for an acknowledgment. I could see the colonel sitting at his desk at the end of a long and narrow room. There was no acknowledgment from the colonel, so I popped my heels together for the second time. Still there was no acknowledgment, and I felt that anyone could have heard my heels popping together from two blocks away.

I was getting somewhat irritated and was just in the process of raising my hand to knock hard on Colonel Aykut's door when all of a sudden he looked up straight into my eyes. I'll never forget those very piercing black eyes of Colonel Aykut's. We must have stared at each other for maybe a full ten seconds before he finally smiled and said, "What the fuck-over." It was an instant bonding moment for both of us, and as a result Colonel Aykut is a man whom I shall never forget. Ike, as he preferred to be called, and I did become better than just good friends. We not only planned our daily activities together but also ate lunch together almost every day, usually in the American mess hall. Many a night Ike and I could be found in our open mess drinking and arguing the world's many problems and philosophies. One of Ike's most profound statements was that we Americans just didn't know how to hate. In the long run I guess he was correct, but it was not my way of thinking. One thing that I quickly discovered about Ike was that he was incredibly intelligent. He could think, speak, and write in seven separate languages. I even felt many times that his command of the English language was better than mine!

As I mentioned, Murted Air Base was located approximately eighty-five miles due southwest of the city of Ankara. The primary mission of the base was to train Turkish fighter pilots to react and respond to the secret NATO operational plan regarding the delivery of nuclear weapons on mutually assigned Soviet targets. To accomplish this mission the Turks had one squadron of F-104 Starfighter aircraft and three squadrons of old American F-102 Air Defense fighters. There were eight similar NATO fighter bases scattered throughout Turkey, all with the same mission. Each base had both a Turkish base commander and an American base commander. The American forces on each base amounted to about 140 troops.

The Turks insisted that the American forces live on one side of their base while the nuclear weapons storage site was located on the other side of the base. The American base commander's responsibility was to maintain the security and control of the nuclear weapons. Should there be an increase of hostilities to the point of war between the United States and the Soviet Union, then the American base commander would release the nuclear weapons to the Turkish base commander. It was to become a very sensitive job, especially since Turkey had gone to war with Greece over the Cyprus Islands and the United States had virtually cut off foreign aid to Turkey. Both Greece and Turkey were NATO allies, and up to a point both countries enjoyed total American foreign aid packages. The point was quickly reached when the U.S. government canceled the foreign aid package to Turkey while it continued to provide support aid to Greek military forces. This action upset the Turkish military forces as well as most American military men. The problem as we saw it was due to our involvement with the Greek OPEC oil fleet, yet the Greek people at the time for some reason hated Americans. Thus the security of our nuclear weapons on Turkish soil was suddenly a critical one.

It really galled me at the time, because Turkey as a nation had always fully supported the NATO missions. They were the first country to send combat troops into Korea in 1950 to help support American forces. In addition, they were the only country, according to historical documents from the Korean War, that ever paid off their loans for foreign aid from the USA. During the Cyprus War, both Greece and Turkey were using the same American fighter aircraft (F-86s) and American bombs and ammunition to bomb and strafe each other's military forces. The problem was that the Turks were very quickly running out of bombs and ammunition as a direct result of their American foreign aid being cut off. Fortunately, the stalemate ended before a disaster occurred. I was aghast that our country would do such a thing. In my opinion the real issue was political in nature, as our country at the time couldn't seem to get by without the support of the Greek OPEC oil industry. The fact that we would totally neglect our allies the Turks was beyond my comprehension.

In any event, this was what made my job most difficult during my tour of duty in Turkey. I really learned to like the Turks and could not believe what the U.S. government was doing to our relationship with them. Each day in 1975 the trust level became worse between the Americans and the Turks. Throughout the year of 1975 our nation continued to shut down the American foreign aid programs to Turkey. These were especially trying times for the Turks, as they had been receiving foreign aid from America for the past thirty-three years. It seemed that everything that the Turks had was produced in America, from common lead pencils, to advanced modern technology in computers, to parts for their military aircraft fleet.

General Jones had reminded me that times might become critical for American military forces stationed in Turkey. As I mentioned earlier, all of the nuclear weapons that we were responsible for were located on one side of the base, while we, the Americans, were located on the other side of the base. We actually had six underground nuclear storage bunkers located on about an acre and a half of land that was surrounded by a double row of steel ten-foot-high fences about five feet apart. The four corners of the double fencing had .50-caliber machine guns manned by Kurdish soldiers. The Turkish general allowed me to maintain only four American guards armed with rifles at night who were located inside the fenced compound. This was always a bothersome point simply because the Turks, should they chose, could have taken the nuclear weapons away from us at any given time. Thus Turkey would quickly become a third nuclear power in the world. This situation was of grave concern to American commanders stationed throughout Europe. To prevent this from occurring each day, we removed an internal item from the stored nuclear weapons, thus rendering them useless.

This really became a cat-and-mouse game that would have made James Bond's actions seem like nothing. I felt that the worst part was my having to remain on base every day. I coordinated my weekly plans for removing certain parts of our nuclear weapons with my boss, who was stationed in Ankara. I couldn't begin to describe all of the places that we hid parts of these weapons. Some might be in pots located overnight in our mess hall, while some were located in a particular airman's toolbox, et cetera. Fortunately, we never got caught, nor did the need ever exist to use our nuclear weapons. Thank God.

Our support base at Bulgat in downtown Ankara was something else. We relied on their support to maintain our vehicle fleet, supply us with food and medical supplies, and integrate new personnel into our ranks. I could never prove it, but I always felt that the CIA ran Bulgat. Too many times I would be seated in my boss's office in Bulgat and some guy in civilian clothes would enter and begin asking me all sorts of questions about what the Turks were doing at Murted. I was quick to remind these civilians that I was a base commander and that if they wanted information regarding the Turks' activities they would have to rely on their own agents.

One of the things that my troops did for recreational entertainment besides playing softball was build and fly gas model airplanes. Our detachment area was located right next to the area that housed all of the three or four hundred Kurdish troops assigned to Murted. It didn't take long to discover that there was a very definite difference between the Turkish troops and the Kurdish troops. The Kurdish soldiers, when drafted from eastern Turkey, were always sent to Turkish infantry units or to Turkish air bases as guards. They only had one uniform and it was made of heavy wool. I don't know how they managed these uniforms in the extreme summer heat of the Turkish plateaus. Mehmet told me that their monthly salary in American dollars equaled twenty-three cents.

Whenever one of my troops would fire up a gas model engine, within several minutes there would be a hundred or more Kurdish soldiers on hand to watch the air show. And a truly great show each performance was! We had some NCOs who could really fly these model airplanes. Usually there was a lot of betting going on, and once the odds were established, the two contestants would attach colored paper to the tails of their individual aircraft before launching them. As the commander and only rated pilot among the Americans, I accepted the challenge and built a gas model. Invariably, every time I tried to fly one of these very unstable models, I crashed on takeoff or was quickly shot down by my competitor, and my guys loved every minute of it. They really razzed me for my inability to fly.

One day a new NCO arrived in the detachment, and whoever his sponsor was had told him about our flying club. The sergeant brought with him a radio-controlled model of a Cessna 172 type aircraft. The first time that the sergeant flew this model he created a sensation and almost an international incident. The young sergeant, after getting the engine running, taxied the model out onto the nearby road and quickly took it off. The Kurdish soldiers went wild and began running all over the place. The sergeant flew the model around our detachment area for a while with everyone in attendance watching the show. Unfortunately for us, the Turkish base control tower was located only two blocks away, and for fun the sergeant decided to fly the Cessna over and buzz the tower. As the small plane began circling the tower, a Kurdish guard appeared out of the tower and began firing submachine guns at the aircraft in an attempt to shoot it down. Bullets were flying everywhere and people were running all over, while the sergeant was trying to get his model back on the ground.

Within minutes the base siren went off, and here came General Tuncman's staff car followed by a whole host of Turkish officers. Speaking to Mehmet, the general requested that the sergeant land the aircraft immediately. Once it was on the ground and with the engine shut down, the Turks quickly grabbed the model and at the general's orders began cutting the paper off the fuselage. General Tuncman was convinced that this was an American spy plane equipped with hidden cameras, and he was really upset. Mehmet finally was able to calm the general down and convinced him that it was only a toy radio-controlled model flown by a new member of my command who didn't realize what he had done. Several weeks later, I was to learn more than I wanted to know about Turkish military discipline.

Maybe it was from my Marine Corps training, although I'm not really sure, but there were a lot of things I did during my tenure in the service that could have easily gotten me into quick trouble. Two days after this tower fly-by I discovered in talking with Ike that the general had disciplined the Turkish tower officer for allowing this embarrassing incident to occur. That afternoon, with Ike accompanying me, I took a case of Budweiser beer and climbed the standard ninety-four steps up to the control room of the tower and apologized to the Turkish officers on duty. I was astounded to discover that there was no elevator in the building. All of the Turks and Kurds on duty were dressed in typical Turkish military wool uniforms. I couldn't believe the temperature inside the tower control room. It was about 120 degrees Fahrenheit, with no air-conditioning and no windows. I asked Ike about this deplorable condition, and he responded that that was just the way that it was. There were no air conditioners available and no money for them should they become available. I told Ike that I thought that it was a flying safety hazard and that I would do my best to do something about it.

Several days later after this incident, I drove into Bulgat to talk to my boss about some business. This was my first trip into Ankara, so I had several of our NCOs bring one of our trucks along that needed some minor maintenance and also show me how to get to Bulgat. While I was visiting with my boss, I discovered that almost every room in the headquarters section building had air conditioners in their windows. I questioned my NCOs about air conditioners, and they suggested that we pay a visit to the civil engineering (CE) squadron there on Bulgat. There was a railhead there in the CE area, and they were unloading large commercial air conditioners as we arrived. While no one was paying attention we borrowed a forklift and loaded one of the large air conditioner units onto our truck. The unit was two feet wide by four feet tall and eight feet long, so it constituted a good load. Before leaving the area, we discovered a warehouse stacked full of window-sized air conditioners. We quickly loaded sixteen of them onto our truck and took off before anyone became suspicious.

I called Ike the next morning and told him to bring a large truck and crew with him and come over to our detachment area.

When the Turks arrived, I told Ike that I wanted the large commercial unit installed somewhere in the tower building complex, while most of the other smaller units could be used anywhere the general wanted them. Needless to say, General Tuncman was ecstatic beyond words. Because I had insisted, the Turks did install three of the window units in the control tower. I later learned that the general had the large commercial unit installed to air-condition his underground Command Post. Two of the units went into the windows of his office, and each of the fighter squadron commanders received a window unit. Mehmet informed me that I could do no wrong from that day forward. I don't think the folks at Bulgat ever figured out what happed to their missing air conditioners, but the Turks loved them. I did later inform my boss what I had done, and he just looked at me and said that it was a good thing that I didn't get caught.

Coming back to Turkish military discipline, I need to describe an incident that left me speechless. I mentioned earlier that I was only allowed four American guards inside our nuclear storage area at night. Besides the Kurds who manned the machine-gun towers, there were between four and eight Kurdish guards who performed a roving patrol at night in between the fences at the storage site. Another incident that occurred one afternoon shall live with me forever. I must admit that there is a great cultural difference between our two nations and probably I'll never fully understand why some things happen in one culture, yet are strictly forbidden in another. In this particular case one of the Kurdish roving guards at the storage site got a little smart with one of my guards and demanded an American cigarette from him. The American guard refused the Kurdish guard's request, and the Kurdish guard spit in the face of the American guard and they both wound up pointing rifles at each other through the inside fence. The senior American guard on shift at that time called me immediately.

In like manner the senior Kurdish soldier had called his Command Post. The captain of the Turkish Military Police had already arrived by the time I got there, and he had all four of the Kurdish guards lined up at attention. To this day I do not know what the captain was saying to the guards, but it was harsh. The captain didn't seem to be talking; he was enraged and yelling at all of them. The

384

captain grabbed one of the Kurdish soldiers and slapped the soldier's face so many times that the soldier dropped his weapon. The captain reached down, picking up the M-1 rifle by the barrel, stepped back, and with all of his might swung the rifle at the guard's head. His swing was so hard that the Kurdish soldier body landed a full five feet away. I have never witnessed such brutality as that, and it made me sick to my stomach. I made no effort to try to talk with the Turkish captain.

That afternoon I conducted a mandatory commander's call. I explained to all of my troops what had happened over at the SAS site. I further informed them that no matter what, there would never be another incident like this one, with either the Kurdish soldiers or the Turkish forces on Murted Air Base. I was appalled by the discipline, and I think it made all of us realize that we were in a foreign land and that we were not necessarily protected by American laws. I told my troops to try their absolute best to remain friendly at all times regardless of the situation and, no matter what, never point a gun at anyone short of an actual war. I don't think that any of us who were there at the time will ever forget this incident.

I mentioned earlier in this journal that in 1956–57 while at Lackland AFB I had met and become very good friends with a captain in the Turkish Air Force. Captain Nevzat and I maintained contact for a number of years before I eventually lost his address. I told Ike one evening that I had a friend who was in the Turkish Air Force and could he possibly help me to locate him? I gave Ike Nevzats' full names and Ike said the name sounded familiar and that he would do his best to try to locate the good captain for me. Two days later Ike came over and informed me that when I picked friends I really picked successful ones. He said that Captain Nevzat was now General Nevzat and that he was currently the chief of staff of the Turkish Air Force. Ike also told me that it would be impossible for me to contact him, as he was located in the Turkish TGS, which was the equivalent of our Pentagon in Washington D.C., and Americans were not allowed inside that complex. Ike went on to explain that the hostility that currently existed between the Turks and the American government as a result of the United States cutting off the Turkish foreign aid was at a peak. Current relations between the two countries had gotten so bad that the Turks had refused to allow any American aircraft to enter their country for the time being.

Ike told me to forget General Nevzat for the time being. Being one to not take no for an answer, I invited Ike over for dinner a few nights later and proceeded to get him drunk during the course of the evening. I informed Ike again how close General Nevzat and I were and that it was extremely important that I see him. Ike finally gave in and agreed to try to get me inside the TGS. The next day we went over to one of the Turkish fighter squadrons and located a major who was about my size and was also bald. We borrowed the major's uniform and credentials, with Ike doing all of the talking. Ike mentioned that most all Turkish officers carried concealed weapons and could shoot to kill without questions. As we were driving into Ankara the next day, Ike told me that this situation was so delicate that if anything went wrong while inside the TGS he personally would have to kill me. I told him that I was so sure of Nevzat that I would accept that risk.

After parking the staff car, Ike inspected my Turkish uniform and gave me a black briefcase with the inscription of TOP SECRET in Turkish letters on the outside of the brief case. As we approached the first guard station Ike told me not to say anything no matter what and should I have to cough do it in Turkish and not English. We got through the first cluster of Turkish guards outside the TGS without a hitch. The guards inside the corridor where the general officers were located were much more thorough, and for a few seconds I wasn't sure that my disguise was going to work. Ike screamed something in the guard's face that had momentarily detained me, and he quickly passed us on through. It seemed like we walked two blocks before Ike finally located the door that he wanted. Ike pressed a buzzer and shortly a Turkish colonel opened the door from the inside. Both the colonel and Ike got into a heated discussion, which eventually resulted in the Turkish colonel slamming the door in Ike's face.

I watched Ike get really mad and he turned and banged on the door again. This time as the Turkish colonel answered the door, Ike grabbed him by his tie and stuck a pistol in his face, pushing him back past the door. Once we were both inside the general's office, Ike quickly closed the door that we had just come through.

Looking to our left into the next room, we saw four Turkish general officers seated at a low coffee table. For a microsecond I wasn't sure what to do, as they were all reaching for their handguns. I quickly removed my wheel hat and threw it at the table just as Nevzat had done so many times in my BOQ room back at Lackland AFB. General Nevzat shouted something in Turkish to the other Turkish generals and charged me. He threw both arms around me as he hugged and kissed me on each cheek. It took a few minutes for the pandemonium to settle down, and then I explained to Nevzat where I came from and how I forced Colonel Aykut into bringing me to his office.

Nevzat introduced me to the other three generals before dismissing them, and then he insisted that we sit down and talk for a while. Ike apologized to Nevzat's aide, telling him what a crazy American I was, and they all got a laugh out of that. Nevzat told me that he had already heard about me from General Tuncman but he had not made the connection with my name. General Nevzat thanked me for providing the air conditioners to General Tuncman and told me what a great job I was doing at Murted. We talked for probably fifteen minutes before Nevzat indicated that he had a meeting to attend. General Nevzat asked if Colonel Aykut and I would accept an invitation to a formal party the next evening. I looked at Ike and told him that we would be delighted to attend and that I would look forward to meeting his wife. General Nevzat's aide escorted us back out to our staff car, shaking his head all the way. On our way back to Murted I asked Ike to swing into Bulgat so that I could meet with General Elliot for a few minutes. I told Ike to accompany me, as I wanted him to meet General Elliot.

General Elliot was extremely pleased to meet Colonel Aykut. General Elliot told Ike that he was the first Turkish officer to ever enter his office and that he was so pleased that relations were so good between our forces at Murted. I told General Elliot that we had just come from the Turkish TGS, where I had renewed old friendship with General Nevzat, and that I had been invited to a state-level party the next evening. General Elliot then told me that I needed to go down to Room Ten and sign some paperwork. He said that he was going to show Colonel Ike around Bulgat while I was tied up. I thought this was a rather strange request, but who was I to question a general's order?

Arriving in Room Ten, I was met by two CIA officers who begged me to help them. These CIA officers informed me that I was the only American officer they knew of to ever be invited to a state-level party, and they wanted me to take notes for them on who was there, et cetera. I politely informed them that I was an American base commander and not a spy and that if they needed information on who attended Turkish parties they would have to look elsewhere. They were not happy with me, but there was nothing they could do. Returning to Murted, I gave Ike a bottle of Scotch and told him to thank the Turkish major for the loan of his uniform.

By March of 1975 the Turks were really feeling the pangs of having the American foreign aid cut off. Approximately 80 percent of the F-102 fighter interceptors were grounded for lack of parts. At Murted the Turks had three squadrons of F-102s, and of the seventy-five aircraft available only ten were flyable. One evening as Ike and I were going over the day's activities, I got a wild idea and asked Ike if he could get me a list of the F-102 parts that were needed there at Murted. Ike came back several days later with a complete list of what they needed, and only then did he ask why I wanted such a list. I told him that I was going to call General Jones in Germany and see if he could help us out. Ike thought I was crazy and told me so. Ike said that even if General Jones's headquarters could release some of the parts, how would they get the parts into Turkey? I told him that I would worry about that after I spoke with General Jones.

General Jones had told me to call him personally should I need any help, so I thought, *Why not!* That evening I placed a call to his office, and when he came on the line I told him why I needed his help. General Jones first congratulated me on the fine job that I was doing at Murted, especially under the current international circumstances. General Jones also told me to send an ops immediate message to him for his eyes only, with a complete list of the parts that I needed. General Jones said that he had heard about my intervention into the Turkish TGS and again congratulated me. I told General Jones that I had refused to spy for the CIA, and he told me not to worry about that. General Jones was in a good mood and told me to give him a week to try to locate the parts that we needed.

One week later General Jones called and told me that he had the parts that we needed and that they were being loaded onboard a C-130 aircraft as we spoke. Since the Turks had refused permission for any American aircraft to enter their airspace, General Jones said, I would have to coordinate the flight plan with the Turkish government. He gave me the aircraft call sign, the UHF radio frequency that the C-130 would be monitoring, the tail number of the C-130, the aircraft's departure time from Ramstein Air Base in Germany, and finally the arrival time at the Turkish air defense zone. General Jones informed me that it was to be a secret mission and that I should send him a secret ops immediate message when all things were cleared with the Turks. I quickly called General Tuncman and told him that I needed to see him immediately. I took Mehmet with me to the general's office to help translate all of the information for me.

After I informed General Tuncman of what I wanted, he picked up a telephone and called the Turkish TGS. Whoever General Tuncman spoke with refused to allow permission for the American C-130 to enter Turkish airspace. I then asked General Tuncman to contact General Nevzat informing him of my request. About an hour later the TGS officer called back and informed General Tuncman that the flight had been cleared. They also informed him that Turkish air defense fighters would meet the C-130 and provide escort from their air defense zone to Murted. I subsequently sent an ops immediate message to General Jones with all the details.

Two nights later General Jones's aide called me and said that the C-130 would depart Ramstein that evening and would arrive at Murted around 0300 in the morning. I told the aide that Turkish fighters would meet the C-130 as it passed through the Turkish air defense zone and would escort it to and from Murted. I also mentioned that I would personally meet the aircraft once it arrived on-station. I had our cooks prepare an airborne meal for the crew for their return flight sparing nothing. General Tuncman, Colonel Aykut, and I met the C-130 as it came to a stop on Murted's main runway. The aircraft commander of the C-130 wanted to unload the cargo right on the runway. I informed the AC that the Turkish F-104s who had escorted him needed to land as soon as possible to refuel for their return escort mission. The AC agreed to taxi to an off-ramp and down-load his cargo. At first the AC did not want to shut his engines down, as he said that they had to be airborne again immediately. I told the AC that I wasn't sure what his weather was like en route or at Ramstein, but that it would be a pretty good idea if he took on a full fuel load. The AC was very hesitant but finally did shut down all of his engines. It was very clear that the crew of the C-130 was scared, as they had not been told about the Turkish fighter escort. The copilot told me that the Turkish F-104s got so close to them that they feared that the craft might shoot them down. I assured him that that wasn't the case.

After all of the pallets were unloaded and the refueling was complete my cooks delivered a banquet to the crew for their return flight. I informed the AC that I would forward a message to General Jones explaining what an outstanding job the crew of the C-130 had done and again thanked him for the flight. I also reminded the AC that the same F-104 fighters would escort his aircraft to the Turkish air defense zone. Later that same day General Tuncman sent a message through General Nevzat to General Jones, again thanking him for his support. That evening I called General Jones and told him how appreciative the Turks were. General Jones informed me that no American aircraft had departed Ramstein AB for Turkey and that our conversation regarding F-102 parts never took place. General Jones did remind me in his parting words to keep up the good work while I was in Turkey.

General Elliot's aide called me the next morning and said that the good general wanted to see me in his office. Several hours later, over a cup of coffee, General Elliot asked me about an ops immediate message from General Jones that I had received. I told General Elliot the complete story, leaving no details out. General Elliot turned several shades of gray but continued drinking his coffee. He told me that it was not a good idea for me to be going outside of regular military channels and especially to be bothering General Jones with such small problems. I told General Elliot that General Jones had told me during my in-brief to call him personally should I ever need any help, and that was what I had done. I also apologized for not bringing General Elliot in on the situation before the fact and said that I would never do it again. In closing, I asked him if he would be kind enough to come out to Murted and to have lunch with General Tuncman, and General Elliot said that he would be delighted. Our mission at Murted was so classified and sensitive that

General Elliot had never been invited onto a Turkish fighter base by anyone.

After returning to Murted, I called upon General Tuncman and asked if he would mind inviting my boss, General Elliot, out to Murted for a luncheon. General Tuncman thought that would be a great idea and said that he would have his aide take care of the details. Once informed of the luncheon date, I quickly held a commander's call and informed all of the troops that General Elliot would be visiting us in three days and that we needed to make sure that everything was spotless and ready for his inspection. General Elliot arrived and after he had lunch, General Tuncman took him on a tour of the base, visiting all of the Turkish fighter squadrons. Each squadron presented General Elliot with a squadron plaque, and the F-102 squadrons in addition gave him a scarf. By the time General Elliot arrived in our area he was overwhelmed with the rapport that existed between the Turks and the Americans. Because of the conflict that currently existed between the Turks and American forces assigned to the other four SAS bases in Turkey, General Elliot expressed the thought that my guys walked on water, and he was really impressed with what he saw. While speaking to the entire detachment, General Elliot reminded us that everywhere else in Turkey at the moment the relationship between the Turks and the American forces was very precarious, so he doubly thanked the guys in our detachment for such an outstanding job.

The entire time that I was stationed at Murted as a base commander I had my own staff car. It was always easy exiting the base, but coming back onto the base was another story. Murted was located about four miles off the main Turkish highway to Ankara, by a very narrow two-lane country road. About a mile after exiting the main highway there was a barrier across the country road with a machine-gun tower next to it. At night the Americans were required to come to a complete stop, rolling down all of the windows and turning off the vehicle's headlights 1,000 feet from the barrier. The Americans were also required to turn on the vehicle's dome lights and to shout out the vehicle's window, "American Commuton!" Should the guards believe the driver, one of them would then blow a whistle, and the driver was then required to proceed slowly toward the barrier at five miles per hour. Upon his arriving at the barrier, both guards would approach each side of the vehicle, sticking their submachine guns inside while letting the gun's bolts go home. It was always a very unpleasant experience, especially since I knew that they knew who I was, but it was a necessary game that they seemed to always enjoy.

Once through the outside barrier, the American had to again proceed toward the main gate at a maximum of no more than five miles per hour with all of the car's windows rolled down. This was especially not fun in the dead of winter. Upon his arriving near the main gate, the procedure was basically the same, except here three guards would meet you. Two of them would again stick their submachine guns inside the car while the third, an NCO, would stand directly in front of the vehicle with his arm extended pointing a .38-caliber pistol directly at the driver. Most of the time the NCO would cock the pistol as he lowered it toward the person's face. Again, all of the guards knew who I was, but I still had to go along with their game before they would allow me to enter the base. I'm certain that the minute I went through they all had a good laugh as I drove off.

One evening as I approached the main gate, the road was covered with both ice and a thin layer of snow. As the NCO brought his pistol down to point it at me, he slipped and the gun went off. The bullet burned a furrow down the top of my car. This of course created a very unpleasant incident. I got out of the vehicle immediately, while the Turks were all shouting at one another. Shortly I heard the siren of the of the base security police headed toward us. The captain, whom I already knew from the previous encounter, jumped out of his vehicle and had all three guards in a brace at attention. The captain ripped the NCO's rank right off his sleeves and began beating him with a club. By the time the captain was through with his discipline, the NCO was covered with blood, handcuffed, and thrown in the back of a nearby truck. The captain apologized to me the best he could. The next morning I asked Mehmet to go over to the Military Police headquarters and check up on the incident. Mehmet returned shortly and informed me that by Turkish law they were probably going to execute the NCO. I called Ike and told him that I needed his assistance immediately.

Once Ike arrived, I told him what had happened and that it happened every time I came back through the main gate after dark. I also insisted that it was not the NCO's fault, as he had slipped on the ice. We drove over to the Military Police headquarters, where the NCO, who was still handcuffed, was brought before us on his knees. Mehmet told me that the NCO was greatly ashamed of the incident and was doing his best to apologize to me. I told Ike that I was certain that the entire incident was an accident and that I insisted on a full pardon for the NCO. Ike wasn't sure that I could do this, as the atmosphere was pretty hostile for a few minutes. Mehmet, bless his heart, defused the situation and came up with a great solution for everyone. Mehmet suggested to Colonel Aykut that since General Tuncman had a staff flag on the left front fender of his staff car and possibly since we both were base commanders, I should have a flag installed on my staff car. A day later I was probably the only lieutenant colonel in the U.S. Air Force that had a flag with a silver leaf flying from the left front fender of my car. The Turks also painted a large silver leaf on a blue background for my front license plate.

Never after this incident did I have a problem with the Turkish guards. They never stuck their submachine guns in my windows and always smiled as I passed through their checkpoints. The Turkish NCO was returned to duty and given his rank back. The NCO, since he couldn't speak English, later came to Mehmet and offered his sincere thanks and apologies to me. The NCO presented me with a small Turkish tea set. I had Mehmet go and get a bottle of American Scotch, and I presented it to the sergeant, telling him that I was glad that he wasn't a better shot with his pistol.

Several days later I was called to General Tuncman's office. In a small ceremony he presented me with a medallion to wear on my Air Force uniform that would inform other members of the Turkish military and civilian citizens that I now possessed the same privileges as other Turkish officers. Although I did not carry a concealed weapon, I was astounded the next time that I went into Ankara wearing the medallion and walked down one of the main streets. People walking toward me got out of my way and stared as I passed them. I was so proud that I wore that medallion on all of my uniforms from then on to the day that I retired from active duty. The medallion still hangs on the left breast pocket of my Class A uniform, which is hanging in our closet at home.

An incident occurred, and as horrible as it was, the results of what happened still make me smile today. One spring day I was returning in my staff car from our SAS site on the opposite side of the base back to our detachment area. As I neared the end of the active runway, I pulled over to watch an F-102 that was preparing for a full stop landing. Watching aircraft take off or land is something that all pilots seem to enjoy, and this day was no exception. I gave the landing aircraft a very careful once-over as it passed over my head about fifty feet in the air. I was horrified to discover that the right landing gear was not fully down and locked.

I watched in dread as the F-102 touched down on the runway and began swirling around in 360-degree turns as it careened down the runway. I quickly stepped on the accelerator and was probably going in excess of sixty miles per hour as I rounded the north end of the runway headed for the crash site. In flying terminology we call this landing experience a ground loop. Normally this maneuver scares the hell out of the pilot involved, and in most cases the pilot is able to walk away from the aircraft once it comes to a complete stop. In this case that didn't happen! Colonel Ike arrived on the scene about the same time that I did. We both watched, horrified, as the aircraft caught on fire while the pilot was still in the cockpit. As we watched, a Turkish fire truck arrived on the scene and immediately began spraying the aircraft with water hoses.

I couldn't believe my eyes, as the pilot was unable to get out of the cockpit and burned to death while we watched. I know that I yelled at Ike in a rage, asking him where the other fire trucks were. This particular fire truck had only water onboard, and water just will not put out a JP-4 (jet fuel) fire. In fact, water seems to increase the intensity of the flames as it is sprayed on jet fuel. Ike informed me that this was the only fire truck that they had on-base, and I just couldn't believe him. I said, "How could you operate four squadrons of jet aircraft on a base without proper fire protection equipment?" Ike just said that that's the way that it was, as the American foreign aid was cut off and the Turkish Air Force just didn't have the funds to purchase new fire trucks.

I was out of control at the time, and I knew it. I just couldn't believe that we had stood there and watched a pilot burn to death with no one able to help him. It was difficult to believe that the Turks had twenty-four brand-new Messerschmitt F-104 fighters plus seventy-five American F-102s and weren't able to adequately provide adequate protection for the planes or pilots.

Several days later, I was at Bulgat on business when I noticed two Air Force P-2 fire trucks sitting on the ready line at the Vehicle Maintenance Section. In asking around, I discovered that there were four P-2 fire trucks assigned to Bulgat. P-2 fire trucks from what I knew were designed strictly for emergencies involving aircraft fires. They do not shoot water on fires but have a foam-type substance that very definitely retards jet-fueled fires. I couldn't understand why Bulgat would have four of these P-2 fire trucks when the base had no runway or aircraft assigned to it. Bulgat was just a small administrative-type support base with maybe thirty to sixty military-type quarters inside their perimeter.

That night after arriving back at Murted, I called in four of my most trusted NCOs and explained to them what had happened to the Turkish pilot and what I planned to do about it. Bulgat had the responsibility for maintaining all of our vehicles, and in many cases one or more of our guys would stay in town until our vehicle was fixed. Using this pipeline, it was an easy task to determine when the next P-2 fire truck was going to be going into Bulgat's maintenance facility. We knew that once the maintenance was completed on a vehicle there at Bulgat, the vehicle was placed outside their maintenance building on what they called their ready line. Oftentimes vehicles sat on the vehicle maintenance ready line for days before an outfit would pick them up. This was the opportunity that we were waiting for. Several days later one of our guys called and said that there was a P-2 sitting on Bulgat's ready line.

The next morning all four NCOs dressed in white coveralls drove a pickup truck loaded with twenty jerricans of gasoline in the back into Ankara, arriving at Bulgat around 0800 hours in the morning. I had accompanied them in my staff car. The reason for so many jerricans of gasoline is that none of us had any idea what kind of mileage a P-2 fire truck got and it was eighty-five-plus miles back to Murted. Arriving at Bulgat, we drove straight to the ready line. I told my guys to just get into the P-2 like they normally would be picking it up and to drive it off. The reason for the white coveralls was that the firemen at Bulgat always wore white coveralls. I told the NCOs to drive around the perimeter road toward the main gate. When they were about a block from the main gate, the NCOs were to turn on the vehicle's overhead red lights and proceed out the gate as if they were going to a nearby fire. It was an incredible theft, and it went off like clockwork. The NCO in the pickup truck followed the P-2 out the main gate as if he were a part of the emergency response team. The NCOs were to proceed to the highway to Murted as fast as they could get there and stop for no one.

I made my way to General Elliot's office and requested to see him. Over a cup of coffee I explained what had happened the week before at Murted with the death of the F-102 pilot and why the pilot had died. I knew that General Elliot was a command pilot and hoped he would understand what I was about to tell him. I then told the general that one of his four P-2 fire trucks was missing and that he now had only three fire trucks. General Elliot jumped up from his desk shouting at me. The general asked if I had any knowledge about the cost of a P-2 fire truck, and I replied, "Yes, sir, about two hundred thousand dollars." General Elliot then told me that I was absolutely crazy and that I was going to get us both fired. General Elliot then told me to get the hell out of his office and not come back to Bulgat unless I was invited by him. General Elliot shook his fist at me as I was leaving, but he also had a large smile on his face. I hurried from his office as quickly as I could, as I wanted to catch up with the fire truck.

About ten miles outside of Ankara, using my handheld radio I quickly figured out where the NCOs were located and proceeded to catch up to them. We stopped twice before reaching the turnoff for Murted, in order to refuel the P-2. With my car in front, the machine-gun tower guards just waved us on to the main gate. Arriving at the main gate, I stopped and got out of my car and called Mehmet using my hand radio. I told Mehmet to locate Colonel Aykut and to have him report to the main gate as fast as he could.

Several minutes later I heard the general's car approaching with the red lights and siren wailing. I knew that Ike would think that I had another run-in with the security guards and he wasn't wasting any time getting there. Colonel Aykut skidded the general's car to a stop, jumped out, and came running toward me. Colonel Aykut was in such a hurry that he failed to notice the large P-2 fire truck behind me. Very casually I handed Colonel Aykut the keys to the P-2 and suggested that he get it on base as soon as possible. I also reminded Ike that they might want to quickly repaint the truck in Turkish vehicle colors and to file off the engine numbers. I returned to my vehicle, started it up, and drove on through the main gate, leaving Ike standing there speechless.

Of the many state-level Turkish parties I had the pleasure of attending, I was always amused at the military protocol. The men would stand at one end of the room while all their wives and girlfriends remained at the other end. If anyone danced, it was usually several of the men. They always reminded me of pictures that I had seen of Russian Cossack officers doing their leg-busting dances. The men dancers would be bent at the waist while thrusting their feet straight out in front of them, accompanied by the noise of their polished boots striking the floor. Everyone formed large circles around the dancers, and they clapped while keeping time to the music. One would have to work to not have a good time at these functions, and I always enjoyed them.

One day Mehmet and I were eating lunch in the open mess when Mehmet asked me if I knew that Alexander the Great in A.D. 323 had wintered here, where Murted was currently located. I was completely taken by surprise by Mehmet's comments, as I had not done a very good job on my world history lessons. I got so interested in what Mehmet was telling me that I could hardly stand it. Mehmet suggested that we take a drive over to the small hills located about two miles southwest of the base. We drove as far as the dirt road would allow us before getting out and hiking up into the hills. Mehemt showed me numerous small caves that had religious pictures painted inside them. Some of them were so clear that they looked like that had only been painted yesterday. I truly could not believe my eyes.

The next day I drove into Ankara and went to the downtown officers' club. This officers' club catered to military officers and political officials from all nations, and downstairs in the basement of the building was a large international library. I checked out every book that I could find having to do with Alexander the Great. Alexander's army must have been a large one, as history also says that Alexander's army wintered in Ankara during the same time period. I spoke with the club steward before leaving, and he told me that I should come into the club on a Saturday night, as there were always interesting people to talk with. The following Saturday I again drove into Ankara and went to the downtown officers' club for dinner. I met an absolutely fascinating man by the name of John Williams there that night. John, who was a research scientist, worked for the Creative Science Research Center, which was located in San Diego,

California. John told me that in 1959 he was a member of a French geodetic team headed by a Dr. Fernard Navarra. This team had received permission from the Turkish government to conduct a search on Mount Ararat for Noah's Ark.

Upon reaching Mount Ararat, John said that Dr. Navarra had the team split up into two smaller teams. The A Team was to be led by Dr. Navarra, while the B Team would be led by a Dr. Cummings. John said that he was a part of the B Team, led by Dr. Cummings. The idea of the two teams was to be able to cover more area during their search. Apparently the A Team located a 120-foot beam of wood at the 10,000-foot level that they believed to have been a part of Noah's Ark. Many pictures were taken of the beam of wood, but it was too large for the team to carry down the mountain. Before John explained what the B Team had found he told me a rather unusual story. John said that sometime around the year 1274, Marco Polo, who was en route to China, had traveled through what is now Turkey. Mr. Polo had written in his diary that as he neared the Mount Ararat area there were some Roman legionnaires that were pursuing a group of Christians up a long stairway which was located on the side of Mount Ararat. Shortly after the legionnaires started up the stairway a large earthquake struck without warning. The ensuing earthquake made a shamble of the stairway and frightened the Romans so badly that they broke off the pursuit.

John said that as his team started down the mountain at the 9,000-foot level they came across what appeared to be a small chapel that had been constructed of stone. The weather was turning bad, so they decided to camp near the stone structure. That evening around a fire they had built, the team was discussing the strange place for a chapel, as it was not listed on any documents that they had. One of the team members, according to John, happened to turn over one of the rectangular stones that he was sitting on. What they discovered on the other side of the stone was a Maltese cross inscribed into the stone face. This got the team really excited, and they quickly began looking at all of the stones nearby. When the team finished their search, they had discovered eight stones with Maltese crosses inscribed in them. What excited the team members so much was that according to legend, there were eight human beings onboard Noah's Ark.

The next morning they began a careful study of the small chapel and discovered a sealed entrance to a vault located under the chapel. There was a Turkish member of the B Team who absolutely refused to allow any of the team members to break the seal on the vault. The teams both returned home with this new and exciting evidence that they had discovered. Dr. Navarra felt that they had made a significant discovery, one that would validate to the world that indeed there was a Noah's Ark, and that it did indeed come to rest on the side of Mount Ararat. John went on to tell me that the reason that the Turkish government would not allow the team to open the vault was that should it actually contain the remains of Noah's crew, it would then disprove the writings in the Holy Koran. Apparently the Koran indicates that there indeed was a Noah's Ark, but that it came to rest on a mountain located about 430 kilometers to the southwest of Mount Ararat in Iran. John told me that he was there again in Ankara in 1975 to try to get permission from the Turkish government to open the vault. John's story was so incredible that I obtained permission from General Tuncman for John to come out to Murted and put on a slide show for all of the American troops.

Turkey had become such a delight for me historically. The more I learned about history, the more excited I got. I spent many weekends in Ankara wandering through the copper alleys. Mehmet had taught me the Aramaic alphabet and numbering system, which was to prove essential in dating pieces of copper. I purchased a number of copper bowls, rice plates, pans, et cetera, all with significant historical dates to me. One particular pan that I located was dated in 1492, while a rice plate was dated in 1066, which historically was the year of the Battle of Hastings. I treasure these art pieces today.

The International Olympics were first held in Greece, which had originally been a part of Turkey. Two things that the Turks are known for are the invention of snow skis and the original Santa Claus, who was born in a small town called Demre. While in Turkey I had the pleasure of skiing just outside of Ankara and, most importantly on the original Mount Olympus, which is located near the town of Bursa. The ski lifts were not exactly up to the standards that I was familiar with, but I just wanted to be able to say that I had skied on Mount Olympus. The Hittite museum is located in downtown Ankara, and it is such an exceptional place to visit. The building that housed the Hittite Museum was 862 years old in 1975.

The first, third, and fourth floors hold much of Turkey's historical artifacts. What is so significant is the second floor. I have been to Fort Knox and gazed on the gold reserves of the United States, but never have I seen anything like the gold artifacts located on the second floor of the Hittite Museum. The entire second floor was filled with gold artifacts that were removed from King Midas's tomb. As I wandered through the floor, I truly began to believe that everything King Midas touched indeed turned to gold.

Leaving Turkey was very difficult, as I had gained so many new and good friends. Life at Murted was enhanced by being able to occasionally fly with one of the Turkish squadrons in the F-102s or in one of their new Messerschmitt F-104 Starfighters. I didn't actually get to complete my assigned tour of duty in Turkey. While coming down a marble staircase in a hotel in Istanbul, I slipped and fell, rupturing two discs in my lower back. I was evacuated out of the country and flown to Lundstul Army Hospital in Germany, where an Air Force surgeon operated on my back. When I was finally able to get out of bed and walk, I convinced the hospital administrators there in Lundstul to allow me to fly back to Spain to complete my postoperative recovery with my family. After three weeks in Spain, the Air Force reminded me that the Date of Return from my overseas assignment was up and that I was being reassigned to duty in the States. My new assignment was to SAC as a deputy commander of resources (DCR) at Fairchild AFB in Washington State.

I cannot leave Turkey without reflecting back on those members of the Turkish military with whom I was associated. Living on a daily basis with the Turks was simply an incredible experience. The evidence of their long devotion to their friends was unbelievable. I shall always respect the Turkish intelligence, loyalty, comradeship, and trustworthiness.

Back in the States, doing work at a desk for SAC was not one of my favorite things to do, although the job of being a DCR was great. I was no longer allowed to fly as my primary job, and I resented it. While I was there at Fairchild my name came out on the new promotion list to full colonel, which was exciting. However, like all things, there is the "good news," and the "bad news." In this case the bad news was that SAC headquarters called and told me that I had my choice of four SAC bases that needed DCRs. Two of those bases (K. I. Sawyer and Kinchlow AFB) were located on the border of what we called the Michigan-Canadian dew line while the other two (Minot and Grand Forks AFB) were located in North Dakota. None of these assignments were appealing to us due to the extremely cold climate in the areas where the bases were located. Since I had twenty-six years of active duty in the service, I decided to retire.

We found the house of our dreams on Lake Steilacoom in Lakewood, Washington. It was a perfect place to raise a family. Our oldest daughter, Jane, started college, while both David and Anne graduated from Clover Park High School. The field of education had always attracted me, so I spent the next twenty-four years as a teacher, principal, and football coach in both junior high and high school. Since retiring from the Air Force, I have volunteered to go on active duty for every war that the Air Force has been subsequently involved in. It was never very much fun having fought in two political wars, especially when both of the killing fields were on foreign soil. During those time periods, no one seemed to care much about how many young Americans lost their lives during these political battles. There were memorials built around the country to honor our dead, but in most cases they were built by funds donated by American veterans' organizations, not the U.S. government.

The Korean War today is frequently called the Forgotten War, and a whole lot of Americans can't even remember what happened there. The Vietnam War most certainly was a wakeup call for our American government, as the protests became violent all over the country. Many people hated our military forces, and it was not a popular time to be in uniform. In spite of all the protestors, I never lost faith or gave up on my country.

My life was molded in the Boy Scouts of America, where, as I was an Eagle Scout, honor and duty to my country were extremely important. From those early days of my youth forward, it was additionally impacted by the words of Gen. Douglas MacArthur's final speech to the cadets in the Long Gray Line at the U.S. Military Academy, where he invoked them to place "Duty, Honor, and Country" above all else. As a young Marine warrior, I was intrigued by the Japanese Samurai warrior's Bushido's creed, where his life was defined as honor and duty to country. When the chips were down, as they often were during lonely and cold winters of the Korean War, I also remembered Gen. George Patton's remarks when he took over the U.S. Third Army during WW II. General Patton said, "No one ever won a war by dying for his country. They won it by making the other son of a bitch die for his." It's amazing to me how truthful statements like these continually impact an individual's life.

The U.S. Marine Corps had converted me from civilian life into a sophisticated warrior, who tried to be impervious to the horrors of war. Probably the greatest lesson that the Marine Corps gave to me was understanding exactly what the Corps meant by *esprit de corps.* A Marine was the best of the best, and that Marine was trained to understand the concept of how important teamwork was. Marines never left one of their own on the battlefield. Marines are *semper fidelis* (always faithful) to the bitter end. It was true that in the heat of battle I oftentimes felt that I was fighting just for my buddies and not for the political war effort. The background that the Marine Corps drilled into me in 1950 was to set the stage for the rest of my life. The Marine creed taught me to be proud of myself, to live honorably, to love life, and to love my country beyond anything else. That very same philosophy remained with me throughout my twenty years as an Air Force pilot. My eyes always mist, even today, whenever I hear people singing "God Bless America" or verses from "America the Beautiful." The more recent 9-11 disaster in New York City to me was a lot like Pearl Harbor, as it really woke Americans up as to how precious our way of life really is. The 9-11 incident was a lot like the bonding of friends, only in this case it cemented and bonded our nation together once again. I truly applaud all of the American citizens who now appreciate and display just how important it is to let the world know how much we love life and our country.